INSIGHT GUIDES

ITALY

Designed and Directed by Hans Johannes Hoefer
Edited by Kathrine Barrett
Photography by Joe Viesti with
introductory photo essay by Albano Guatti

APA
PUBLICATIONS

Italy

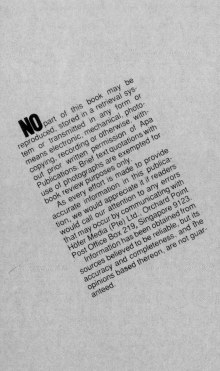

First Edition (2nd Reprint)
© **1991 APA PUBLICATIONS (HK) LTD**
All Rights Reserved
Printed in Singapore by Höfer Press Pte. Ltd

ABOUT THIS BOOK

What can a travel book say about Italy that has not been said before? How to describe, explain and simply cover a subject that has inspired poets, novelists and composers for centuries? It is all there: snowy mountains, green valleys, ancient beautiful cities, exciting street life and unchanged villages. Never far away is a great meal with a choice of memorable wines. In one direction is the deep blue Mediterranean and in the other the green Adriatic sea.

Insight Guide: Italy therefore simply applied its particular formula for travel journalism to this well-known and beloved subject. The goal of all Apa Publications books is to inspire and inform the serious traveler with a solid background of history and current information, good writing, exciting photographs and honest reporting of their subjects, warts and all. Apa Founder **Hans Höfer** first compounded this formula in 1970 with his *Insight Guide: Bali*, a prize-winning edition that has been followed with a series of books that repeat and uphold that standard. A native of West Germany, Höfer is a follower of the Bauhaus tradition, trained in photography, design and production. From his headquarters in Singapore, Höfer has extended the reach of Apa Publications across the entire world of travel. He names a project editor for each volume and that editor assembles the most expert local writers and photographers for each edition.

The work of putting this book together fell to **Katherine Barrett**. Like so many Americans, Barrett first saw Italy from the window of a bus. A student at Harvard, she was intrigued by the possibility of becoming an archaeologist and had signed up for a semester in Rome. She was attracted by all of Rome's layers: from its antiquities to its churches to its shop windows. Her research into the writings of past travelers eventually led to an undergraduate thesis on

Henry James' use of Rome in his novels.

After graduating from Harvard College, Barrett spent a year living in Rome traveling all the time around Italy. The editorship of *Insight Guide: Italy* presented the perfect opportunity for Barrett to combine her interests in Italy, travel writing and journalism. Barrett penned the chapters on Travellers and on Rome.

The most prolific writer in this volume was **Clare McHugh**. Her travels in Europe have taken her to Austria, France, England, Ireland, West Germany and, of course, Italy. A graduate of Harvard College, she has written for the *East Village Eye* and contributed to Frommer's *New York Guide*. She is currently a staff writer at *Scholastic Magazines* in New York City. McHugh wrote the chapters on Italy's history through to the beginning of the 20th century and on the northern provinces.

It is to **Alberto Rossatti** that the book owes a substantial portion of its native expertise. As well as assisting Clare McHugh in her own researches, Ferrarese Rossatti interpreted Italian manners and customs in his chapter on the Italian people and provides insight into Italy's great sense of style with his chapter on fashion. In addition, Rossatti has been a lawyer, teacher, actor, director and translator of literature.

New Yorker **Benjamin Swett** first saw Italy at the age of 14 from the back of a Citroen station wagon; since then he has been back many times and most recently, drove through the wilds of Apulia, Basilicata and Calabria with editor Barrett in a rented Renault during the preparation of this book. Swett's European travels have taken in Greece, Turkey, France and Spain. He has written for *Insight Guide: New York,* and the *Patent Trader Newspaper* where he began his career as a reporter.

Claudia Angeletti abandoned the elegant arcades of hometown Turin to investigate the sorcerous island of Sicily. She also compiled the all-important, nuts-and-bolts Travel Tips.

McHugh

Rossatti

Swett

Angeletti

She received her doctorate in Classical Culture and Literature from the University of Florence. She has also done archaeological work in the Parco Orsiera in the Italian Alps and exhibited photographs of her findings there.

Jacob Young studied history at Stanford University before entering journalism. He now writes about international affairs for *Newsweek International* where he is an associate editor. His knowledge of history and politics is apparent in his informative, fast-paced introduction to 20th-century Italian history. Young's more whimsical side comes out in the piece he wrote with wife **Kathleen Beckett** about Florence and Tuscany. Another experienced New York journalist, Beckett is currently a contributing editor for *Vogue* where she has her own column of fashion essays called "F.Y.I." Her work has appeared in *USA Today, EQ, Redbook, Mademoiselle* and *Harper's Bazaar* and *Glamour* where she has been on staff. In addition to writing about Tuscany, Beckett turned her aesthetic eye to Italian Art.

Melanie Menagh was yet another New Yorker whose mission was to "forsake the grey canyons of Manhattan for the green hills of Umbria and the Marches." She fell in love with Italy's most restful regions, as will be clear to any reader of her contribution. She is a freelance journalist in New York whose work has appeared in *Vanity Fair, USA Weekend, Entertainment Tonight* and *Savvy*.

Peter Spiro's undergraduate training as a historian served him well when he set about unearthing the fascinating history of the Vatican. Spiro contributed the excellent historical introduction to *Insight Guide: New England*. His essays have also appeared in *The New Republic* and *The Christian Science Monitor*.

George Prochnik, a New York writer, studied film while he was an undergraduate at Harvard; he studied Italian cuisine, "the best food in the world," he claims, while a resident of Boston's North End. He also sampled many of the delicacies which he so tantalizingly describes in his piece during a lengthy trip through Italy with his wife **Anne Ketchum**, another New Yorker whose early convent education left her with an eternal fascination for monasticism.

New York based photographer **Joe Viesti** took most of the pictures in this book. The subject was undoubtedly beautiful, but Viesti brought humor, sensitivity and a great aesthetic sense to his images. An American of Italian descent, Viesti had an opportunity to discover his roots during the six weeks he spent taking pictures of people and places from Milano to Palermo. Viesti's fascination with different cultures led him to specialize in photographing festivals around the world. In 1984 his colorful collection provided the pictures for the UNICEF Engagement Calendar. His work has also appeared in *Geo, Stern, Pacific* and *The New York Times*.

Peter Namuth, a free-lance photographer located in New York, did the archival photography. His work for animated films and award-winning documentaries has also been seen on Public Television. Additional photographs were contributed by **Albano Guatti**, Rome-based **Susan Pierres**, and Florentine **Gaetano Barone**, **Catherine Desjeux** of Brinon sur Sauldre and **Thomas Schöllhammer** of Munich.

Martine Singer applied her precise eye to the maps. Amilia Medwied of the Ente Nazionale per il Turismo in New York and her colleague Signora Lantini in Rome offered assistance in planning itineraries and arranging for accommodation. Finally, thanks to Harvey, Giuliana and Umberta Telfner, who have always shown their American cousin how hospitable the Italians are.

—Apa Publications

Young

Menagh

Spiro

Prochnik

Viesti

HISTORY

PEOPLE

SITES

TRAVEL TIPS

THE ETERNAL SEDUCTRESS

Italy, like sorceress Circe tantalizingly beautiful and at the same time treacherous, has been sought after by kings, scholars, saints, poets and curious travellers for centuries. The spell of the "Eternal Seductress," as men have called her, was strong enough to draw people in the past across stormy mountains and seas, and today, into hardly less tumultuous airports and train stations.

Italy has always seemed somewhat removed from the rest of Europe: physically by mountains and sea, historically because of her antiquity, spiritually by virtue of the Pope. In the eyes of outsiders her people have been characterized by extremes: on the one hand, the gentle unworldliness of St. Francis, and on the other, the amoral brilliance of Machiavelli; on the one hand the curiosity of Galileo or the genius of Michelangelo, on the other, the repressive dogmatism of Counter Reformation Jesuits. There have been those who thought the Italians unworthy of Italy, and others, like E.M. Forster, who have considered the Italians "more marvellous than the land."

The editors and writers of this book believe that Italy and its people are equally worthy of the visitor's attention and that there are few countries more fascinating to explore. We introduce you to the land and its people from Calabrian villagers to Milanese sophisticates. We show you the country's artistic treasures from a mysteriously smiling Etruscan statue to Botticelli's radiant Venus. We have also included special features on some contemporary expressions of Italian creative genius: films, fashion and food. In the history section we take you through the highpoints of Italy's past from the founding of Rome by Romulus and Remus to the Eternal City's becoming capital of a reunified Italy almost 3,000 years later.

Italy is not just a museum of the past, but a country where the past is always present; where a housing development rises above a crumbling Roman wall; where an ultra-modern museum displays pre-Roman artifacts; where old people in tiny mountain villages preserve customs centuries old; where youths in those same small villages roar into the future on Vespas.

This is the country which inspires imagination in the dull, passion in the cold-hearted, rebellion in the conventional. Whether you spend your Italian sojourn lying under a brightly colored beach umbrella on the Riviera, shopping in Milan or diligently examining churches and museums, you cannot leave Italy unchanged. At the very least, you will receive a highly pleasurable lesson in living. Whether you are struck by the beauty of a church facade rising from a perfectly proportioned piazza, the elegant line of a dress worn by a mannequin in a shop window, a piece of salty prosciutto wrapped around melon, or the view of animated, well-dressed passersby spied from over the foam of your cappucino, there is the same superb sensation: nowhere else on earth does just living seem so extraordinary.

Preceding pages: Pisa's leaning tower; a celebrant during Venice's carnival in the guise of the Roman God of the New Year, Janus (who looks both backwards and forwards); street games in Palermo, Sicily; St. Peter's Square, Rome; Milan's eclectic style — Gothic cathedral and new-wave fashion. Left, Piazza San Marco in Venice.

CARTA GEOGRAFICA GENERALE DELL' ITALIA

I SVIZZERI Walese · I GRIGIONI · Valtellina · VESCOVATO DI TRENTO · Vicentino

Chambery · Aosta · Vagona · Como · Lago d'Iseo · Bergamasco · Trento · Rivea · Feltre · Cenea

DUCATO DI SAVOJA · DUCATO DI Seregna · STATO DELLA REPUBBLICA DI VENEZIA

S.Gio.di Morienna · Inurea · Novara · MILANO · Milano · Bergamo · Iseo · Brescia · Vicenza · Verona · Padova

PIEMONTE · Vercelli · MASSERANO F. · Vigevano · Crema · Bresciano · Castiglione · Veronese · Legnago · Rovigo

Brianton · Pinarolo · Torino · MONFERRATO · Pavia · Lodi · Cremona · Tartarano · MANTOVA · Guastalla · Ferrara

Gap · Embrun · Susa · Alessandria · Vogera · Tortona · Piacenza · SABIONETA · BOZZOLO · Zelo Rovigo

Barcellonetta · Saluzzo · Alba · Aqui · Piccinino · Parma · DUCATO DI PARMA · LOZARI · MIRANDOLA · Pieve · FERRARESE · Cunae

Glandere · Mendovi · TORRIGLIA · Edifici · Fiorenzuola · Rassena · Reggio · MIRANDOLA · Modena · Romagna

CONTADO DI NIZZA · REPUBBLICA DI GENOVA · Brugneto · DUCATO DI MODENA · Bologna · Bolognese · Faenza

Beglio · Tenda · Genova · Serenaza · Frignano · Vergato · Pistoia

Grace · Gilete · Niza · Albenga · Finale · Pergola

Venta · Ventimiglia · MARE DI GENOVA · MASSA · REPUBBLICA DI LUCCA · Fiorenza · Valli Ombrose

Antibo · MONACO · Sestri di Levante · Lucca · Pisa · Arno F. · GRAN DUCATO

Frejuls · I. di S.Margarita · Pisano · Fiorentino · Voltera · Arezzo · S.Gimno · Siena

I. de Gorgona · Livorno · Vado · Colle · Cusole · Ore

I. de Capri · Piombino · Porto Terraio · Vdi · Montieri · Monzano · TOSCANA · Chu

S.Fiorenzo · Bastia · I. d'Elba · Porto Longone · Massa · Grossetto · Pligi

Nebbia · Mariana · Pianosa I. · MARE DI TOSCANA

C.Rosso · Calvi · Aleria · ISOLA DI CORSICA · Orbitello

Corsica · Aleria distrutta · Mare Tirreno

Golfo di Aiaro · Russo · Corbini · Porto Vecchio · I. delle Corsi

Bonifacio · Isole della Maddalena · Terranoua · Taulara

I. Asinara · Castel Aragonese · Lusa · Sant · 38

Sassari · Terra Nova · C. Comin

C. della Cacca · Algeri · Oucar · Orse · 37

C. de Bosa · Bosa · Tartista · ISOLA · Valle di Mazara · Palermo

C. S. Marco · E REGNO DI · Dasalo · S.Vito · Iato · Trapani · Tori

Orosthione · Cagliari · SARDEGNA · Marara

Isola S.Pietro · S.Michele · M.Serato · 36

I.S.Antioco · Isola di Ghisci · MARE MEDITER

Capo Tavolaro · 36

MARE DI TOSCANA · Mare Tirreno · MARE MEDITERRANEO

THE LAND

As school children have noticed for years, Italy looks like a boot. The long, narrow peninsula sticking out of Europe's underbelly is perpetually poised to kick Sicily westward. Because of this peculiar shape, Italy was a natural site for early civilization. The Alps, which cut across the only land link with the rest of Europe, protected the peninsula from barbarians who in ancient times roamed the plains of Northern Europe. On all other sides Italy is surrounded by the calm Mediterranean, thus even in the earliest times she was linked to the ideas and people of three continents. The sea first served as a highway to bring civilization to the peninsula, later it became a route outward, controlled by the Italians and used for the spread and domination of ideas born in Italy.

The land itself encompasses two separate regions: the northern continental, and the southern peninsular. Together the two parts cover an area of about 91,000 sq miles (146,500 sq km). The smaller, northern section is a plain, bordered on the north and northwest by the Alps and on the south by the Apennines. This plain was once a vast bay of the Adriatic. Gradually the bay filled with silt brought down from the Alps by the Po, the Adige and other rivers. These deposits made the plain into rich farmland, the most fertile in all Italy.

The Apennine range, the so-called backbone of Italy, dominates the peninsular section of the country. These mountains zig-zag down the peninsula from the French Alps and the coast of Liguria in the northwest, through northern Tuscany southeast to the Adriatic coast, and veer west again to the Strait of Messina, between Sicily and the toe of the boot. They reach their greatest height in the central province of Abruzzi where the peaks of the Gran Sasso d'Italia soar as high as 9,700 feet (2,912 meters).

It is no coincidence that the early inhabitants of Italy flourished in the west, on the lowland plains north and south of Rome. Here there are a few natural harbors and long rivers. The Tiber, Arno, Livi and Volturno are easily navigated by small craft, and their valleys provide easy communication between the coast and the interior. The plains of Tuscany, Latium and Campania are fertile

farmland, because they are covered by a thick layer of ash and weathered lava from the many, once-active, volcanos.

Around 200,000 years before the founding of Rome, only cavemen lived on the Italian peninsula. These early inhabitants hunted and gathered for food. Italy became more fully populated when, with the Indo-European migrations (between 2000 and 1200 BC), tribes of primitive peoples poured into Italy from Central Europe and Asia.

Archaeological evidence suggests that these tribes lived in round huts clustered in small villages. The Villanovans, as the tribesmen are called, were farmers who could make and use iron tools. They cremated their dead and put the ashes into tall clay or bronze urns.

Villanovan culture spread from its original center around Bologna south to Tuscany and Latium. Nowhere, however, did Villanovan settlements grow to the size of towns; Italian life at this time centered around mean little villages. Nor, were the artistic achievements of the Villanovans very great. Their funerary urns were shaped crudely, and no tomb or wall paintings have ever been found.

The transformation of Italy from a primitive backwater to the center of the ancient world came about once two groups of outsiders landed. The Greeks and the Etruscans both came across the sea seeking rich new land. They sowed the first seeds of civilization on the peninsula in the early 8th Century BC.

The Greeks in Italy

Greek colonists settled in Sicily and on the west coast near where Naples sits today. Most came in search of land to farm; in Greece not enough arable land was available to feed or employ the entire population. Others were political refugees. When a Greek king was overthrown, all his followers would be required to seek a new home.

Once they arrived in Italy, Greek settlers formed independent cities. Each city was weakly linked to the parent city on the Greek mainland where its settlers had originated. One of the earliest colonies was at Cumae, on the shores of the Bay of Naples. Greeks from Euboea, a large island northeast of Athens, settled there in approximately 770 BC. Other Euboeans founded Rhegium (modern Reggio-Calabria), at the tip of the boot, a few years later. The Corinthian city of Syracuse on Sicily ultimately became the most powerful of the

Preceding pages, 18th Century map shows Italy when it was still divided into many states. Left, Etruscan statue of the god Apollo has the mysterious smile characteristic of these early inhabitants of Italy.

Greek colonies.

The colonists farmed the land around their cities, and engaged in trade with mainland Greece. They soon prospered in the fertile land, and made important contributions to Italian agriculture. They were the first people to cultivate the vine and the olive on the peninsula; previously these plants had grown only in a wild state.

In the 5th Century both Syracuse and Athens tried to establish empires out of the Greek colonies in Italy. Numerous battles were fought, and some are recorded in the histories of Greece written by the ancients. Many Italian natives were forced to participate in the hostilities as drafted soldiers. But after years of fighting neither side achieved total victory, and the Greek leaders gave up the struggle.

letters. By example the Greeks also taught the Italian natives about modern warfare, lessons that the natives would eventually use against their Greek teachers. The Italians saw how the Greeks fortified their towns with high walls of smooth masonry, and in battle used shock troop tactics with armored spearmen.

But all this wealth and knowledge did not provide the Greeks with the unity that they needed to control Italy. Their civil wars kept the Greeks too busy to consider expansion and conquest. They were willing to trade with the natives, but not able to unify them under Greek leadership. This left great political opportunities wide open.

Like the Greeks, the Etruscans were newcomers to Italy. In approximately 800 BC, they settled on the west coast where Tuscany

The colonists continued to argue among themselves, a state of affairs that prevented them from becoming a dominant political force in Italy. They did however become the major cultural and artistic force. Italian natives were eager to trade for Greek luxury goods, the like of which they had never seen before. Soon Greek bronze and ceramic ware was dispersed throughout Italy and providing natives with new and sophisticated art patterns to imitate. The sculpture and architecture in the Greek cities also served as models for the Italians.

The civilizing influence of the Greeks went beyond the visual arts. The natives adapted the Greek alphabet for their own Indo-European tongues. Each native group soon had its own

(Etruscany) and Lazio are today. Questions about the origins of the Etruscans still puzzle scholars. The Greek historian Herodotus said that the Etruscans came from Asia Minor, and that revolution and famine at home drove them to seek new lands. This has been a popular theory ever since. However, recent archaeological evidence suggests that the Etruscans were indigenous to Italy. A small group of Phoenicians from Palestine may have landed in Italy, taught the natives the knowledge they had brought with them from the East, and Etruscan culture was the result.

Wherever they came from, there is no doubt that the Etruscans were a highly civilized people. Little is known of the details of their lifestyle because their language is incomprehensible to modern scholars, but the archaeological remains reveal that the Etruscans enjoyed life to the fullest. Hundreds of Etruscan tombs have survived, many of them decorated with lush wall paintings. In the paintings men and women are seen dancing, playing music, and enjoying elaborate dinner parties lying on their reclining couches. Other paintings show battle and hunting scenes, and these too attest to the spirited nature of Etruscan life.

The Etruscans were also skilled craftsmen. Their speciality was metal-working and they were lucky enough to live in a land rich in mineral resources. Trade in metal goods became the basis of an active urban society. Etruscan cities sprang up where previously there had been only simple farming villages.

Tuscany to learn how to read the entrails of animals for signs from the gods.

Each Etruscan city supported itself by trading with the other cities and with the Greeks in the South. The Etruscans were eager to obtain luxury goods that the Greek colonists had to trade, and they developed overland routes to reach Greek cities. These routes cut straight through Latium, the plain south of the Tiber that was occupied by Italian natives called Latins.

The Etruscans Rule Rome

The Etruscans chose as one of their outposts on the route south a Latin village called Rome. By choosing Rome for their trading post, the Etruscans converted a cluster of mud huts into

Each Etruscan city was independent and unique, but the cities (12 in all), were grouped in a loose confederation for religious purposes. Representatives of the cities would gather at regular intervals to worship the twelve Etruscan gods, but that was the extent of their political unity. Their fascination with religion far surpassed their desire for political power. Indeed, long after Etruscan power was eclipsed by Rome, the Etruscan's reputation for skill and devotion to religious practice lived on. Young men of imperial Rome would be sent to

Left, ancient Greek dives gracefully into the hereafter. The fresco is from a tomb at Paestum. Above, Etruscan statue of the she wolf is Rome's symbol.

a thriving city. Their prosperity attracted Italic tribesmen from the surrounding countryside, and soon Rome's population swelled. To make Rome better serve their needs, the Etruscans drained the swamp that became the Roman Forum and built grand palaces and roads.

For 300 years, starting in the late 8th Century BC, Etruscan kings ruled Rome and directed its growth. But by the 5th Century, Etruscan power was fading. In the north, Gauls overran Etruscan settlements in the Po Valley. Next Italic tribesmen from the Abruzzi threatened the main Etruscan cities. Then in the south, the Etruscans went to war against the Greeks. The Romans took advantage of this moment of weakness to rebel against their Etruscan masters.

ROME RULES THE WORLD

The historians of ancient Rome wrote their own version of the events leading to the overthrow of the Etruscan kings. For this version they drew upon accepted legends about Rome's past, which stated that the city never really was Etruscan, but had only fallen under Etruscan rule temporarily. According to legend Rome was founded by the descendants of gods and heroes.

In his epic the *Aeneid*, the Roman poet Virgil tells how Aeneas, a hero of Homeric Troy, came west after the sack of Troy to live and rule in Latium. In the 8th Century one of his descendants, the Latin princess Rhea Silvia, bore twin sons: Romulus and Remus, fathered by the god Mars. Her uncle, King Amulius was angry because the princess had been sworn to chastity as a Vestal Virgin. He locked her up and abandoned the boys on the river bank to die. They were found there by a she-wolf who raised them.

When they were young men the brothers led a band of rebel Latin youths to find a new home. They chose the site of Rome because when they approached it a flight of eagles passed overhead. This was interpretated as a sign from the gods that they approved of the site and gave their blessing to the new city.

Rome was ruled by Etruscan kings until 509 BC when the son of harsh king Tarquinius Superbus raped a Roman noblewoman, Lucretia. She killed herself in shame, and Roman noblemen used the incident as an excuse to revolt against the Etruscans.

The leader of the Roman revolt, Lucius Junius Brutus, may have been an actual historical figure. In Roman legend he's larger than life: the founder of a republic, a vigorous leader, and a puritanical ruler. The historian Tacitus wrote that Brutus was so loyal to Rome that he watched without flinching as his two sons, arrested as traitors, were executed in his presence.

In the war against the Etruscans, Rome was also aided by a talented soldier named Cincinnatus. The legend "merits the attention of those who despise all human qualities in comparison with riches, and think there is no room for great honors or for wealth but amidst a profusion of wealth" wrote the Roman historian Livy. Cincinnatus was a simple Roman farmer who left his plow to help his

Left, Augustus of Primaporta shows a youthful emperor looking to Rome's future of *Imperium sine fine* – rule without end.

city. He was so able that he quickly rose to the rank of supreme general. But once the fight was won, he surrendered his position of power and returned to life as a plain citizen.

These stories of Rome's early heroes are very revealing of the Roman character. For the Romans, nothing was as important as *pietas* — dutiful respect to one's gods, city, parents and comrades. They turned to the heroes of the past to illustrate this point and they used it to build a powerful society.

Upon the overthrow of the Etruscans, Rome's leaders declared that no more kings would rule Rome. A republic based on the Greek model was founded and the Senate, a group of Rome's leading citizens who had previously had only an advisory role in government, took control of the city.

The Punic Wars

During the next 200 years Rome conquered most of the Italian peninsula. But Carthage, a city in North Africa first founded by the Phoenicians, controlled the western Mediterranean. If Rome was ever to expand it's borders across the Mediterranean, Carthage would have to be defeated.

The initial clash between the two cities came in 264 BC. This first Punic War began as a struggle for the Greek city of Messina on Sicily. By the time it was over, in 241 BC, the Romans had driven the Carthaginians out of Sicily completely. The island became Rome's first province. Three years later Rome annexed Sardinia and Corsica as well. Further military triumphs followed. Rome was able to conquer Cisalpine Gaul (northern Italy) and thus extend her borders to the Alps. Once Roman command posts guarded the Alpine passes, Rome was far more secure from the constant threat of an invasion by the Gauls.

War broke out once more in 218 BC when the brilliant Carthaginian general Hannibal, who at age nine had dedicated his life to the destruction of Rome, embarked on an ambitious scheme. He led his soldiers, supported by many war elephants, out of Spain, over the Pyrenees and Alps, and aimed to attack Rome from the north. Rome eventually counter attacked Carthage, and Hannibal was forced to return and defend his homeland. There he was defeated in 202 BC at the battle of Zama 80 miles from Carthage.

The Third Punic War was almost an afterthought. Carthage had been stripped of many of her possessions 50 years before, but had become once again an important commercial power. When the Carthaginians challenged Rome indirectly, the Romans took the opportunity to rid themselves of their bitter rival forever. The city of Carthage was razed, and the site sowed with salt. The Carthaginians themselves were sold into slavery.

Revolution at Home

The blessings of peace were mixed. Rome was now more prosperous than ever before, but only the middle class and the rich benefitted. For the common people, many of whom had served their city faithfully during the wars, peace meant only greater poverty. Menial jobs they had depended on for their

livelihood now were filled by the increased number of slaves so cheap that any Roman who could afford to feed them, could have them. Independent farmers, a group that traditionally formed the backbone of the Roman state, were bought out in large numbers by the owners of great estates who used slaves to work the land efficiently. These displaced farmers joined the Roman mob or wandered Italy in search of work.

The Senate's usual tactic of dealing with the potentially explosive situation that their wealth and power created, was to feed the masses bread and entertain them with circuses. But eventually one man from the patricians' ranks, challenged the exploitive system and worked to change the lot of the common man.

His name was Tiberius Gracchus, and in 133 BC he was elected tribune. He proposed that an old law limiting the size of the great estates be revived, and that farming and grazing land owned by the state be distributed amongst the poor. The Senators would have none of this; many of them were large landowners who did not want to see their influence checked. Similarly the public land under discussion had fallen into the hands of powerful citizens not about to give it up. The Senate blocked Tiberius' plan, but when he persisted and ran for re-election as tribune, they hired thugs to kill him and many of his followers.

But Tiberius' spirit did not die with him. Eleven years later, his younger brother Gaius was elected tribune. A volatile personality and an effective speaker, Gaius was even more popular than Tiberius with the Roman masses. Once in office he immediately called for sweeping land reform. And once again the Senate struck back viciously. The Roman people were incited to riot, and Gaius was blamed. He then was either killed, or forced to kill himself, and all his followers were imprisoned.

The power of the army commanders now became the determining factor in Roman politics. The heroic general Gaius Marius, son of a farmer, returned to Rome from triumphant campaigns in Africa determined to smash the power of the despised Senate. To the Roman people Marius was a god-like figure. He had transformed the Roman citizen legions into a professional standing army. Now he and his supporters butchered the senatorial leaders and thousands of other aristocratic Romans.

This fateful action, done in the name of liberty, opened the way to dictatorship. The Senate turned to Sulla, a rival general and a patrician by birth, who answered Marius's violence with a blood bath of his own. After Marius's death in 86 BC, Sulla posted daily lists of people to be executed by his henchmen. He proceeded to conduct equally bloody campaigns abroad and to return to Rome to rule as absolute dictator. There was no check the Senate could put on him; it was they who had opened the door for him to take power. But even if they had not done so, he and the army were so powerful that he could have forced himself on them. The Republic was dead, victim of three centuries of empire building.

The Rise of the Emperors

For two years Sulla made the streets of Rome run with blood. But in 79 BC he suddenly grew tired of ruling and retired to his estate near Naples. Civil war broke out once more. The eventual successor to Sulla was another general, Gnaeus Pompeius, called Pompey the Great. Pompey restored many of the liberties that Sulla had suspended, but that was not enough for the Roman citizens. The rioting masses demanded that all the Republican liberties be restored.

Pompey's solution was to join forces with two other military men, Crassus and Caesar, and form a three-man ruling body of considerable power and influence called the Triumvirate. This arrangement was successful at first but did not last long. Crassus died in 53 BC, and the two remaining leaders quarreled. For several years Pompey and Caesar eyed each other warily, then Caesar took a fateful step. Against the orders of the Senate he crossed the flooded Rubicon River (the border

was divinely appointed to rule Rome. For the first time in decades no riots plagued the capital's peace. But the upper classes were less content. They were accustomed to exercising considerable power through their control of the Senate, and Caesar's obvious monarchic tendencies made them nervous. This did not stop various factions within the Senate from heaping honors on the new ruler, as they hoped for favors in return. However many patricians watched suspiciously as Caesar had statues of himself raised in public places, and as his image began appearing on coin faces. Soon a conspiracy formed against him.

An Etruscan soothsayer had warned Caesar to beware of misfortune that would strike no later than March 15th 44 BC. On that day — the Ides of March — Caesar was scheduled to

between Cisalpine Gaul and Italy) with his army. With Caesar heading toward the capital, Pompey quickly left for Greece taking *his* army and most of the Senate along with him. Pompey had planned to strike back at Caesar from Greece, but Caesar moved first. He attacked Pompey's allies in Spain and then in Greece, forcing Pompey to flee to Egypt where he was eventually killed.

Caesar returned to Rome in triumph. No one could challenge his authority now, and the masses believed that his victories proved he

Left, Julius Caesar raised patrician eyebrows when he put his face on a coin. Above, Emperor Augustus built the monumental *Ara Pacis* to celebrate peace.

address the Senate. As he travelled from his house to the Senate chamber he passed the soothsayer. Caesar laughed and remarked that the Ides had come safely. The Etruscan replied ominously that the day was not over yet.

In the chamber, the conspirators surrounded Caesar and stabbed him 23 times. When Caesar saw that Marcus Junius Brutus, a patrician he had always treated like a son, was among his murderers, he is said to have murmured, "You too, Brutus," and died.

After Caesar's death, Mark Anthony, Caesar's co-consul and Octavian, his grandnephew, worked together to pursue and murder the conspirators. Despite their cooperation, the two were never the best of friends. For awhile they joined with an army leader called Lepidus to form an uneasy Second Triumvirate, but this arrangement was shattered when Anthony fell in love with the Egyptian queen Cleopatra. He rejected his wife, Octavian's sister, to marry the queen. Octavian got his revenge by turning the Senate against Mark Anthony, and then declared war on his former partner. When defeat was imminent, Anthony and Cleopatra committed suicide.

Octavian's triumphant return to Rome marked the beginning of a new era. He called himself simply "Augustus" meaning "the revered one," but in actuality he was the first emperor of Rome. His authority could not be challenged now that Mark Anthony was dead. But unlike his grand-uncle before him, he took care not to offend the republican sentiments of the Romans — therein lay his success. He was

creating a personal bureaucracy within his household. Not only did he have footmen and maids working for him, he also had tax collectors, governors, census takers, and administrators as his "servants." He allowed this personal civil service to grow to a size sufficient to run the empire, but always kept it under his tight control. At first many members of the nobility would not join because they believed that any office in the household, however influential, was too close to personal service. But poor men of talent joined Augustus readily, and throughout his reign the Empire was run smoothly.

With peace came a flourishing of art and literature. The poet Virgil, who had lived through the civil wars and military dictatorships, was so impressed by Augustus' achieve-

not interested in the trappings of power; he lived and dressed simply. The Republic was allowed to function outwardly as it always had, while he ran the show, very effectively, from behind the scenes. The competence and sensitivity with which Augustus reigned made for a period of peace and prosperity the like of which Rome had never seen. Indeed for 200 years after Augustan reform, the Mediterranean world basked in a "Pax Romana," a Roman peace.

Before Augustus had assumed power, the republican institutions had proved unable to administer the vast territories Rome now controlled. Military dictatorship had been the result. Augustus met this daunting administrative challenge, without resorting to tyranny, by

ments, that he wrote in the *Aeneid* of the divine origins of the emperor's family. And he wrote of the Roman's mission:

Roman, remember by your strength to rule
Earth's peoples—for your arts are to be these:
To pacify, to impose the rule of law.
To spare the conquered battle down the proud.
(Translator Robert Fitzgerald)

Another poet, Horace, was similarly impressed with Augustus. He likened the

Above, a reconstruciton of the Coliseum. Right, the philosopher emperor Marcus Aurelius rears above Rome's Campidoglio.

emperor to a helmsman who had steered the ship of state into a safe port. Horace's own achievements were considerable. After years of study he mastered the Greek poetic forms and used them to write beautiful Latin verse.

Augustus himself took part in the artistic resurgence. Among his projects was the rebuilding of the capital. The Roman historian Suetonius says that Augustus claimed he had found Rome a city of brick and left it a city of marble. He also worked to rebuild the character of the Roman people. He outlawed drunkeness and prostitution, and strengthened the laws governing divorce.

Augustus reigned for 41 years and set the tone of Roman leadership for the following 150. None of the men who succeeded him had the same breadth of interests nor the ability to

actually by their children—and the relatives forbidden to go into mourning."
(Translator Robert Graves)

Rome was relieved when Tiberius died, only to find that there was worse to come. Caligula, the successor, ruled ably for three years, then ran wild. His derangement may have been the result of illness, or simply the pressures of his high office. He insisted that he was a god, formed his own priesthood and erected a temple to himself. (In the temple was a life-size statue of the emperor, that was dressed each day with the clothes he was wearing.) He proposed his horse be made consul. Finally a group of his own officers assassinated Caligula, and Rome was rid of its most hated ruler.

The officers took it upon themselves to name the next emperor. Their choice was

do what he had done. Some were merely adequate rulers, others were quite mad. But the institutional and personal legacy of Augustus did much to preserve peace in the flourishing Roman world.

The Emperor Tiberius had none of his step-father's sense of proportion, nor his steadiness. He began his reign with good intentions, but he mismanaged many early problems, and soon grew sour and suspicious. He spent the last 11 years of his reign at his villa on Capri, from whence he issued execution orders. Suetonious wrote, "Not a day, however holy, passed without an execution; he even desecrated New Year's Day. Many of his men victims were accused and punished with their children—some

Claudius, the grandson of Augustus, whom they found hiding behind a curtain in the palace after the assassination. Many people thought Claudius a fool, for he stuttered and was slightly crippled, but he turned out to be a good and steady ruler. He oversaw the reform of the civil service, and the expansion of the Empire to include Britain.

Claudius was poisoned by his ambitious wife Agrippina, who pushed Nero, her son by a previous marriage onto the throne. Like Tiberius before him, Nero started out with good intentions. He was well-educated, an accomplished musician and showed respect for the advice of others, especially senators. But the violent side of his nature soon became apparent. He poisoned Brittanicus, Claudius' natural son. He then tried to do in his mother using the same method, but she had foresightedly built up an immunity to the poison. Nero was forced to accuse her of plotting against him, and had her executed.

Many of Nero's other excesses caused discontent among Rome's citizens. So much so that when a fire destroyed the city in 64 AD, Nero was accused of setting it. He was actually away from the city at the time and stories of him fiddling while Rome burned are probably untrue.

Nero lost his throne after the Roman commanders in Gaul, Africa, and Spain rebelled. When the news reached the capital riots broke out and the Senate condemned him to death as a public enemy. With no hope left, Nero killed himself in 68 AD.

His suicide threw the empire into greater turmoil. He left no heir. The commanders who had risen against Nero, fought among themselves for a year until out of the bloodshed a legion commander named Vespasian emerged as the new emperor.

Vespasian, whose last name was Flavius, proved to be a wise ruler, and the dynasty he started led Rome through a period of peace. There was a short time of troubles when Vespasian's younger son, Domitian became emperor after his father's and older brother's death, but upon Domitian's death the Senate was powerful enough to appoint its own Emperor, Nerva, a highly regarded lawyer from Rome.

Nerva was the first of the "five good emper-

ors" who reigned from AD 96 to 180. Trajan, Hadrian, Antoninus Pius and Marcus Aurelius ruled in turn after Nerva. All of these five were educated men, interested in philosophy and devoted to their duties. Not only were they loved by the people of Rome, but all over the Empire their names were spoken with reverence. They administered their vast territories efficiently and tolerantly and built up a successful defense of the Empire's borders against the barbarians who lived just outside.

During the period between the death of Marcus Aurelius and the sack of Rome in the 5th Century, it became more and more difficult to defend the Empire from barbarians. Between 180 and 285 AD, Rome was threatened in both the east and the west by barbarian tribes. To fight off these threats, the Empire doubled the size of the army. The drain on manpower and resources caused an economic crisis, and the increased power of the army meant that the army could place emperors on the throne and remove them at will. Most of these "barracks emperors" served for less than three years and never even lived in the capital.

Plague also struck Rome, which weakened the Empire and made it more vulnerable to enemy attack. On all sides wars raged. In the east the revived Persian Empire threatened Syria, Egypt and all of Asia Minor. Franks invaded France and Spain.

Major political reform was undertaken by Emperor Diocletian in 286. He believed the Empire could no longer be ruled by one man, so he divided it into an eastern and western region. He chose Nicomedia in Asia Minor as his capital and appointed a soldier named Maximinus to rule the west from Milan.

Unfortunately this arrangement did not end quarrels about the succession. Constantine marched on Rome in 311 to assert his right to the throne. On the road he had a vision. The sign of the cross appeared in the sky with the words "By this sign win your victory." When Constantine emerged as the sole Emperor in 324, he ruled as a Christian. This established Christianity, which had been spreading through the empire since the time of Nero, as the religion of the Roman state and thus the Western world.

Despite the conversion to Christianity the Empire continued to deteriorate. In 324 Constantine decided to move the capital east, and make a fresh start in his new city of Constantinople. Back in Italy, the barbarians moved closer. The city of Rome was sacked in 410.

Above, one of the late "barracks Emperors," probably Valentian. Right, this fresco is at the casa dei Vettii in Pompeii.

DAILY LIFE IN THE EMPIRE

As the political influence of Rome spread through Italy so did its customs. The residents of towns all over the peninsula considered themselves Romans and lived according to Roman rituals and customs. Most important among these was the primacy of the family, the basic unit of Roman life.

In Roman families the paterfamilias ruled like a king over his wife, sons, daughter-in-laws, unmarried daughters and grandchildren. By law he was allowed to punish them with death, although by the time of Augustus this right was rarely exercised. When a child

would adjoin.

The Romans enjoyed feasting, and wealthy citizens made a point of eating a big meal, called the *cena*, in the middle of every day. Servants would wait on each family member, and hover close to the couches to wash the diners' hands between courses. Food was rolled out from the kitchens on low tables and set before the couches.

After the *cena* Roman men were likely to go to the bath houses for their afternoon's entertainment. There they would not only bathe, but play dice games, listen to lectures

was born into a Roman family, he was placed at the father's feet for ceremonial acceptance. He grew up learning that the father's authority was absolute in the home, just as government authority was absolute in society. For a Roman, obedience was a way of life.

Romans lived in homes that appeared very simple from the outside. There were no windows opening onto the street. But inside, the homes of rich men had elaborately patterned mosaics on the floors. The walls were painted with scenes from Greek mythology. Poor families lived in only one room, called an *atrium* because the roof was partially open to the sky. In a rich man's house the *atrium* would be the parlor. A dining room with enough space for several reclining couches

and musical entertainments, do calisthenics, and gossip. The bath houses were so popular that larger and larger ones were built. The magnificent Baths of Caracalla in Rome (which are very well-preserved) had room for 1,600 bathers a day. The water was heated by underground furnaces.

But in addition to these comforts, Roman cities had great drawbacks. Getting around was very difficult. There were no sidewalks lining the narrow, winding streets. Crowds filled the streets at all hours of the day. A pedestrian had always to beware of falling garbage, since housewives threw their trash out the window. A stranger in a Roman city needed a guide. The streets had no names, and the houses no numbers.

POPE GREGORY.   *Frontispiece.*

THE MIDDLE AGES

For four centuries after the sack of Rome in 410, barbarian invaders including the Goths and the Lombards, battled with local military leaders and the Byzantine emperors for control of Italy. Under these conditions, the culture and prosperity of ancient times faded. The Roman Empire had unified Italy and made her the center of the world, but after the Empire's demise, Italy was no more than a provincial battlefield upon which these rival claimants to Rome's political legacy fought bitterly, and unsuccessfully, for complete victory. Since none of the rivals was powerful enough to control the whole of Italy, eventually the land was divided. Italy would not again be a unified territory until the 19th Century.

The Dark Ages began with a series of Visigoth invasions from northern and eastern Europe. The emperors in Constantinople were still in theory the rulers of Italy, but in reality for many decades they accepted first the Visigoth and later the Ostrogoth leaders as *de facto* kings. Justinian I who became emperor in Constantinople in 527 had dreams of reviving the earlier splendor of the Empire. He sent his brilliant general Belisarius to try to regain direct control of Italy for the imperial crown. This effort was successful initially, (he captured Ravenna from the Goths in 540) but eventually crumbled when a new group of barbarians appeared on Italy's borders.

The Lombards were German tribesmen from the Danube valley who as fierce warriors had no trouble conquering most of what is now Lombardy, Venetia and Tuscany. Many citizens of the northern Italian cities fled the Lombard armies and settled in the remote eastern coastal regions where they were protected by the Byzantines, who still controlled the seas. One area that became the home for many was the lagoon of Venice.

Meanwhile, in the areas they controlled, the Lombards radically changed how Italy was governed. They replaced the centralized Roman political system (which previous barbarian invaders had respected) with new local administrative units called "duchies" after the Lombard army generals who were known as "duces." Within each duchy a duce ruled as king. The land was distributed to groups of related Lombard families. Each family was headed by a free warrior, who owed only

Left, 6th Century Pope Gregory the Great was one of many early Popes to be canonized.

limited feudal allegiance to his king. On his land he was allowed to do as he wished. This, plus the fact that the Byzantines continued to control many provinces, meant that the effect of the Lombard invasion was to divide Italy.

The Power of the Popes

The radical changes that the Lombards brought to Italy's administration did not touch the church. In Rome, the bishopric rose to new prominence because the emperors in Constantinople were too far away to exert any temporal or spiritual authority.

Greatest among the early popes was Gregory I (589-603), a Roman by birth, a scholar by instinct and training. He instituted many liturgical reforms — the Gregorian chant is named after him. He was also a great statesman. He persuaded the Lombards to abandon the siege of Rome, and then helped bring about a general peace in Italy. He sent missionaries to Northern Europe to spread the word of God and the influence of Rome. One day on the street in Rome he saw a group of blond slaves whom he thought were the most handsome people he had ever seen. "They're Angels not Angles," he punned upon learning they were Britons. He later sent the first missionaries to the British Isles.

Gregory's successors reorganized the municipal government of Rome, and became rulers, in fact if not in name, of the city. It was inevitable that the popes would eventually clash with the emperor in Constantinople.

The clash came over a spiritual matter. In 726 Emperor Leo decreed that the veneration of images of Christ and the saints was forbidden, and that all those images were to be destroyed. The popes opposed his decree on the grounds that the church in Rome should have the last word on spiritual matters, and they organized an Italian revolt against the Emperor. The Lombards joined the revolt on the side of the popes and used it as an opportunity to chase the Byzantines out of Italy.

After the imperial capital, Ravenna, fell to the Lombard army in 751, the popes realized they were more directly threatened by the powerful Lombards than an absent emperor, so they sought a new ally from across the Alps. Since Gregory's time, they had sent missionaries to the Frank kingdom in Northern Europe to convert the Franks to Christianity. Now the Franks answered the popes' cries for help.

Pepin, king of the Franks, invaded Italy in

754. With his army he reconquered the imperial lands but he gave them to the Pope not to the emperor. Twenty years later, Pepin's son Charlemagne completed his father's work by defeating and capturing the Lombard king, confirming his father's grant to the papacy, and assuming the crown of the Lombards.

A New Empire is Formed

After Charlemagne conquered the Lombards, he returned to the north and campaigned against the Saxons, the Bavarians and the Avars, making himself ruler of a large part of Western Europe. In recognition of these accomplishments, and in an effort to unify his vast territories under Christian auspices he had Pope Leo crown him Holy Roman Emperor at

half centuries Sicily was an Arab state. Sicily also became a base for raids on the Italian mainland, and Charlemagne's great-grandson Louis II who was emperor for 25 years, tried but could not raise an organized defense against them. The Lombard dukes in the South whom Charlemagne had not conquered completely, allied themselves with these invaders against the Carolingian emperor. What successes Louis did have were overshadowed by Pope Leo IV's defense of Rome and naval victory against the Saracens at Ostia.

The Normans in the South

In the early 11th Century small groups of Normans arrived in southern Italy. They were adventurers and skilled soldiers who were

St. Peter's in Rome on Christmas Day 800.

Charlemagne was an extraordinary man who used his position to promote religion, justice and education among the people he conquered. But he lived only 14 years after his coronation, and none of his successors was as able as he. Instead, the new authorities in Italy were Frankish counts, who as vassals of Charlemagne had accompanied him south and were granted land of their own. As representatives of the crown they were required to raise troops from among the population on their grants. But the counts often used these troops to fight among themselves for more land and power.

This period of feudal anarchy was also marked by invasions. In the south the Saracens invaded Sicily in 827, and for the next two and

seeking their fortunes in a sunny land. The region was divided into so many conflicting states that the Normans' abilities as fighting men were in great demand. In southern Italy they would fight for anyone who would pay: Greek, Lombard and Saracen alike. As payment they asked for land.

Soon landless men from Normandy began to arrive in a steady stream to fight, settle and conquer for themselves. The papacy quickly allied with this powerful group of Christians. In the 1050s the Norman chief, Robert Guiscard, conquered Calabria in the toe of Italy. Pope Nicholas II "legitimized" Norman rule of the area by calling it a papal fief and then investing Guiscard as its king.

Robert's nephew, Roger, conquered Sicily.

He was crowned king in Palermo in 1130 and ruled over the island and his uncle's mainland possessions. He was an efficient and tolerant ruler. All the different groups under his authority: Greeks, Saracens, Italians, and Frenchmen, were for the most part allowed to live as they wished. The Norman court became a meeting place of Jewish, Greek and Arabic scholars. Still visible today are the architectural achievements of this sophisticated culture. Brilliant examples of Arab-Norman architecture can be seen in Palermo (San Giovanni degli Eremiti, the Zisa and the Cuba,) and at the cathedrals of Monreale and Cefalú.

Despite some external opposition (from both the eastern and western emperors) and occasional domestic rebellions, Roger's son and grandson were able to preserve the regime.

named an appropriate candidate. But by reforming the papacy, the emperors started a trend that would later cost them more than they anticipated.

In the 11th Century, the Popes strove to reform the church further by organizing a strict clerical hierarchy. Throughout the Holy Roman Empire, bishops were to be answerable to the pope, and priests to bishops. A single legal and administrative system would bind all members of the clergy together. These reforms immediately angered all lay rulers from the emperor on down.

The struggle reached a climax when Emperor Henry IV invested an anti-reform candidate as archbishop of Milan in 1072. As a result, Pope Gregory VII decreed in 1075 that such investiture by a non-cleric was forbidden.

Only when William II died in 1189, leaving no legitimate male heir, did civil war break out and Norman control of southern Italy end.

Church and Emperor Clash

During the 9th and 10th centuries, the papacy was completely controlled by Roman nobles. The men they picked for the office were often corrupt. After the Emperor Otto I arrived in Rome in 962, he insisted that no pope could be elected until the emperor had

Left, glittering mosaics, such as this one of the Emperor Justinian, are reminders that Ravenna was once the capital of Byzantium. Above, fresco in Siena's town hall.

At the same time the pope excommunicated Henry IV. For three days in the cold winter of 1077, the humbled emperor stood in the courtyard of a Tuscan castle where Gregory was staying, and pleaded for a reconciliation with the Pope.

Henry was forgiven, but Gregory had no way to be sure that he would keep to his promise to recognize the claims of the Papacy. As it turned out he did not, and a new civil war broke out. Gregory's supporters were defeated initially and he was carried off to Salerno to die, but the years that followed witnessed the triumph of his cause. The men who succeeded him worked gradually for the reforms Gregory died fighting for. The emperors were forced to give up their rights of investiture in 1122.

The Rise of the City-States

During the years of the investiture controversy and ensuing civil wars, the cities of northern and central Italy became richer and more powerful. The emperors were too distracted to administer them directly. Simultaneously, Mediterranean commerce, which for decades had suffered constant interruptions at the hands of the Saracens, was now revived. With new wealth and independence at their disposal the cities forced the nobles in the surrounding countryside to acknowledge their supremacy. The Italian city states were born.

The maritime republics of Venice, Genoa, and Pisa were foremost among the Italian cities because they had fleets for trade and protection. The prosperity of inland cities was due to

their locations on rich trade routes. Milan and Verona lay at the entrance to the Alpine passes, Bologna was the chief city on the Via Emilia, and Florence had a route to the sea by the river Arno and controlled two roads to Rome.

The growing political power of the city-states was an important factor in renewed conflict between emperor and pope during the 13th Century. Emperor Frederick II (1197-1250) tried to build a strong, centralized state in Italy. The cities that supported him kept their rights of self-government, but were forced to join an imperial federation. Many more cities opposed him because they wanted complete political autonomy. They found an ally in Pope Gregory IX who secretly had imperial designs of his own for Italy. Northern

Italy became a civil war battlefield where the "Guelfs," supporters of the Pope, and the "Ghibellines," allies of the emperor, clashed.

When Frederick died in 1250 without instituting his reforms, the Guelf cause had won. The alliance of pope with city states had ruined the imperial plans for a unified, centralized Italy. Frederick's heirs, his illegitimate son Manfred and his grandson Conradin fought 15 years longer for his Italian policy, but they too could not defeat the combined forces of Pope and townspeople.

The Age of Dante

The Guelfs won decisively over the Ghibellines, but soon a feud broke out between two factions within the Guelf party: the Blacks and the Whites. This split was especially severe in Florence where the Blacks defended the feudal tradition among the nobility against the Whites, rich magnates who were willing to give rising merchants and the people a voice in government.

Pope Boniface VIII sided with the Blacks and worked to have all the prominent Whites exiled from Florence in 1302. Among them was Dante Alighieri, who in his exile wrote a masterpiece, *Divina Commedia*, that was a powerful enough literary work to promote Dante's language, Tuscan Italian, to the status of a national tongue. The *Divine Comedy* also reveals much about the politics of the period.

"Rome used to have two suns, which lighted the roads of the world and of God. Now one has extinguished the other . . ." Dante wrote of the papacy and its assumption of temporal power. Dante was biased because Pope Boniface was in part responsible for his exile, but he also sincerely believed that it ill-fitted the supreme spiritual power in the world to play at politics. "Christ has been made captive in the person of his Vicar," Dante wrote.

Dante believed that Italy needed a new form of political unity. He put his faith in the weakened Holy Roman Empire, convinced that it could and should usher in a new period of cultural and political prominence for Italy.

When Henry VII became Holy Roman Emperor in 1308 an opportunity arose for testing Dante's scheme for Italian salvation. Henry wanted to revive imperial power in Italy and establish a government that was neither Guelf nor Ghibelline. But when he came to Italy, the cities refused to support him. Dante's home town of Florence was the center of resistence to imperial plans.

Above, the Middle Ages live on in Siena's famous Palio race. Right, a pensive Dante stands over a quiet piazza in Verona.

THE RENAISSANCE: ITALY ALONE

The constant fighting in Northern Italy ended in the early 14th Century when both the popes and the emperors withdrew from Italian affairs. After Henry VII's demise the emperors turned their attention to Germany. They came south occasionally during the next 200 years, but they could not maintain real control of Italy and follow their dynastic interests in Germany at the same time. The influence of the papacy declined after Pope Boniface quarreled with King Philip of France in 1302. The Pope insisted that the King had no right to tax the French clergy; the King's response was to send his troops to capture the Pope. French pressure insured that the next Pope was a Frenchman, Clement V, and he moved the papacy from Rome to Avignon, where it remained until 1377.

As a result of these events, the people of Italy were free of outside interference during the 14th Century. The Italian cities, already stronger, richer and bigger than any others in Europe, gained even more power as the power of the popes and emperors faded. Against the political background of the supremacy of the city state, a new culture bloomed. The independence of the cities combined with the ever-increasing wealth meant that new ideas flourished. Rulers could try new methods of administration. Scholars were allowed to rediscover and explore the pagan past. Merchants were rich enough to become lavish patrons of the arts. Through their commissions, artists experimented with a new, more realistic style.

Not even the Black Death — the terrible outbreak of bubonic plague that ravaged Europe in the 14th Century — could smother the new cultural awakening. But the plague did cause great human suffering and a prolonged economic depression. During several months of 1347 the death rate was as high as 60 percent in some Italian cities. The merchants' solution to the declining profits of the period was to change the way they did business. Their innovations included marine insurance, credit transfers, double-entry bookkeeping, holding companies, all of which later became standard business practice.

To be a good businessman in the early Renaissance required a basic education. Anyone who intended to get rich needed to know how to read, write and figure. With profits growing and opportunities increasing many Italians were taught these fundamental skills. But the more complicated business practices became, the more knowledge was needed in addition to basic skills. An understanding of law and diplomacy, and a general appreciation for the ways of the world were valuable commodities in this period of expansion. The traditional theological studies of the Middle Ages were replaced by the reading of ancient authors and the study of grammar, rhetoric, history and moral philosophy. This type of education became known as *studia humanitatis*, or "humanities."

Despite its rejection of much of medieval scholarship, humanism was not atheism. Humanists believed in God, but they simultaneously embraced many ideas of classical, pagan civilization. For them life was much more than a long preparation for paradise. Instead, they thought life should be enjoyable, and a chance for a man to serve his fellow man.

Humanism developed partly out of the need for greater legal expertise in the expanding world of Mediterranean commerce. To learn how to administer their new, complex societies lawyers looked back at the great tenets of Roman law. As they struggled to understand the codes of the ancients they grew to appreciate the cultural riches of that long-buried classical civilization. All aspects of Italian life were re-examined in the light of this new humanism. Classical beliefs about education, character and science were embraced wholeheartedly. One way of life was thought to be ideal —that of the all-round man based on classical models. The Renaissance man was a reincarnation of rich talented Roman philosophers.

Despots and Republics

Italians of the 14th Century considered themselves citizens of particular cities, not members of a large national unit. They worshipped local saints, believed myths that explained the origin and uniqueness of their city, and carried on feuds with other cities. The competition between the city states even played a role in art patronage. Italian rulers desired paintings and literature to glorify their towns.

There were a few experiences and conditions that many cities shared. As the authority of the Popes and the emperors declined, life in the cities became increasingly violent. Leading

Michelangelo's *David* is a splendid illustration of Renaissance Italy's rediscovery of the beauty of the human form.

families fought each other constantly for power, and often came into conflict with groups lower on the social ladder who wanted to play a role in the political life of the city. The remedy to this bloody civil strife, was the rule of one strong man. The pattern was repeated over and over again in Northern Italy. Traditional republican rule which could not keep order was replaced by a dictatorship. Sometimes a leading faction would bring in an outsider, known as a *podesta*, to end the chaos — the lordship of the Este family in Ferrara was established this way. More often, the future despot was originally a captain of the people, their representative against the growing power of the rich families. Over time, this captain would extend his powers until he controlled the entire city. Then he was in a strong enough

flourish, for the merchants dominated the organs of the republican government completely.

During the 14th and 15th centuries northern and central Italy changed from an area speckled with innumerable, tiny political units to one dominated by a few much larger states. Both republics and despots had a tendency to expand. They would conquer their smaller neighbors, and construct out of the lands they won a new regional state. These larger states greatly increased the economic resources a city had to draw upon, but they were costly in military terms. The citizens of the absorbed towns resented outside rule and were likely to revolt at any time. Furthermore, the new territory had to be defended from encroachment by the other states.

position to make his office hereditary. This was how the della Scala family in Verona, the Carrara in Padua, the Gonzaga in Mantua and the Visconti in Milan came to power.

Once established, a despot would centralize all agencies of the government under his personal supervision. His power would only be threatened if he overstepped what his subjects could tolerate. The united population could overthrow him. But even that was difficult as he controlled all the military force.

Some cities, including Venice and many important communities in Tuscany (Florence, Siena, Lucca, and Pisa) never resorted to despotism. In these places, the merchants were so powerful that class warfare never broke out. But even in these cities republicanism did not

Of the Italian city states, the most successful and the most powerful, was Milan. During the 14th Century, the authoritarian Visconti family led the city to innumerable military and political victories until it was the largest state in northern Italy. The famous historian of the Renaissance, Jacob Burckhardt, admired Visconti Milan for its "strict rationalism," he considered the Milanese government "a work of art."

The Visconti regime may have been, in it's deliberateness and efficiency unlike anything

Above, Italian city states were constantly at war with each other. Right, Cosimo the Elder established the Medici family as rulers of Florence.

Europe had seen for centuries, but for the Milanese people it had great drawbacks. Their freedom was severely limited. The personal brutality of the Visconti, rather than a modern bureaucracy, controlled Milan. The regime could not rely on the loyalty of the populace for its survival. When the Visconti line died out in 1447, the Milanese took the opportunity to declare a republic. Unfortunately this republic was not strong enough to rule over all the restive towns Milan now controlled. When in 1450 Francesco Sforza, a famous general who had served the Visconti, overthrew the republic and became the new duke, ruling with his wife Bianca Visconti, many Milanese were relieved.

The Republic of Florence

The spectacular transformation of Florence from a small town in the 1100s to the commercial and financial center it was by the end of the 14th Century, came about because of the profitable wool trade. The wood guild of Florence, called the *Arte Della Lane* imported wool from Northern Europe and dyes from the Middle East. Using its own secret weaving and coloring techniques guild members produced a heavy, red cloth that was sold all over the Mediterranean area. Profits from the wool trade had provided the initial capital for the banking industry of Florence. Since the 13th Century Florentine merchants had lent money to their allies. the pope and other powerful Guelf nobles. This early experience led to the founding of formal banking houses, and a fine reputation that made Florence the financial capital of Europe.

The leading merchant families of Florence spent their wealth on art. They made their city a showpiece of the best of Renaissance sculpture, painting and architecture. In the second half of the 13th Century a building boom began with the construction of the Bargello, the Franciscan church of Santa Croce, and the Dominican church of Santa Maria Novella. Arnolfo di Cambio designed the cathedral and the Palazzo Vecchio. The *Arte Della Lana* paid for the construction and decoration of the cathedral. The guild hired Giotto to design the Campanile which is named after him, and in 1434 they had Brunelleschi finish the great dome.

The rich men of Florence controlled the city government through the *Parte Guelfa*. With membership came the right to seek out and persecute anyone with "Ghibellistic tendencies." Other political non-conformities were also not tolerated. When members of lesser guilds demanded a greater share of power, or joined with the lower classes to fight the *Parte*

Guelfa, they were met with quick and effective annihilation. However, in the early 15th Century the violence of class warfare escalated. The unenfranchised artisans struck back more and more. At this point the rich merchants allowed Cosimo de' Medici to rise to the leadership of Florence.

The Fifteenth Century

This was the golden age of the Renaissance. All the economic, political and cultural developments of the previous century had set the stage for a period of unprecedented artistic and intellectual achievement. To live in Italy at this time was to live in a new world of cultural and commercial riches. Italy was truly the center of the world.

The political history of the century can be conveniently divided into two parts. Until 1454 the five chief states of Italy were busy expanding their borders, or strengthening their hold on territories they already, in name, possessed. These developments required fighting many small wars. The soldiers who fought them were for the most part *condottieri* — mercenaries. After 1454 there was a period of relative peace, during which the states tried to further their own interests through alliances rather than resorting to war. These later years were ones of the greatest artistic achievement, when Italian states of all sizes became cultural centers.

Italian wars of the Late Middle Ages and Early Renaissance had traditionally been fought by foreign mercenaries, but by the 15th

Century the mercenaries were more likely to be Italian. Men of all classes and from all parts of Italy joined the ranks of the purely Italian companies to fight northern wars for rival nobles. The *condottieri* looked upon war as a professional, technical skill. In battle the object was to lose as few men as possible but still win. Soldiers were too valuable to be sacrificed unnecessarily. The countryside however, always suffered heavily as village after village was given over to plunder. The *condottieri* did not hesitate to take what they could get in the field despite the fact that they were very well paid. They were bound by no patriotic ties, only by a monetary arrangement. The result of this system was the ever-present danger that an important captain would be bought up by the enemy. Rulers were constantly trying to satisfy the *condottieri*'s needs for wealth, fame and territory. Then, they could only pray that there would be no higher bidder.

Among the *condottieri*, one of the greatest was Francesco Sforza. Sforza had inherited the command of an army upon his father's death in 1424. He fought first for Milan and then for Venice in the northern wars until Fillipo Visconti sought to attach him permanently to Milan by marrying him to his illegitimate daughter Bianca.

Visconti died in 1447 leaving no heir, and Milan declared itself a republic. Sforza was expected to be the captain of the new republican forces. Instead he went into exile, when the republican government proved incompetent he turned his forces on the city and was able to starve Milan into surrender. The chief assembly of the republic invited the former mercenary to be the new duke of the city.

Peace and the Italian League

Sforza, the great soldier, was instrumental in bringing peace to northern Italy. He signed and encouraged others to sign the Treaty of Lodi out of which followed the Italian League of 1455. This was a defensive league between Milan, Florence and Venice that the king of Naples and the pope also respected. The League was intended to prevent any one of the great powers from increasing at the expense of its weaker neighbors, and to present a common national front against attack.

The smaller states of Italy benefitted most from the new arrangement. Previously they had spent vast resources, human and monetary, on maintaining a defense against the larger, more aggressive states. "This most holy League upon which depends the welfare of all Italy," wrote Giovanni Bentivoglia a leading citizen of Bologna in 1460.

Life in peacetime in Renaissance Italy centered around business. The new worldliness of the culture and education meant that making money was the most respectable of occupations. Petrarch among others associated the values of bourgeois life with the politics and economics of ancient Rome. The state was valued because without state protect'on business would be impossible. Children were taught the virtues of thrift, honesty and public duty.

Florence Under the Medici

During the decades of peace in Italy, Florence experienced its own golden age under the rule of the Medici family. The historian Guicciardini wrote later of the Florence of Lorenzo de' Medici where he had spent his childhood:

"The city was in perfect peace, the leading citizens were united, and their authority was so great that none dared to oppose them. The people were entertained daily with pageants and festivals; the food supply was abundant and all trades flourished. Talented and able men were assisted in their careers by the recognition given to arts and letters. While tranquility reigned within her walls, externally the city enjoyed high honors and renown." All these features that Guicciardini mentions were due in large measure to the leadership of the

Above, Francesco Sforza married the natural daughter of the last of the Visconti rulers of Milan and became despot of Milan. Right, his beloved wife Bianca.

Medici family.

In part, the success of the Medici was a public relations coup. They allowed the Florentines to believe that the city government was still a great democracy. Only after Lorenzo's death when Florence was briefly ruled by his arrogant son did the citizens realize that their state, for all its republican forms, had drifted into the control of one family. They then quickly exiled the Medici and drafted a new constitution. But until that time, the Medici managed to dominate Florence but never appear to be more than prominent private citizens. They did this partly by manipulating the elections for the *Signoria* — the Florence city council — but the real base of their power lay in their complete acceptance by the city's leading citizens.

The Medici did more than simply rule and, successfully keep the peace. They promoted art and culture in Florentine life. When the famous humanist Niccolo Niccoli died, Cosimo acquired his book collection and attached it to the convent of San Marco, creating the first public library in Florence. Cosimo also had Marsilo Fucino trained to become head of the new Platonic Academy and make Florence a center of Platonic studies. He supplied Donatello with classical works to inspire his sculpture. Lorenzo de' Medici grew up in the atmosphere his grandfather had created and when he became leader of Florence he was also a great patron of the arts. For his employees he was also a peer as well as a patron. His poetry was widely admired.

When the political theorist Machiavelli wrote *The Prince*, his famous advice book for rulers, he was inspired by Lorenzo's example when he named the qualities that a successful ruler must have. "A ruler must emulate the fox and the lion, for the lion cannot avoid traps and the fox cannot fight wolves. He must be a fox to beware of traps and a lion to scare off wolves."

When Lorenzo de' Medici died in 1492, the fragile Italian League that had successfully kept Italy at peace and protected her from foreign attacks died with him. Ludovico il Moro, the lord of Milan, immediately quarreled with the Neopolitan king and proposed to the king of France that he, Charles VIII, conquer Naples and the surrounding states. Ludovico offered financial assistance and safe passage through the north of Italy. Charles readily accepted the offer and so began one of the most demoralizing chapters of Italian history.

The internal disarray in Italy at the time was so great that the French troops faced no organized resistence. The new leader of Florence, a Dominican friar named Girolamo Savonarola went so far as to preach that Charles was sent by God to regenerate the church and purify spiritual life. Other Italians also welcomed the French. They believed that the invaders would rid Italy of decadence and set up model governments with worthy natives in the principle posts. Only when these ideas proved to be illusionary could Italian patriots recruit an army and challenge the French.

The French and Italians met near the village of Fornovo on July 6, 1495. At first it appeared that the Italians led by general Francesco Gonzaga would be certain victors: they outnumbered the French two-to-one, and they could launch a surprise attack against their enemy. But in the pitch of battle, the Italian strategy fell apart. Crucial troops could not cross the river to the French position. General Gonzaga entered the fiercest fighting and did not direct the battle as a whole. Some soldiers were distracted by the sight of the French king's booty, and left the battle to capture it. When the battle ended, Charles escaped with what was left of his troops. Four thousand men had died — the majority of them Italian.

"If the Italians had won at Fornovo, they would probably have discovered then the pride of being a united people ... Italy would have emerged as a respectable nation ... a country which adventurous foreigners would think twice before attacking," wrote Luigi Barzini in his book *The Italians*. Instead, Fornovo broke the Italian spirit and opened the way for 30 years of foreign interventions, bloody conflicts, civil wars and revolts.

RENAISSANCE ART

Italian art shone brightest during the Renaissance when, as in most disciplines, a revolution took place. The Early Renaissance (1400-1490/5), or Quattrocento, introduced new themes that altered the future of art. Ancient Greece and Rome were rediscovered and, with them, the importance of man, in all his glory, in the here and now. As a consequence, the human body surfaced as a new focal point in painting and sculpture. The discovery of perspective, also stemming from study of the ancients, changed architecture.

The Early Renaissance centers on Florence. The city wished to be considered "the new Athens" and public works projects abounded. First was Lorenzo Ghiberti's (1378-1455) commission for sculpting the gilded bronze north doors (1403-1424) of the Baptistry, captured after a competition in 1401 with Filippo Brunelleschi. Ghiberti's later east doors (1424-52) are the more famous, so dazzling in their depiction of scenes from the Old Testament —and in their use of perspective— Michelangelo called them "the Gates of Paradise."

It was Filippo Brunelleschi (1377-1466) who championed perspective. After losing the Baptistry door competition, he set off for Rome to study ancient buildings, noting their exact measurements. You can see the result of these studies in his masterpieces of design: the interiors of the church of San Lorenzo (1421-69), the Pazzi Chapel of Santa Croce (begun 1430/3), and Santo Spirito, all in Florence. You need not get out your yardstick to appreciate the mathematical proportions and ratios: They come through, unmistakably, in the sense of harmony, balance and calm.

If Brunelleschi was the most noted architect, Donatello (1386-1466) ruled the realm of sculpture. His work expresses a whole new attitude about the human body.

The body of St. Mark (1411-1413) at the church of Orsanmichele is clearly a separate and solid form, distinct from the drapery that covers it. His *Gattamelata* (1445-50) in Padua is the first cast-bronze equestrian statue since Roman times. Donatello also sculpted the figures in five of the niches of Florence's Campanile: the most famous, an unidentified (and bald) prophet called *Zuccone*, or pumpkinhead (1423-25) is so realistic its creator is said

Left, Titian's portrait of Pope Julius II. He wasn't much of a priest, but was a great patron of art. He hired both Raphael and Michelangelo.

to have commanded it, "Speak!" The sensual beauty of the human form is exalted in his bronze *David* in the Museo del Bargello (1430-32). The sinewy youth, clad only in boots and a hat, is the first free-standing nude statue since antiquity.

The Birth of Painting

The groundwork for the revolution in painting had been laid a century earlier by Giotto (1267-1337). His frescoes — in Santa Croce, in Padua's Cappella degli Scrovegni, and, most notably, in Assisi's San Francesco — depart from the flat Byzantine style and invest the human form with a new solidity and volume, and the setting with a sense of space and depth. His breakthrough was carried further by the Early Renaissance's most noted painter, Masaccio (1401-28). In his fresco *The Holy Trinity with Virgin and St. John* in Santa Maria Novella (1425), and in the Brancacci Chapel of Santa Maria del Carmine (1427), you can see the coalescence of the Renaissance's new themes: the importance of the human form, distinct under its clothing; the display of human emotion; and the use of perspective.

Domenico Veneziano moved to Florence in 1439 and introduced a new color scheme: pastel greens and pinks awash in cool light. The palette was picked up by his assistant, Piero della Francesca (1416?-1492) for his frescoes at San Francesco in Arezzo (1460) — marvels of pale tone as well as mathematics: heads, arms and legs are variations of geometric shapes; of spheres, cones and cylinders.

The artistic revolution in Florence soon reached other parts of Italy. Leon Battista Alberti (1404-72), an author of famous treatises on sculpture, painting and architecture, spread his design development of tracing classic motifs (columns, arches) on the exteriors of buildings from the Palazzo Rucellai in Florence (1446-51) to the Malatesta Temple in Rimini (1450).

Giovanni Bellini (1430/1-1516) triumphed in Venice. In his *Madonna and Saints* in San Zaccaria (1505), you can see the grandeur of Massacio's influence tempered by a newer concern: Flemish detail and intimacy.

Detail most delicately expressed is the hallmark of Sandro Botticelli (1444/5-1510). The Uffizi Gallery houses his most beloved canvases: the enchanting, allegorical *Primavera* (1480), and the lovely *Birth of Venus* (1489).

The *High Renaissance* (1490/5-1525) was the heyday of some of the most stellar artists in the entire history of art: Leonardo, Michelangelo, Bramante, Raphael, Giorgione. These men unlike their predecessors, were considered creative geniuses rather than craftsmen, geniuses capable of works of superhuman scale, grandeur and effort. Their extravaganzas were made possible by a new source of patronage: the papacy. Having returned to Rome from exile in Avignon, the popes turned the Eternal City once again into a center of culture. The art itself is marked by a move beyond rules of mathematical ratios or anatomical geometrics to a new emphasis on emotional impact. The increasing use of oil paints — another technique from the north, introduced to the Italians in the late 1400s — began to replace egg

Da Vinci also pioneered new techniques in painting. *Chiaroscuro* (literally, light-and-dark) — the use of light to bring out and highlight three-dimensional bodies — is vividly seen in the whirl of bodies in the *Adoration of the Magi* (1481-1482) in the Uffizi. Another invention was *fumato* — a fine haze that lends paintings a dreamy quality, enhancing their poetic possibilities.

In 1503 the great art patron, Pope Julius II, commissioned the most prominent architect of the day, Donato Bramante (1444-1514) to design the new St. Peter's. Bramante had earlier made his mark with the classically inspired gem, *The Tempietto* (1502) in the courtyard of Rome's San Pietro in Montorio. The pope's directive for the new project: create a monument to surpass any of ancient Rome. Working

tempera and opened new possibilities for richness of color and delicacy of light.

Leonardo da Vinci (1452-1519) was born near Florence but left the city to work for the Duke of Milan, primarily as an engineer and only secondarily as a sculptor, architect and painter. In Milan, da Vinci painted the first great work of the High Renaissance, the *Last Supper* (1495-98), in Santa Maria delle Grazie. The mural — an unsuccessful experiment in oil tempera, which accounts for its poor condition — is nonetheless a masterpiece of psychological drama. The personalities — indeed, the inner thoughts — of each of the apostles is revealed as da Vinci depicts "the intention of man's soul": his statement of the highest purpose of painting.

with a stock of classic forms (domes, colonnades, pediments) Bramante revolutionized architecture with his revival of another classic technique: concrete. Used by the ancient Romans and abandoned in the Middle Ages in favor of brick or cut stone, concrete enables greater flexibility and monumental size — size as mammoth as St. Peter's.

Bramante died with little of his design for the church actually realized. It was not until 1546 when Michelangelo was put in charge of the project that St. Peter's reached its present form, more a reflection of Michelangelo's ideals than Bramante's.

Michelangelo Buonarroti (1475-1564) first astounded the world with his sculpture: human figures with a dignity, volume and beauty inspired by Hellenistic precedents, yet given new emotional impact. It has been said that Michelangelo sought, in his art, to liberate the form of the human body from a prison of marble: an allegory for the struggle of the human soul, imprisoned in an earthly body, and a condition ripe for themes of triumph and tragedy. The resulting tension imbues his most famous works: *David* (1501-4) in Florence's Galleria dell' Accademia; *Moses* (1513-1515) in Rome's San Pietro in Vincoli, and the beloved *Pietà* in St.Peter's.

Julius II commissioned Michelangelo to paint the Sistine Chapel ceiling. The result, completed in only four years (1508-12) is a triumph of human emotions unleashed by the human conditions: man's creation, his fall, and his reconciliation with the Lord.

While Michelangelo was busy on the Sistine Chapel ceiling, working nearby decorating a series of rooms in the Vatican Palace was the artist known as the premiere painter of the High Renaissance: Raphael (1483-1520). His masterpiece of this series is the *School of Athens* (1510-11). The dramatic grouping of philosophers surrounding Plato and Aristotle suggests the influence of Michelangelo; the individualized intention of each recalls da Vinci's *Last Supper*; the architectural setting is a perfecting of the Early Renaissance tradition.

In Venice, Giorgione da Castlefranco's (1476/8-1510) paintings have all the lightness, delicacy and charm of predecessor Bellini's. In addition, they favor poetic mood over subject matter (*The Tempest* (1505) in Venice's Galleria dell'Accademia is a perfect example), pre-

Michelangelo returned to the Sistine Chapel in 1534 to paint the spectacular *Last Judgement*. In the intervening years he went to Florence to complete the Medici Chapel of San Lorenzo (1524-1534) and the Laurentian Library (begun 1524) where the drama of the design outweighs many functional considerations. Michelangelo's architectural genius culminates in his redesign of Rome's Campidoglio (1537-39). This open piazza, flanked by three facades, has become the model for modern civic centers.

Left, Botticelli's ethereal *Venus* rises modestly from the sea. Titian's goddess of love, painted a hundred years later, has a more earthy sensuality.

figuring the Romantic movement of centuries to come.

Also looking ahead to the freer brushwork and shimmering colors of the Impressionists is the Venetian Titian (1488/90-1576). Titian mastered the technique of oil painting, and left behind a legacy of opulently-colored and joyously-spirited religious pictures as well as masterful portraits.

The drama of da Vinci, the theatricality of Michelangelo, the poetic moodiness of Giorgione, set the stage for the last movements of Renaissance art: Mannerism and the Baroque, when art became its most flamboyant.

The term *Mannerism* (1525-1600) refers to an artificial — or mannered — style, and words such as cold, formal, elegant, languid, mystical and distorted are used to define it.

This highly unnatural look stems, surprisingly, from High Renaissance antecedents, as elements of Michelangelo, Raphael, and Titian were embraced, then exaggerated. Expressing an "inner vision" at the expense of reality was often the artist's driving force. In a work that anticipates the new movement — Rosso Fiorentino's *The Descent from the Cross* (1521) in Volterra's Pinacoteca, the unlikely placement of angularly draped figures bathed in an unreal light stirs feelings of anxiety and tension. (It has been claimed that the artist later committed suicide.) His friend, Pontormo (1494-1557) is similarly known for works of unexpected coloration, unnaturally elongated figures and disquieting mood.

Agnolo Bronzino (1503-1572),Pontormo's

pupil and adopted son, epitomizes Mannerism's barren formalism in his remarkable portraits, of Cosimo I and of his wife Eleanora of Toledo and her son Giovanni de' Medici (1550) in the Ufizi Gallery. The characters are remote, expressionless, elegant; Eleanora's elaborate gown is the true star of the painting.

The work of Parmigianino (1503-40) also exemplifies elegance, remoteness, and coldness with another twist: a distortion of form that is the painter's trademark. In his *Madonna with the Long Neck* (1535) in the Uffizi, the figures are elongated beyond any reality, the setting is fantastical, and the inspiration for the work — Raphael's fluid grace — is exaggerated beyond recognition.

In Venice, Jacopo Tintoretto (1518-94)

combined the bold style, rich colors and glowing light inspired by Titian with a mystical inclination. His attempt to depict one of religion's greatest mysteries — the transubstantiation of bread into the body of Christ — results in the haunting *Last Supper* (1592-94), San Giorgio Maggiore, Venice, with its swirling angels created out of vapors.

In architecture, Andrea Palladio (1518-80) stands out. Like his predecessor Alberti, Palladio wrote theoretical studies of ancient architecture. His own designs — the Villa Rotonda (1567-70), Vincenza; San Giorgio Maggiore (1565), Venice — are based on a repertoire of classic forms and concepts, and have influenced later architects from Inigo Jones to Thomas Jefferson.

The Baroque

The Baroque (1600–1750) was born in Rome, and nurtured by a papal campaign to make the city one of unparalled beauty "for the greater glory of God and the Church."

One artist to answer the call was Caravaggio (1573-1610). A stormy individual, Caravaggio was at odds with society in his personal life as well as his art. His early secular portraits of sybaritic youths revealed him to be a painfully realistic artist. His later monumental religious paintings such as *The Calling of St. Matthew* in Rome's San Luigi dei Francesi shocked the city by setting a holy act in a contemporary tavern.

The decoration of St. Peter's interior by Gianlorenzo Bernini (1598-1680) was more what the Romans had in mind: a bronze tabernacle with spiralling columns at the main altar; a magnificent throne with angels clustered around a burst of sacred light at the end of the church; and, for the exterior, the classically simple colonnade embracing the piazza (1657).

Bernini's rival was Francesco Borromini (1599-1667), whose extravagant, eccentric, romantic designs were the complete opposite of Bernini's classics. Many of Borromini's most famous designs hinge on a complex interplay of concave and convex surfaces, seen in the undulating facades of San Carlo al le Quattro Fontane, Sant'Ivo, and Sant'Agnese in Piazza Navona (1653-63) with its unexpected positioning of towers and dome.

The influence of the Italian Baroque spread quickly to Germany and Spain. The impact of the Italian Renaissance continues to excite the entire world.

Above, portrait of Cosimo de' Medici by Bronzino. Right, Caravaggio's Bacchus half-heartedly raises an ample glass to the good life.

BIRTH OF A NATION

"A white Devil, a radiant daughter of sin and death, holding in her hand the fruit of the knowledge of good and evil, and tempting the nations to eat: this is how Italy struck the fancy of men in the 16th Century. She was feminine and they were virile; but she could teach them and they could learn. She gave them pleasure they brought force," says J.A. Symonds in his book *Renaissance In Italy*. After Fornovo, all the armies in Europe came to Italy. An international free-for-all resulted as they fought among themselves for a share of the spoils.

Spain, the most powerful nation in Europe at the time, eventually emerged as the clear master of Italy. The Pope crowned King Charles V of Spain Holy Roman Emperor in 1530. He and his descendants then ruled Italy with a heavy hand for 150 years. This period has often been called the dullest in Italian history. The burden of high Spanish taxation and the exploitation of Italy's resources by petty Spanish officials killed all native energy and initiative. The Papacy was no less oppressive. The rules of the Inquisition, the Index and the Jesuit Orders forced many Italians to flee the country because of their opinions.

Under the oppressive rule of the Spaniards and later (after the 1713 Treaty of Utrecht) under the equally oppressive Austrians, Italy was no longer a cultural center as it had been during the Renaissance. But the French Revolution inspired many Italians. The ideas of liberty and republicanism spread like wildfire throughout the country. Patriots began dreaming of an independent Italian republic modeled after the French.

When Napoleon invaded Italy in 1796, the people rose against the Austrians and a series of revolutionary republics were founded. For three years the whole peninsula was republican and under French domination. Unfortunately, in March 1799 an Austro-Russian army expelled the French from Northern Italy and restored many of the local princes. In Naples, the republicans were able to hold out for a few more months, but eventually they too had to give in and they suffered greatly for their brief resistence. The British Lord Nelson had the republican Admiral Caracciola hung from the yardarm of his flagship.

Preceding pages, Italian rebels storm the city of Palermo in the fight for a unified Italy. Left, Garibaldi, who led the 1,000 men on the expedition against Sicily. Right, Cavour, Italy's first great statesman.

To work against the new foreign oppressors and their local sycophants, many Italian patriots joined clandestine organizations, of which the most famous was the Carbonari. In their love of ritual and oath they resembled the Freemasons, but they had a deadly serious goal: to liberate Italy.

The Risorgimento

In 1800, Napoleon managed to win back most of Italy. The kingdom that he founded lasted only briefly, but was an important stage

CAVOUR.
(From a contemporary print in Bianchi's *Cavour.*)

in Italian history. By proving that the country could be a single unit, it gave Italian patriots new inspiration and direction. From the time of the Congress of Vienna in 1815, which reinstated Italian political divisions, until Rome was taken in 1870 by the troops of King Victor Emmanuel II of Savoy, the history of Italy is one continuous struggle to be unified again.

The period is a complex one because although many Italians both in the North and South wanted the peninsula to become one nation there was no agreement as to who would rule the new nation, or how its creation was to be achieved. Some believed in peaceful, slow, evolution. Others, like Mazzini, wanted to revive the Roman Republic. Still others were for a Kingdom of Italy under the leadership of the house of Savoy. A writer-priest, Vincenzo Giobetti, argued in his book, *The Moral and Civil Primacy of the Italians*, for a federated Italy, with the pope as President. When Pius IX was made pope in 1846, those who followed Giobetti hailed the new Pope as their leader. Unfortunately, Pius himself rejected these liberal plans.

In 1848, a year of revolution all over Europe, the first Italian war for independence was fought. First, local rebellions in Sicily, Tuscany and the Papal States forced rulers in those areas to grant constitutions to their citizens. In Milan, news of Parisian and Viennese uprisings sparked the famous "five days" when the occupying Austrian army was driven from the city. A few days later, Charles Albert of Savoy sent his army to pursue the Austrians,

skills as a mercenary in the revolutions of South America, where he had been forced to flee after being convicted of subversion in Piedmont. Now he and his men faced the combined strength of the Neopolitans, the Austrians and the French. It was French forces that entered the city on July 3, 1849, the day after Garibaldi escaped into the mountains. The following month the Venetians succumbed to Austrian siege.

The peace treaty they signed with the House of Savoy kept the Austrians out of Savoy, so it was now the only Italian state with a free press, an elected parliament, and a liberal constitution. Piedmont was also blessed from 1852 on with a brilliant prime minister — Count Camillo Cavour — who was devoted to the cause of Italian unity. Cavour went to England

and the revolution began in earnest.

Charles Albert was soon supported by troops from other Italian states and the war was going well. The tide turned when the Pope refused to declare war on Catholic Austria. With that, the Austrians regained confidence and drove Charles Albert's army back into Piedmont. After Charles Albert's abdication a few months later, the House of Savoy signed a peace treaty.

Venice and the Roman Republic continued the fight. In Rome, Mazzini led a triumvirate that governed the city with a true democratic spirit despite the siege conditions. The commander of the city's armed forces was the colorful Giuseppe Garibaldi. Garibaldi, a lifelong Italian patriot, had honed his fighting

and France to raise money and support for the Italian cause. He had Piedmontese troops fight in the Crimean War, and thus won a seat at the peace conference. There, he brought the Italian question to the attention of Europe's most important statesmen. Although Cavour made no tangible gains at this meeting, he did win moral support for the Italians.

Europe was thus not surprised when France and Piedmont went to war with Austria three years later. The French king, Napoleon III and

Above, Garibaldi and Victor Emmanuel II of Savoy join forces at the town of Teano. Right, celebration of Italian liberty in Turin, a leader among Italian cities in the fight for freedom.

Cavour had agreed in secret that after the expected victory, an Italian kingdom would be formed for the Piedmontese king Victor Emmanuel and Nice and French Savoy would be returned to France. The people of the Italian dukedoms rushed to proclaim their allegiance to Victor Emmanuel.

Unfortunately, the French soon tired of fighting and decided to make a quick peace with Austria. The Austrians agreed to let Lombardy become part of an Italian Federation (with Austrian troops still in its garrisons), but the Veneto region went back to Austria and the dukes of Modena and Tuscany were reinstated.

In Italy, everyone was outraged. Cavour resigned in protest, although first he arranged plebiscites in Tuscany and Modena. Citizens

Pope preached against the patriots, and the French garrisoned troops there to protect the city. The victorious nationalists were divided on how to deal with Rome. One group wanted to take the city by force; the conservative majority wanted to negotiate.

Finally in 1870, after the French were weakened by a defeat in the Sudan, Italian troops fought their way into the city through Porta Pia. The Pope barricaded himself in the Vatican. For half a century, no pope emerged to participate in the life of the new Italy.

The new government of all Italy was a parliamentary democracy with the king as the executive. The most powerful men in the early days of the Italian state were the sober, loyal Piedmontese parliamentarians who were largely responsible for its creation. They designed

refused to have their dukes back and voted to become part of Piedmont.

Garibaldi and 1,000 volunteers sailed for Sicily from Quarto near Genoa on May 5, 1860. Shortly after landing on the island, Garibaldi declared himself dictator of it in the name of Victor Emmanuel. He and his troops had to fight hard, but with the help of Sicilian rebels Garibaldi entered Palermo in triumph. Because of his success, men from all over Italy now came to help him, and on September 7, Naples fell to the patriots.

Meanwhile, Victor Emmanuel gathered troops and began marching south to link up with Garibaldi. The two groups met at Teano, and the kingdom of Italy was declared. However, one gaping hole remained — Rome. The

the original administration, and established standard weights and measures for the whole peninsula. But once the government moved down to Rome, this group began to splinter. The left came to power under a new prime minister, Agostino Depretis.

Depretis had been a skilled legislator and manipulator when he was a member of the parliament, but once he became prime minister he was less effective. He could not organize his party or set forth a coherent program for administering the nation. His rivals on the right had done no better, but their opposition made it hard for Depretis to accomplish much. This was the beginning of the breakdown of the party system in Italy, the effects of which are still discernable today.

THE TWENTIETH CENTURY

As governments so often do during times of rapid change and relative instability at home, the young republic began to look abroad for confirmation of its hard-won independence. Relations with France had already cooled during the final fight for unification; when Paris occupied Tunisia, a traditional area of Italian influence, they became positively chilly. Italy's response was to sign the Triple Alliance with Germany and Austro-Hungary, providing for mutual defense in the event of war.

Under the conservative governments of Francesco Crispi (1887–1891, 1893–1896), Italy also joined the scramble for colonies in North Africa. Crispi successfully pushed into Eritrea, but when he tried to subdue Ethiopia, the Italian army suffered a humiliating loss at Adwa. The defeat immediately brought Crispi's second administration crashing down. Italy's only other unqalified success at colonization during this period came during the Italo-Turkish War (1911–1912), which ended with Rome's victory and the occupation of Libya and the Dodecanese Islands.

At home, the years leading up to World War One were already marked by the division that still plagues the country today: relative wealth in the north and extreme poverty in the south. The economy was overwhelmingly agricultural, and the government's staunchly protectionist policies left Italy increasingly isolated from other European markets. The industrial boomlet of the late 1800s, mostly in textiles and refining, was confined to the north. The crushing economic conditions in the south drove an ever-increasing wave of emigration. In the last years of the century, nearly half-a-million people a year set out for the New World.

When World War One began with Austria's attack on Serbia in July 1914, Italy was caught almost completely unaware. Prime Minister Antonio Salandra reasoned that since his government had not been consulted before the Austrian advance, Italy was not bound by the terms of the Triple Alliance. On August 2, he declared Rome's neutrality. If anything, public opinion began to swing away from the Germans and Austrians and in the direction of the Allies. To help bring Italy over to its side, the Allied governments dangled the possibility of territorial gains: among other things, Rome was offered the chance to gain *Italia irredente*, the "unrecovered" provinces of Trieste and

Left, Benito Mussolini, in 1928, making one of his fiery speeches.

Trentino, long held by the Austro-Hungarian Hapsburg Empire. In addition, Italy would receive the upper valley of the Adige River, plus various north African and Turkish properties. Finally swayed, in April 1915 Italy signed the secret Treaty of London. A month later, the government broke the Triple Alliance and entered the war on the Allied side.

Seldom had an army been so ill prepared for battle. The armed forces were poorly equipped, and Austrian troops had already dug into defensive positions in Alpine strongholds along the 300-mile border the two countries shared. The only real hope of advance was at the eastern edge of the front, near the city of Gorizia and the Isonzo River. The Italian commander, General Luigi Cadorna, threw most of his troops here, but through 11 major battles he could never advance more than 10 miles. For the Italian army, the war turned into a stalemate, albeit a costly one; of the 5.5 million men mobilized, 39 percent were either killed or wounded.

Then, on October 24, 1917, the opposition forces stormed the Italians at Caporetto (now Kobarid, Yugoslavia). Pounding away, they quickly drove Cadorna's army to within 20 miles of Venice. Some 40,000 Italian soldiers died, and another 250,000 were taken prisoner. Eight months later, however, the Italians got their revenge. In a last-ditch effort to win a battle — almost any battle — the weary Austrian army again attacked, this time plunging at the Italian defense spread along the Piave River. They quickly pushed the Italians back, and an Austrian victory looked certain. But the Italians held fast, and the battle of Vittorio Veneto became their Caporetto. By November, the Austrian forces had virtually collapsed. Pushing east as the enemy retreated before them, at last the Italian forces could march into the longed-for cities of Trieste and Fiume (now Rejeka, Yugoslavia). *Italia irredente* was finally theirs.

Unfortunately, the war's true end came not on the battlefield but at the conference table. Although Prime Minister Vittorio Emmanuele Orlando sat with the victors — Prime Ministers David Lloyd George of Great Britain and Georges Clemenceau of France and United States President Woodrow Wilson — he was hardly regarded as an equal. Despite Orlando's protests, which at one point included storming out of the peace conference and returning to Rome, the Treaty of London was ignored. In the end the Treaty of St. Germain (September

10, 1919) gave Italy Triento and the Alto Adige, as well as Trieste. But Fiume, Dalmatia and the other promised territories were negotiated away by the Allies.

The Rise of Fascism

The disappointments at the peace table, combined with the social and economic toll of the war, produced chaotic domestic conditions. Soon there was talk that Italy had won only a "mutilated victory" despite its wartime sacrifice. Inflation soared. Urban factory workers regularly took to the streets, and rural peasants clamored for land reform. The wealthy and upper middle classes were horrified at the progress of events. But parliament was seriously divided along ideological lines, and about all the government could do was try to keep a semblance of public order.

Into his power vacuum marched Benito Mussolini and his Fascist Party. When he founded the party in 1919, Mussolini's philosophy was more one of opportunism than anything else. A vivid, moving speaker, he played on the worst fears of all Italians. To those who fretted over the "mutilated victory," he was a chest-thumping nationalist. To placate the wealthy, he denounced Bolshevism, although he himself had once been an ardent socialist. To the frightened middle classes he pledged a return to law and order, and a "corporate" state in which workers and management would pull together for the good of the whole country. The Fascists also gained a reputation for radical-bashing, and clashes between the socialists and communists and gangs of Mussolini's black-shirted thugs became increasingly common.

By mid-1922, Fascism had become a major political force. The government still could not control the factories or quell the street demonstrations, and the solid *borghese* class longed for relief from the almost constant turmoil. When workers called for a general strike, Mussolini made his move. On October 28, 50,000 members of the Fascist militia converged on Rome. Although Mussolini's supporters held only a small minority in parliament, the sight of thousands of menacing Fascists flooding the streets of the capital was enough to topple the already tottering government of Prime Minister Luigi Facta. Refusing to sanction a state of siege, King Victor Emmanuel II instead turned the reigns of government over to Mussolini.

Who was this man who had suddenly bullied his way to power? Italy's youngest prime minister — he was only 39 — had been born in 1883, the son of a schoolteacher and a blacksmith-cum-socialist-revolutionary. Kicked out of two schools for fighting, Musso-lini nevertheless graduated and obtained a teacher's diploma. In 1902 he fled to Switzerland to avoid the draft, where he spent two years, living mostly hand-to-mouth. Back in Italy, his politics drifted steadily leftward, and he began to hone the formidable rhetorical skills that would one day draw many thousands to his palace on Rome's Piazza Venezia. Although frequently jailed for his political activities, Mussolini also developed a reputation as a writer of leftist propaganda, and in 1912 he was appointed editor of the socialist party organ *Avanti!* But service as a sharpshooter during World War One changed Mussolini. He returned a committed anti-socialist with a mission to remake his country in his own image.

Once in control of Italy, he did just that. Mussolini quickly rammed through an act assuring the Fascists a permanent majority in the parliament. After questionable elections in 1924, he completely dropped the pretense of collaborative government. Italy was now a dictatorship. At Christmas of that year, he declared himself head of the government, responsible only to the king. Fascist fronts took over all the rights once held by unions and management organizations, lockouts and strikes were banned, and national corporations were set up to supervise every phase of the economy. Within two years, Mussolini had completely co-opted his political opponents. All parties except the Fascists were banned, and opposition activists were jailed and forced into exile or the underground. Anyone Mussolini could not subject by will or law he crushed with force, hauling "offenders" before a political crimes tribunal or dispatching bands of thugs to do his dirty work.

Despite its ugly underbelly, on the surface Fascism seemed to work. Weary of inflation, strikes and street disturbances, Italians eagerly embraced their severe new government and its charismatic *Duce*, or leader. This spontaneous response to Fascist rule was reinforced by a relentless propaganda campaign, featuring Mussolini's hypnotic speeches: staccato bursts of verbiage, punctuated with long silences, and rhetorical questions answered by roars from the crowd. Mussolini had promised to restore to Italy the glories of ancient Rome, and for a time promises were more than enough.

Soon, however, the government could also show some results. The economy firmed, the trains, so they said, ran on time, massive public works projects were launched, and Mussolini even managed to make up with the Vatican, hammering out the Lateran Treaty (1929), which ended the 50-year drift between Rome and the Catholic Church. He also set out on an ambitious imperial campaign, restoring control over Libya, which had been ignored during World War One and its immediate aftermath. And in October 1935, Italian troops crossed the border of Eritrea, headed for the Ethiopian capital of Addis Ababa. The League of Nations howled in protest, but took no real action to stop Mussolini. Six months later, *Il Duce* announced to a hysterical Piazza Venezia crowd that, finally, Rome had begun to reclaim its empire.

World War Two

The international outcry over the Ethiopian occupation left Rome badly isolated. The one government willing to overlook Mussolini's expansionism was in Berlin, where Adolf Hitler's Nazis had held power since January

require an automatic military response. In any case, most Italians opposed intervention, and the army, again, was poorly prepared for war. But as Hitler racked up victory after victory — in Denmark, Norway and Belgium, and with France near collapse — the lure of sharing the spoils of war finally proved irresistible. On June 10, 1940, Italy entered the war, just in time for the fall of France. From the start, however, it was obvious even to Mussolini that he was definitely Hitler's inferior in their alliance, a realization that deeply hurt the proud *Duce*. To make matters worse, the security-obsessed Germans kept their specific combat plans secret, for fear they might leak out through the Italian officer corps.

Eager to pull off his own battlefield coup, in autumn 1940 Mussolini set his sights on

1933. Both Germany and Italy had supported Generalissimo Francesco Franco's nationalist troops in the Spanish Civil War (1936–1939), and this cooperation on a foreign battlefield led eventually to the signing of the Pact of Steel between Berlin and Rome in May 1939. Three months later, Hitler invaded Poland. Within days, Britain and France declared war on Germany.

At first the Rome government held back, as it had during World War One, arguing that Berlin's surprise attack on Poland did not

Above, Enrico Berlinguer was head of the Italian Communist Party (PCI) from 1972 to 1984.

Greece, in his estimation an easy target. But the Greeks fought back fiercely. The prospect of a total Italian defeat was eliminated only after the Nazis came to the rescue, steamrolling through Yugoslavia to back the Italians up. The war was also going badly for the Axis in North Africa, and eventually even the battlefield genius of General Erwin Rommel could not prevent the collapse. Heartened by their desert victories, in the summer of 1943 American and British troops captured Sicily. The beginning of the end was in sight.

From their base in Sicily, the Allied forces began bombing the Italian mainland, and the already slumping Italian public morale sunk even lower. On July 25, 1943, the Grand Council of Fascism voted to strip *Il Duce* of his powers. In keeping with his character, Mussolini refused to step down. The next day, however, King Victor Emmanuel ordered him arrested, and Mussolini was taken on the steps of the Villa Savoia immediately following a royal audience. Well aware that the Nazis would try to rescue Mussolini, new prime minister Marshal Pietro Badoglio ordered him to be taken to a remote island and then later moved him to a resort high in the Abruzzi Mountains. There, despite all predictions that the prisoner was untouchable, a crack team of German air commandos did manage to get to Mussolini and spirit him off to Munich.

Chaos broke out in the final days of the war. To placate the Germans, who would have otherwise occupied the entire country, Badoglio publicly declared that Italy would fight on. In the so-called "Gothic line" in the Apennines, but by spring 1945 that effort too had collapsed. Mussolini, only a few months before the supreme leader of the entire country, tried to sneak into Switzerland disguised as a German soldier. Italian partisans found him, however, and the next morning Mussolini was shot. His body was hauled into Milan and hung by a rope for the passing public to see.

Recovery and Resiliency

In the immediate post-war period, Italy suffered greatly. This time there was no representative from Rome at the meetings that dictated the terms of peace; those seats were taken by the victorious governments of the United States, Great Britain, France and the Soviet

secret, however, he entered negotiations with the Allies, who by now had fought their way as far north as Naples. Above that line was the hastily organized *Repubblica Sociale Italiana*, headed by the liberated *Duce*. But the Italian Social Republic was nothing more than a puppet regime under the thumb of Berlin, and a morose Mussolini spent most of his time brooding about the judgement that history would pass on him.

As the Allies fought north, the Italian Resistance, or the Corps of Volunteers for Liberty, finally felt safe enough to begin widespread activities. Combined, the forces managed to liberate Rome on June 4, 1944; Florence followed on August 12. The Germans, and Mussolini managed to last out the winter behind

Union. All of the Italian colonies, won at such great cost, were taken away. Reparations had to be paid to the Soviet Union and Ethiopia. The political system was in need of a complete overhaul. In elections in June, 1946, voters decided 54–46 in favor of making the country a republic, thus formally ending the days of the monarchy. The economy was in a shambles, although Italy's inclusion in the European Recovery Program, otherwise known as the Marshall Plan, helped ease the burden from 1948 on.

The first order of business was to get a

Above, feminist protest march in Rome's Piazza Venezia. Their banner proclaims "I accuse the society of males."

government going again. After the June 1946 elections, and a brief alliance that included the Socialists and Communists, Christian Democrat leader Alcide De Gasperi gained control of government, booting out his leftist partners. For more than a decade after that, centerist coalitions of one sort or another ran the country. The rift between right and left was not healed until the *apertura a signistra*, or opening to the left in the early 1960s, under which the Christian Democrats, Socialists, Social Democrats and Republicans formed a coalition government. The combination proved remarkably durable, ruling, in various combinations, until 1968.

Marx But No Marx

One of the most distinctive features of Italian politics — at least by Western standards —has been the influence of the Italian Communist Party (PCI). In the immediate post-war years, the PCI cleaved to the political line set by the Soviet Union, and the centerist government that sat in Rome kept the Communists at arm's length. But under the leadership of Enrico Berlinguer, who became PCI secretary in 1972, the party's orientation changed dramatically. Under the charismatic Berlinguer, the PCI often led the so-called "Eurocommunism" movement, which advocated a greater independence from Moscow. Under Berlinguer, the PCI scolded the Soviets for human rights abuses and for the invasion of Afghanistan in 1979. On economic issues, it grew ever more centerist, prompting some to dub it a "Marxist party without Marx." By 1981, this platform had attracted nearly 2 million members, and could regularly count on about a third of the vote in nationwide elections. That made it the largest communist party in Western Europe and second largest political group in Italy after the Christian Democrats. In 1984, Berlinguer collapsed at a political rally and died shortly thereafter. He was replaced by Alessandro Natto, one of his long-time lieutenants.

Fueled by the availability of cheap labor, there was an economic surge at the end of World War Two. Heavy industry such as chemicals, iron, steel and autos took off. In 1958, Italy became one of the founding members of the European Economic Community, or the Common Market. By the mid-1960s, manufacturing overtook agriculture as the major source of GNP, and observers hailed the Italian "economic miracle." Only a few years later, however, the boom had gone bust, and Italy was dubbed the "sick man of Europe." In recent years, government policies have at least begun to set the economic house aright. Dogged effort helped cut inflation, and

in 1985 the Craxi government pushed through tightened tax-collection regulations, which boosted national revenues. Still, inflation remained in the high single digits, and the lira proved unsteady against such stalwart currencies as the U.S. dollar.

In 1946, Italy was still a primarily agrarian society, and many of the largest cities had suffered severe damage under the Allied bombing campaign. The rapid growth of industrialization soon altered that forever; throughout the 1950s there was a steady migration from the country to the cities and from south to north, especially into the big manufacturing centers of Milan, Turin and Genoa. The economic and social changes severely disrupted traditional lifestyles, and as the bloom faded from the "miracle," inevitable social ills set in.

By far the worst was terrorism: from the late 1970s on, kidnappings, kneecappings and murders became an all-too common fact of life. The most horrifying incident was the kidnapping in March 1978 of former Christian Democratic prime minister Aldo Moro by the left-wing *Brigate Rosse*. The Red Brigade wanted a group of their comrades released from jail, but the government refused to negotiate any deals with the terrorists. Nearly two months later, Moro's body was pulled from the trunk of a car parked on a Rome street. The slaying spurred a new round of anti-terrorist measures, and eventually 32 Red Brigade members were convicted and sentenced to life in prison for the deaths of Moro and 16 others.

Crime of another sort gripped the nation in May 1981, and when there was an attempt on the life of Pope John Paul II as he rode through a crowd-packed St. Peter's Square, Turkish-born Mehmet Ali Agca was convicted and sentenced to life for shooting the much-loved Pope. In rambling testimony in the months after his conviction, Agca implied that he had had help in his plot to assassinate the Pope, and relations between Rome and Bulgaria, whose agents Agca said had assisted him, became strained.

Still, Italy endures. Despite its deep economic and social problems and a system of government that often seems predestined *not* to rule effectively, the country manages to cope. Perhaps, in some small way, it is the glory of their history that allows the Italians to manage so well in the reduced circumstances they live in today. Although the Empire is long vanished and the Renaissance ended 400 years ago, the Italians are steeped in the influence of history, and are surrounded by its sweep, not only in their national consciousness but even in the streets that they walk. Fortunately for the traveller, those streets — and that link with the past — are open to all.

THE ITALIANS

"And don't, let me beg you, go with that awful tourist idea that Italy's only a museum of antiquities and art. Love and understand the Italians for the people are more marvellous than the land."

— E.M. Forster

It has been said that the Italians do not exist, that until now very few Italians have been discovered, and that those who go by the name "Italian" eventually turn out to be Piedmontese, Tuscans, Venetians, Sicilians, Calabrians and so on. Apparently no one has ever been able to classify the Italians: to be born in Palermo, Sicily or in Turin, Piedmont is a classification and a differentiation by itself. One can die of Mafia, the other of unemployment. In Germi's movie, *Il Cammino Della Speranza* (*The Path of Hope*), there is a tiny little women who says: "There's bad people in Milan, they eat rice." Another witty writer, Ennio Flaiano, with one of his typically bitter remarks, once said that there is no such thing as Italian nationality. According to him being Italian is a profession, it doesn't require much studying, one just inherits it. It has always been this way: our great-grandfathers, in order to survive learned the complex art of "arrangiarsi," of getting along in all kind of difficult situations. Having to deal with and adjust to quick political changes and foreign conquerors requires a flexible mentality and encourages a certain detached attitude towards political institutions and regimes, all of which in the end are considered unsacred and ephemeral. Having to move through a forest of rules, a tropical tangle of statutes, norms, regulations, some of them hundreds of years old, others of obscure interpretation, some forgotten but lying there ready to be revived suddenly for the benefit of one group against another, forces one to distrust the state, and encourages one to find one's own way. The popular saying *fatta la legge, trovato l'inganno* (a law is passed, a way past it is found) expresses adequately the criteria along which Italian good sense and experienced juridical sensibility tends to operate.

There is no denying that Italian genius, especially during past centuries, has achieved peaks of extraordinary, almost miraculous,

greatness. The testimonies of art, culture, and philosophical and scientific thinking of the Renaissance, and the very architectonic and urban structure of most Italian cities, exercise an irresistible spell on visitors from all countries. Yet the Italian nation — as an autonomous state is a relatively recent creation. The Italians gained their idependence and unity a little more than a century ago. So one can easily understand why they do not have a well-developed sense of nationality. The most obvious feature of this retarded process of nation building — easy to detect even by the

eye of a foreigner — is the large economic, social and cultural gap between the north and south of the country.

North Versus South

Since the very first years after Italian unification, the problem of the south came to the attention of rulers and political thinkers. Camillo Cavour, minister of the King of Savoy and one of the architects of Italian unity, turned his final political thinking to the problem of "mezzogiorno" and "the poor Neapolitans." He denounced the corruption of that part of Italy, which he attributed to the previous rule of the Bourbons, and exhorted his successors to bring morality, education and

Preceding pages: glittering gala at Milan's 200-year-old La Scala Opera House; a woman in Positano. Left, a Sardinian beauty decked out in native costume. Above, a Neapolitan man.

liberty to the area. Since that time, spending money in an attempt to solve the problems in the South has been a constant feature of government policy, and yet the gap between the two Italies still exists. At the turn of the century, hundreds of thousands of Southerners fled hunger and underdevelopment by moving to New York and South America. During the 1960s even more Southerners, 2.5 million, migrated to northern Italy, where the nation's industries are concentrated. The causes of underdevelopment in the South have been attributed to a variety of factors: previous rule of oppressive foreigners, residues of the feudal system, distance from markets, lack of sources of energy and raw materials.

Conditions in the South are complicated by the presence of the Mafia. *Gli amici* as Mafia

ians' skeptical attitude toward politics is not unjustified. The history of their young republic has been characterized by enormous scandals, sensational thefts against the community, and gigantic tax evasions, sometimes with the help and complicity of the Vatican banks. The Italian courts have acquitted Mafiosi of international renown, corrupt politicians, and terrorists plotting with the national intelligence services. During recent years, Italian citizens have undergone dangerous limitations of their liberties. They can be sent to jail for years (some have languished for as many as nine) without trial. A simple confusion over names, or the accusation of one already in jail, who hopes for a lesser sentence in return for naming names, can be enough to land an Italian in jail. On the other hand, what can one

men call themselves, are most dominant in Western Sicily, where nothing happens without their approval. And indeed, their influence insures that very little in the name of progress does happen in the area. Little northern capital is invested where the secret organization of friends can stop any activity that does not please them.

At election time, a higher proportion of Italians go the polls than many other European countries. Consequently, they appear very aware and mature politically. But the man in the street, when he is questioned, expresses a total repulsion for politics: *La politica e una cosa sporca* (politics is a dirty thing). He believes all parties are the same, and that politics work only for politicians. Actually the Ital-

expect from a state that, if a citizen loses an eye in war, will give him US $12 a month, US $14 for a foot, and US $21 for a right arm. And it could be that the veteran's neighbors consider him fortunate to receive such a stipend.

It's no wonder then that the Italians continue today to cultivate their ancient attitude of skeptical detachment from the state. It's no surprise that the Italians cannot conceive of abstract solutions for their problems or put their trust in ideologies. Everyone in Italian political culture, even members of the Marxist parties who were traditionally attached to ideological thinking, has long since given up on ideology and ridicules utopian solutions and idealistic institutions with a cynicism that was unknown ten years ago. As for the man in the street, he believes that institutions of government are useless burdens invented by the politicians, and that things would go better if everything were left to the common sense and free initiative of those "who work and produce." Behind this generic political formula, often lies an unrestrained individualism that denies any social responsibility. Existing side-by-side with this single-minded entrepreneurship, is another attitude of the man in the street, which corresponds to a dangerous temptation always threatening to reemerge. This is the nostalgic yearning for "The Strong Man." One whose power and will can be seen in his set face, one whose voice captures the needs and desires of the people as it carried over the loudspeakers, one whose gestures command and direct the fate of a nation — like the one who once

Sicily was once an Arab kingdom, and the Semitic ethnic type is still noticeable there. The Normans, who succeeded the Arabs in Sicily and in Southern Italy left clear traces of themselves. The peasants of the Veneto near the Yugoslav border have strong Slav strains; the Gothic, Lombard and other Germanic conquerors of the period following the fall of the Roman Empire, though relatively few, left distant traces of themselves, especially in the population of Lombardy and Piedmont. Today there are Albanian and Greek areas in Calabria and Sicily; the region of Friuli-Venezia Giulia has a very large Slavic population, and there is a whole German province —South Tyrol — within the frontiers of the Republic. It has been observed that even in areas south of the Tyrol — in Treviso for

appeared regularly in Piazza Venezia.

Appearances

The Italian "look" defies easy definition. Among the Italians, the Mediterranean type may prevail, yet there are innumerable varieties: the Latin strain, in other words the "Julius Caesar" type, (the one you can see in the faces of status at the Capitolium Museum) can still be found in certain places, especially in the remoter regions of the mountains near Rome.

From left to right: a quizzical nun in Rome; mounted police patrol, Piazza S. Pietro; a modern-day gladiator teaches fencing in a studio in Rome.

example — you can see walking around a type of blond that you may easily meet punching a hole in your ticket at Düsseldorf railway station, but the blond Germanic type represents only about two percent of the whole Italian population. The general complexion of the Italians, at least in the eyes of a foreigner, is dark. But despite the fact that the Mediterranean type, with abundant black hair, olive skin and dark eyes prevails over all other types, the population is really rather varied.

The Language

The Italian language is the closest to Latin of any of the so-called Romance languages. It's the official language at public occasions, in the

Parliament, on radio and television, and for literature and newspapers. It is taught to foreigners and supposedly in Italian schools. It's a result of the ideas and labors of various writers from the 14th to the 19th centuries, from Dante Alighieri to Alessandro Manzoni. These authors assumed as their standard the educated language of Tuscany, and the best form of speech is said to be *la lingua toscana in bocca romana* (the Tuscan tongue in the Roman mouth). The vocabulary of the Italian language comes mainly from Latin and the grammar is also clearly derived from that ancient tongue. Italian is said to be the most musical language in the world: Emperor Charles V — his biographers maintain — would use Spanish with God, French with men, German with his horse, but Italian with women. The

tinued by the subtle preachers of the Counter-reformation in the following century, and then revived by the later theoreticians of the juvenile protests in the 1960s. The Anglo-Saxons always talk about concrete things. Among Italians talking about concrete things, *pane al pane e vino al vino* sounds a little irritating and shocking.

Up until recently, a large number of dialect existed side by side with the official Italian language. Over 1,500 of these dialects were counted, and at one time they were incomprehensible from one village to another. You can still hear dialect spoken among the old people in the countryside, but among the younger generations dialects are fading away as a combined result of school, radio, television and military service.

Italian language is capable of expressing many subtleties of thought and feeling in a delicate and sweet manner. It can be as precise as any other language, yet sometimes it falls victim to verbosity and cloudiness. The style of newspaper editorials, art criticism and political speeches in particular is often abstract, obscure and boring. In Italian, lack of ideas may be easily disguised by elegantly ambiguous prose. Yet under these senseless structures of words, under those mysterious and vague terms, one can discover a certain constant of national characteristics: superficiality, inconstancy, irresponsibility, and incompetence. The non-communicating style has an ancient origin: it was introduced by learned humanists in the courts of the 15th Century. It was then con-

Unlike the official Italian language, the dialects were unable to resist the imprint of hundreds of years of foreign occupation. The dialects of north Italy, for example, contain a number of German words; Spanish, French, and German words are also frequent in Neapolitan. Piedmontese was strongly affected by the French, and Spanish; French and Arabic have a large part in the dialects of Sicily. In addition to dialects, French is spoken widely in Val d'Aosta; the population of South Tyrol speaks German; about half-a-million people in

Above, bicyclists in Calabria. Right, time out from skiing in a posh resort in the northern mountains.

Friuli-Venezia Giulia speak Slovene and other Slav tongues, and Slav dialects are also found in the Molise region to the South of Rome. Ladin, a direct descendent from Latin, related to the Romansh language of Switzerland, is spoken in some valleys of the Dolmites; Greek and Albanian are spoken in Calabria and Sicily. Sardinia has its own language, and Catalan is spoken at Alghero in Sardinia.

Regional Differences

Up until 50 years ago, horizontal and vertical differences between classes and towns were very obvious in Italy. Such differences were due not only to geography or distance between social classes, but to a long historical process of separatism. It was possible by simply moving from one town to a neighboring one to observe marked differences: "pasta" was cooked in a different way, and the vowels pronounced in a different way. The same could be said for clothes and haircut, and even eroticism. "Oh, those unforgettable years on the Autostrada del Sole (the main highway from Milan to Calabria) when at each exit and every toll booth you could experience a different way of making love," sighs the writer Alberto Arbasino. The American writer Gore Vidal, who chose Italy as his second home, also complains that modern mass culture has had a homogenizing effect on the Italians. "Towns that were once different to the point of hostility are now all unified by TV, Fiat, festivals and soccer matches."

These two writers may be right to complain of the progessive disappearance of some original and fascinating features of Italy, but deep cultural divisions between various areas are still observable today, and will probably continue to be found for many years to come. The Venetian with his mildness, sweet talk and respectful fear of authority will stay quite different from the more aggressive Roman; the Piedmontese type will maintain his dignified, reserved, slightly conceited attitude that shows French influence; the Milanese will still look commercial, and efficient in the German style; the Florentine will exhibit his cool, classical perennial Renaissance traits; the Sicilian will be easily distinguished by mainland Italians, though foreigners may not see this distinction unless they harass his daughter. And when we speak of general national characteristics one can be sure that, be it virtue or flaw, its quality, tone and intensity changes and increases as one moves from North to South.

One revealing aspect of the Italian character is to be found in the way Italians relate to foreigners. Many Italians, particularly those who have reached a certain level of culture and have had some chances to travel abroad accompanied by their fellow countrymen, have experienced a sense of national self-loathing. The trip abroad is often the occasion of some traumatic and painful confrontation whereby the Italian is forced to judge his own countrymen lacking. Such Italians tend to worship the supposed technical efficiency of the Germans, the self-control of the British, the elegant rationality of the French, the optimism and straightforwardness of the Americans, the sexual openness of the Scandinavians, and the refined sensuality of the Orientals. These Italians cannot see that these are generous abstractions, generalizations that naturally favor the foreigners; and yet their generous attitude means that foreigners are accepted with unabashed openess when visiting our country.

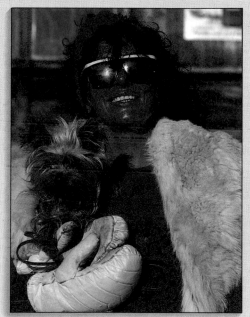

And open cosmopolitanism saves Italians from uprighteous nationalism.

The lively temperament of the Italians, expressing itself as it does in a sunny and beautiful natural environment and within cities that have retained their human scale, may seem to the ear of the foreigner to be jarringly loud. Simply put, the Italians are noisy. Each instrument from the voice to a car exhaust pipe is a good pretext to make noise. When you hear a chorus of car horns beneath your window it's not easy to know what it is: the joy of the fans over their soccer team's victory, the mourning of policemen who are remembering a recently fallen colleague, the enthusiasm of a wedding party who moves through the streets with white carnations stuck in the bodies of their cars and in the hair of their women.

Another characteristic of the Italians is individualism. The persistence for centuries of political and religious authoritarian structures which oppressed the values and needs of the individual and forced him to fall back on cunning self-reliance seems to have produced, among many Italians, an over-blown ego. You can see the strong sense Italians have of their own existence by simply observing the way they line up, or rather, don't line up, at the window of government offices, at the bus stop, or in the tobacconist.

In their relationship with the environment, Italians are consistently elegant. If one observes the crowd in cities and villages, and compares it to those in other countries with the same, if not higher, standard of living, one

aspect of the environment — natural or man-made.

Sex and the Family

There exists in the minds of many, especially foreigners, the image of the Italian man as the great Latin lover: passionate, impetuously sentimental, and powerful in bed. This myth has pushed many a foreign woman into coming to Italy in search of a romantic encounter. But what is the truth behind this cliche? How does the Italian male really relate to females?

The principle characteristic of Italian men seems to be attachment to their mothers. Their bond goes far beyond the natural tie to a parent. And it's a feeling that hardly ever changes into a more mature affection. Its residue is

must admit that the Italians are among the best dressed. Shoes, ties, beautiful fabrics, and freedom and liberty of the imagination all contribute to the make up of one's own "costume." The same fastidious care put into this exterior representation of self is extended even to the car or the motorcycle which becomes an appendix of the personality. Motorcycles are now coming into fashion even for women. Similar care or engagement one does not see in the care of homes, or the development of a civil conscience, nor in respect for the landscape. The creative genius of the Italians, with its great sculpturistic and chromatic capacity, which in the past achieved incomparable heights, seems to be focused today mainly on personal appearance more than any other

always there: the need to feel loved, understood, the tendency to constantly receive affection while never giving any in return. The Italian mother herself, tender, anxious and generous, often does much to strengthen this feeling.

The Italian male carries with him this mother image as he looks for someone to spend his life with. He searches for his ideal: a woman who is tender, sweet, willing to give up anything for him and put his wishes first. The search is the first step in the development of

Above, young Italians dress in the international casual style. Right, a Sardinian patriarch preserves traditions at the Calvacata festival.

that family morality, or amoral familism (so-named by the British sociologist E. Bumfield in the 1960s) which cannot see beyond the family into the community and that strengthens arrogant individualism in relation to the state.

Female virginity is one of the pillars of the official morality. In Italy the Christian ideal of virginity has been, especially in the South, affected and strengthened by the influence of Islam. As it is for Muslims, virginity for Southerns is part of the honor and wealth of a family. After a woman is married, faithfulness is the natural extension of her duty. If dishonor comes to a family in the form of a departure from the code of virginity and later unfaithfulness, it can be repaired by a resort to a "Crime of Passion." During the 1970s, about 1,500 such crimes were reported each year. A

less cruel solution is to marry the shamed girl to her seducer.

Italians of the South divide women into two groups: those who have to be respected and the others. Among the others may be included blond foreigners, and as a whole the group represents all that is attractive about sex and sin. In the South they talk very much of sex, often in an obsessive way. At the bar, while sipping coffee, standing on a street corner or at work the talk is of either sex or soccer. The most experienced strip with their eyes women who pass by, and tell with careful attention to detail of their real or imaginary adventures, evoking for the youngest listeners visions of extraordinary pleasures.

The persistence of this morality that still considers women along the Islamic model, does not conflict with the tyranny, within many Italian families of the wife. Her value in society is so restricted that she compensates at home where she exerts all her power. Many women impose their will through hysterical scenes, laden silences, constant nagging. Many men end up fearing their wives, and all go out a lot to find comfort in companionship with male friends, soccer, cards, and a little sex.

If it's true that extra-marital sex is the security valve of marriage, then Italians use it a lot. More than half of Italian males have had extra-marital affairs. They get along with their wives, and feel that they could never do without them. Each prefers his wife to other women, and yet betrays her. Why? More than anything else male adultery is a habit, as is the consequence of regarding the wife as a nice, clever woman who takes care of the house and the children and who is in exchange financially supported by the husband. The husband loves her, but being faithful to her is not necessarily the concomitant. To have affairs is natural he would explain: "Only stupids don't have women." But it would be unthinkable for women to enjoy the same sexual scope. Why? The common answer is that women don't have the same physical need for sex as men.

In the 1970s, under pressure from the feminist movement, the scaffolding of this centuries-old sexual and family morality started to give way. Italian women refused their role as dolls, sex objects, or angels of the fireplace, and claimed their economic and sexual independence. Old taboos were overturned. But in the 1980s these issues are no longer at the forefront. The image of the woman which is proposed by the media and which more and more eagerly strive to imitate, is one who is more and more beautiful and naked for the enjoyment of the Latin sultan.

How can one judge the national life of the Italians? Many would say that Italian life is a failure because of the persistence of many seemingly solvable problems. There are so many things, from the traffic in Rome to the cumbersome paperwork that's attached to the simplest official action, which restrict and frustrate Italians. And Italians seem unable to believe in the possibility of constructive change. For them, the ethic of life is not work and progress, but survival and individualism. And yet on the other hand, and perhaps for that reason, Italian life sparkles. The people have perfected a style of life that may be short on efficiency but long on enjoyment. Simple things, eating a meal, taking a walk, watching the world go by, become special. They are enjoyed to their fullest, with the practice and skill that have been refined over centuries.

Between 40 and 50 million foreigners visit Italy each year. Their numbers have increased so dramatically since World War Two that tourism is now Italy's number one industry. Why do so many come? Their reasons are as various as the resources Italy has to offer. The cognoscenti travel back roads, hoping to find some undiscovered medieval village, some precious fresco hidden in a dusty town. Tour groups speed from Rome to Florence to Venice, admiring the important sights from the air-conditioned comfort of a bus. Students crowd inexpensive pensiones near train stations, eating bread and cheese from markets, travelling cheaply to see in the flesh paintings their professors have flashed on the screen back home. The pious make pilgrimages to St. Peter's, Monte Cassino and Assisi. The affluent stay in the Hassler in Rome and the Danieli in Venice, visit the collections in Milan and shop in the boutiques in Rome's Via Condotti and Milan's Via Monte Napoleone.

The one thing these travellers share is a feeling that the presence in their favorite places of swarms of other non-natives is obnoxiously unpicturesque. "Though there are some disagreeable things in Venice," wrote Henry James in 1882, "there is nothing so disagreeable as the visitors" — and this remark has been echoed throughout the ages. So, though some may feel that the speed and affordability of modern travel have turned Italy, the Eternal Seductress, into a cheap trick packaged for the masses, tourists are really as characteristic of the Italian landscape as the towers of San Gimignano or the pigeons of Piazza San Marco.

For centuries Europeans and Americans have been crossing mountains and oceans in search of what John Keats called "a beakerful of the warm south." Italy's admirers have included some of the world's greatest writers and painters. The country has found a prominent place in so many journals, poems, letters, paintings and novels that the Italy of the artist's imagination has become almost as real in our minds as the actual geographical country. No other place, we feel, lends itself more to profound thoughts about mortality or to raptures on the splendors of nature and the

Left, the heroine of Hawthorne's *Marble Faun* has an assignation in a piazza in Perugia. Right, Mme de Stael led an even freer life than the heroine of her novel, *Corinne*.

intricacy of civilized man's mind. Nowhere else have northerners felt so free to throw off the restraints of society and discover the pleasures of the sensual life.

Pilgrims

The earliest peaceful visitors to Italy were pilgrims. Their destination was Rome where they found, along with the shrines of St. Peter and St. Paul, much of the imperial city still standing. As early as the 12th Century there was a guidebook to the Eternal City called the

Mirabilia Urbis Roma. But the pilgrims themselves left none of the ruminations on ruins that characterize later writings. They wrote topographical descriptions of interest now only to antiquarians. Rome, despite her declining state, was still considered to be the center of civilization as the well-known saying of Anglo-Saxon pilgrims indicates: "While stands the Coliseum, stands Rome; when falls the Coliseum, falls Rome and also falls the world."

The first major incursion of foreigners, unsurpassed until modern times, occurred in 1300 when Pope Boniface VIII established a jubilee (Holy Year). He granted plenary indulgences (previously preserved for those who made the more arduous trip to Palestine)

to pilgrims who visited, during this special year, the shrines of St. Peter and St. Paul. The crowds astounded contemporary historians, one of whom reported that there were never fewer than 200,000 visitors in Rome at any one time during the year. Estimates ran to 2 million visitors for the entire year. "In the streets and churches," wrote Edward Gibbon, "many persons were trampled to death by the eagerness of devotion." One unfortunate English monk had his leg fatally crushed while he was admiring the famous relic of St. Veronica, still in the Vatican today.

The establishment of the Holy Year was most probably motivated more by the need to replenish Rome's coffers than by any real desire to save the souls of the faithful. Undoubtedly this dramatic influx of hungry, tired foreigners was a great economic boon to the citizens of Rome, who discovered a thousand ways to turn their city's past into a goldmine. They sold numerous religious trinkets — cheap metal pins with pictures of St. Peter and St. Paul, not unlike the gew-gaws found in the Vatican today! A number of edicts were passed against greedy innkeepers who, in their eagerness to attract business to their hotels, often forcibly dragged guests away from the inns of competitors.

The humanists, starting with the poet Petrarch in the 14th Century, increasingly applied their knowledge of ancient texts to the ruins they saw. In addition to this scholarly interest, they began to respond imaginatively to the ruins. A 15th Century scholar, Poggius, wrote a dialogue called *De Varietate Fortunae* (*On the Varieties of Fortune*) that reveals an early tendancy to view Rome as a symbol of the mortality of man's creations and the supremacy of God. Inspired by the ruins of the Capitoline Poggius wrote: "The spectacle of the world, how it is fallen! How changed! How defaced! The path of victory is obliterated by vines, and the benches of senators are concealed by a dunghill."

Certainly one of the most significant journeys to Italy for the history of western civilization was that made by a young German monk, Martin Luther, in 1510. In his eagerness to see Holy Rome, Luther rushed through Milan, Bologna and Florence. Arriving at his destination, he found on the throne of St. Peter, Pope Julius II, a warlike Renaissance prince more interested in military conquest than in celebrating the mass. "I would not for a hundred thousand florins have missed seeing Rome," wrote the disillusioned Luther many years later. "I should have always felt an uneasy doubt whether I was not, after all doing injustice to the Pope. As it is, I am quite satisfied on that point."

Gentlemen of means from the 16th to the 17th centuries considered an extended trip to Italy the final step in their education both as humanists and as courtiers. Italy, wrote one 17th Century traveller, "hath always been accounted the nurse of policy, learning, music, architecture and limning (painting), with other perfections which she disperteth to the rest of Europe." (The bible of 16th Century English gentlemen was Castiglione's *The Courtier*, available in an English translation.) Others, however, felt differently. For them Italy was less the cradle of civilization than a center of papist corruption and court intrigue. "The art of atheisme, the art of epicurizing, the art of whoring, the art of poisoning, the art of sodomitrie," were some of the "fine arts" the early English novelist Thomas Nashe felt one could acquire in Italy. In the popular imagination of Elizabethan England, the Italian political theorist Machiavelli was identified with the Devil. A famous expression of the time declared "*Un inglese italianizzato e il diavolo incarnato.*" English nationalists bridled at the influence of sophisticated Italian manners. In Shakespeare's Richard II, one of the King's uncles speaks contemptuously of the Italian pretentions of the Royal court: "Proud Italy/Whose manners still our tardy, apish nation/Limps after in base imitation."

Despite such hesitations, the list of well-known visitors to Italy before the French Revolution is impressive: the essayist Montaigne, the diarist John Evelyn, the poet Milton, painters Reubens and Velasquez. Horace Walpole travelled with the poet Thomas Gray; the result of their journey was *The Castle of Otranto*, Walpole's blood-curdling Gothic romance that established Italy as the proper setting for thrilling tales of innocent damsels defiled by outrageously wicked dukes. Edward Gibbon claims to have received the inspiration for his mammoth *The Decline and Fall of the Roman Empire* while musing one day amidst the ruins of the Capitoline in Rome.

Travel during the days of the Grand Tour lacked the comforts of even the cheapest expedition today. (To describe a hotel as "lousy" had an uncomfortably vivid meaning.) The novelist Smollett found 18th Century travel difficult. He offers the prototype of the cantankerous traveller so preoccupied by his physical discomfort, that he ignores some of the world's most extraordinary places. (You find this type today complaining bitterly and loudly about the dirty bathrooms.) Undoubtedly, Smollett's description of his hotel does inspire some sympathy: "the house was dismal and dirty beyond all description; the bedclothes filthy enough to turn the stomach of a muleteer; and the victuals cooked in such a manner, that even a Hottentot could not have beheld them without loathing ... here I took my repose, wrapped in a greatcoat, if that could be called repose which was interrupted by the innumerable stings of vermin."

By the end of the 18th Century the "Proud Italy" of the Renaissance had been humbled by foreign invasions and the repression of the Counter-Reformation. Travellers still admired the Italians' aesthetic sensibility, but the respect was tempered by a feeling of their own political superiority. The English and the French saw their nations headed towards a glorious future. As a country Italy seemed condemned to remember only her two glorious pasts: the Roman and the Renaissance. Now she was ruled by foreigners and her

Coliseum, to Dickens, was an inspiring spot for "moralists, antiquaries, painters, architects, devotees." The number of visitors increased dramatically throughout the century, since travel was no longer limited to aristocrats. Travellers' accounts abound as almost every visitor of note felt inspired to publish his thoughts on Italy. Superlatives crowded the rhapsodies of dewy eyed romantics. "Sister land of paradise," Italy was called, as well as "the promised land," "the land that holds the rest in tender thrall," "the whole earth's treasury," and "men's mother, men's queen."

Northerners' worship of Italian ruins had already started in the 18th Century. (English gentlemen used to build ruined temples to make their gardens look more picturesque.)

great artists and statesmen were all dead. Visitors came to view Italy more and more as a mere storehouse of the past — a past somehow unconnected to the present, degenerate people. John Ruskin, the art critic who taught the world to rave about early Italian art, often claimed to loathe modern Italians.

The Romance of Ruins

The interests that brought visitors to Italy by the 19th Century were quite varied. The

Above, Piranesi's fanciful drawings of ruins, such as this one of Hadrian's Villa at Tivoli, contrasted crumbling buildings with luxuriant vegetation.

Giambattista Piranesi, dubbed "the Rembrandt of the ruins," had familiarized thousands with his fantastic images of the Italian landscape. The pathetic charm of greatness brought to its knees attracted many, especially the romantics. Percey Shelley, the English poet, contended that the Coliseum was more sublime in its ruined state, half-fallen, wreathed with weeds and flowers, than it had been during the days of the Roman empire when it glistened with marble. Where more pious visitors had seen the hand of God in the ruins, the romantic Shelley saw the triumph of nature: "Rome has fallen, ye see it lying/ Heaped in undistinguished ruin;/Nature is alone undying."

For Shelley, and his close friend Lord

Byron, Italy provided a retreat from the repressive morality of England. (Shelley's belief in free love and abandonment of his wife had caused a scandal back home; the discovery of Byron's incestuous relations with his half-sister forced him to leave England.) Both men felt alienated in their native land and spent years wandering from city to city in Italy. Byron wrote many poems set in Italy, the most famous of which was *Childe Harolde*. With its lengthy and evocative descriptions of Italy's most famous sights, the poem became a standard guidebook for visitors. In fact, by mid-century, most of the famous passages could be found excerpted in the standard guidebooks. For Byron's hero the journey to Italy became nothing less than the journey to his own soul. The spiritual pain of the

Stael's *Corinne* (1807) and Nathaniel Hawthorne's *The Marble Faun*. *Corinne*, little known today, was enormously popular in the 19th Century. The novel tells the love story of the animated Italian poetess Corinne and the brooding Scottish Lord Nevil. In the course of their courtship, Corinne instructs Nevil — and the reader — in the beauties of Italy. Chapters with such titles as "On Italian Character and Manners," "The Statues and Pictures," and "The Tombs, Churches and Palaces" reveal this romance to be a thinly disguised guidebook. De Stael was highly esteemed for her sympathetic portrait of the Italian character, so often maligned as superficial, immoral or faithless. In fact, it is the proper, dutybound Nevil who proves to be faithless.

Like so many northerners, Nevil goes to

romantic exile, misunderstood and despised by his own country, was only, finally, adequately reflected in the mighty ruins of Rome. As Childe Harolde cries "Oh, Rome! my country! City of the Soul!/The Orphans of the Heart must turn to thee." Neither Byron nor Shelley ever returned to England: Byron went onto Greece where he died at the age of 36; Shelley drowned off the coast of Liguria while sailing to Lerici in his boat *The Don Juan*. Their compatriot John Keats, another romantic poet, also died in Italy, in a little room overlooking the Piazza di Spagna in Rome.

Two other imaginative works taught the average traveller what to see and how to respond to what he saw. These were Mme De

Italy to develop his "taste." Corinne gently shows him how to appreciate things sensuously rather than intellectually. But once back in Scotland "his thoughts begin to steady from the Italian intoxication which had unsettled them." With Nevil as the stiff northerner and Corinne as the southern temptress, the novel was read as an allegory of England and Italy. Underlined are the contrasts between reason and passion, art and duty, society and the individual, the intellect and the senses.

Hawthorne's *Marble Faun* reveals a 19th

Above, Goethe, the German poet, posed in front of an idealized Italian landscape. This great traveller to Italy had to wait 37 years before making a pilgrimage to the peninsula.

Century New Englander's ambivalent feelings toward Italy. The novelist is openly hostile to Catholicism, a religion depicted as seducing its followers with a "multitude of external forms." He sees a similar superficiality in Italian paintings which "show a marvelous knack of external arrangement instead of the live sympathy and sentiment which should have been their inspiration." Despite a distaste for the Baroque aspects of Italian culture, Hawthorne appreciated the rich history and mysterious atmosphere that Italy offered. His own country, he admitted, lacked such an intriguing presence of the past. *The Marble Faun*, like *Corinne*, contained extensive descriptive passages in chapters entitled "A Stroll on the Pincian" or "A Moonlight Ramble."

The inevitable result of all the publicity — the novels, poems, guidebooks, lithographs — showered on Italy in the 19th Century was disappointment once the traveller was actually there. Ruins rarely looked like Piranesi etchings, and few people were capable of feeling that Rome was truly the city of their soul. The escalating numbers of uneducated tourists just didn't have the preparation in the Italian language, history and classical culture traditionally recommended for the earlier traveller. Thus Daisy Miller, Henry James's specimen of silly, light-hearted American girlhood, was unabashedly bored by antiquities. But she also fell victim to a tourist trap: her eagerness to see the Coliseum by moonlight, a must on any tourist's itinerary, led her to contract malaria and eventually die in Rome.

Perhaps the most entertaining expression by an American of impatience with the cult of Italy is Mark Twain's *The Innocents Abroad* (1869). Though Twain did poke fun at American smugness as well as at the pretentions of Italophiles, he basically defended American common sense. He refused to ooh and aah at what he considered to be the Emperor's New Clothes Italian style. "But isn't this relic matter a little overdone?" he asked. "We find a piece of the true cross in every church we go into, and some of the nails that held it together. . . I think we've seen as much as a keg of these nails." Admiration for Michelangelo he also found excessive: "Enough! Say no more! Lump the whole thing! Say that the creator made Italy from designs by Michelangelo!"

It is hard to think of a 19th Century American writer of any importance who didn't go to Italy and leave some record of his impression: James Fenimore Cooper, Melville, Hawthorne, James, Washington Irving, William Dean Howells. Most of the painters and sculptors went as well. Many artists stayed on for inspiration, for an environment more conducive to creativity than the business world back home, and for the cheap marble and skilled craftsmen. The neo-Classical sculptor William Wetmore Story rented out a suite of 50 rooms in the Palazzo Barberini in Rome. There he hosted frequent receptions for the numerous American and British expatriates living in or around the Piazza de Spagna. In Florence Casa Guidi, home of Robert and Elizabeth Barrett Browning, was the nucleus of the community of foreigners.

Some scrimped and saved to make their one trip to the "promised land." It was the dream of a lifetime for many a small town school teacher or minister. For others, such as James's nouveaux riches Millers, it was a status symbol, a means of acquiring culture, of rubbing off some of that provinciality and new money. Europeans tended to be less hostile to raw Americans with bundles of money than was upper class society in New York or San Francisco. Many of these millionaires, advised by such connoisseurs as Bernard Berenson, would purchase Italian art. It is to these travellers that Americans can attribute the presence of so many Italian masterpieces in museums across the United States.

At first glance modern travellers may seem to have little in common with their predecessors. Most visit Italy for only a week or two and few have a classical education. How many feel these days, as Bryon did, that the Forum "glows with Cicero?" Yet there persist throughout the centuries certain attitudes and behaviors. For example, the law that first-time visitors to Italy must go to Roma, Venezia, Firenze was pretty much laid down in the 19th Century. The Puritanical distaste that Hawthorne felt for the Baroque is shared by many of his spiritual descendants today. Confronted by coping with a strange culture, tourists still often like to comfort themselves with the thought of how much better things are at home. (Complaints about Italy's sanitation are clearly eternal!) Many, like Shelley and Lord Nevil, feel that in Italy they can at last forget their duty and let loose. How many girls hope to fall in love with a handsome, passionate Italian man, freed from the watchful eyes of parents back home? With him they can forget their self-conscious northern ways and abandon themselves to the pleasures of the senses. And if our appreciation of the picturesque has decreased (and after all, Italy is less picturesque than it was 150 years ago), don't we still satisfy our sensual longings through the appreciation of the edible? As for religious pilgrimages, the oldest type of Italian travel, one only has to go to the Pope's public audiences in Piazza S. Pietro to see that not since the Middle Ages have the devout swarmed to Rome in such great numbers.

PLACES

Often, when you approach an Italian town and see it in the distance clinging with stony fingers to its hilltop, you imagine yourself a modern day Guidoriccio da Foligno riding through a landscape painted by Simone Martini or Giotto — a Guidoriccio who has turned in his steed for a speedy FIAT. But drive a little closer and try to find the center of town, and you will probably feel that you're lost in the Minotaur's labyrinth. Negotiating the tangle of one way streets of an Italian city takes years of experience. Often a helpful native will point the way, even take you personally to your hotel, restaurant or museum. But if no one materializes, don't panic, simply follow the tourist signs for "Centro Storico" and "Duomo," and remember that "senso unico" means one way. Then find the first *parcheggio* and abandon your car. Most Italian cities from San Gimignano to Rome are best explored on foot. If you arrive by train, the station will inevitably be in the seedier part of town, so leave it behind for the greener pastures of the *Centro Storico*.

That is as far as generalizations about Italy will take you. Modern life has stamped most places with a bar and a large population of motor-cycle-riding youths. Every town has its Duomo, but how different is the austere Romanesque in Apulia from the lavish Baroque of Turin. Every town has one or more piazzas: in the south they are crowded with men who smoke and play cards; in the North, the men are still there but so are the ladies and the tourists.

Our favorite places in Italy include many spots less frequently visited than the tried and true trio of Roma, Firenze, Venezia. For example, we suggest that after visiting Rome, you take an excursion east into Abruzzo or Molise, those hitherto remote regions whose architecture, parks, mountains and beaches make them among the most refreshing vacation spots in the country. Or if you happen to be exploring the Bay of Naples, why not rent a car and continue on down to Italy's heel and toe — Apulia, Basilicata, Calabria.

The North has Florence and Venice, of course, but also Milan and Turin, two very modern cities packed with art and history. Or you could follow the path of generations of travellers who, with Dante and Ariosto in hand, toured the cities of Lombardy, Venetia, Emilia-Romagna and Tuscany. And if you want to catch your breath and relax, why not retreat into the green hills of Umbria, home of Italy's beloved saint, Francis of Assisi.

As for the many beautiful places the demands of space compel us to bypass we can only quote Dante's apology for similar oversights in his journey through the inferno: "Io non posso ritrar di tutti a pieno,/ pero che si mi caccia il lungo tema,/ che molte volte al fatto il dir vien meno." ("I cannot describe all of them in full, because my lengthy theme so drives me on that many times my words fall short of the fact.") We hope you will go on where we leave off. Italy can never be fully explored, not even in a lifetime. Who knows? You might, like many others before you, fall under the spell and never leave.

Preceding pages: a roadside image of the Tyrrhenian Sea; Reflections of an Italian townscape; the Campo in Siena is the scene for the twice-yearly Palio; walking through marble mazes. Left, woman behind a veil, Palermo.

ROME

"Oh Rome! my Country! City of the Soul
The orphans of the heart must turn to
thee,
Lone mother of Dead Empires! and
control
In their shut breasts their petty misery.
What are our woes and sufferance? Come
and see
The cypress – hear the owl – and plod
your way
O'er steps of broken thrones and temples
– Ye!
Whose agonies are evils of a day –
A world is at our feet as fragile as our
clay."

— Byron

"City of the Soul" was the epithet Lord
Byron gave Rome (Roma). Though few
today would indulge in such romantic
hyperbole, the poet's characterization still
conveys the complexity and beauty of The
Eternal City. In her history, her people
and her landscape, Rome encompasses
the splendor and the squalor of civilization. Less efficient and sophisticated than
Milan, less picturesque and well-preserved than Florence or Venice, she surpasses all those cities in her intricate warp
and woof of past and present. Rome is not
an easy town to know or love; at times the
visitor will curse her foul-smelling traffic
and aggressive inhabitants. Yet you cannot visit Rome without being changed in
some way. If it is impossible to compre-
hend the city completely (after all, the
saying goes, "Rome, a lifetime is not
enough"), she helps us understand our-
selves, our "petty misery" and the fragility
of our world.

The Picturesque Palatine

Spend at least a week, preferably two or
three in Rome. Sightseeing here is
exhausting and is best done on foot, so
have comfortable shoes and don't overlook the simpler pleasures of food and
shopping. After a morning of walking
around, you will be extremely grateful for
that long Roman lunch hour and for the
fact that there are more *trattorie* here than
in any other Italian city. If you come in
the spring be sure to try *abbacchio*, a
tender suckling lamb. Roman specialties
are many, but try: *spaghetti alla matri-*

ciana and carciofi alla romana (stuffed
artichokes).

The best introduction to Rome is not
Piazza Venezia, that terrifying traffic circle at the center of the modern city, but
the more pastoral **Palatine Hill** where the
history of Rome itself began. The ancients
believed that here was the home of Rome's
mythical founder Romulus; recent discoveries of early Iron Age dwellings in the
southwest corner of the hill lend support to
this legend. Nearby these early remains is
the **Tempio di Cibele** picturesquely planted with an ilex grove. The cult of the
eastern goddess of fertility, also known as
Magna Mater, was introduced to Italy
during the Second Punic War (218–201
BC). Mystical rites characteristic of this
and other such cults — throngs of fren-
zied female worshippers, self-mutilation
of priests, sacrifices of bulls — were dis-
tasteful to old fashioned Romans. Nevertheless, adherents continued to expand in
numbers throughout the imperial era.

The name Palatine, said to be derived
from Pales, the goddess of shepherds, has
in turn given us our word "palace." In
Roman times this hill was celebrated for
the splendor of its princely dwellings. Earliest, and simplest of these, was the
Domus Augustana. A portion of it
erroneously called the **Casa di Livia**
(Augustus's wife) is renowned for its illu-
sionistic wall paintings. To the north,
alongside the **Palazzo di Tiberio** (now
mostly covered by the Farnese Gardens)
runs the **Criptoporticus**, a cool underground passage with a delicately stuccoed
vault, built by Nero to connect the palaces
of Augustus, Tiberius and Caligula to
Nero's own sumptuous Golden House on
the Esquiline Hill. To the southeast of this
passage extend the remains of the **Palazzo
dei Flavi** built at the end of the 1st Century AD by the Emperor Domitian. This
infamous sadist, who took pleasure in tor-
turing everything from flies to senators,
also suffered from an obsessive fear of
assassination. According to the ancient
historian Suetonius, an entertaining if
not completely trustworthy source, the
Emperor covered the walls of the palace's
peristyle with reflective moonstone so no
assassin could creep up on him while he
was taking his daily walk. (This room is
the one with an octagonal maze.) Next to
the peristyle lie the remains of a splendid
banquet hall, hailed by contemporaries as
"the Dining Room of Jove." Its buckling
pavement, still covered with pink and yellow marbles, gives some sense of its

receding
ages, the
un sets over
he Eternal
ity. Left,
he Victor
mmanuel
nonument
rovides the
ackdrop to
Roman
vedding
arty.

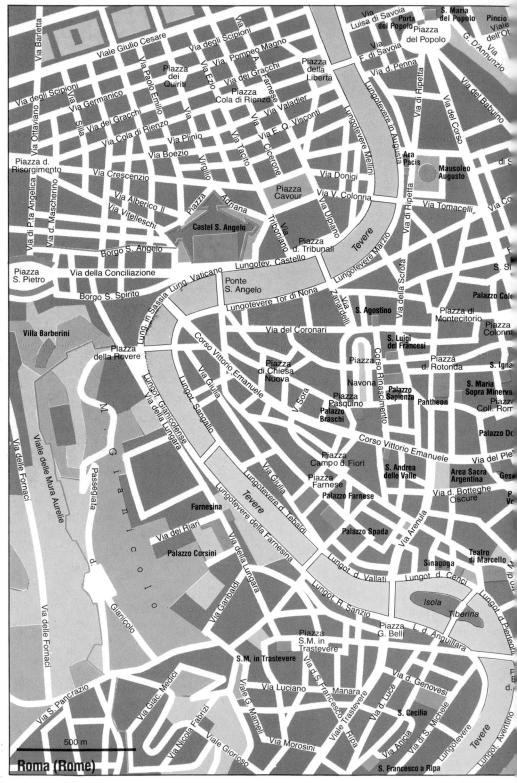

Roma (Rome)

93

former grandeur. To the south lie the extensive remains of the **Domus Augustana**, and the **Stadium**.

Following the fortunes of the city as a whole, the imperial palaces fell into disuse during the Middle Ages; monks made their home among the ruins; the powerful Frangipani family built a fortress there. Then in the Renaissance, when a surge of new building occurred throughout the city, Cardinal Alexander Farnese bought much of the Palatine and laid out the gardens on the slope overlooking the Forum. The **Orti Farnesiani** are remarkable for symetrical but lush plantings, the soothing sounds of fountains and birds, and good views over Rome.

For the lovers of the picturesque, the ruination of the Palatine was a fortunate thing. Even the investigations of archaeologists cannot deprive this location of its wild charm. It is the last remaining place in Rome where you can find a landscape as it might have been drawn by Piranesi or Claude Lorraine. Roses, moss, bright poppies growing amidst the crumbling bricks and shattered marble give this location a romantic rather than an imperial splendor. It is the perfect place to wander, sketch or picnic.

The Roman Forum

The **Clivus Palatinus** leads from the domestic extravagances of the Emperors down into the **Forum**, the civic center of ancient Rome. This area, once a swamp used as a burial ground by the original inhabitants of the surrounding hills, was drained by an Etruscan King in the 6th Century BC. Until excavations began in the last century the Forum, buried under eight meters (25 feet) of dirt, was known as the "Campo Vaccino" because *contadini* tended their herds among the ruins. Today it reveals a stupendous array of ruined temples, public buildings, arches and shops. The overall effect is impressive, but identifying individual buildings can be a bit of a chore. We will wander through stopping at only the most interesting sights.

At the bottom of the Clivus Palatinus rises the **Arco di Tito** which commemorates that emperor's destruction of Jerusalem and its sacred Temple. This event marked the beginning of the Diaspora and the shift from the Temple to local synagogues as the focus of Jewish worship. Until the 20th Century when Israel was founded and the return to Palestine

Classical, Medieval a Baroque coalesce i and aroun the Roma Forum.

became possible, pious Jews refused to walk under the arch.

The **Via Sacra** leads past the three remaining arches of the **Basilica di Constantino**, a source of inspiration for Renaissance architects. Bramante is said to have bragged about his design for St. Peter's: "I shall place the Pantheon on top of the Basilica of Constantine." **The Tempio di Antonino e Faustina**, also known as **San Lorenzo Miranda**, is a superb example of Rome's architectural sedimentation. The layers began with a Temple erected in 141 AD by the Emperor Antoninus Pius; it was then converted into a church in the Middle Ages. During the 17th Century, as was the case with so many Roman churches, a Baroque facade was slapped on. Across the Via Sacra rises the lovely round **Tempio di Vesta**, (goddess of the hearth), where the six Vestals took turns tending the sacred fire. The punishment for allowing the fire to die down was scourging by the priest. Service was for 30 years and chastity was the rule. Few patricians were eager to offer their daughters and the Emperor Augustus had to pick girls by lot. Laxity about vows was also common and the Emperor Domitian resorted to the traditional punishment of burying the errant Virgin alive and stoning her lover to death in the comitium. The lovely **Casa delle Vestali** suggests that this demanding life certainly had its compensations. The ruined buildings and their garden now provide the weary sightseer with a place to sit and enjoy the smell of roses.

If the Roman religion seems very strange to us, their legal practices were much closer to our own. Like 20th Century Americans, the ancient Romans were mad for litigation. Walk past the three elegant columns of the **Tempio dei Castori** to the **Basilica di Guilio** on the left of the Via Sacra. Here trials were held, as many as four at one time. The acoustics were terrible and on one occasion the booming speech of a particularly loud lawyer was applauded by audiences in all four chambers. In case an advocate wanted a little help with his cause, professional applauders, called "supper praisers," were for hire. These claquers, when not employed, would loiter on the steps of the basilica and play games. Their roughly carved boards can still be seen. The senate met across the way in the **Curia**, the best preserved building in the Forum. Its

A fragment of a glorious past.

somber, solid appearance suits the seriousness of its purpose — though there too, as in the Basilica, conditions could be chaotically overcrowded.

At the western end of the Forum rises the famed **Rostra**. Here the orator Cicero declaimed to the Roman masses and here, after his death in Octavian's anti-Republican proscriptions, his hands and head were displayed. Opposite the rostra is the single **Colonna di Foca**. For centuries the symbol of the Forum, it was described by Byron as the ·"eloquent and nameless column with the buried base." Unburied and named, it is still, as the Italians say, *molto suggestivo*. To the right is the **Arco di Settimio Severo**.

At the end of the Via Sacra, in the shadow of the Capitoline Hill, rise the eight ionic columns of the **Tempio di Saturno**. The God's festival, called the Saturnalia, marked the merriest days in the Roman calendar when gifts were exchanged and distinctions between master and slave forgotten. Behind the Temple can be seen from left to right, the graceful **Portico degli dei Consenti**, the **Tempio di Vespasiano e Tito** and the **Tempio della Concordia**.

Outside the Forum excavations, across from Pietro da Cortona's **Chiesa di SS Luca e Martina** is the **Carcere Tulliano** (Mamertine Prison) home of some of Rome's most famous prisoners. A plaque on the wall lists the unfortunates and how they met their unhappy ends: strangling, starvation, torture, decapitation. This dank, gloomy dungeon, according to Catholic legend, was where St. Peter was incarcerated and where he converted his pagan guards. Miraculously, a fountain sprang up so he could baptise the new Christians.

Capitol

If the Palatine was the womb of Rome and the Forum its heart, the Capitoline was, and is, its soul. From here the splendid Temple of Juppiter Capitolinus (dedicated 509 BC) watched over the city. And here, in an inharmonious yoking of past and present characteristic of Rome, modern Italians raised their tribute to Italy's unification after 1,400 years of fragmentation. The **Vittoriano** (Victor Emmanuel monument), completed in 1911 and dedicated to Italy's first King, captures all the neo-Classical bad taste of the last century. Natives and visitors alike claim to despise

The Campidog designed b Michelangelo.

this "Typewriter" and "Wedding Cake."

Throughout the centuries the hope for Italy's future has focused on this hill. Here in 1300, the poet Petrarch was crowned; here in 1347 Cola di Rienzo roused the Roman populous to support his short-lived attempt to revive the Roman Republic; there in the 16th Century Michelangelo planned the elegant Campidoglio and made the Capitoline once again the architectural center of the city; here the historian Edward Gibbon was inspired to write his history of *The Decline and Fall of the Roman Empire.*

If you're feeling energetic, climb the 124 steps to the medieval **S. Maria in Aracoeli** (the midnight mass at Christmas is lovely). The weak-kneed will prefer Michelangelo's regal staircase (known as **La Cordonata**), flanked, at the top, by monumental statues of Castor and Pollux. In the back of the **Campidoglio** the **Palazzo Senatorio** surmounts the ancient **Tabularium**, one of the few remains of Republican times. On the left rises the **Palazzo dei Conservatori**, on the right, **the Palazzo del Museo Capitolino**, both housing important art collections. For insight into ancient Roman character, study the busts of emperors in the **Sala degli Imperatori** in the **Museo Capitolino**. Realistic portraiture was Rome's greatest contribution to the art of sculpture.

Roman Empires

Piazza Venezia marks the center of contemporary Rome. You may feel you risk your life by crossing its wide expanse but usually the torrents of traffic will part to allow a pedestrian passage. The **Palazzo Venezia** dominates one side. Rome's first great Renaissance palace (built 1455) was Mussolini's headquarters from 1929 on. From the balcony he gave some of his most fiery speeches. The light burning in his bedroom at all hours of the day and night reassured the Italians that the "sleepless one" was busy solving all the nation's problems. But according to Luigi Barzini, the light was often left on when Mussolini was not there, a piece of showmanship typical of his rule. Now the palace contains the **Museo del Palazzo Venezia** with a good collection of paintings, sculptures and tapestries.

"Ten years from now, comrades, no one will recognize Italy," proclaimed Il Duce in 1926. One of the most dramatic changes the fascists wrought on Rome

The Dying Gaul, Capitoline Museum.

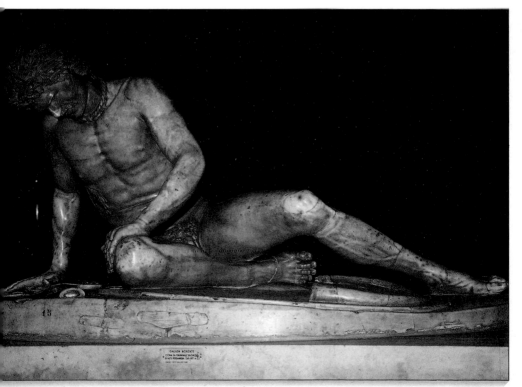

was the **Via dei Fori Imperiali**. Mussolini cut down old neighborhoods (reminders of Rome's decadent period) in order to excavate the fora and build the road. Thus he made a symbolic connection between Rome's glorious, distant past and his regime.

Westernmost of the Imperial fora is **Trajan**'s dominated by its famous **Colonna**. Behind are the splendidly preserved **Mercati Traiano**, one of the favorite haunts of Rome's ubiquitous *gatti*. In ancient times the five storeys of the market were abundantly stocked with exotic fare. The top floor contained two fishponds, one of which received water from an aqueduct, while the other held sea water brought all the way from Ostia. Cunning vendors attracted customers by displaying monkeys whose clever antics proved to be an effective magnet.

Augustus and Nerva both built their fora to accommodate Rome's growing population and passion for litigation. Statues of the emperors stand opposite their fora.

Finally, at the end of all this ruined splendor, rises the **Coliseum**, stripped of its picturesque wildflowers and weeds, surrounded by buses and snack stands, encircled by a swirling moat of traffic. This symbol of the Eternal City is less splendid than it was in its marble-clad, imperial days, less picturesque than in its tumble down Romantic period; but now, scientifically excavated, much of it roped off to ensure the safety of both visitor and building, crowded with tourists from all over the world, it is a suitable emblem of 20th Century concerns.

The Coliseum was built in 79 AD. when the Emperor Vespasian drained the lake of Nero's **Domus Aurea** (Golden House). The message was clear: where Nero had been a profligate, opening the coffers of the empire to construct his own personal pleasure palace, the Flavian prince built a public monument.

Now the public can also enjoy Nero's domestic extravaganza on top of the **Esquiline Hill**. Upon the completion of the Domus Aurea, the emperor is said to have remarked "At last I can begin to live like a human being!" Also near the Coliseum is the **Arco di Constantino**, swathed in scaffolding indefinitely (1985).

Roman Sedimentation

Via San Giovanni Laterano brings you

An anonymou 17th Centu painting of the Colisie

to **San Clemente** one of Rome's most fascinating churches. Here the archaeologically inclined may explore three levels of building. You descend from a 12th Century basilica to a 4th Century basilica to a 1st Century Roman *palazzo* and an apartment building whose courtyard contained a Mithraic temple, honoring one of the popular cults of imperial Roman times. The excavations are extremely well documented in a little booklet called *St. Clement's Rome*, well worth the 2,000 lira (1985).

A little farther along, Via San Giovanni opens up into the piazza of that name. There the pilgrim finds some of the most important buildings in Christendom. The **Obelisk** is the tallest and oldest in Rome; a suitable marker for the Church of Rome, **S. Giovanni in Laterano**, founded by Constantine the Great. Not surprisingly, such an important church is a hodgepodge of building styles, from the exquisite 4th Century Baptistry (Custodian will show mosaics) to the peaceful Medieval Cloister, to the majestic Baroque interior. The **Palazzo Laterano** was home of the Popes until the Avignon exile in 1309. The pious will want to ascend the nearby **Scala Santa**, on their knees of course,

since these most holy steps are said to be the ones Christ walked down after being condemned by Pontius Pilate. Constantine's mother, St. Helena, retrieved them from Jerusalem.

The Ghetto

Rome's old **ghetto** lies to the west of the Capitoline Hill, near the ruins of the **Teatro Marcello**. The city has had a Jewish community since the Republican era, but the credit for isolating the Jews in an overcrowded residential area goes to the Counter-Reformation bigot and inquisitor Pope Paul IV (1555–1559). From his time on, the gates to the ghetto were locked from sunset to sunrise. Jewish men had to wear a yellow hat, the women a yellow scarf, and most professions were off-limits. "The iron of persecution and insult is every day driven into their souls," wrote one outraged 19th Century American. At that time the Jews were forced several times a year to listen to a tirade from a Dominican friar in **S. Angelo in Pescheria**.

Today when wandering through the narrow streets or visiting the **Synagogue** on the Tiber, one has little sense of those

Enduring
and
immutable,
the
Coliseum
today.

years of confinement. A plaque on **Via del Portico Ottaviano** however, is a reminder that it was only 40 years ago that over 2,000 Roman Jews were deported to a concentration camp.

The V.del Teatro Marcello leads to **Piazza Bocca della Verita** which harmoniously yokes together two Roman Temples (**Tempio di Portuno** and, the round, **Tempio d'Ercole**), a baroque fountain and the medieval **S. Maria in Cosmedin**. In the portico of the Byzantine rite church is the **Bocca della Verita** a marble slab that resembles a human face and is considered to be one of the world's oldest lie detectors. If a perjurer puts his hand in the mouth, so the legend goes, it will be bitten off. In fact, the slab's origin is sadly prosaic: it once covered a drain. Those interested in sewers should not miss the **Cloaca Maxima**, the most ancient drain in Rome, visible from the Ponte Palatino, and said to have been built under the Etruscan Kings.

The oldest and largest of the famed Roman circuses, The **Circus Maximus**, lies in the valley between the Aventine and Palatine Hills. It once seated 250,000 people who, in addition to the extravagant main event, were also entertained by the vendors, fortune tellers and prostitutes who plied their trades beneath the arcades. The last of these still light their fires along the banks of the ruined circus.

If the circus has earned the ancient Romans a bad reputation, their public baths have inspired great praise. For the Romans, the baths were much more than a place to keep clean. The **Terme di Caracalla** boasted, in addition to the three pools (hot, warm and cold), exercise rooms, libraries and lecture halls. Bad behavior did occur, especially when mixed bathing was permitted. And some took their cleanliness to an extreme. The Emperor Commodus is said to have taken 8 baths a day! But for the most part, the baths represent a triumph of the Roman public spirit. Cleanliness was not limited to those rich enough to have private facilities. These Terme di Caracalla are now used for performances of Opera in the summer.

The Affluent Aventine

For a contrast to the dusty and barren remains of the circus and baths, visit the Aventine, one of modern Rome's most desirable residential neighborhoods. As

Piranesi's etchings were the f
glimpse ea
travellers
caught of
Rome. He
the Theate
of Marcell

you climb the **Cliva dei Publici** the smell of roses wafts down from the pretty garden at the top of the hill. The Via Sabina leads to **Santa Sabina**, a perfectly preserved Basilican Church of the 5th Century. Inside it is splendidly simple. Shafts of Rome's golden sunlight light up the immense antique columns of the nave. Outside in the Portico, are some of the oldest wooden doors in existence (5th Century).

On the other side of the Aventine, in the shadow of the **Pirimido di Cestio**, lies the **Cimitero Acattolico** or Protestant Cemetary, without doubt one of the most picturesque spots in Rome. Here were buried scores of unfortunate travellers who never returned home from a Wedding Trip or the Grand Tour. In the old part of the graveyard is Keats' tomb with its melancholy epitaph: "here lies one whose name was writ in water."

The modern part of the cemetery contains the grave of Shelley's heart. His body was burned on the shore near Pisa, but as his dear friend Lord Byron described; "All of Shelley was consumed, except his heart, which could not take the flame and is now preserved in spirits of wine."

Outside the **Porta San Paolo** is the basilica of **San Paolo Fuori dei Muri**, one of the major basilicas of Rome. It is believed to house the tomb of St. Paul.

The Beauty of Baroque

Americans and northern Europeans tend to find Baroque architecture garrish, pompous and oppressive. But once you put aside prejudice and stop looking for the austerity of a New England clapboard church or a Romanesque Cathedral, you might find endless fascination in the Baroque. The style is exuberant, awe-inspiring, outrageous. There is such an over-profusion of detail, painting, gilt, marble that it is easy to feel overwhelmed, exhausted, impatient. But what pleasure there is in discovering a particularly winning putto winking at you from an architrave, to crane your neck upwards to a fantastic vision on a ceiling by Pietro da Cartona or Andrea Pozzo, to calculate the wealth it must have taken to cover every inch of a building in marble, gilt and precious metals; or to see saints and Biblical characters made flesh and blood by Caravaggio or Bernini.

The Baroque dominates in Rome and

Baths of
acalla.

the best place to start appreciating it is the **Gesù**. The church was started in 1568 for the recently approved Jesuit order, champions of the Counter-Reformation. The Council of Trent (1545-1563) laid down the rigorous principles for strengthening the Catholic church against the Protestant heretics. Originally, the Gesù was meant to be austere; the church's Baroque makeover was performed in the late 17th Century. By this time the counter-reformers had discovered the usefulness of art as a tool of persuasion, especially as a means to connect worldly and spiritual experience and so make the intangible more accessible to the faithful. At the same time, Baroque art would impress the masses with the great power of the church. Andrea Pozzo's altar to St. Ignatius in the Gesù is particularly sumptuous.

But it is the Gesù's ceiling, with Baciccio's painting *The Triumph of the Name of Jesus*, that shows what Baroque is all about. White statues cling to the gilt vault, some holding up the central painting which spills out of its frame. Here is the characteristic Baroque blend of architecture, painting and sculpture, all working to reinforce the meaning of a church as a place between this world and the next.

The vault of the church seems to dissolve into the vault of heaven.

If you're converted to the style, then head immediately over to **S. Ignazio**, another Jesuit church, this time with a ceiling by Andrea Pozzo. To appreciate its fantastic perspective stand in the middle of the nave and look heavenwards: the vault seems to disappear as an ecstatic St. Ignatius receives from Jesus the light he will disperse to the four corners of the earth. Pozzo also painted a fake dome, since the fathers were unable to find the money to build a real one. The **Piazza S. Ignazio** reveals another side of the Baroque: the theatrical. The perfectly balanced palaces were designed by Philippo Raguzzini to look like the wings of a set. Center stage: the church!

Carnevalian Corso

Via del Corso stretches from Piazza Venezia to **Piazza del Popolo** for nearly a mile. Lined with elegant palaces and crowded with shoppers, this central artery has always been a good place to take the pulse of the city. In ancient times it was the main route north, known as the Via Lata (Wide Way), which gives an idea of

Left, Baroque ceiling at Jesuit Church. Below, Via del Corso

how very narrow most ancient streets were. Its present name derives from the races that were run down its length during the Middle Ages. More recently (between the 18th and 19th centuries) it was the scene of the wild Roman Carnival. During the time of high gaiety before Lent, aristocrats and riff-raff used to pelt one another with flowers, bon-bons and confetti. Masked revellers abandoned all discretion; to facilitate the ogling of ladies and the hurling of missiles, temporary balconies were attached to the palaces. This chaotic setting provided a dramatic background for the climax of Hawthorne's *Marble Faun*. Alas, Rome has sobered up since it became the nation's capital. So for Carnival, head to Venice.

First stop on a tour of the Corso is **Palazzo Doria**, home of the **Galleria Doria-Pamphilj**. The collection is superb (great paintings by Titian, Caravaggio and Raphael), but nothing is labelled, so unless you're a connoisseur of 16th and 17th Century art, its a good idea to buy their catalogue. The star of the collection is Velasquez's *Innocent X*.

Via delle Muratte, off the Corso, brings you to the most grandiose and famous of Roman fountains: **the Fontana di Trevi** in whose waters the voluptuous Anita Ekberg frolicked in Fellini's *La Dolce Vita*.

But the ancient city rears its head even in the most up-to-date places. **Piazza Colonna**, also off the Corso, is home to the **Colonna di Marco Aurelio** (180–193 AD). Sixtus V (1585–1590) crowned this column with a statue of St. Paul and Trajan's column with one of St. Peter. (Sixtus was always eager to appropriate Roman triumphal symbols to Christianity. He placed many fallen, forgotten obelisks in front of churches.)

Two of the most splendid remains of the Augustan era cleaned up and reassembled during the fascist era are the **Mausoleo di Augusto** and the **Ara Pacis Augustae**. The emperor's funeral pyre burned in front of the mausoleum for five days. In the Middle Ages the ill-fated Cola di Rienzo was cremated there. The Ara Pacis, built between 13 and 8 BC to celebrate peace throughout the Empire, was for centuries broken into pieces. Fragments were to be found as far away as the Louvre in Paris and the Uffizi in Florence. Finally, in 1938, the altar was reconstructed with actual fragments and copies of missing parts.

The Trevi Fountain.

The Gate of Rome

Nowadays most people enter the **Piazza del Popolo** from one of the three fingers that lead to its south side: Via del Corso, in the middle; Via di Ripetta on the left (from the Mausoleum of Augustus); and Via del Babuino on the right, from Piazza di Spagna. But the Piazza was intended to be seen from the north. Everyone from Emperors in Triumph to pedestrian Pilgrims used to enter the Eternal City through the **Porta del Popolo** (Porta Flaminia). On the east rises the lush green of the Pincian where, in the Middle Ages, the Emperor Nero's ghost was believed to wander. According to Church legend, a walnut tree infested with crows, grew up from the nefarious Nero's final resting place. The 11th century Pope Paschal II had a dream that the crows were demons and the Virgin Mary wanted him to cut down the trees and build her a sanctuary. The existing church of **S. Maria del Popolo** dates from the late 15th Century and contains many splendidly decorated chapels of different periods, with works by Pinturrichio, Raphael (Chigi Chapel) and Caravaggio (*Conversion of St. Paul* and *Crucifixion of St. Peter*).

Take the Via del Babuino on the left of the twin Baroque churches to the **Piazza di Spagna**. The piazza is shaped like an hour glass or bow tie. In the southern section is the **Palazzo di Spagna**, once the residence of that country's ambassador. Thus the name. But it is in the northern part that the famous **Scalinata della Trinita dei Monti** rise. Neither New York's Times Square nor Paris' Champs-Elysées provide the idle with a better location to watch the world go by. Caricaturists quickly sketch self-conscious tourists; crones sell roasted chestnuts or coconuts dripping with water; gypsy children solicit alms, often with the help of a cacophonous accordion or endearing kitten; tired sightseers rinse their hands in Pietro Bernini's fountain; backpackers sunbathe on the steps; the last of the hippies play guitar while shoppers crowd the windows of stores below, discussing the elegantly displayed merchandise. (Italian good taste even extends to window displays, among the most discreet and effective in the world.) Off this Piazza stretch the most fashionable shopping streets in Rome: **Via Condotti**, **Via Frattina**, **Via Borgognona**. Underneath the Pincian, the quiet

Left, one o many obelisks brought fro Egypt to Rome, in Piazza del Popolo. Below, the Church of Trinità dei Monti.

Via Margutta is the place to buy art.

Years ago the Piazza di Spagna was the habitat of English and American expatriates. Keats died in the house overlooking the steps, which contains a cluttered collection of memorabilia. The **Keats and Shelley Museum** is a must for all romantic ghost seekers. Keep an eye out for plaques all over this area commemorating the residences in Rome of illustrious foreigners. Henry James stayed in the **Hotel Inghilterra**; Shelley in the Via Sistina and Via del Corso; George Eliot in the Via Babuino; Goethe at 20 Via del Corso, where you can visit a museum devoted to the poet's travels in Italy. One of the most grandiose of plaques marks James Joyce's residence at 50/52 Via Frattina. Joyce, it says, "made of his Dublin, our universe." Joyce would not have returned the compliment to Rome, which, according to his biographer Richard Ellman, he said: "reminds me of a man who lives by exhibiting to travellers his grandmother's corpse."

Climb La Scalinata, which at Christmas time has a lovely Crèche, to the church of **Trinità dei Monti** where Felix Mendelssohn listened to the famous choir of nuns who could be heard but not seen.

Legend has it that in the 19th Century one of the demure maidens would admit the public, but make sure all handsome young men were excluded. The church contains paintings by Michelangelo's most talented pupil, Danielle di Volterra, but was greatly destroyed when French soldiers were quartered there in 1816.

The Bones and the Bees

The street between Trinità dei Monti and S. Maria Maggiore was cut by Sixtus V, a pope bent on improving Rome and glorifying his own name. The view down the length of the road is dramatic — climaxing in the obelisk which Sixtus had raised in front of S. Maria Maggiore. Once called Strada Felice, the street now changes its name three times as it cuts through the tangled Roman streets.

The first leg, **Via Sistina**, brings you down to **Piazza Barberini** in the center of which is Bernini's magnificently sensual **Fontana del Tritone**. The musclebound sea creature blows fiercely on a conch shell while a geyser of water shoots above him. In the base is the unmistakeable coat of arms of the Barberini family: three bees. The family palace nearby is the han-

ne Spanish eps.

diwork of, among others, Carlo Maderno, Bernini and Borromini. In the 19th Century William Wetmore Story, a second rate neo-Classical sculptor from Boston, was able to rent a 50-room suite in the palace for a song, but today the **Palazzo Barberini** houses the **Galleria Nazionale**. Don't miss Pietro da Cortona's *The Triumph of Divine Providence*, an elaborate Baroque celebration of the Barberini Pope Urban VIII — the same who, because he quarried so much of his building material from the ruins of ancient Rome, inspired the Pasquinade: "What the Barbarians didn't do, the Barberini did."

Via Veneto swoops off the Piazza Barberini. But before strolling along its wide streets or staring at the people from a cafe, be sure to stop in at the **Chiesa dei Cappuccini**. Its burial ground is one of the most fascinating sights in Rome. A group of artistically and goulishly inclined friars decided to put the dead brothers' bones to a moral and artistic use. The result is four rooms of Rococo sculptures: a playful filigree of hip bones in one room, a garland of spines in another, in yet another skulls stacked as neatly as oranges and apples in a fruit vendor's stall. In case the visitor

should forget these are bones and begin to look on them as mere elements in an elegant design, there are also a few rotting corpses, still swathed in their humble brown robes.

La Dolce Vita

The **Via Veneto** became famous in the post World War Two era as the center of Rome's "Dolce Vita," but today it seems more sleazy than glamorous. Yes, some of the best hotels are around here — the glitzy **Excelsior** and the ultra-comfortable **Jolly** — but so are the prostitutes and fast-food restaurants. Buy an English magazine, put on your dark glasses and sit down in one of the streetside cafes. Then move onto the **Villa Borghese** where you can picnic or visit the **Giardino Zoologico**. Near the Via Veneto entrance to the Park is the **Galleria Borghese**, a great museum with many works by Bernini, Caravaggio and Raphael. If you're curious about Italy's more recent achievements in the arts, visit the **Galleria Nazionale d'Arte Moderna**.

To the north of the Villa Borghese is another aristocratic pleasure palace built for Julius III. The **Villa Giulia** has a beautiful Renaissance garden, and inside, the **Museo Nazionale di Villa Giulia**, full of fascinating pre-Roman art. Especially interesting are the Etruscan terracotta sculptures: a touching sarcophagus of a husband and wife and a magnificent statue of Apollo.

Bernini and Borromini

From the intersection of Via Sistina and **Via XX Settembre** you can admire the drama of Roman urban planning: in three directions you see obelisks proudly scraping the sky. The Via XX Settembre contains a number of splendid Baroque churches. First is **San Carlo alle Quattro Fontane**, also known as **San Carlino**. This tiny church, whose interior is the same size as one of the piers under the dome of St. Peter's, was designed by Francesco Borromini (1599-1667). An undulating facade is characteristic of this eccentric architect's style. The all-white interior is a fantastic play of ovals. The financially pressed monks who commissioned the church were impressed by Borromini's ability to keep down the costs of the church — by using delicate stucco work rather than marble or gilt — without in any way lessening the beauty.

Triton Fountain, Piazza Barberini.

Up the Via Quirinale is another oval gem by Borromini's arch rival, Gianlorenzo Bernini (1598–1680). **San Andrea al Quirinale** offers quite a contrast to its neighbor. Every inch of this church is covered with gilt and marble. *Puttis* ascend the wall as if in a cloud of smoke. Yet there is a simplicity to this church due to the architect's masterful, classical handling of space.

For another Bernini masterpiece head the other direction to **Santa Maria della Vittoria** in Largo Santa Susanna. Here in the Cornaro chapel is Bernini's sculpture of the 17th Century Spanish mystic **S. Theresa of Avila.** The artist captures her at the moment when she is being struck by the arrow of divine love. Her look of ecstasy might seem to be sexual rather than spiritual to the unenlightened, but read the saint's description of her vision to see how accurate Bernini's portrayal is:

I saw a long golden spear and at the end of the iron tip I seemed to see a point of fire. With this he seemed to pierce my heart several times so that it penetrated to my entrails. When he drew it out, I thought he was drawing them out with it and he left me completely afire with a great love for God. The pain was so sharp that it made me utter several moans; and so excessive was the sweetness caused me by this intense pain that one can never wish to lose it, nor will one's soul be content with anything less than God.

(From *The Life of Teresa of Jesus* Translated by Allison Peers. Image Book 1960)

Into the Bowels of the Earth

Dip back into the secretive beginnings of Christianity at **S. Agnese Fuori le Mura** about two km beyond Michelangelo's **Porta Pia** on the Via Nomentana. Beneath the church run extensive catacombs where the martyred Roman maiden St. Agnes was buried. (For her story, see Piazza Navona.) Also in the complex is the incomparable **S. Costanza**, the mausoleum of Constantine's daughter. The ambulatory of this elegantly proportioned round building is encrusted with some of the most beautiful mosaics in Rome.

For those enamored of torturous tunnels winding endlessly past burial niches dusty with disintegrated bones, there are

orghese
ark.

countless catacombs outside the walls of Rome. Perhaps the best way to see them is by spending a day on the picturesque **Via Appia Antica**. You can picnic amidst the remains of the **Villa Quintili** or some unnamed crumbling edifice overgrown with wildflowers and inhabited by bright green lizards. Above ground sits the "stern round tower" (Byron) of the **Tomba di Cecilia Metella**. Below spread the **Catacombe di S. Callisto** (most famous in Rome), **S. Sebastiano** and **Domitilla**.

To get a sense of how huge Roman baths were, see **Santa Maria Degli Angeli**, a church Michelangelo created from the tepidarium of the **Terme di Diocleziano**, the largest baths in Rome, constructed between 298 and 306 AD. They now also house the **Museo Nazionale Romano** one of the greatest collections of ancient art in the world. Sculptures include the Venus of Cyrene, two copies of Myron's Discobolus and the Ludovisi throne. Roman wall painting is seen at its best in the delicate frescoes from the Villa of Livia. They represent a refreshing garden scene with fruits, trees and birds, and were in the dining room where they soothed the digestion of the Empress's guests.

Mary and Moses

Perhaps the Italian attitude toward "Mamma" explains why Rome has more churches dedicated to the Virgin Mary than to any other Saint. The largest and most splendid of these is **Santa Maria Maggiore** one of the four patriarchal churches of Rome. Here the melange of architectural styles is surprisingly harmonious: early Christianity is represented in the Basilican form and in the 5th Century mosaics above the architrave in the nave (binoculars are a must if you want to decipher them). Medieval input includes the Campanile (largest in Rome), the Cosmatesque pavement and the mosaic in the apse. But, no surprise, the overwhelming effect is Baroque. The coffered gold ceiling seems miraculously suspended (it was supposedly gilded with the precious ore Columbus brought from America). The **Cappella Sistina** and **Cappella Paolina** vie for position of most lavish chapel in Rome. Pope Paul probably takes the prize since he intentionally aimed to outdo his predecessor Sixtus V.

If your head is spinning with the folderol of gilt and marble, head down the **Via Cavour** to **S. Pietro in Vincoli** where you will find Michelangelo's massive and dignified *Moses*. Originally the statue was to be part of an enormous freestanding tomb for Pope Julius II, but politics and lack of money curtailed Michelangelo's imagination. Of this one statue Giorgio Vasari, artist and biographer of artists said: "No modern work will ever approach it in beauty, nor ancient either." Moses sits three meters (10 feet) high, every inch the powerful lawgiver. Today the tomb provides entrance, not to another world, but to a cluttered gift shop, where you can buy, among other things, replicas of the statue out front.

The Heart of Historical Rome

During the Middle Ages, most of Rome's population was crowded either into the region between Via Del Corso and the **Tiber** (**Campus Martius** to the ancients) or into Trastevere across the River. When wandering through the cobblestoned streets of these areas, especially late at night, the traveller can easily imagine himself back in the Rome of the medieval tyrant Cola di Rienzo, or of Pope Julius II, or even of Byron — until the

Michelangelo's *Moses* at the Church of Pietro in Vincoli.

spell is broken by the roar of a speeding motorcycle. Perhaps an even better time to tour Trastevere or the Campus Martius is in the early morning. Then you will be able to admire the facades of buildings alone, enter churches with only the faithful as your companions, and watch the modern Romans starting their day. Windowless shops give directly onto crooked, narrow streets and workers leave their doors open for light and air. Look in and you will see bakers kneading loaves of delicious *Casareccio* bread, furniture restorers rubbing down wood with strong smelling ointments, cobblers hammering heels onto worn boots. Children walk to school and women drag metal carts to market. Occasionally a door glides open in the side of a crumbling stucco facade to release a shiny black Fiat.

Just One *Cornetto*

ne antheon is e best-eserved ncient uilding in ome.

Have a *cornetto* (Italian croissant) and a cappuccino in the **Piazza del Rotondo** and admire the outside of the **Pantheon** — the best preserved of all ancient Roman buildings. For those who question the greatness of Roman architecture and dismiss it as inferior to Greek, the Pantheon is an eloquent answer. This perfectly proportioned round temple proves how adept the Romans were in shaping interior space. Rebuilt by the Emperor Hadrian, its architectural antecedents are not the Republican round temples such as the one in the Forum Boarum, but the round rooms used in baths. Western architecture owes the Romans a great debt for their skillful work with vaults and domes.

Near the Pantheon in front of **Santa Maria Sopra Minerva**, Bernini's much-loved elephant carries the smallest of Rome's obelisks. Inside the church (the only one in the Gothic style in Rome) are a chapel decorated by Fra Lippo Lippi and, to the left of the main altar, Michelangelo's statue of Christ bearing the cross. Other ecclesiastical treasures are just a few blocks away. Caravaggio frescoes adorn both **San Luigi dei Francesi** (*Calling of St. Matthew*) and **S. Agostino** (*Madonna of the Pilgrims*). Borromini's **S. Ivo** is tucked into the courtyard of **Palazzo Sapienza**. Like San Carlino's, this church's interior is dazzlingly white. Most startling, however, is its spiralling Campanile.

Even the crowds of people milling

around eating ice cream, the artists sitting on beach chairs hoping to sell their paintings, and the Roman youths zooming through on their motor bikes cannot disguise the elegant proportions of the **Piazza Navona**. This completely enclosed space was once the Stadium of Domitian, parts of which can still be seen outside the northern end. Hagiographers claim that when the youthful S. Agnese was exposed naked in the vaulted areas of the circus beneath the church that bears her name her hair grew to shield her modesty. S. Agnese had refused to be married because she had sworn herself to be a virginal bride of Christ. In another version of her martyrdom her punishment was to be sent to a brothel where her chastity was miraculously preserved; a subsequent attempt to burn her was also unsuccessful; finally, she was beheaded. The church **S. Agnese in Agone** has another curvacious facade by Borromini. Rival Bernini designed the **Fontana dei Fiumi** in the center of the piazza. A popular tale claims that the statue of the Nile which faces S. Agnese is covering its eyes for fear the church will collapse. While in the piazza be sure to gorge on a *Tartuffo* from **Tre Scalini**.

Stony Words

Piazza Pasquino contains a beat up old statue that was formerly the underground newspaper of Rome. The papal censors allowed so little criticism that irrepressible satirists attached their bonmots to several statues throughout the city. Most famous was **Pasquino**, whence our word pasquinade. In one of the quips the writer claimed he had received the worst insult of his life when some one called him, horrors, a Cardinal. Near the piazza is the elegant little church of **S. Maria della Pace**. The facade and piazza may be as much as you see, since the church is rarely open. If you do make it inside there are frescoes by Raphael and a beautiful cloister. To the north **Via dei Coronari** burns with torches every night. The picturesque street is full of pricey antique stores. At the end of Via dei Cornari, take a left and you will soon arrive at the **Chieso Nuovo**.

The Light-Hearted Apostle of Rome

St. Philip Neri is, without question, one of the most *simpatico* saints in the calendar. He arrived in Rome in 1533 and spent the rest of his life there gently trying to reform the population of that sinful

city. He started inviting young men off the streets and into his room for informal discussions of the Gospel, prayers and song. From this simple beginning arose his Oratory. St. Philip refused to withdraw from the world or condemn it, preferring to work steadily and with great humor to save as many souls as he could. He once advised an overly zealous penitent to wear his hairshirt on the outside of his clothes. The Baroque splendor of the Chiesa Nuova was never intended by this humble man, who had a weakness for practical jokes. But for fans of the style, Pietro da Cortona's interior is sumptuous. Behind the altar are three paintings by Reubens.

Our last Baroque church (excluding St. Peter's) is perhaps the most ornate of all. Puccini chose **S. Andrea della Valle** for the opening act of his dramatic opera *Tosca*. Act II takes place at the nearby **Palazzo Farnese**, most splendid of Renaissance palaces and suitably intimidating as headquarters for the villainous Scarpia. The palace is now the French Embassy and, alas for the visitor who would like to pop in to see Annibale Carraci's frescoes, it is open to the public Sundays only (11 a.m. to noon). Other palaces in the neighborhood: **Palazzo della Cancelleria** and the **Palazzo Spada**, which has a good gallery.

Act III of Tosca takes place across the river in the **Castel S. Angelo**. The Mausoleum of Hadrian became in turn a fortress and then a prison; it is now a museum. The view from the parapet from which Tosca plunges to her death is splendid, enhanced by the presence of an enormous bronze angel.

Trastevere

The heart of medieval Trastevere literally, "across the Tiber" is south of the Castello. Here you can find many reasonably priced restaurants and, at **Porta Portese**, a popular flea market each Sunday. Traditionally it has been a working class neighborhood with strong Communist leanings.

South of Viale Trastevere are two churches worth visiting. **Santa Cecilia** was built on top of the house of a Christian martyr whom the Roman authorities attempted to burn to death in her own caldarium. She was then sentenced to beheading, but the executioner failed to kill her after three blows and she lived for three days (enough time to consecrate her house as a church). Carlo Maderno's touching statue of the fetally curled saint was inspired by the sculptor's observations when her tomb was opened in 1599.

A contrastingly sublime statue of a woman in her death throes is Bernini's **Blessed Luisa Albertoni** in nearby **San Francesco Ripa**. This late work of the master captures even more powerfully than his St. Theresa (see above), the conflict between pleasure and pain: joy and sorrow felt by a woman who is in between this world and the next.

Piazza S. Maria in Trastevere is a hangout for some of Rome's more anti-establishment types. The church itself, one of the oldest in Rome, has some beautiful mosaics illustrating the life of Mary. (This was the first of many Roman churches to be dedicated to the Virgin.)

After these sobering places of worship with their emphasis on the horrors of this world and the glories of the next, it is a relief to come to the **Farnesina**, a jewel of the Renaissance, worldly and pagan. A ceiling fresco by Raphael details the love of Cupid and Psyche. The figures are robust, fleshy, almost Rubenesque. Bosoms and buttocks are unabashedly displayed in a rollicking sea of banquet-

ers. In the next room Raphael's *Galatea* captures the moment when the nymph, safe from the clutches of her pursuer, the cyclops Polyphemus, looks back. Upstairs Baldassarre Peruzzi, who designed the entire villa, devised a fantastic *trompe l'oeil* so that the room seems to open upon a restful village scene. In the bedroom: Sodoma's erotic painting: *The Wedding of Alexander and Roxanne*.

To reach another important Renaissance monument, this time ecclesiastical, climb the stairs up the Gianicolo to **S. Pietro in Montorio**. In the courtyard is Bramante's **Tempietto**, a circular church that marks what was mistakenly believed to be the site of St. Peter's martyrdom. Climb a little farther to the **Fontana Paola**, an impressive Baroque monument that now serves as a popular car wash.

The **Passeggiata del Gianicolo** provides an appropriate place to bid Rome farewell. Stroll along its shady way and enjoy the panoramas over the Eternal City. If you've been here a while, you should be able to pick out some of your favorite monuments. Easiest to spot are the flat dome of the Pantheon, the twin domes of S. Maria Maggiore and the Victor Emmanuel Monument.

astel Sant'
ngelo.

THE VATICAN

If size were the only measure of a nation's power or importance, the Vatican would demand even less heed than we pay to such countries as Djibouti or Nauru — perhaps a passing curiosity, nothing more. Yet the Vatican serves as an exception to the rule that postage-stamp sized nations are famous for little more than their postage stamps.

Steeped in an age-old tradition of political and spiritual might, for many centuries the unchallenged center of the Western world, the Vatican invites continued fascination. Its symbolic significance, both past and present, and its enduring international role, as both a religious and diplomatic force, have in many ways elevated this tiny city-state to a position of equality with nations many millions of times larger. No matter how secular our world has become, divine right of authority seems still to count and to make the Vatican much more than a geographic oddity, much more than the academic footnote it might otherwise be.

Covering a total area of only a little more than 100 acres, Vatican City is by far the world's smallest independant sovereign entity. Indeed, what other nation is as small as New York's Central Park? What other nation can lock its gates at midnight, as the Vatican's doorkeepers do each night, opening them only at the ring of a bell? What other nation can be traversed, at a leisurely pace, in well under an hour?

This is not to say, however, that the Vatican is situated on any ordinary plot of land; the area enjoys a unique history dating even from pre-Christian times. In imperial Roman days, the lower part of what is now Vatican City was an unhealthy bog, famous among caesars and consuls for its vinegary wine and as a good place to catch a nasty fever or an oversized snake. In the 1st Century AD, the dowager empress Agrippina ordered the Vatican valley drained of its marshes, to be etched instead with tranquil imperial gardens. The notorious emperors Caligula and Nero conceived a less quiet use for this area; under their reigns the raucous spectacle of the circus, Roman style, became a regular event at the spot where now stands St. Peter's Piazza. Chariot racing and executions — including that of St. Peter himself — were the norm where today God's

Left, one of the world's greatest figureheads, Pope John Paul II, the first Polish pontiff, resides in the world's smallest sovereign state, the Vatican, right.

representative on earth performs a weekly mass.

The Lateran Treaty of 1929, concluded between Pope Pius XI and Benito Mussolini, established the present territorial limits of the Vatican. The city is roughly trapezoidal in shape, bounded by medieval walls on all sides except on the corner, where the opening of St. Peter's Piazza marks the border with Rome and the rest of Italy. Roughly even areas of flat pavement, buildings and, to the northwest, sloping hills and gardens make up the topography of the tiny nation. Of the six

openings to the Vatican, only three are for public use: the Piazza, the Arco delle Campane (south of St. Peter's Basilica), and the entrance to the Vatican Museums. Pius XI had a special Vatican Railway station built in the early 1930s, a facility through which no paying passenger has ever travelled and of which even popes have availed themselves infrequently. A heliport has been laid down on a spot where British diplomats, restricted to the confines of the city, whiled the days away during World War Two.

Aside from an impressive array of palaces and office buildings, there is also a Vatican prison, a supermarket, and the printing press which churns out the daily *L'Osservatore Romano* and is capable of handling linguistic scripts ranging from Coptic to Ecclesiastical Georgian to Tamil. In short, the Vatican is much more than an oversized museum.

Subjects of the Holy See

As with other states, the Vatican has those it protects as citizens. Anyone wishing to immigrate, however, had better not hold his breath, for to hold a Vatican passport is to be a member of one of the world's more exclusive clubs. About 400 individuals enjoy Vatican citizenship, all of whom either live or work permanently in the city or are abroad on diplomatic mission for the Catholic Church. The privilege hinges on a continuous direct relationship with the Holy See. When ties are severed, the privilege is lost.

Servants of God. His role is perhaps best characterized by the root of the word "Pope" itself. In Greek "pappas" meant simply "father" — in this case the spiritual father of all mankind. And although the papacy's claim to universality has undoubtedly eroded in the two millenia since St. Peter assumed the mantle as a heavenly representative on earth, the Pope's image remains decidedly paternal, ordinarily demonstrated by a benevolent concern for the advancement of humanity, occasionally by more stern warnings against theological or spiritual deviation. John Paul II, elected in 1978, the year of three popes, has done much to restore this sense of papal prestige and energy. The path of 262 predecessors has not always been so virtuous.

In briefly considering the history of the

There is one person for whom severence ordinarily comes only with death. He carries passport no. 1 (although he is unlikely ever to have to use it); he rules absolutely over Vatican City and he holds ultimate authority within the Catholic Church. He is, of course, the Pope himself. Within the Vatican and Catholic hierarchies, his power is unchallenged. A glance at his official titles, as listed in the *Annuario Pontificio*, the official Vatican directory, sheds any doubt of this supremacy: Bishop of Rome, Vicar of Christ, Successor of the Prince of the Apostles, Supreme Pontiff of the Universal Church, Patriarch of the West, Primate of Italy, Archbishop and Metro-politan of the Roman Province, Sovereign of the State of Vatican City, Servant of the

papacy, it is important to remember that the papacy's powers and significance were for many centuries more temporal than spiritual. The pope until modern times was a mighty piece on the chessboard of European politics; and just as there have been good and bad kings, there have been good and bad popes. Such immensely centralized authority cannot consistently elude the grasp of ill-motivated men. With that in mind, some facts: the shortest reign of a pope was that of Stephen II, who died four days after his election in March

Above, a public mass draws thousands to St. Peter's Square. Right, the Vatican's Swiss Guards are responsible for the safety of the Holy See.

114

752. At the other extreme, the 19th Century's Pius IX, famous for his practical jokes and his love of billiards (he had a table installed at the Vatican Palace), headed up the Holy See for 32 years. The youngest pope on record, John XI, was a wise 16 when he took the helm in 931; the oldest, Gregory IX, managed to survive 14 years past his election in 1227 at the age of eighty-six. While the great majority have been of either Roman or Italian extraction, Spain, Greece, Syria, France and Germany have all been represented in the seat of St. Peter; there was at least one of African birth (Miltiades, 311-314), one hailing from England (Hadrian IV, 1154-1159). John Paul II is himself the first Pole to lead the Catholic Church. At least 14 popes abdicated or were deposed from office (Benedict IX in the 11th Century was elected and then deposed three times). Some 10 have had their reigns end in violent death, including a record three in a row in the grizzly days of the early 10th Century. Popes have been arrested, imprisoned, and otherwise humiliated by various disrespectful lay leaders, and many have never ruled from Rome at all.

Some 80 popes have been canonized by the church, most recently Pius X (1903-1914). Many others are unlikely ever to climb out of the inferno. The decidedly unchristian Stephan VII (896-897) exhumed the body of his predecessor, Formosus (891-896), re-dressed it in papal vestments, and put it on trial on charges of usurping the throne and of being guilty of ambition, among other offenses. In what has become known as the Synod of the Corpse, Formosus was predictably convicted on all counts, his body stripped, dismembered, and thrown into the waters of the Tiber. The prosecutor got his just deserve, however, as a Roman mob rose up and strangled Stephan.

Perhaps more notorious, if less gruesome, is the case of Alexander VI (1492-1503), the famed Borgia pope. Even before the Spaniard won election to the throne, gained by means of powerful family connections, Alexander had developed a rather unsavory reputation as a womanizer and profligate. He flaunted a dalliance with the lovely Vanozza de' Cataneis. A party he hosted in 1460 in Siena provoked an angry rebuke from Pius II: "We leave it to you to judge if it is becoming in one of your position to toy with girls, to pelt them with fruits ... and, neglecting study, to spend the whole day in every kind of pleasure."

Alexander improved little during his tenure as Holy Primate, casting papal favors in the direction of his mistresses and ten illegitimate children. One son, Cesare Borgia, was made a cardinal even though he had never been ordained. Other progeny openly fiddled in the mire of Italian court escapades. The family's only saving grace, in fact, seems to have been one of Alexander's great-grandsons, Francisco, who became head of the Jesuit order and went on to an honor his ancestor would never have — sainthood.

For all the high primates remembered for unseemly deeds, there are, of course, many more of undoubted virtue. St. Peter himself, crucified upside down by the Emperor Nero in AD 64, was only the first in a long line of those reigns characterized by distinguished leadership. Take, for instance, St. Gregory the Great (590-604), who emptied the Vatican treasuries to feed thousands of starving refugees from the Lombard wars. Or St. Leo IX (1049-1055), who brought the church out of a steep decline by cleaning up rampant corruption, including the common practice of trading in holy offices,

among the clerical ranks. Or the more recent example of John XXIII (1958-1963), who transformed the papacy into a more caring and humane institution through the simple gift of a warm personality. "We are not on earth to guard a museum," he once said of the Church, "but to cultivate a garden." Pope John also throttled the Vatican's tendency towards pomposity: where the L'Osservatore Romano used to write, "following is the allocution by his Holiness as we have gathered his words from his lips," John ordered a simple "the Pope said." John Paul II, an eminently pastoral pope who has successfully availed himself of advances in communications, will one day join those leaders who have done credit to the Church and to humanity.

Picking the Pontiff

The process of electing a new pope is as fascinating as it is unusual. The papacy is the world's only elective monarchy. The Sacred College of Cardinals, a largely titular body of 120 bishops and archbishops appointed by the pope, assumes full responsibility for the selection, convening for a conclave from points the world over soon after death tolls in the Vatican Palace. The electors are sealed into the Sistine Chapel — sorry, no cameras or tape recorders allowed — and are not permitted to leave until their task is done and a new successor to St. Peter has been chosen. Voting can proceed by any of three methods: by acclamation, whereby divine inspiration provokes the cardinals all to shout the same

ordained that cardinals should be reduced after five days to a diet of bread and water.

Paper ballots are burned after each tally, and onlookers eagerly await the smoking puffs from the chapel's small chimney, for this provides the outside world with the only clue as to how the election is progressing. With every inconclusive vote, the smoke remains dark; white plumes denote a winner. (Electors are provided with special chemicals labelled *bianco* and *nero* to render the signal more clear.) The cardinal dean announces to the faithful, "*Habemus Papam,*" and the newly chosen soon after appears in one of three robes (sized small, medium and large) kept on hand for the occasion. The coronation takes place on the following day in St. Peter's Basilica.

Although popes have absolute legislative,

name at the same time; by scrutiny, in which four ballots are cast daily until one candidate has captured a two-thirds majority plus one; or, at last resort, by compromise, entrusting a small group of perhaps two dozen to hammer out a resolution.

All modern popes have been selected by the second method. Although most conclaves have seen to their duty with relative dispatch (John Paul II prevailed after two days; his predecessor, the short-lived John Paul I, after only one), outside authorities have occasionally hurried the cardinals along with little incentives. After the death of Innocent III (1216), local magnate Matteo Rosso Orsini forced the electors to enjoy the company of the dead pope's corpse. Gregory X (1271-1276)

executive, judicial and doctrinal authority over both Vatican City and the church as a whole (they were declared infallible in matters relating to faith by the First Vatican Council in 1870), the immensity of their responsibilities obviously necessitates substantial assistance.

Governance of the Vatican itself is handled by the Pontifical Commission for the state of Vatican City, which consists of seven cardinals, and a lay official, who directs the city-state's administrative affairs. But it is the task of shepherding the spiritual deportment of

Above, the Vatican Museum - seemingly endless corridors of artistic treasures. Right, view from the Vatican dome over the Tiber. Next page: mass in St. Peter's Cathedral.

more than 800 million catholics worldwide, and of managing a global religious bureaucracy composed of 4,000 bishops, 400,000 priests, and at least 1 million nuns, that occupies the great majority of those who work within the Vatican walls. This highly organized body of institutional supervisors, known collectively as the Roman Curia, directs everything from the Church's diplomatic and missionary affairs to the interpretation of Catholic marriage law.

Of the 4,000 or so employed in Vatican City, most operate within the Curia. This Vatican civil service was once considered plump with sinecures. As one story goes, an eminent Italian visited Pius IX to speak of concern for his maturing son. "Holiness," the suppliant began, "he is now grown up, he doesn't want to work, he spends his whole time idling and he wastes

within its ranks. As late as 1860, the Vatican and Church governments employed almost 200 laymen for every priest; today, the proportion is reversed. Most prominent among the remaining non-initiates are the Swiss Guards, who are exclusively charged with protecting the Holy See. This corps of 120 men, all Catholic, all Swiss, all brightly garbed in blue, red and yellow uniforms allegedly designed by Michelangelo himself, may seem no more than an ornamental regiment destined only to lure the shutter of many a tourist's camera. In fact, the Guards have a history of very real military bravery dating back to the early 16th Century, and today perform a function for the pope much like that which the United States Secret Service performs for American presidents.

And so the Vatican is distinguished by much

time with horses and carriages." The Pope serenely replied "We have understood. You consider him suitable for employment in Our service." Although this traditional bureaucratic flab has been markedly pared in recent times, the tightening could go further still. The position of Secretary of Briefs to Princes and of Italian Letters, for instance, is responsible primarily for adapting the dead language of Rome for such new words as "telephone" and "airport." A standard lampoon of the government's extravagance has it that the city's "SCV" license plates stand not for "Stato della Citta del Vaticano" but rather for "Se Cristo Vedesse" ("if Christ could see . . .").

While chipping away at waste, the Curia has also largely turned from elevating lay officials

more than the artistic masterpieces it is so fortunate to shelter. Blessing the Catholic Church with an independant sovereignty upon which to stand, it assures that institution a unique and enduring position among the world's many religions. Blessing the papacy with all the privileges that come with the leadership of a state, it assures the continued respect and deference of other national leaders before the person of the pope. His powers and those of the church would undoubtedly survive without the advantage of Vatican City. Backed by the tradition of the ages, however, the foothold will not likely be lost, and perhaps it is best that a body of the spirit maintains this small perch against the onslaught of governments answering to less thoughtful authorities.

A TOUR OF THE VATICAN

Church, museum, mausoleum, St. Peter's is all three. No other temple surpasses it in terms of historical significance or architectural splendor. Some may feel that the immensity of the interior is more suited to moving commuters through a railway station than to inspiring the faithful to an act as intimate as prayer. The cathedral is, in fact, very much a place of worship, though there is no doubt its many architects and patrons intended it to astonish the faithful with the worldly power as much as the spiritual piety of the Catholic popes. A tour of the Vatican should be divided into two parts: first, the piazza and Church, then the museums.

Bernini's spectacular, colonnaded **Piazza S. Pietro** is, according to one's perspective, either the welcoming embrace or the grasping claws of the Mother Church. The **Via della Conciliazone**, put through in 1937 to commemorate the reconciliation between Mussolini and Pope Pius XI, changed the original impact of the space. Before this thoroughfare provided a monumental approach to St. Peter's, the pilgrim arrived by way of a series of smaller streets, winding through the old **Borgo**, to arrive, finally, in this enormous enclosed open space, with the biggest church in the world at one end, and an enormous, Egyptian obelisk in the center.

Just about every important Renaissance and Baroque architect from Bramante on had a hand in the design of St. Peter's. The idea for rebuilding the original 4th Century basilica was as old as the mid-5th Century, but not until Julius II became Pope did a complete reconstruction get under way. He hired Bramante, who over the years was succeeded by Raphael, Baldassare Peruzzi, Michelangelo (usually credited with the dome), Giacomo della Porta and Bernini.

The hugeness of the interior is offset by its proportions: thus the cherubic *putti* are actually six feet tall, as are the mosaic letters of the frieze that runs around the church. On the right as you walk in is Michelangelo's **Pietà**, which has been inspiring sympathy in viewers since the 25-year old sculptor finished it in 1500. At the end of the nave is the bronze statue of St. Peter, its toe worn away by the kisses of generations of pilgrims.

Over the high altar, which is directly above the tomb of St. Peter, rises Bernini's garrish bronze **Baldacchino**, thought by many to look like the canopy of an imperial bed. Pope Urban VIIIth stripped the bronze for it from the portico of the Pantheon. But Bernini outdid himself in the design for the **Cathedra Petri** (chair of St. Peter), in the apse. Four gilt bronze figures of the church fathers hold up the chair. Above, light streams through the golden glass of a window crowned by a dove (symbol of the holy ghost). The chair itself bears a relief of Christ's command to Peter to "feed his sheep." Thus the position of the Pope is explained and bolstered by Christ's words, and the teachings of the church fathers, and blessed by the Holy Ghost. Further confirmation of the Pope's sacred trust is inscribed in the dome. Christ's words contain the most important pun in Christendom: "You are Peter and on this rock I will build my church and I will give to you the keys to the kingdom of heaven."

The **Musei e Gallerie del Vaticano** merit a lifetime of visits. But for those who have only a few hours, a few sights must not be missed. The **Museo Pio-Clementino** contains the Popes' collection of antiquities. Be sure to visit the **Belvedere Courtyard**, home of the celebrated and cerebral *Apollo Belvedere* and the contrastingly, writhing, muscle-bound sensual *Laocoon*. The Vatican **Pinacoteca** contains superb paintings including Raphael's *Madonna of Foligno* and *Transfiguration*. There are also entire rooms painted by the masters. The **Stanze di Raffaello**, commissioned by Julius II, comprise three rooms painted by Raphael: **Stanza dell' Incendio di Borgo**; **Stanza della Segnatura**; **Stanza di Eliodoro**. Downstairs, delicate and colorful frescoes by Pinturricchio decorate the **Appartamento Borgia**. But the triumph of fresco painting, not only of the Vatican Palace but of the entire world, is the **Cappella Sistina** (Sistine Chapel). On the walls are paintings by Botticelli Pinturicchio, Ghirlandaio; on the ceiling and behind the altar, of course, by Michelangelo. No reproduction can ever do justice to the interplay of painting and architecture, to the drama of the whole chapel, alive with color and human emotion. "All the world hastened to behold this marvel and was overwhelmed, speechless with astonishment," Vasari wrote. The astonishment is no less today than it was in the Renaissance, and now the panels are slowly being cleaned, revealing once more their bright colors.

ROME ENVIRONS

The boast of the fascists that they represented the continuation of ancient Rome has been often ridiculed. Mussolini's claim to imperial inheritance was based on his aggressive foreign policy towards two East African countries — Ethiopia and Somaliland — which the other colonialist nations, greedy more for resources than for empty power, had left behind. But, in 1936 Mussolini could proclaim from the balcony of Palazzo Venezia to an enthusiastic mob that "the hour struck by destiny had finally arrived" and the imperial eagles — signs of the power in ancient Rome — had come back again to shine on the hills of Rome.

The official art of the regime also would stick to canons and forms of Roman grandeur. Mosaics in the style of ancient Roman floors pave the avenue and decorate the walls of the **Foro Italico**, the ambitious sports center created in 1931 northeast of the capital. Bulky square columns support the **Palazzo della Civiltà e del Lavoro** — commonly called the "Square Coliseum" — at EUR. Sixty colossal statues of athletes adorn the **Stadio Olimpico** in the Foro Italico. Stark lines and impressive bulk are the features of the church of **SS Pietro e Paolo** at EUR. The esthetic of the regime did succeed in creating some striking effects, but mostly the result is one of phony grandeur. In the city itself, urban planners ruthlessly drove roads through areas of historical importance, tearing down medieval quarters, which they considered an inheritance of dark times, and ripping through the very heart of Rome a triumphal way for the new eagles of the regime. From this point of view EUR (Esposizione Universale di Roma), is the least offensive of Il Duce's efforts in town planning. EUR is an area south of Rome which was previously undeveloped. Here in 1938 Mussolini undertook to build, with the designs of Marcello Piacentini, a third Rome to rival in grandeur the Imperial Rome and the Rome of the Renaissance. The Exposition, which was to open in 1942 in commemoration of 20 years of fascism, never took place because of World War Two. The overall design was only partially completed. In the 1950s new buildings were added and government offices and

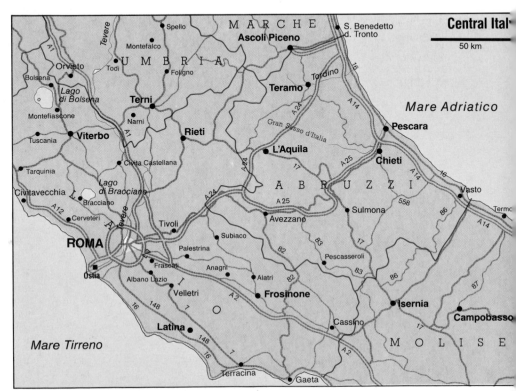

museums moved here. EUR became a smart residential quarter.

Roman history buffs should visit the **Museo Preistorico ed Etnografico** and the **Museo della Civiltà Romano**. The latter contains the famous **plastico di Roma**, a reconstruction of the city in the time of Constantine.

Ancient Apartment Dwellers

The town of **Ostia Antica** was founded around the end of the 4th Century as a fortified city to guard the mouth of the Tiber. Later it developed into the commercial port of Rome as well as its naval base. Vital supplies of produce, mainly corn, arrived from Ostia to the capital through the **Via Ostiensis**. When Ostia became inadequate for its trade, another port, Portus Augusti, which had been originally planned by Augustus, was built by Nero northwest of the town. By the time of Constantine, Ostia had been definitely eclipsed by Porto and turned into a residential town for Romans of the middle and lower classes. Ostia's ruins rival those of Pompeii in showing the layout of an ancient Italian city. The example of houses unearthed in Ostia *insula* are,

therefore, of the utmost importance for the knowledge of the type of dwellings the same classes presumably had in Rome. The *insula* was usually a four storey house built in brick, reaching a maximum height of 15 meters. It had numerous rooms, each with a window. (Mica was used instead of glass for the panes.) The *Domus*, the typical Pompeiian residence built for the very rich, usually on one floor only, was very rare in Ostia.

The Roman theater, enlarged in the 2nd Century by Septimius Severus to hold 2,700 persons has perfect acoustics and houses the summer season of the **Teatro di Roma**.

The **Lido di Ostia** is an overcrowded seaside resort for Romans. The sea there looks dirty and polluted. Nature lovers are advised to drive about 7 km (4.5 miles) south (Tor Vaianica). Along those beaches, served by very primitive facilities, nudists of all ages and kinds of sexual tastes and attitudes meet in a very laid-back Roman-type atmosphere.

Palestrina and Tivoli

The ancient **Praeneste** is one of the oldest towns of Latium. According to the myth, Telegono, son of Ulysses and Circe, founded it. The town was already flourishing in the 8th Century BC and in the following centuries was successful at resisting the attacks of the Romans. Only in the 4th Century, after the end of the Latin War against Rome, in which Praeneste had a leading role, did the town become a subject of Rome. Later, during the bloody civil war between Marius and Sulla, Marius fled to Praeneste. The town was besieged by Sulla's troops and eventually destroyed. But Sulla wanted to make amends and ordered the reconstruction of the famous sanctuary of **Fortuna Primigenia**. The temple, which occupied an area of about 32 hectares, was one of the richest and grandest of antiquity. It consisted of a series of terraces down the slopes of mount Ginestro that were connected by vaulted ramps. The temple housed an oracle believed to tell the future. Its cult lasted until 4th Century AD when the temple was abandoned. On its ruins the Medieval town rose. The bombing of 1944, which destroyed the part of the town which stood on the third terrace, brought the temple to light again and started excavations and studies. The **Museo Nazionale Archeologico Prenestino** houses many of the local finds includ-

receding ages, Barberini mosaic in the Archaeological Museum of Palestrina. Below, the excavations Ostia Antica.

ing the incomparable **Barberini Mosaic**.

At the height of the Roman empire the ancient site of Tibur (Tivoli) on the lower slopes of the Sabine hills, was a favorite retreat for poets and the rich. Lavish villas scattered around sacred woods and scenic waterfalls, had such guests as Horace, Catullus, Maecenas, Sallust and the Emperor Trajan. In the year 117 AD the Emperor Hadrian began to build his luxurious place of retirement on the gently sloping plain below the foothills on which Tivoli stands. The villa, which occupies 180 acres of land, is the largest and richest in the Roman empire. They say the Emperor attempted to recreate the monuments and places which had impressed him the most during his extensive travelling in the East. (The peaceful **Canopus** was modeled on a sanctuary of Scrapis near Egyptian Alexandria.) But Hadrian's overall conception is extremely sophisticated and goes beyond mere imitation. What one sees in the endless succession of terracings, and water basins and baths, is the design of a great esthetical toy, a divertissement against trivial functionality — no matter how sumptuous it can be — and common sense. Yet there is nothing in the state of this general tired of the war and the world, of this man at the end of a loveless life, which may be associated with decadent baroque taste for artifice and tromp-l'oeil. His architectonical and decorative vision turns out to be of a rigorous, geometrical, classical controlling nature. The building which stands in the heart of the villa and that a romantic archaeology had previously labeled **Teatro Marittimo** is an example of this. It's a circular building with a columnated portico and an island in the middle surrounded by a strange moat. It is, on the one hand, a place of the mind, a *locus mentis*, a synthesis fantastic and symbolic of space, perhaps a theater of the world. And at the same time it is the equivalent of a medieval cloister, or of the '*hortus conclusus*' of the courts of the Renaissance princes. So it's a place of the metaphysical suggestion, of escape from reality, of retreat into the memory, perhaps also of the lucid contemplation of death.

The spirit which pervades the **Villa d'Este** in Tivoli — the sumptuous residence into which Cardinal Ippolito d'Este had the skillful Pietro Ligurio transform a Benedictine convent is very different, less complex, not metaphysical at all. On the

Villa Adria at Tivoli.

contrary, it is immediately light and gay. The palace, whose facade overlooks the park, with its rooms decorated with frescoes, is a typically Renaissance princely mansion. And Ippolito, of the Dukes of Este, more absorbed by mundane business than spiritual care, was a prince indeed, though of the church. But the real splendor here lies in the symmetrically terraced garden sloping down the hillside, covered with luxuriant vegetation and the unrestrained plays of water. Water is here the prime element in architecture and decoration. Water — and its necessary co-medium light — is given shape, moulded in infinite faces and kinds of motions. Long pools of quiet water, escorted by rows of elegiac cypresses multiplying the distance, give the suggestion of infinity. Water spouts squirt out from obelisks or gurgle out from the mouths of mythological creatures and monsters lurking behind an accretion of green slime, or gayly spring from the nipples of a sphinx or the many breasted Artemis of Ephesus. In this monument dedicated to the ephemeral, in this superb triumph of an astonishing theatricality, one can perceive the beginnings of the baroque taste of the following century.

Renaissance la d'Este Tivoli, with fountains d gardens.

The Etruscans

Before any of the many Romes, before modern Rome, capital of unified Italy, or Renaissance Rome, capital of the Popes, or Imperial Rome, capital of the world, Italy could claim a highly refined civilization: the Etruscans. Their apparent zest for life and their emphasis on physical vitality fascinated the novelist D.H. Lawrence, who saw them as a happy contrast to the "Puritan" Romans.

The "Etruscan Places" (so Lawrence named his travel book) were in the ancient region of Etruria northwest of the Tiber, that encompassed parts of modern Tuscany (Etruscany), Umbria and Lazio. Around 500 BC, at the height of their political domination, the Etruscans occupied a large part of ancient Latium and had established colonies in Corsica, Elba, Sardinia, the Balearic Islands and the coast of Spain. The Etruscans were not organized under a centralized government, but rather formed a loose confederation of city-states tied together for religious reasons. Etruscan wealth and power was partly based on knowledge of metal working and their exploitation of iron deposits in Etruria.

Cerveteri

The small Medieval town of Cerveteri, north of Rome on the via Aurelia, was built on the site of the Etruscan town of Caere. The ancient settlement occupied a much wider area and in the 6th and 5th centuries BC, (the period of its maximum prosperity and power) was one of the most populated towns of the Mediterranean world. It had strong ties with Hellenic lands whose merchants and artists formed communities and made Caere the center of a lively and sophisticated cultural life. The decline began in 384 AD, when Pyrgy harbor, its main port, was devastated by a Greek incursion. Eventually the rude, haughty, still barbaric strength of rising Rome blindly wiped away what had been a highly refined and joyous civilization. Nothing remains today of the ancient town of Caere except for a few walls.

Caere's necropolis, the city of the dead, is placed on a hill where it could be seen from the ramparts of the city of life, gay with its painted houses and temples. The oldest tombs (8th Century BC) have a small circular well carved into the stone where the urns with the ashes of the dead were placed. (Two modes of burial, cremation and inhumation, continued side by side for centuries.) The first chamber-tombs, also cut into the stone and covered with rocky blocks and mounds (tumuli), appeared as early as the beginning of the 7th Century. The noble Etruscans were either enclosed in great sarcophagi with their effigies on top, or laid out on stone beds in their chamber tombs. Placed beside them in the tombs were treasures they would need in the next world: a miniature bronze ship in which to travel to the other world, rich jewels for adornment, dishes for eating, statuettes, tools, weapons, armor. Etruscan women, the great ladies, sometimes lying beside their husbands, were sumptuously attired for their journey: a mirror, comb, box of cosmetics, jewels were all at hand, available for future use. A profound belief in life seems to have been the basic philosophy of the Etruscans. And if life on earth was so good, then the life beyond could only be a continuance of earthly pleasures.

Excavations of the tombs, not already rifled — the Romans were the first big collectors of Etruscan antiquities — have brought to life outstanding grave-goods of gold, silver, ivory, bronze and ceram-ics. The vases show the strong influence of the Greek world as well as the excellent quality of the Etruscan craftmanship. Much of this material is now on display in the **Museum of Cerveteri**, housed in the **Ruspoli castle**, in the Museo di Villa Giulia and the Vatican Museum in Rome.

Tarquinia

The Etruscan town of Tarquinia stood on a hill northwest of the present picturesque Medieval town bearing the same name. The town already existed as early as the 9th Century BC and two centuries later was at its height. It is difficult to say whether the Roman dynasty of the Tarquini held the crown because of the military conquest of Rome or merely because of the political, economic and cultural influence they exerted on Rome. Starting from the 4th Century BC the roles switched and Tarquinia died like all other Etruscan cities. It had a Medieval rebirth when part of the population, escaping from the barbarian invasions, moved to the hill nearby and founded another town, Cornetum, which in 1922 the Fascist regime, wanting to recapture the spell of the past, renamed Tarquinia. In 1924

Monastery St. Benedi Subiaco.

the **Museo Nazionale Tarquinese** was founded. In it are many Etruscan treasures, including the famous terracotta winged horses.

The **Necropolis** of Tarquinia, together with that of Caere, is the most important of the Etruscan necropoli. It is located on a hill south of the old Etruscan Tarquinia and occupies an area which is 5 km long and 1 km wide (three miles by half-a-mile). Since the Necropoli was in use until the Roman age, not counting the archaic age, the whole area is covered with tombs of a great variety of forms. There are well-tombs, hall-way tombs and chamber tombs with or without tumuli. The painted tombs with frescoes are not only the most important document of Etruscan painting but also a very precious document of the life of the Etruscans, their costumes and beliefs. Horizontal ribbons of bright colors frame the animated scenes below: the banqueters and musicians in the **Tomba dei Leopardi**; the hunters in the **Tomba del Cacciatore**; the erotic scenes in the **Tomba dei Tori**; the prancing dancers, diving dolphins and soaring birds of the **Tomba della Leonessa**; the beautiful maiden from the Velcha family in the **Tomba di Polifemo o**

dell'Orco. One leaves these dusty, decayed houses of death feeling reaffirmed in one's faith in life and its many joys and mysteries.

Subiaco did not yet exist when the emperor Nero started building his villas overlooking one of the three artificial lakes he had created by deviating the course of the river Aniene. Apparently the slaves employed in the construction of the dam and then of the villa founded the town. Five centuries later a rich young man from Norcia, Benedict, escaping the corrupt life of his dissolute contemporaries, came to the site in search of a place to retreat for meditation and prayer. He chose a cavern and there he stayed for three years. The cavern is now known as the **Sacro Speco** (Holy Grotto). Subiaco remains, in history, the birthplace of western monasticism. It is a series of convents with their numerous cloisters and churches, and bell towers, and superimposed churches, and chapels decorated with frescoes and grottoes hewn out of the mountainside, connected by picturesque stairs, forming one of the most interesting monumental complexes of the region.

Around 529 Benedict and a bunch of his faithful monks left Subiaco and chose **Monte Cassino** as the place to continue their mystical experience. Here they established one of the most important religious and cultural institutions of Medieval Christianity. Benedict died in 543. Five centuries later the Abbey that he had founded was considered the richest in the world. The artistry of the monks in the illumination of manuscripts, and in frescoes and mosaics was so highly developed that it became a model for the rest of medieval Europe.

In World War Two, the area around Cassino and the Monte Cassino itself became the theater of a major military event. After the American forces entered in Naples, the Germans established in Cassino the main stronghold of the Gustav line. This was a fortified front-line designed to defend the environs of Rome. The repeated attacks of the Allies were smashed by the powerfully strengthened bulwark, causing enormous losses. This provoked the Allies' decision to bomb, which ended in the total destruction of Cassino. The ancient Abbey, — within which apparently there were no German military installations — was swept away. What one sees today is a faithful, loving reconstruction of what existed before the catastrophe.

Allied bombs reduced the abbey at Monte-cassino to rubble in World War Two.

MONASTIC LIFE

Where are the monks? Have they shut us out for so long that we cease even to wonder about them? We walk through the passages and arcades of the churches of Subiaco, Fossanova, Montecassino and admire the magnificent frescoes, paintings, statuary and architecture —the cloister itself thrown open for our examination — but we catch few glimpses of monks. As the world advances toward him, the monk retreats, leaving us the shell of monasticism while spiriting away the substance.

Monks are usually imagined in quasimedieval settings, trailing darkly along after the triumphal processions of prince and pope, putting a damper on the penant flapping festivities with all their talk of Hell and damnation. Medieval cobwebs trail around them still — their long dark robes, cowls and cords bear little resemblance to anything worn by man, or woman for centuries. They live in environments largely untouched by modern technology: until quite recently, neither radio, nor television, nor even newspapers were allowed in a monastery. Monks live a life which is in most respects, identical to that led by the community's founders, as many as 10, or even 15 centuries ago.

The distinguishing features of the life have always been *Ora, Labora,* and *Vita Communis* — prayer, labor, and communal life. To help them achieve their spiritual goals, all monks and nuns take vows of poverty, chastity, and obedience, which are intended to curb the most persistent of human failings: greed, lust, and pride. Only a truly humble and loving person will have the strength to pursue such a strenuous life, to forgo the comforts and distractions of family, ambition, private property, vacations, entertainment, in order to know a more sublime satisfaction in God.

The daily routine recalls the cycle of Christ's life. The monk rises well before daybreak to pray and confess his sins in preparation for the Resurrection at dawn. At that time, the community gathers to celebrate the newly risen Saviour, singing Lauds — prayers of praise and thanks. Then they separate to do the Lord's work, the *Opus Dei*, through reading of the Scripture and contemplation of its meaning, as well as manual tasks of cultivating the earth, and building necessary shelter. The monk's daily labors are interrupted at specific times by

Monks live a life which is little changed from more than 1,000 years ago. Left, a monk at the Monastery of Vallombrosa.

the Hours, when he either pauses to recall his purpose with a prayer to God, or gathers for the Divine Office, prayers sung or chanted in unison. At Vespers thanks are given for the day, and at Compline the cycle is complete. The monk enters into the tomb of sleep, until, by God's grace, the soul is again resurrected at dawn.

A Life of Prayer

The unifying thread which runs through every activity is prayer. No matter where he is, or what he is doing, the monk is praying. The ultimate aim of his prayer is to reach a state of contemplation in which he "receives the revelation of God." The latin term *contemplare,* to observe carefully, was a term of augury. Contemplation is an active, ecstatic state in which one may see visions, hear voices, speak in tongues. Even if one remains perfectly quiet and calm, the experience is of an animating force. St. Basil told one of his pupils: "If you will, you can become all fire. You cannot be a monk unless you become like a consuming fire." What the fire consumes is the self — its petty individual concerns, weakness, and mortality — leaving the soul innocent and loving as God intended it to be.

This basic pattern, with only local or temporal modifications regulates the life of every Catholic monk in every part of the world, from Italy to the United States, China to Latin America. Contemporary monasticism of course bears the stamp of its 20th Century members, who invest the traditional rituals with renewed meaning. Today, you may find your "medieval" monk is well versed in the works of contemporary as well as ancient mystics, eastern as well as western; perhaps he even twists into a lotus position to meditate — with the permission of his abbot, of course.

This broadening of the monastic tradition shouldn't be confused with a relaxation of spiritual standards. *Acedia* — Latin for spiritual sloth — is still the vice most diligently scouted out. Browsing instead of reading, daydreaming instead of contemplating, going through the motions of the liturgy without real inspiration, even working to the exclusion of prayer are the laxities which eat away at the monk's spirit. The austerity of a monk's life; the fasting, unheated quarters, narrow wooden beds — and in extreme cases, flagellation, hair shirts, iron cuffs and chains — is ultimately intended to curb *acedia,* by depriving the monk of the material comforts which often encourage a spiritual easiness.

The major source of confusion about the monastic vocation springs from a tendency to lump all Catholics in long dark robes together. Priests, bishops, cardinals, popes, and particularly the members of the Religious Orders should not be thought of as monks who work in society. They may become monks, but in so doing they change the fundamental tenet of their vocation; they must renounce all former ecclesiastical rank, and devote themselves exclusively to the labor of prayer.

A word about the Religious Orders, also referred to as the Mendicant Orders as distinct from Monastic Orders. The Franciscans, Dominicans, Jesuits, Carmelites, Ursulines, Daughters of Charity and others all take vows of poverty, chastity, and obedience, as do members of the Monastic Orders. Before 1965, they wore distinctive habits, very similar to the brown or black or white robes of the monks; they have traditionally maintained abbeys, and have lived a communal life equally simple and rigorous. They seek the revelation of God through the same means of prayer and contemplation. However, the revelation of God's will has marked these individuals out for active service — teaching, preaching, missionary work, nursing, maintenance of charitable and other community organizations.

In 1965, the Second Vatican Council called for an "adjustment of the community to the changed conditions of the time." This "Decree on the Appropriate Renewal of the Religious Life" was intended to foster an easier interchange between the religious man and woman and the society which they were dedicated to serve, by removing the "barriers" of the habit, liturgical Latin, and often insular living arrangements.

As might be expected, the monastic orders, for whom direct community involvement was never an issue, did not change much, although the spirit of renewal did penetrate. Allowance was made for the more "exotic" monastic traditions of the Far East; some modern appliances were admitted as necessary; he or she (for there are monastic orders of nuns) may on occasion wear street clothes. Nevertheless, the essence of monasticism has remained contemplation. Working monasteries are often situated in remote, undeveloped terrain. Communication with the outside world is still strictly controlled — the abbot reads every letter received and every letter sent. (Censorship is not intended; the practice is meant to breakdown the sense of individual privacy, which has no place in a monastery. God knows all in the heart of man, and all in the heart of man should be freely confessed.) The rituals of

the Divine Office and the Hours are maintained to the extent that they still structure and give meaning to the monastic life.

The First Monks

Monasticism's roots lie at the beginning of the Christian era. When the Emperor Constantine declared Christianity the official religion of the Roman Empire, in 313 AD, he initiated a series of mass conversions. Many of the new Christians were ignorant of the true requirements of the faith, haphazardly trading gods for God, temples for churches, ritual sacrifice for the Mass. This decline in standards horrified the more zealous and orthodox, especially the ascetics. They began leaving their villages and families, going into the Egyptian desert to

regain the purity of their faith in solitude. As they had always been austere in their personal habits, the desert was just what they wanted. Any weakness of the flesh was immediately dealt with by the scourging environment.

Unguided by a community, the hermits had tended to eccentricity, even lawlessness. The desert was as likely to bake a man's brain as it was to bring him close to God! St. Simeon the Stylite (d. 459) chose to live in a basket hovering between heaven and earth — that is, balanced atop a column reputed to be more than 60 feet tall. St. Pachomius organized the hermits (or anchorites, as they were also called) into a *laura*, forming the first monastery at a place called Tabennisi. Pachomius had realized the hermits needed to share their experiences, to guide one another. Besides, Christ required that his disciples love their fellow men; one must live among them in order to love them.

Thus in a laura each hermit has an individual cell and lives for the most part as a solitary; however, they would periodically pray together.

Lauras rapidly formed throughout the vast Roman Empire. They arrived in Italy when St. Jerome, a Roman Christian, translated the teachings of St. Pachomius into Latin at the end of the 4th Century. Inspired by this work, hermits formed *lauras* in the rugged wilderness south of Rome at Subiaco and Vico Varo.

Only the Roman talent for organization could create a rule at once firm and flexible enough to marshal these monks. St. Benedict's Rule, compiled between 530 and 535, reflects

the moderation and common sense of this noble Roman monk. Instead of striving after an unachievable physical austerity, the monk is urged to strenuous discipline in every act and thought to train himself in God's intention.

Benedict was the last of the line of a noble family of Nursia, a Sabine town in central Italy. Born in 480 AD, he was baptized a Christian, and as a young teenager sent to Rome to study literature; however, it is not surprising that he remained relatively untouched by the corruption around him: he had always been a

Left, at Galluzzo Carthusian monastery, near Florence. Above, statue of St. Benedict at the abbey of Montecassino.

serious youth, and his own family numbered several monks. Benedict is said to have been only 14 when he abandoned Rome's pleasures for the life of a hermit. He lived in absolute solitude in *Sacro Speco*, literally "holy cave," at Subiaco, a laura just 50 miles (80 km) east of Rome.

The reputation of the young solitary spread throughout the craggy, cave-riddled region, he was sought out by eager disciples. Monks from the nearby monastery, Vico Varo, asked him to help them achieve a similarly exalted state of holiness; however, they quickly rebelled against the austerity which he imposed. Legend had it that they tried to poison Benedict, but that as he made the sign of the cross over the contaminated chalice, it shattered.

St. Benedict's 35-year residence in Subiaco came to an abrupt end when an envious priest of the neighborhood, who despised the saint for his holiness, defiled Sacro Speco by filling it with prostitutes. Benedict and his closest followers left the gorge for Monte Cassino, 50 miles to the south, in 529 AD.

Monte Cassino was a region scattered with vestiges of paganism and the Roman Caesars. Benedict is said to have found peasants still worshipping the god Apollo in a temple on the site; he converted them, and together they razed the temple and its sacred grove, erecting a monastery in its place.

St. Benedict's Rule established the paramount role of the abbot, who was to function as spiritual father and representative of Christ in the community. The Rule defined the Hours, and the prayers to be sung at every interval of the Divine Office. It laid out the basis for the vows of poverty, chastity and obedience, which have become standard in all monastic orders.

The structure and delegation of duties within the monastery were carefully delineated. As none of the monks have any private property, a common store was established, and the abbot appointed a worthy brother to give out and collect all tools, clothes, and other articles as they were needed. None of the monks were to keep a tool overnight, even if it was to be used again the next day, so as to discourage a sense of private possession and encourage the humility of having to ask each time. In today's monasteries, the monk may ask each morning for the soap, toothpaste and towel he needs in order to wash.

Benedict even specified the disciplinary measures to be taken if a monk was unruly and disobedient, or repeatedly late to meals or the mass. He was disciplined also if he failed to observe the rule of silence or grumbled or stirred up resentment among the other monks. The punishment could be severe and corporal.

A monk could be whipped for blundering the Oratory, the sung prayers. The procedures for admission to the monastery were clarified. After a period of postulancy, in which the aspirant is instructed in the life and observed to have an aptitude and genuine eagerness for it, the novitiate takes vows which bind him for life to the particular monastery. He is technically never to set foot outside those strong stone walls again, never to visit or communicate with his earthly family, which he has exchanged for the family of his brethren in Christ. A monk who needs to travel outside on monastery business must be carefully prepared, and on his return all the brethren prostrate themselves and pray for faults fallen into by hearing or seeing evil things on the road. Neither is the monk to relate anything of what he encoun-

Camaldolese and the Vallombrosans hearkened back to the primitive *lauras* in an effort to preserve the simplicity and zeal of a faith in hard times an integrity all too quickly lost as soon as material prosperity returns. Both orders sought to balance hermetical and community life. St. Romuald left the monastery of San Miniato al Monte, in Florence, and went up into the nearby Apennines, where he began a community of hermits. The rough wooden huts were scattered in a remote mountain wood, and a monastery was built farther down the slope at Camaldoli. Vallombrosa, located near Camaldoli, and founded by a disciple of St. Romuald's was structured along much the same hermetical lines, and met with a similar fate. The impulse for simplicity and solitude was also taken up in the 12th Century by the

tered. The Rule even mentions how the monks are to sleep — fully clothed and girt in their cords, so that they waste no time in dressing; yet they are not to sleep with their knives, "lest perchance they be injured whilst sleeping."

St. Benedict's Rule soon became the rule of every western monastery. By the end of the 8th Century, virtually every monk was a Benedictine monk.

Power and Money

The centralization of monasteries after Benedict brought power; but it also brought corruption. Throughout the Middle Ages new orders arose that sought to rid monasticism of its worldliness. In the 11th Century, the

Carthusians and the Cistercians. The former are the most mystical order within the Benedictine tradition; the monks take vows of absolute silence and communicate in sign language when absolutely necessary. The latter are called the White Monks, for they chose to wear habits of unbleached muslin in contrast to the black robes of the other Benedictines. They stress rigorous manual labor and physical discipline. The Trappists, who practice extremes of physical deprivation approaching those of the Desert Fathers, are an offshoot of the Cistercian Order. Fossanova and Casamari, both

Above, the spartan simplicity of a monk's cell at Galluzzo Carthusian monastery.

located about 100 km (60 miles) south of Rome are the only two Cistercian houses in Italy. The Burgundian Gothic church at Fossanova reminds one of the order's French origins and was the first Gothic structure to appear in Italy.

Despite reforms, the Middle Ages saw the monasteries grow rich through Papal benefice and deathbed conversions, profiting from a society desperately sinning in the face of imminent destruction by plague, famine, wars and barbarian invasion, and yet equally terrified of the hellfire which was thought to await them after death.

Unfortunately, wealth laid the monasteries open to various evils, the worst of these being the infamous practice of commendation, where the position of abbot was awarded like any other noble title. The noble abbots proceeded to milk them for all they were worth, leaving the monks barely enough to survive. In some cases, children in their teens inherited the abbatorial office of several abbeys, none of which they had ever laid eyes on.

Pushing for Perks and Praise

By the time of the Renaissance, the monasteries were in a state of utter decay. Inspectors were sent out by the Church and the orders themselves; the reports which they sent back tell of a shocking state of ignorance, dishonesty, and cupidity among the monks. In some cases they could barely read or write, let alone study the Scriptures, in others, monks held individual livings and considered the abbey a private estate; some of the monks even kept their mistresses with them. One abbot when confronted with his transgression protested that "he could not relinquish the woman because of his affection for the children she had born him; and further, his doctor advised sex as useful treatment for his complaint, the stone." (From a visitation document of Athansius Chalkepoulos, subsequent bishop of Calabria, report made in 1446.)

The moral state of the friars of the Religious orders, Franciscans and Dominicans, was no better. The orders competed for perks and praise for their good works in a manner wholly un-Christian. The Dominicans became particularly involved in politics; the monk Savonarola, of the abbey San Marco in Florence led the people of Florence in a rebellion against the Medici to form a short-lived Republican government.

For a titillating taste of a 14th Century opinion of monasticism, pick up Boccaccio's *Decameron*. Here the monks, friars, and nuns are shown frolicking along with the rest of mankind — an abbess appears to reprimand a young nun caught in the act with her lover, yet she herself is wearing the britches of her own lover, (incidentally, a priest,) on her head, having mistaken them for her veil. Or the Franciscan friar Alberto convinces a vain noblewoman that her beauty is so breathtaking that even the Angel Gabriel has fallen in love with her — and then proceeds to don the guise of the angel to make love to her himself. Or better still, a young hermit in the desert seduces an eager novice by telling her that to render service unto God, she must let him put his "devil" in her "hell," only to find that she enjoys this activity so much that he can't keep her satisfied, and must ask her to find another man's devil.

The monasteries in Italy were finally taken in hand when Ludovico Barbo instituted the Cassinese Congregation in the late 15th Century. The congregation began in Padua, at the monastery of St. Guistina. Barbo's revitalization of this house was so impressive that many other houses put themselves under his direction. Recognizing that the practice of commendation must be stopped for the monasteries to regain any of their integrity, he made the abbatorial office a rotating position with a fixed term of three years, and concentrated administrative power in the hands of an elected council, or chapter. Eventually, all the monasteries in Italy and Sicily joined; when Monte Cassino did so in 1504, it became the mother house of the congregation henceforth called Cassinese.

Monasticism was all but wiped out by the Reformation in England and Germany, by the French Revolution and Napoleonic Wars, and the wholesale secularization of society in the 17th and 18th centuries. Monasteries were suppressed, the monks hounded from their cloisters, killed or forced to flee to safer ground. The Trappists of southern France were driven from their Pyrenee home to northern Italy, Switzerland, Prussia, and finally Russia, always just one step ahead of Napoleon's advancing armies.

Perhaps because of the strong rooted religious devotion of the Italian people, monasticism survived here, whereas elsewhere it all but perished. The Italian government has in the 20th Century returned some of the property confiscated during the Unification in the 19th Century. Although some of the monasteries still are used as police barracks or hotels (San Domenico Palace in Taormina) others have been restored to the monks, either to administer as museums and national monuments, or to live in as before, occupied in the Opus Dei, dedicated to realizing in themselves our all too often unrealized potential for spiritual grace.

ABRUZZO AND MOLISE

"There were bears on the Gran Sasso D'Italia but it was a long way. Aquila was a fine town. It was cool in the Summer at night and the Spring in ·Abruzzi was the most beautiful in Italy. But what was lovely was the fall to go hunting through the chestnut woods. The birds were all good because they fed on grapes and you never took a lunch because the peasants were always honored if you would eat with them at their houses."

— Ernest Hemingway

The Apennine Mountains, in their torturous descent through Italy, unravel into three strands as they twist down between Rome and the Adriatic, creating a geologically unruly region long ignored by mainstream travellers. It is characteristic of this area, formerly denominated by the single name Abruzzo, that it should have been the birthplace of the priest in Hemingway's *A Farewll To Arms*, who recommended it for its winter sport. That has been Abruzzo's traditional image among foreigners and Italians alike, a sort of Italian Montana popular among outdoorsmen. While the image, like all caricatures, leaves out many of the finer points of this old region, it persists today as visitors flock to the Gran Sasso, the central mountain chain, to climb, ski, birdwatch and hunt, and to Pescara and other beach towns, where another form of outdoorsman engages in another form of hunting, often to the intense discomfort of bikini-clad girls. Yet the region has an indigenous history that may be the oldest in Italy, and its lovely towns, surrounded by snow-capped mountains even in June, contain many monuments of the first rank. Molise split off from Abruzzo to form an autonomous region in 1963, and has managed to retain its wild spirit more completely than its populous and faster-growing neighbor.

A Dip into History

Human habitation of the region goes back more than 13,000 years to the so-called Fucino or Marsicano Man, of whom bits of bones have been discovered in caves in Ortucchio and Maritza.

Archaeological evidence of a flourishing indigenous civilization of the 6th Century BC is growing, spurred on by the find of the famous Capestrano Warrior, now at the Museo Nazionale in Chieti. Signs of later Roman domination can be seen throughout the region, particularly at the interesting archaeological site of Alba Fucens, near **Avezzano**. In the middle ages and later, the region came under the sway of the various invading kingdoms from the south. The Spanish were responsible for most of the castles that pepper the region. Earthquakes, particularly that of 1703, have caused considerable damage, as did the two world wars. Despite great migrations of farm workers into the cities after World War Two, which resulted in economic imbalances between town and country, recent efforts to encourage tourism and industry and the completion of the autostrada have begun to reverse a post-war impoverishment. Today the region, thriving and modern, appears linked to the rest of the nation.

Shy Animals

Those whose love for Italy extends to her voluptuous landscape will be particularly charmed by the **Parco Nazionale d'Abruzzo**, where over 400 sq km (154 sq miles) of high-altitude meadows, beech groves and snow-capped peaks have been preserved forever from the encroachments of Abruzzian housing developers. Here, if one is lucky, one may see the shy Apennine Brown Bear (*Ursus arctos Marsicanus*), of which 100 are known to exist in the park today, feeding on berries and insects in remote upper pastures. The Abruzzo Chamois (*Rupicapra ornata*), famous for the black-and-white pattern on its throat, also thrives here, as do the Apennine Lynx and various foxes, wolves, otter, singing birds, hawks and eagles. More than 150 well-marked trails provide access to even the highest sections, most of which can be visited (and returned from) in a day's walk from the main road.

Pescasseroli, the administrative headquarters for the park, was the birthplace of the philosopher Benedetto Croce. Today it is a hiker's and skier's boom town, and accommodations of all kinds are readily available except at Christmas and Easter and during the August vacation time. Buses ply daily between Pescasseroli and **Avezzano**, a more convenient

versa degli
bruzzi, a
naracteris-
c Apennine
llage.

place to stay if one is planning to visit the park only for a day. The dawn busride takes one around the edge of the **Piana del Fucino**, a lake in Roman times which was subsequently, after centuries of effort, drained. In what was once the center of the lake now sits the important *Telespazio* station, consisting of a dozen dish antennas of varying sizes, all pointing up at the sky. In the fields that surround this technological boast of Abruzzo, bright red poppies burst forth in May.

Fountain of 99 Spouts

L'Aquila, chief town of Abruzzo, is known for its turbulent history, its fine architecture and the pleasant coolness of its arcaded streets. Founded in 1240 by Frederick II of Hohenstaufen as an outpost against the papacy, the city converted to papal rule shortly after Frederick's death in 1250. Nine years later, Frederick's son Manfred reclaimed the city after a bloody siege that laid waste to the city walls and caused the town to be abandoned for seven years. Charles I of Anjou began rebuilding it after defeating Manfred at Benevento in 1266.

According to legend, the city of L'Aquila was formed of 99 palaces, 99 churches, 99 fountains and 99 squares; and in commemoration of this numerical coincidence, authorities began constructing a fountain of 99 spouts in 1272. The **Fontane delle Novantanove Cannelle** is one of the highlights of the city. Be forwarned: the water is not drinkable and the pavement leading to the fountain is (1985) weedy and in disrepair. But the pleasant courtyard of red and white stone and the sound of the water issuing from the 99 grotesque masks that form the spouts give a sense of the peace earlier travellers must have felt when they first entered the nearby Porta Rivera from Rome.

L'Aquila's most well-known monument is the 13th Century church of **Santa Maria di Collemaggio**, located outside the city wall on the southeast corner of town. It is impossible to miss its red and white facade, whose three rose windows and corresponding doorways subtly combine the Gothic and the Romanesque. The church was begun in 1277 under the guidance of the famous local hermit Pietro dal Morrone, who was later crowned Pope Celestine V at the age of 85. He only served five months on the job, claiming that his inexperience with the ways of the

Turn of the century beach house in Pescara

world made him unfit to sit on the Throne of Saint Peter. His lovely Renaissance tomb may be seen to the right of the apse inside. The interior, freed of its Baroque garnishes in 1973, has a long wooden ceiling and spartan walls made bright by afternoon sun streaming through its rose windows.

The church of **San Bernardino** is considered by some to be the finest Renaissance monument in the Abruzzi. The interior, completely rebuilt after the earthquake of 1703, is actually dominated by its Baroque ceiling and organ, both designed by Ferdinando Mosca of nearby **Pescocostanza**. The Renaissance tomb of San Bernardino (1488), in a chapel on the right, has a classical precision that is carried over into its delicate floral frieze. The tomb and, in the apse, the Monument of Maria Pereira (1496) are both the work of a local artist, Silvestro dell'Aquila. The floor continues the theme of red and white marble.

Every weekday in the **Piazza del Duomo** there is an open-air market where local products of cane, wood, lace and copper are sold. The Duomo itself, completely destroyed by the 1703 earthquake, was rebuilt in the 19th Century.

One of the best museums in Abruzzo is L'Aquila's **Museo Nazionale d'Abruzzo**, located in the castle at the north end of town. The **Castello** itself, built in 1532 by Pirro Luigi Escriba or Scriba, the architect of Castel Sant'Elmo in Naples, is known for its four protruding "ears" which enabled soldiers to cover every possible angle of approach. There's an amusing frieze of Medusa's head in the archaeological section on the ground floor, while in the section on sacred art on the first floor a pair of wooden doors carved in 1131 have the ancient, dessicated look of driftwood. The modern art section on the second and third floors contains some interesting paintings by Abruzzians of the present day.

Unlike the Parco Nazionale, which is of interest for its wildlife and the majestic peacefulness of its beech groves, the **Gran Sasso d'Italia**, just outside L'Aquila, is known for its interest to the mountaineer, the conqueror of dizzying heights. The Gran Sasso itself, at 2,914 meters (9,560 feet), is the highest peak in the Appennines; and the numerous trails, both for hiking and skiing, that radiate from the nearby *Campo Imperatore* have made the area famous throughout Europe. Trail

maps are available at the Agenzia di Viaggi-Centro Turistico Gran Sasso in L'Aquila.

Sulmona

One of the most spectacular drives in Abruzzo takes Route 261 from L'Aquila to Sulmona, following the Valley of the Aterno river past a number of medieval villages, each with its ruined castle and its church. **Sulmona**, the birthplace of Ovid, is considered by many Abruzzians the most beautiful town in their province. Arrive here at 2 p.m. and you will feel that you have entered a ghost town. The streets will be empty. The stores will be shut. Even the dogs will seem to have gone into hiding. It's the *mezzo giorno*, the hour of the midday nap. Go inside, take a nap, write a letter. Reappear at 6 p.m. The streets will be packed with teenagers thronging arm in arm up the Corso. Mothers are pushing strollered infants past the admiring gaze of grandmothers who gaily gather on the steps of the Palazzo della SS. Annunziata to talk about children and the priest. In the **Piazza XX Septembre**, important-looking men stand in significant circles by the statue of Ovid, discussing soccer. All around, about the narrow medieval streets, snow-capped mountains glisten in the evening sun.

The **Palazzo della SS. Annunziata** stands at the ancient center of town. The much-acclaimed harmony of its facade lies in the way different architectural styles have been brought together in a uniform setting. Each of the three portals has a different size and shape corresponding to each of the three windows above. The left portal is Gothic, dating from 1415, the middle, Renaissance, dating from 1483, and the less interesting and less classifiable right portal from a still later date. A floral frieze running across the face links the three. Upstairs, on the first floor of the Palazzo, is a museum of local archaeological finds, and paintings by local artists. The attached church, originally more visibly connected to the palazzo, had to be rebuilt after an earthquake in 1706.

In Italy, it often seems that the requirement for a town is that a famous person should have been born there. **Pescara's** claim to fame is the writer Gabriele d'Annunzio (1864–1938), whose birthplace may be visited off **Piazza Unione**. But it's

Abruzzian native.

not d'Annunzio that draws the annual packs of tourists from Germany, France, the United States. Nor is it the town's status as a fishing port. What brings the tourists flocking year after year is the beach. Pescara's wide, sandy beach is an excellent point from which to try swimming in the Adriatic. Soothed by the fashionable hotels, cafes, restaurants and bathing huts that predominate here, one could, like Ulysses in Lotus-land or Aeneas in Carthage, dally in Pescara forever — or at least until September, when the elaborate beach umbrellas begin to fold.

Just half-an-hour outside Pescara is the ancient hilltop town of **Chieti**, famous today for its archaeological museum, but known since antiquity for its views out across mainland Abruzzo and the sea. Remains of three Roman temples can be seen off the main Corso Marrucino, just behind the modern-day post office. The recently modernized **Museo Archeologico di Antichita** is located at the far western edge of town in the **Villa Comunale**. Its extensive coin collection is one of the most interesting in Italy, arranged in informative cases with descriptions in both Italian and English. One can follow here the ancient trade routes along which coins were distributed. Particularly interesting is the case containing coins from Alba Fucens. A diagram charts the trenches in which the different coins were found. In the main hall is a colossal Hercules. The **Capestrano Warrior**, in his Huck Finn hat, is upstairs, along with selected ceramics from various stages in Abruzzo's history. Outside, as you descend through the municipal gardens, you pass a small zoo containing pigeons and monkeys.

A Festival in Molise

If you happen to take the train from Termoli to Campobasso between May 25 and May 27 of any year, stop at the medieval village of **Larino**. There you can take part in the *Sagra di San Pardo*, Larino's annual festival, when ox-carts are paraded through the streets in memory of Roman times. While there, visit the old cathedral, with its beautiful facade, and climb up the monumental staircase of the **Palazzo Reale**. Larino, like its province Molise, is one of the least known places in Italy, yet one of the most worthy of a visit.

Termoli, on the Adriatic, is a popular beach resort whose "old town," situated on a promontory, is known for its fine views in all directions. Well garrisoned behind a small castle built by Frederick II, the mazy streets of old Termoli, with their fine cathedral, contain an unexpected reference to American history in a restaurant called "Il Generale Custer." Termoli is the traditional starting point for boats to the **Isole Tremiti**, a group of offshore islands famous—perhaps too famous—for their mysterious grottoes and other marine phenomenon.

The town that most fully illustrates the difference between the old and the new in Molise is **Campobasso**, the region's capital. Presided over by the 15th Century **Castello Monforte**, from which tumble the steeply stepped streets of the old town, Campobasso has a very pleasant modern town spreading out to the train station below. It is in the new town that two of Campobasso's most well-known features are to be found: a top-security prison and a training school for the Carabinieri, the Italian police. It's a startling sight, when one first arrives, thirsting to climb up to **San Giorgio**, the 12th Century Romanesque church whose faint bas-reliefs still show forth after all these years, to find tightly uniformed young men strolling up the streets by twos and threes, or quietly talking in the shade of the trees in the main square. Ask these cadets for directions to the old town.

Ninety minutes by train from Campobasso is **Isernia**, rich in regional lore, and a good starting point for explorations up into the remote hilltowns. The discovery, in 1979, of the ancient human genus *Homo aeserniensis* on the outskirts of modern-day Isernia has projected the town into the archaeological limelight of the world. According to archaeologists, the genus, which existed 1 million years before Christ, is the oldest yet discovered in Europe. These prehistoric humans used fire, as was learned by the discovery of a fireplace. Bones of elephants, rhinoceri, hippos, bison and bear were also discovered near the fireplace, indicating the presence of these animals in Molise at that time.

The town of Isernia, strung out along a single street running downhill from the train station, has an excellent archaeological museum. The old town (turn left out of the station) has been much damaged by earthquakes. Most of it is now held together with scaffolding. The dark lanes that criss-cross through its charming medieval houses are shoulder-narrow.

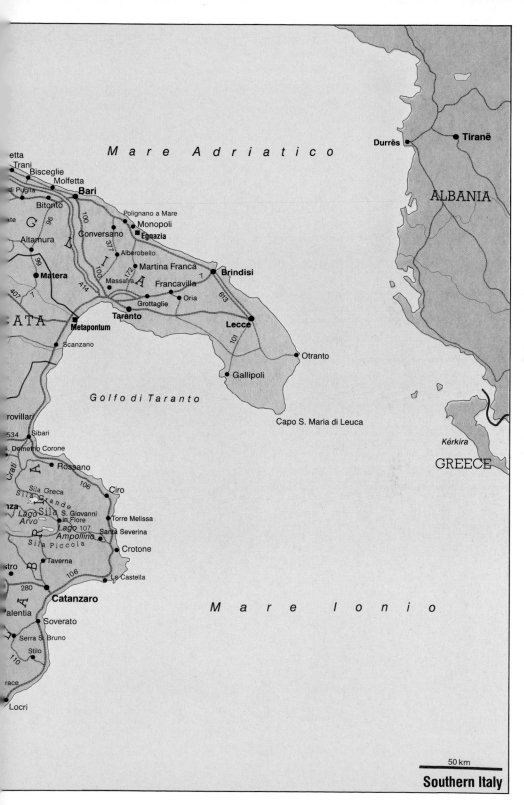

Southern Italy

THE SOUTH

When a foreign traveller visits Apulia, Basilicata and Calabria, he is usually greeted by stares. The stares are not hostile. Nor are they necessarily suspicious. They're just amazed. So few foreigners — so few northern Italians, even — have visited these three sunbaked, poverty-stricken, remote and wild regions that anybody who would do so is looked upon as a bit of an oddball. This was the case when the English writer Norman Douglas visited here in 1911; it was the case when the Italian anti-fascist Carlo Levi was banished here in 1935; and despite growing efforts to encourage tourism, it is still the case today. So few have come here for pleasure or insight that nobody knows of the pleasures and insights to be found. Visitors come, as they have always come, following the Greeks and Romans, to Naples, Pompeii, Cumae, Capri. They flock to Sicily and its temples. But Apulia? Basilicata? Calabria? Oh yes! they remember. Italy's heel. Her instep. Her toe.

Then there is the problem of northern prejudice. Northerners speak of it, southerners speak of it. The northerners are industrial, pragmatic, fair-skinned. The southerners are agricultural, superstitous, dark. The northerners are rich. The southerners are poor. The southerners move north for jobs; they emigrate to America for jobs. Nobody moves south to take their place. So the population stays low, the land stays big, traditional superstitions continue. This is *La Problema del Mezzogiorno*. It is a problem for the north as well as for the south.

The truth is that Southern Italy is one of the most interesting places to visit in Europe. It is a romantic land of castles and churches; vast, wheat-covered plains; misty mountains where itinerant shepherds still wander with their flocks. Apulia is a place for novel architectural forms: the Apulian Romanesque; Leccian Baroque; castles by Frederick II — and of course those odd, conical peasant dwellings known as the *Trulli*. In Basilicata one discovers the *Sassi*, cave-dwellings cut into the side of a ravine, often containing brilliant frescoes. And there is La Trinita, an unfinished 11th Century Benedictine monastery covered with Roman inscriptions. In Calabria the visitor rediscovers the Greeks — two, especially, made of bronze, recently dredged up by fishermen off Riace. There are Norman castles, Byzantine churches, rich red wine, landscapes first described by Homer. The land is redolent with history, culture and tradition.

Naples, the Naples Environs and Sicily are the most richly packed with traditional sights, and we have weighted our sections accordingly. Except for in Naples, where the visitor is happiest moving about on foot or by bus, the descriptions have been geared toward travel by car. A car is especially important in the *Mezzogiorno*, where sights are too scattered to justify spending long hours waiting for infrequent mail trains. Time should be reserved, instead, for contemplation of the south's natural and artistic beauties, for a swim at a beach, a picnic at a castle, a visit to a monastery. Here, as nowhere else in Italy, life really does seem to go on much as it has for thousands of years.

— B. Swett

Preceding pages, Albanian villager in Calabria. Left, an ancient fresco of spring in Naples Archaeological Museum.

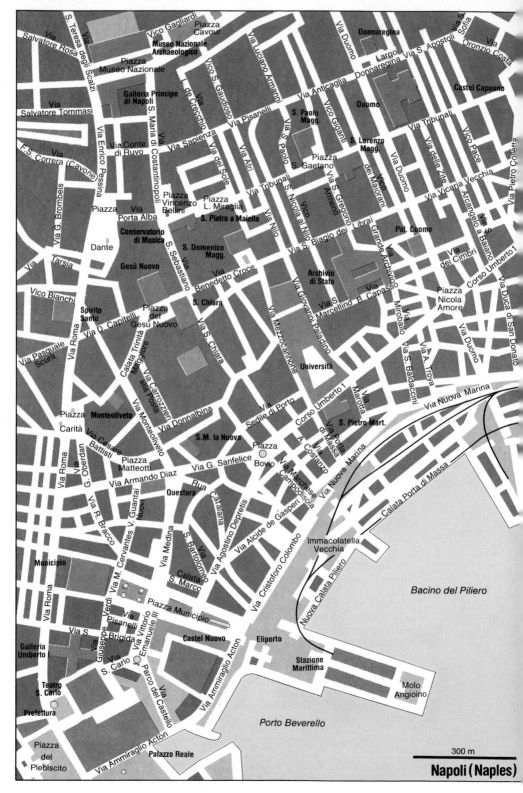

Napoli (Naples)

NAPLES

"It wakes again to Policinelli and pickpockets, buffo, singers and beggars, rags, puppets, flowers, brightness, dirt, and universal degradation; airing its Harlequin suit in the sunshine, next day and every day; singing, starving, dancing, gaming, on the sea-shore; and leaving all labour to the burning mountain, which is ever at its work."

— Charles Dickens

Naples (Napoli) has always been the black sheep of Italian cities, the misfit, the outcast, the messy brother that nobody knew quite what to do with. Burdened by the densest population of any city in Europe, intense poverty, joblessness, bureaucratic inefficiency and organized crime, the city has come to be seen as a cross between Manhattan and Calcutta for human squalor. That Naples is in fact one of the most rambunctiously beautiful of Italian cities, with a friendly population and a long artistic heritage, does not deny its less appealing image. It only colors it, gives spice and fragrance to it, as do its art, its churches, its castles, its pizza. In the end, like all black sheep, troubled Naples is the most interesting member of its family.

Orientation

The city has its own special shape, defined partly by landscape, partly by chance and partly by governmental edict. The only way to get a feel for the place is to spend time walking through its different quarters. To orient yourself, find **Piazza Garibaldi**. From here, the long **Corso Umberto** I juts down to the left (southwest) to the Piazza Bovio, where, changing its name to Via Agostino Depretis, it continues on to the **Piazza Municipio**. The corso is one of the main traffic routes in Naples and at midday is jammed with buses, taxis, cars and motorbikes. At night it is lined with prostitutes. The thoroughfare was forced through the narrow, crowded streets that surround it in 1888, in an effort to improve air circulation after a cholera epidemic four years earlier. The rather drab **Università** hulks about halfway down, on the right side.

The Piazza Municipio and the nearby **Piazza Plebiscito** form a central hinge from which the city fans out to the east, the north and the west. Directly north, up the Via Toledo, also known as the Via Roma, is the red palazzo that houses the **Museo Archaeologico Nazionale**. East of the Museo, in the triangle it forms with the Piazza Plebiscito and the Piazza Garibaldi, lies most of Old Naples, with its medieval streets and its churches. North of the Museo, on a hilltop, stands the picture gallery of **Capodimonte**. Farther south, on a spur of land out in the bay, rises the egg-shaped **Castel dell' Ovo** and, along the waterfront, the Via Partenope, where the city's most expensive hotels overlook the water. The shoreline then curves away west, passing the **Villa Comunale** with its famous Aquarium, to the Marina at **Mergellina**, near Virgil's tomb. From Mergellina one can gaze back on the entire city, with Mount Vesuvius looming in the background haze.

Origins

The name "Naples" derives from "Neapolis," the "New City" founded by settlers from Cumae in the 6th Century BC. Nearby stood "Paleopolis," the "Old City," founded in the 9th Century BC, also by Greeks from Cumae. The two cities grew side by side like brother and sister until their violent overthrow by Samnites from the interior in 400 BC. Rome wrested them away after a three year siege in 326 BC, at which point they began to grow into a single entity, the old and the new conjoined, called by the single name Neapolis.

From the beginning Romans flocked here, drawn by the mild climate, the sparkling bay and the political freedom allowed by the retention of the Greek constitution. Virgil wrote the Aeneid and died here; emperors built gardens and bathed. The Dark Ages were indeed dark in Naples — nobody knows quite what happened — and until shortly after the first millennium the city was ruled by dukes vaguely faithful to Byzantium. Then, in 1139, Roger the Norman took Naples under the wing of his Kingdom of Sicily. The seven dynasties that followed wrought most of the architectural landmarks to be seen today. Their statues, together with that of Roger, peer out from niches in the facade of the **Palazzo Reale** at the center of town: Frederick II of Hohenstaufen, who founded the university but never lived here, preferring the plains of Apulia; Charles I of Anjou, who did live here and made sure everyone knew it; Alphonso I of Aragon, Charles I of Austria, Charles I of Bourbon, Joachim Murat, Victor Emmanuel II. They line up like so many wrinkles in the broad face of the building, testimony to the years that have made the city what it is today.

Castles and Music

When Charles I of Anjou built the **Castel Nuovo** in 1272, he could not have known that seven centuries later it would still serve as the political hub of the city. The Municipal Council of Naples meets in the huge **Sala dei Baroni**, where the cruel Charles is said to have performed some of his bloodiest executions. Perhaps the finest architectural element in this imposing fortress is its famous Triumphal Arch, built in 1454-1467 to commemorate Alphonso I's defeat of the French. It is the only Renaissance arch ever to have been built at the entrance to a castle.

A short walk up the Via San Carlo leads to the **Teatro San Carlo**, the largest opera house in Italy and one of the finest in the world. It is the opera house of one's dreams, all red velvet and gold trim, with six tiers of boxes opening out in the shape of a horseshoe from the stage. Built in 1737 under the direction of Charles III of Bourbon, the theater retains its perfect acoustics, helped by the insertion, after a fire in 1816, of hundreds of clay pitchers between the walls. The monthly tourist magazine *Qui Napoli*, available at tourist offices, gives full listings of the many concerts, operas and recitals performed here throughout the year. Even on the sixth tier, you will sit in your own private box, in a velvet seat, inches beneath the ceiling.

Across the street is the **Galleria Umberto I**, erected in 1887 on a neo-Classical design similar to that of its older brother in Milan. Its glass ceiling, 56 meters (184 feet) high, and its mosaic-covered floor were reconstructed after bomb damage in World War Two. Pleasant cafes permit a moment's rest; a major telephone and telegraph center links it to the outside world.

The wide **Piazza Plebiscito** around the corner is embraced by the twin arcades of the **Chiesa di San Francesco di Paola** (1817-32), modeled after the Pantheon in Rome. The imposing church has unfortun-

Castel dell'Ovo guards Naples harbor.

ately, little to offer the tourist other than the pungent shade of its dingy arcades. The Piazza itself is now a major parking lot, illustrating one of the city's major modern headaches: cars. Buses ply regularly from here to most points in the city.

The sprawling red facade of the **Palazzo Reale** (1600) looms across the street with its eight statues illustrating the eight Neapolitan dynasties (see above). At the foot of its monumental marble staircase — whose lavishness shocked Mark Twain upon his visit here in 1868 — stand the original bronze doors from the Castel Nuovo. The cannonball lodged in the left door is an eery reminder of an early siege. Upstairs are an impressive, if somewhat uncomfortable-looking, throne room and a small, lavish theater. Further rooms stretch off into an endless magnificence of period furniture and Dresden china.

Another famous castle, the **Castel dell'Ovo** on the waterfront, is also in use by modern man. It is a popular spot for scientific conventions. Its oval shape (hence the name) is apparently the responsibility of the Spanish viceroy Don Pedro de Toledo, who reconstructed it in 1532-53. It was originally begun by William I in 1154, finished by Frederick II and enlarged by the not-to-be-outdone Charles I of Anjou. Pleasant restaurants line the shore; children do bellyflops from the causeway; the speedboats of the Guardia Finanza lurk along the Quay.

House of History

The **Museo Archaeologico Nazionale di Napoli** is one of the great museums of the world, housing the most spectacular finds from Pompeii and Herculaneum and some of the finest examples of Greek sculpture visible today. A trip to the museum will take an entire morning.

The ground floor is devoted to classical sculpture and Egyptian art. In the main entrance hall, a monolithic sarcophagus depicts a famous and important scene: Prometheus creating man out of clay. Another awesome sarcophagus presents a raucous Bacchanalian celebration. Through a doorway to the right, a pair of statues of Harmodius and Aristogeiton, who killed the tyrant Hipparchus, fairly leaps out at you as you enter the room. These are actually Roman copies of originals once installed in the Agora in Athens. In a further room stands a Roman copy of the

famous statue of Doryphorus by Polycleitus (440 BC), considered the "canon of perfection" of manly proportions. This statue, found at Pompeii, and others of its period are evidence of the fine tastes brought to Italy by its Greek settlers.

The rich collection of Pompeiian mosaics on the mezzanine floor reminds us that art never gets better through the ages; it only changes its form, as a beautiful model changes her dress during a fashion show. Everything in these rooms comes from the floors, walls and courtyards of houses unearthed at Pompeii. The freshness and color of these works after centuries buried in lava are an amazing tribute to the craftsmanship of their ancient makers. Room LIX contains two of the most famous of the mosaics, both signed by a master of the craft named Dioscorides from the island of Samos. That labeled 9987 depicts, according to some, two women consulting a sorceress, and according to others, three women gossiping. This mosaic and 9985, which shows a dwarf, two women and a man with musical instruments, are thought to represent scenes from a Greek comedy. The Nile scenes in room LX, from a later period, present a world of bright ducks,

crocodiles, hippopotami and snakes. These mosaics originally framed the *Battle of Issus*, now in Room LXI. In this huge scene Alexander the Great is presented in his victorious battle against the Persian emperor Darius in 333 BC. The thicket of spears creates an illusion of an army vaster than that actually shown.

Through the large Salone dell'Atlante at the top of the stairs is a series of rooms containing the fabulous wall-paintings from different Campanian cities. One could spend a whole morning in this section alone. Quite startling is the 6th Century BC *Sacrifice of Iphigenia*, the Greek equivalent of the Biblical sacrifice of Isaac. The deer borne by Artemis in the top of the picture replaced Iphigenia at the last minute, just as Isaac was replaced by a ram. Far happier is *The Rustic Concert*, in which Pan and several nymphs tune up for a Roman shindig.

Churches

A visit to the churches of Naples, as to the churches of any Italian city, is the best introduction to the local streetlife. Unlike in the United States, whose architectural unifiers are primarily shopping malls and

Neapolitan shop in the Galleria Umberto I

banks, in Italy a visit to a church, a quick confession, a curtsy in front of an altar are still a daily reality for large sections of the population. Walking from church to church, one encounters weddings, masses, funerals in progress; rich and poor emerging together into the twilight after services; families, old people, young people, going to their daily mass.

The church of **Monteoliveto**, about halfway up the Via Roma, is a warren of Renaissance monuments hidden away in surprising corners. Far in the back of this aisleless basilica, begun in 1411, stands a bizarre group of terracotta figures by the artist Guido Mazzoni. The eight statues, looking almost alive in the dim light that filters into their chapel, represent the Pieta, and are said to be portraits of Mazzoni's 15th Century friends. Further back, down a side passage, waits the Old Sacristy (*in restauro, 1985*), containing frescoes by Vasari and quite wonderful wood stalls, inlaid with Biblical Scenes. In the very front of the church, to the left of the entrance, another passage leads to the Piccolomini Chapel where a relief of a nativity scene by the Florentine Antonio Rossellino (1475) is a delight to behold.

Unlike in Rome, which is heavily Baroque, no one architectural style dominates the Neapolitan ecclesiastical scene. One learns to phase in and out of the Gothic, the Renaissance, the Baroque with the ease of a true modern dilettante. The church of **Gesu Nuovo**, at the top of the street called **Trinità Maggiore**, presents perhaps the most harmonious example of the Neapolitan Baroque. The embossed stone facade originally formed the wall of a Renaissance palace. At noon on Saturdays, when weddings inevitably occur here, the massive front doors are thrown open to give a splendid view of fully lit baroque at its best. The interior has a unique design, being almost as wide as it is deep. The colored marbles and bright frescoes seem to spiral up into the dome. Directly above the main portal, just inside the church, stretches a wide fresco by Francesco Solimena (1725) depicting Heliodorus driven from the temple. The ubiquitous Solimena ruled Neapolitan painting in the first half of the 18th Century.

A more austere, and older architectural approach is demonstrated by the Gothic church of **Santa Chiara**, just across the street. Founded in 1310-28 by Robert the Wise for his queen, Sancia, the huge church — the biggest in Naples — became the favorite place of worship of the Neapolitan nobility. Extensive bomb damage during the Second World War destroyed many of its most important works of art, but worth more than a moment's gander in its vast, now relatively empty interior is the Tomb of Robert the Wise (1343) behind the main altar, by the brothers Giovanni and Pacio Bertini of Florence. Through a courtyard to the left of the church is the entrance to its immense and peaceful cloister, where majolica-tiled pathways meander through a wild and beautiful garden of roses and fruit trees.

The steep **Via Santa Maria di Constantinopoli** leads up to the **Conservatorio di Musica**, founded in 1537, the oldest musical conservatory in Europe. Its important library and museum are open from 9 a.m. until 1 p.m., but best of all is to wander through its courtyard listening to the music of violins, organs, harps and pianos spilling down from upper storeys. Just down the block, the church of **San Pietro a Maiella**, built in 1313-16, will reward the visitor with one of the most famous ceilings in Italy. The Calabrian Mattia Preti began painting it in 1656, at the age of 43, a few months after leaving his native Taverna for the more rigorous artistic

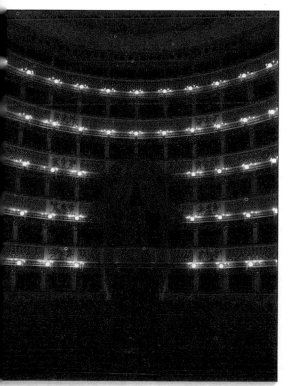

and Opera
ouse, San
rlo.

challenges of Naples. Five years later he completed his work, establishing himself as one of the most talented painters of his generation. The panels in the nave tell the story of Saint Celestine V (see Abruzzo, above), while the panels in the transept present the life of Saint Catherine of Alexandria, the virgin martyr who was beheaded for out-arguing pagan scholars.

The Naples **Duomo** is a magnificent gothic warehouse of relics from every period of the city's history. Here are stored, in a chapel off the right aisle, the head of Saint Januarius, the Patron Saint of the city, and two phials of his blood. The magical powers of the blood are the subject of what the irrepressible Twain called "One of the wretchedest of all the religious impostures in Italy — the miraculous liquefaction of the blood." The miracle has been taking place every year on Dec. 16, Sept. 19 and the first Saturday in May since the saint's body was brought to Naples from Pozzuoli, the place of his martyrdom, by Bishop Severus in the time of Constantine. It is said that if the blood fails to liquefy, some awful unknown thing will happen to the city's inhabitants.

Museums in the Clouds

Two of the greatest museums in Naples stand high on bluffs overlooking the city below. The National Gallery of Naples, formerly in the **Museo Nazionale**, has been relocated to the **Palazzo Reale di Capidomonte**, situated in a shady park directly north of the Museo. Here are gathered the best paintings in southern Italy. Among the high points are Masolino Da Panicale's *Foundation of Santa Maria Maggiore in Rome*, in which Christ and Mary ride a cloud as if it were a magic carpet; Bellini's *Transfiguration*; various works of Titian; two startling allegorical paintings by Peter Breughel the Elder (*The Blind Leading the Blind* and *The Misanthrope*); and, most famous of all, Caravaggio's *Flagellation*.

A trip up the Montesanto funicular brings the visitor to the top of the Vomero hill, home of the **Museo Nazionale di San Martino**, located in the Carthusian monastery of the same name. Here are 90 rooms of paintings, furniture, ceramics and costumes illustrating the life and history of Naples. Some of the top painters of the Neapolitan Baroque are represented here, including Francesco Solimena and the prolific Luca Giordano. Belve-

deres give access to the best views in town. Good views can also be gotten from the **Castel Sant' Elmo** next door, a 14th Century fortress long used as a prison for political troublemakers. The stately gardens of the **Villa Floridiana**, also on the Vomero, are favored among young mothers as a place to teach infants to walk. The gardens house the **Museo Nazionale della Ceramica**, containing one of the most extensive collections of European and Chinese porcelain in Italy.

A secret known to sailors in Navies around the world is that the Bay of Naples is one of the most beautiful ports in Europe. The best way to appreciate the splendors of the bay requires an evening walk through the **Villa Nazionale** to the far-western district of **Mergellina**. The Villa Nazionale itself is a mile-long public garden containing, at its very center, a small Aquarium of dubious importance where 200 species of fish, including eels and sting-rays, cavort in murky tanks. The **Piazza Sannazaro**, at the heart of the Mergellina district, repays the persevering walker with some of the best pizza in Naples. The secret of Neapolitan Pizza, aside from the fact that it is made with fresh mozzarella, lies in the way it is

Mosaic of battle in Naples Archaeological museum.

baked. It is baked in an oven shaped like a mound, over a wood fire, by an old man. The old man, like all dignified chefs, will only work in the evening. Hence it is often difficult to order pizza for lunch. One must make do, then, with other local specialties, such as the excellent octopus (*polpo*), Mussel soup (*zuppa di cozze*), numerous swimming fish, various spaghetti's made with a fish-sauce (such as the Neapolitan catch-all *Spaghetti alla Pescatore* [Spaghetti of the fisherman's wife]); *mozzarella e prosciutto* (favored by fat men from the country), swordfish, baked mozzarella, fried mozzarella, *Spaghetti alla Mozzarella*. The Piazza Sannazaro like most Neapolitian Piazzas, is a major traffic center: the ricketty outdoor tables of the restaurants rest inches from the swirling confusion of the cars. One dines to the surprising odors of carbon monoxide and drinks to the acceleration of engines. While one eats, a basket is lowered from a nearby window, containing a pack of black-market Marlboros for a young man and his girlfriend waiting below, racing the engine of their Vespas. The youth takes out the cigarettes, puts in the money, and slowly steers his machine, with its lovely passenger, off into the traffic. The basket is pulled back up by its owner, a 60-year-old man in long underwear, counting his meager profits on a balcony where his clothes hang to dry.

After dinner, you can take a stroll down to the Marina, where the motor-yachts of the rich congregate. Here German tourists consume their last glasses of Liebfraumilch on the poop deck before walking unsteadily ashore, their sweaters over their shoulders, to join the crowd milling along the quay. A half-dozen cafes with swinging chairs and views of Vesuvius siphon off the wealthier members of this heterogeneous mob; the rest continue on their way, content some of them, some of them not so content, with a bottle of beer, a slice of pizza, the shoulder of a chum for entertainment. Meanwhile, the least wealthy, the barbed and bespattered indigent, also continue on their way, encouraged by the not-so-friendly words, and even less friendly hand-motions, of the waiters.

Naples is a big, brawling city that exists for nobody, ultimately, but itself. It neither actively discourages the visitor nor makes any real attempt to draw him in: it just continues on its crowded, noisy, irremediable way, a gypsy caravan of all that is best and worst in Italy.

ay of
aples at
usk seen
om
lergellina.

ENVIRONS OF NAPLES

The various wonders packed into Campania have acted as a magnet for generations of tourists. "Whether we turn towards the Miseno shore of the splendid watery amphitheater, and go by the Grotto of Posilipo to the Grotto del Cane and away to Baiae: or take the other way, towards Vesuvius and Sorrento, it is one succession of delights," marveled Charles Dickens. At least a week should be devoted to exploring the area, preferably tied to a visit to the Museo Archaeologico in Naples, where the region's most important works of art are kept.

The Entrance to Hell

In Greek times, Naples was a mere stripling overshadowed by its powerful parent **Cumae**, 30 km (19 miles) to the west. Founded by Aeolians from Asia Minor around 750 BC, by the 6th Century BC Cumae had become the political, religious and cultural beacon of the coast, control-

ling the Bay of Naples and its islands.

Here Aeneas came to consult the Sybil before his descent into the underworld. The famous **Antro della Sibilla Cumana** (Cave of the Cumaean Sybil), recently uncovered by archaeologists, consists of a trapezoidal *dromos*, or corridor, 44 meters (144 feet) long, punctuated by six airshafts. At the far end is a rectangular chamber cut with niches where the Sybil apparently sat and uttered her prophecies. The eery echo of your footsteps in the corridor recalls Virgil's description of "a cavern perforated a hundred times,/having a hundred mouths with rushing voices/carrying the responses of the Sybil." (Translated by Robert Fitzgerald). From the cave's mouth the visitor may climb up the acropolis, whose ruined, lizard-haunted temples offer fine views of the coastline and the sea.

The region between Cumae and Naples, known traditionally as the **Campi Flegrei** or "Burning Fields," has been a center of volcanic activity for as long as mankind can remember. Unexpected rumblings underfoot and gaseous exhalations from the soil have caused the area to be associated with Hades. The **Lago di Averno**, a once gloomy lake in the crater

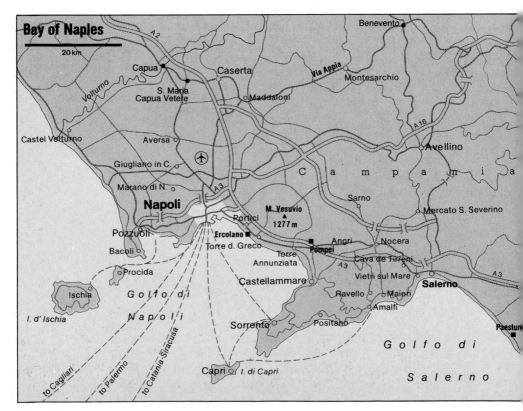

of a now extinct volcano, is the legendary "dark pool" from which Aeneas began his descent into the underworld. No bird was said to be able to fly across this lake and live, owing to the poisonous gases that erupted from it. A cruel experiment along these lines was conducted for many years at the **Grotto del Cane** on the nearby Lago d'Agnano. An innocent dog was subjected to the carbon dioxide that issued from the floor of the cave until he was knocked out or killed. "The dog dies in a minute and a half — a chicken instantly" reported Mark Twain. The experiment was repeated nine or ten times a day for the benefit of tourists.

Pozzuoli, a wealthy trading center in Greek and Roman times later devastated by wars and malaria, is now chiefly famous for its **Solfatara**, a volcanic crater from whose fissures sulfureous gases ascend in jets. The Solfatara is thought to have influenced Milton's description of Hell in *Paradise Lost*. Pozzuoli also boasts a magnificent Amphitheater. On the waterfront, enclosed in a small park, lies a rectangular structure formerly known as the **Serapeo** (Temple of Serapis), but now thought to have been a *macellum* or marketplace. Evidence of

shellfish encrustation around the bases of its four Corinthian columns has led archaeologists to speculate that the ground once sank 5 meters (16 feet) below sea level before rising again to its present height.

Baia apparently derived its name from Baios, Odysseus's navigator. Here Roman society came to swim. The modern town, with its view across the Gulf of Pozzuoli, contains extensive ruins of Roman palaces enclosed in a picturesque **Parco Archaeologico** on the hillside. At the lowest level of the park is a rectangular *piscina* from which an arched pathway, hidden in foliage, leads to a domed building believed to have been a bath. Archaeologists have pinpointed this perfect circular structure as an architectural model for the Pantheon in Rome. Today the hall, partially filled with brackish water, is a natural echo chamber of unusual sensitivity. Even the slightest scuff of your shoe is picked up and broadcast through the dome.

Pompeii

The tremendous interest of Pompeii

yrrhenian
ea at dusk
ff the
oast of
Campania.

and Herculaneum, the two Roman cities buried by the eruption of Mount Vesuvius in 79 AD, lies in their answers to what the archaeologist Amedeo Maiuri has called "the essential problem in the history of civilization: the origin and development of the house." Pompeii, originally settled by indigenous Oscans some time before the 8th Century BC and later ruled by Etruscans, Greeks and the warlike Samnites, was by the time of its sudden immersion in pumicestone and ash a thriving commercial center under Roman administration. It was a city of shops, markets and comfortable townhouses, with paved streets, wide sidewalks, a stadium, two theaters, temples, baths and houses of prostitution. Its rediscovery during land reclamation operations in the 16th Century, and subsequent years of sometimes piratical but increasingly respectful excavation, have allowed us today perhaps our most intimate vision of life in a Roman city of the 1st Century.

The Pompeiian house is thought to have evolved from the relatively simple design of the Etruscan farmhouse. The structure was built around a central courtyard (*atrium*) whose roof sloped inwards on all four sides to a rectangular opening in the center known as the *compluvium*. Through the compluvium rainwater fell into a corresponding rectangular tank beneath called the *impluvium*. Around the atrium itself spread the various rooms of the family including the bedrooms (*cubicula*), the dining rooms (*triclinia*), and, directly opposite the narrow entranceway (*vestibule*), the living room (*tablinum*), the most important room in the house. As the plan developed, a further peristyle courtyard appeared in back, often containing a fountain. Shops were built into the front of the house; sections of the house were blocked off and rented out, with separate entranceways, to strangers (**Villa di Julia Felix**); another storey was added up top, until the Etruscan prototype had metamorphosed into the comfortable and palatial townhouses typified by **Casa dei Vettii** and the **Casa Del Fauno**.

Wedding Whips

A striking feature of the Pompeiian house was the colorful and often highly refined frescoes that covered its walls. Many of the most beautiful of these have been taken to the Museo Nazionale in Naples, but at the **Villa dei Misteri**, just outside the Porto Ercolano, a series of 10 scenes apparently depicting the initiation of brides into the Dionysiac mysteries has been left in *situ* for the benefit of the curious. The exact meaning of these splendid paintings, which depict, among other things, the whipping of a young bride, is still unclear, though it is agreed that the Mantled Woman in the final scene is probably a portrait of the mistress of the house, who may have been a Dionysiac priestess.

There is something for everybody at Pompeii. No visitor can leave the place without remembering some small sign on a shopfront, some view into a gated garden, some mosaic-covered fountain of unexpected beauty. Often one sees, carved into the polygonal paving stones of the streets, small phalluses pointing off into the center of the city. These are thought by some to have warded off evil spirits, by others to have pointed to the red light district. The walls of houses, shops and public monuments are covered with inscriptions of every kind, from lists of upcoming shows at the theater to the scribbled figurings of shopkeepers, from election notices to the private declarations of lovers. "It is a wonder, O Wall," wrote one cynic on the wall of the Basilica, "that thou hast not yet crumbled under the weight of so much written nonsense."

Herculaneum

Unlike Pompeii, Herculaneum was a bedroom community built for the enjoyment of its sea breezes and its views out across the Bay of Naples. Instead of the compact townhouses of Pompeiian businessmen, one finds here wealthy villas of wealthy patricians. There is a freer, more spontaneous form of architecture, and the houses, finally freed of the mud in which they were encased for so long, are generally in a better state of preservation than those of Pompeii. One of the pleasures of Herculaneum (aside from the fact that it is less crowded with tour groups than Pompeii) is the carbonized pieces of wood furniture, door mouldings and screens that can still be found in the original positions in the houses. Fine frescoes, such as that of the *Rape of Europa* in the so-called **Casa Sannitica**, adorn the walls, and carpet-like mosaics cover the floors. Particularly striking are the black-and-white mosaics on the floor of the **Casa**

dell'Atrio a Mosaico which have become rippled through the centuries. The city derives its name from Hercules, and was originally called *Herakleia* by its Greek founders.

Herculaneum is the best starting point for an afternoon ascent of **Mount Vesuvius**, which looms directly over the modern city of **Ercolano**. No longer is it necessary, as in Dickens's time, to be carried up the mountain on a litter borne by 15 attendants. Buses leave regularly from the Ercolano train station and drop you off at the roadhead, from which a well-beaten track continues up (20 minutes — sneakers may be rented) the final steps to the crater. Since the volcano's first eruption about 10,000 years ago, periods of violent activity have alternated with periods of relative peace. Just before the infamous eruption of 79 AD, Vesuvius was planted with trees and olive groves to its very peak. In this century, a constant plume of smoke billowed from a cone inside the crater until 1944, when, during the volcano's last eruption to date, the cone was destroyed. Now only a few scattered *fumarole* (whisps of smoke) around the lip of the crater indicate that the volcano is still active and could erupt again.

road in the ⁙ined city of ⁙mpeii.

Of the three islands just outside the Bay of Naples, **Capri**, on the Sorrento side, has traditionally been the most popular among travellers owing to its odd shape, its mild climate and the luxuriant vegetation that grows among the rocky recesses of its seemingly inaccessible coast. Here the Roman emperor Tiberius retired in 27 AD, some say to pursue his lifelong love of privacy, others maintain to indulge in the secret orgies with which the historians Tacitus and Suetonius branded the closing years of his reign. While on Capri, writes Suetonius, the emperor "devised little nooks of lechery in the woods and glades ... and had boys and girls dressed up as pans and nymphs posted in front of caverns or grottoes; so that the island was now openly and generally called "Caprineum," because of his goatish antics." The modern English writer Norman Douglas, who also lived many years on Capri, has attributed such legends to the idle exaggerations of resentful peasants.

The modern traveller, arriving by ferry or hydrofoil from Naples or Sorrento, may visit the remains of Tiberius's **Villa** by bus from the town of Capri. This is the

site of the cliff from which the emperor allegedly threw his victims. The most famous sight on the island, however, is the **Grotta Azzura** or Blue Grotto, a cave on the water's edge whose bizarre light effects have made it perhaps the most visited tourist attraction in Campania after Pompeii.

From **Anacapri**, located on the far side of the island, one may ascend, via chairlift, **Monte Solaro**, the central mountain whose 360-degree view encompasses the Southern Apeninnes, Naples, Vesuvius, Sorrento and Ischia. Butterflies and lizards inhabit the stone wall buttressed concrete slab at the peak. In Anacapri itself the church of **San Michele** is worth a visit for its majolica-tiled pavement depicting the *Story of Eden* by Francesco Solimena.

On Capri, as on its fellow islands Ischia and Procida, the pleasures of the body take precedence over the pleasures of the mind. **Ischia**, the largest island off Naples, is famous among Germans for its hot mineral springs. The island is entirely of volcanic origin. Some say the Giant Typhoeus, struck by Zeus' thunderbolt, was buried under Ischia, causing the occasional groanings and shakings that

have marked its long history. Visitors generally stay in one of the comfortable hotels in **Porta Ischia**. One of the most pleasant, with a luxurious spa, is the modern **Jolly Hotel**. The town of **Lacco Ameno**, on the coastal road, is known for its mud baths, which contain the most radioactive waters in Italy. **Sant' Angelo** has some of the best beaches on the island. At **Ischia Ponte**, a causeway crosses to the **Castello Aragonese**, built by Alphonso I of Naples in 1450. The crypt of the ruined cathedral is adorned with frescoes in the style of Giotto, and the nearby convent has an interesting cemetery where the dead sisters were placed upright in chairs. **Procida**, the smallest of the islands, has good beaches and a thriving fishing industry. It is quiet and serene and generally empty of tourists.

Old Campania

Inland from Naples, at **Santa Maria Capua Vetere**, are the remains of the second largest amphitheater in Italy. Few tourists are aware of this magnificent crumbling structure, yet it may be the one amphitheater in Italy were visitors can

Left, a fisherman Ischia harbor. Below, a well-dress horse waiting to ferry tour around.

actually climb down into the subterranean passages where wild beasts roamed.

The basilica of **Sant' Angelo in Formis**, 6 km (four miles) north of Capua, is an ancient, musty structure in an ancient, musty village, containing bright Byzantine frescoes illustrating the life of Christ. **Caserta**, often called the "Versailles of Naples" for its lavish **Palazzo Reale**, is otherwise of little interest, but **Caserta Vecchia**, on a mountaintop 10km (six miles) to the northeast, is one of the most beautiful towns in Campania. Founded in the 8th Century, it still looks much as it did then, with stone streets, stone houses and good views. Its Romanesque cathedral has a wonderful facade with a cow over the central portal. Inside are a pair of holy water stoups supported by lions and a monolithic 4th Century baptismal font in which baptism by total immersion was practiced. There are some excellent restaurants scattered around the town where you can indulge in the local specialty of wild boar.

One of the most important cities in Campanian history is **Benevento**, where the noble king Manfred voluntarily died in battle after the defection of his allies in 1266. The city was named Beneventum upon becoming a Roman colony in 268 BC. Before that it was called Maleventum, apparently for its bad air. Its original settlers, the fierce Samnites, called it Malies.

In the center of town, on the route of the ancient **Via Appia** from Rome to Brindisi, stands the **Arch of Trajan**, one of the best-preserved triumphal arches in Italy. Of the splendid reliefs of scenes from Trajan's life, those on the side facing Rome celebrate the emperor's domestic policies while those on the side facing Brindisi record his foreign policies. The **Museo del Sannio** is worth visiting not only for its collection of local antiquities but also for the hunting scenes on the column capitals that surround its 12th Century cloister.

Paradise Regained

The visitor to **Sorrento**, whether arriving from the noisy streets of Naples or from the scorched ruins of Pompeii, will find this a cool and peaceful town of lemon groves, with a small beach and a plentiful supply of cafes. There's not much more to Sorrento, save for a 15th

Century **Loggia** with fine column capitals on the Via San Cesareo, and the fact that the poet Tasso was born here in 1544, but that is exactly why the town is such a popular resort among Italians and foreigners alike. It's a good place to relax, and an excellent starting point for excursions to Capri and the **Amalfi Coast**.

This coast, cliff-hung, convoluted, stretches from **Positano** to **Salerno**, and possesses some of the most spectacular scenery in Italy. The **Amalfi Drive** faithfully follows its length, keeping at a respectful distance above the waves while dutifully following each frightening twist of the shoreline. Bright houses cling to the slopes, surrounded by gardens that descend in steps to the sea. Its pleasant climate, breathtaking views and picturesque gorges have made it a favorite haunt of artists and honeymooners.

Positano consists of a semi-circle of houses set back in a cove, with numerous hotels, places to swim and lookouts on which to pose for photographs. The road then passes through several tunnels before reaching the **Grotto di Smeraldo**, famous for its greenish light. The road continues through more tunnels (watch out for bicyclists) to **Amalfi**, a major trading cen-

ter in Byzantine times and now a major tourist center. From the main piazza, with its naughty fountain, a flight of steps ascends to the 11th Century bronze door of Amalfi's **Duomo**. Here, in the crypt, lies the body of Saint Andrew the Apostle, delivered from Constantinople in 1208. On either side of the main altar are interesting ambones (pulpits) with fine mosaics.

Ravello

The most beautiful town on the Amalfi coast is surely Ravello, famous for its architecture, its gardens and its generations of admirers. Here Richard Wagner found the inspiration for the Magic Garden of Klingsor in *Parsifal*. Ravello's **Cathedral** is celebrated for its bronze doors by the Apulian Barisano da Trani. Cast in Trani in 1179, the doors were carried to Ravello by ship. Inside, the floor slopes upwards towards God and a fine marble ambo supported by pillars resting on the backs of six hungry lions. The ambo was presented to the church in 1272 by Nicola Rufolo and his wife Sigilgaida, who built the splendid **Villa Rufolo** across the street. Their lush gardens and

Left, off th
Amalfi co
Below, a
street cafe
Positano.

Moorish cloister overlook the sea several kilometers below. The best view, however, is from the more extensive gardens at the **Villa Cimbrone**, built at the end of the 19th Century by a wealthy Englishman, Ernest William Beckett, whose ashes are buried beneath the **Temple of Bacchus** he built on the edge of the cliff. The gardens blend box, cypress, roses, wisteria into a peaceful park ending in a belvedere so high it seems as if it were built upon a cloud.

Salerno and Paestum

It was just south of Salerno that the Allies began their assault of Italy on Sept. 9, 1943. The city, strung out along the shore of the gulf named after it, has a good beach and one of the loveliest cathedrals in southern Italy. The **Cathedral** is reached through an atrium with 28 columns from Paestum. Inside, as the removal of 18th Century plaster continues, more and more medieval frescoes are coming to light. Particularly beautiful is a fresco of the virgin behind the fourth pier in the right aisle. As at Ravello, this cathedral contains a pair of exquisite ambones, dating from the 12th Century, with Byzantine decorations. The great Hildebrand is buried in a tomb in the right apse. The crypt contains the body of Saint Matthew.

When George Eliot visited the **Temple of Neptune** at Paestum, she thought it "the finest thing, I verily believe, we have seen in Italy." Her words echo the sentiments of many 19th Century travellers for whom this Greek city, founded in the 6th Century BC, was the final stop on the Grand Tour. There are few sights so arresting as Paestum's three well-preserved Doric temples standing empty on the grassy plain that surrounds them. The Temple of Neptune, the most majestic of these, was built in the 5th Century BC of a reddish travertine whose warmth, as Eliot wrote, "seems to glow and deepen under one's eyes." The so-called **Basilica** beside it, of a greyer tinge, is older, having been built in the 6th Century BC. The third temple, the **Temple of Ceres**, is separated from the other two by the **Roman forum** and **baths**, and a **Greek theater**. Across the street, in the **Museum** (*in restauro*, 1985), one may see the famous mural paintings from the **Tomb of the Diver** (480 BC), rare and beautiful examples of Greek painting.

pectacular mains of eek temples Paestum.

APULIA

*"Who will complain of the trees?
Only a few makers of bad pictures.
They can go elsewhere. Our country,
dear sir, is encrusted with old castles
and other feudal absurdities."*

— Norman Douglas

Some visit Apulia (also known as Puglia) for its architecture, some for its landscape, some for its archaeology and some for its food, but all go away haunted by memories of a single man: Frederick II of Hohenstaufen. Known to Dante as "the father of Italian poetry" and to his 13th Century contemporaries as *stupor mundi et immutator mirabilis* — the wonder of the world and the extraordinary innovator — Frederick built most of the castles that are still a dominant architectural feature of the region. He also founded many of Apulia's most splendid churches, carrying on the tradition of the Apulian Romanesque begun by his Norman predecessors a century before. An enlightened ruler who waged a bitter and ultimately unsuccessful feud with the popes in Rome, he was also an avid sportsman whose brilliant treatise on falconry still ranks among the most accurate descriptions of the subject. His just laws and tolerance of the religious beliefs of the Saracens are remembered by Apulians to this very day. Frederick's death in 1250 and the tragic defeat of his illegitimate son Manfred at the Battle of Benevento in 1266 ushered in a period of economic and spiritual decline that is only now being reversed.

If Frederick II is the dominant figure in Apulia's long and varied history, the Apulian Romanesque is its most important architectural legacy. The style, fusing Byzantine, Saracenic and Italian decorative techniques with the French architectural forms introduced by the Normans, first appeared in the Church of San Nicola at Bari in 1087. The plans of most other Apulian churches of the period derived from this elegant cathedral: short transepts; three semicircular apses corresponding to three naves and three portals; a tall, plain facade; richly decorated doorways carved with animals, flowers and biblical scenes. The visitor learns very quickly to detect these elements, for they are visible in one form or another in nearly every church in the region.

The food of Apulia is fresh and simple, making good use of the tomatoes, wine and olive oil which are among the region's chief products. The most famous pasta here is *orecchiette*, an ear-shaped variety occasionally made with whole-wheat flour.

The Visiting Archangel

The landscape of northern Apulia is dominated by vast inland plains planted with wheat whose color changes from white at midday to a deep gold at sunset. The only real mountains are clustered on the Gargano Promontory, a thickly forested peninsula that juts out into the Adriatic to form the "spur" of the boot of Italy. Here, in the medieval town of **Monte S. Angelo**, one may visit the famous **Sanctuario di San Michele**, a cave where the Archangel Michael is said to have revealed himself to local bishops in 490, 492 and 493 AD. The cave is entered through a pair of bronze doors manufactured in Constantinople in 1076. Brass rings in the doors were supposed to be knocked loudly to wake up the Archangel within. This pleasant town also has a fine municipal museum devoted to the popular arts of the Gargano. Particularly interesting are the presses once used for creating wine and olive oil, and a stone flour mill originally turned by mules.

Monte S. Angelo is a good place to buy materials for a lunch in the **Foresta Umbra**, a parkland in the center of the peninsula where centenarian beech trees, oaks and chestnuts shade winding trails and pleasant picnic spots. From here one may drive down along the coastline to **Vieste**, a bright town on the tip of the promontory containing a castle built by Frederick II. The road continues west, passing an odd, phallic rock formation known as *Pizzomunno*, along a torturous coastline studded with beaches and grottoes. Signs indicate where to turn off for the grottoes. **Manfredonia**, back on the mainland, is a booming industrial center of little interest except for its Castello, begun by Manfred in 1256 and later enlarged by Manfred's enemy, Charles I of Anjou. Near Manfredonia are the beautiful medieval churches of **Santa Maria di Siponto**, with a 5th Century crypt, and **San Leonardo**, with a wonderful facade guarded by two stone lions.

*receding
ages, Trulli
ouses at
lberobello.
eft, getting
round on
orseback,
argano.*

South to Bari

The coastal route to Bari is lined with seaport towns of various degrees of importance, all carrying on a brisk trade in vegetables, fruit and wine. One of the oldest, most important and, today, least attractive of these towns is **Barletta** where Manfred established his court in 1259. Here, at the intersection of the Corso Garibaldi and the Corso Vittorio Emanuele, stands the intriguing **Colosso**, a 4th Century Byzantine statue thought to represent the emperor Valentinian I (364–375). Only the head and torso are original, the rest having been recast in the 15th Century. Behind rises the **Basilica di San Sepolcro**, with a nice Gothic portal and an octagonal cupola reminiscent of Byzantine designs. Barletta's **Duomo** (*in restauro*, 1985) is a confusing edifice built on a Romanesque plan, with five radiating apses in the French Gothic style and a Renaissance main portal. By the sea rises Manfred's castle (also *in restauro* 1985).

A far more picturesque town, located 13 km (8 miles) south of Barletta, is **Trani**, whose Romanesque cathedral, founded in 1097 but not completed until the middle of the 13th Century, is perhaps the most beautiful church in Apulia. Beneath its richly carved rose window is a small monofora window flanked by pillars resting on the backs of elephants. The wonderful bronze doors are the work of the local artist Barisano da Trani, who is also responsible for the celebrated doors on the Cathedral at Ravello. The interior of the church, bright and austere, has the usual three apses and three naves, with triforium arcades above the side-aisles supported, here, by six pairs of columns on either side. Steps descend to the underground church of **Santa Maria della Scala** and the crypt. Even further down is the underground **Ipogio di San Leucio**, 1.5 meters (five feet) below sea level, containing two crude and delightful frescoes.

Windy Bari

The ancient Barium, founded by Greeks, developed by the Romans as an important trading center, destroyed by William the Bad in 1156 and restored by William the Good in 1169, is today the largest and most important commercial center in Apulia. The city is divided into two distinct parts: the *Citta Vecchia*, a labyrinth of tightly tangled medieval

A limeston grotto on Apulian coast.

streets and dazzling white houses, and the *Citta Nuova*, the modern city, with wide boulevards laid out at perfect right angles to each other. It is said that the torturous alleyways of the old city protected the inhabitants from the wind and from invaders who became confused when they tried to penetrate the winding streets. The modern traveller may feel equally vulnerable, and should keep a firm grip on his pocketbook.

The church of **San Nicola** was founded in 1087 to contain the relics of St. Nicholas, stolen that same year from Myra in Asia Minor by 47 sailors from Bari. Its facade bears many resemblances to the facade of the cathedral at Trani, though it is even plainer. A small round window, or *oculus*, crowns three bifora windows, a monofora window, and a richly carved portal flanked by columns borne by a pair of patient and time-worn bulls. The interior of the church is best visited in the evening, when sun shoots through the windows of the facade, creating unusual light effects among the three great transverse arches (a structural addition of 1451) that are the first thing one notices when walking inside. Among the many noteworthy objects in this church are the beautiful column capitals of the choir screen separating the nave from the apse and the ciborium over the high altar, the oldest of its kind in Apulia, built in the early 1100s. Behind the ciborium is the church's most well-known work of art, an 11th Century episcopal throne supported by three grotesque telemones. To the left is a Renaissance altar-piece, *Madonna and Four Saints*, by the Venetian Bartolomeo Vivarini. The crypt formerly contained the precious relics of St. Nicholas, said to exude a wonder-working oil. They have since been removed for safekeeping. The Byzantine icon of St. Nicholas in the central apse of the crypt was presented to the church by the King of Serbia in 1319.

Bari's **Cathedral**, a short walk west of S. Nicola, was erected between 1170 and 78 over the remains of a Byzantine church wrecked by William the Bad during his rampage through the city in 1156. Basilican in plan, the church follows San Nicola in most details of its design, with deep arcades along both flanks and a false wall at the rear that masks the protrusions of the three semicircular apses. A particularly fine window adorns the rear facade. Nearby, off the Piazza Federico II di Svevia, is Bari's **Castello**, built in Norman

ieste, on he Gargano oast.

times, refurbished by Frederick II, and considerably enlarged by Isabella of Aragon in the 16th Century.

Bari's **Pinacoteca Provinciale**, containing paintings from the 11th Century to the present, is located in the Citta Nuova along the Lungomare Nazario Sauro. The best painting in the museum is undoubtedly Bartolomeo Vivarini's *Annunciation* in Room II. Further rooms contain Giovanni Bellini's startling *S. Pietro Martire* and a number of works by Neapolitan Baroque painters including Bernardo Cavallino, Andrea Vaccaro and the prolific Luca Giordano. Francesco Netti, the Italian impressionist, a native son of Bari, is also well represented. Bari's small but worthwhile **Museo Archaeologico**, in the Piazzo Umberto I, has a rich collection of attic black- and red-figure vases.

Around Bari

An interesting one-day excursion into Apulia's architectural past begins 18 km (11 miles) west of Bari in the town of **Bitonto**, whose famous cathedral, built between 1175 and 1200, represents perhaps the most complete expression of the Apulian Romanesque. The beautiful facade, tall, plain, yet finely adorned, is dominated by a rose window and an elegantly carved portal, flanked by the usual lions. The pelican pecking her breast above the doorway is considered a symbol of Christ. Of the pulpits inside, the larger one, beneath the last arch in the right nave, is a masterpiece signed by a famous local artist, Nicolaus *sacerdos et magister* (1229), known as "Maestro Nicola." A relief on the side depicts Frederick II and his family, while, in front, the bent head of a telamon supports an eagle which in turn supports a marble bookstand.

The town of **Ruvo di Puglia**, 18 km (11 miles) farther west, was known as Rubi in Roman times, when it was famous for its ceramics. The 12th Century **Cathedral** was widened in the 17th Century to provide room for Baroque side-chapels, and though restorations have narrowed the interior back to its original Romanesque proportions the wide facade retains its Baroque girth, giving the church a somewhat squat appearance. The seated figure at the top of the facade is thought to represent the ubiquitous Frederick II. Beneath the church lie the recently excavated remains of some Roman houses, a Roman cistern, Roman floor mosaics, and Christian tombs from the 12th through the 17th centuries. The dark stains in the tombs are from the blood of the corpses that were stacked here. Ruvo's excellent **Museo Jatta** is devoted to Rubian ceramics excavated from nearby necropoli.

On a hilltop 30 km (19 miles) west of Ruvo stands, all alone, the **Castel del Monte**, often compared to the Coliseum in Rome as a supreme example of the architectural aims of an age. Historians differ on whether Frederick II erected the small fortress as a hunting lodge or a military outpost, but all agree that it was here that he married off his daughter, Violanta, to Riccardo, Count of Caserta, in 1249, and here that in 1266 the implacable Charles I of Anjou imprisoned the hapless sons of Manfred after their father's tragic defeat — and voluntary death — at Benevento. The castle served as a refuge for the noble families of Andrea, a nearby town, during the plague of 1665, and was later abandoned, becoming a hideout for brigands and political exiles. Restoration began in 1876. The present emptiness of the building and its isolation in the middle of arid, wheat-covered plains produce a strong effect on every traveller.

An entirely different kind of architectu-

In the old city of Bar

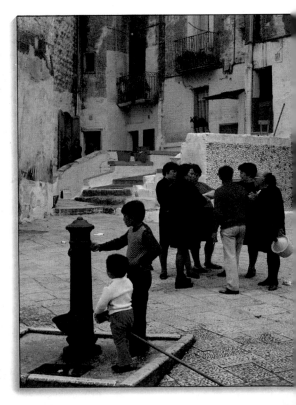

ral unit — the odd, conical peasant dwellings known as the *Trulli* — proliferates in the town of **Alberobello**, 50 km (31 miles) southeast of Bari. Nobody know the exact origins of these houses, but their special shape has turned them into one of Apulia's prized tourist attractions. Unfortunately, the visitor will probably find himself speculating, as he visits the town, whether the Trulli were not actually built relatively recently, for the sole purpose of housing gift shops. The **Grotte Castellane**, another of the region's great tourist attractions, are also surrounded by gift shops, but the caves themselves (20 km [12.5 miles] back towards Bari from Alberobello) are really quite interesting, containing pools, grottoes and ceilings that literally drip with stalactites.

Spartan Taranto

Taranto, the ancient Taras founded by Spartan navigators in 706 BC, was in the 4th Century BC the largest city in Magna Graecia, boasting a population of 300,000 and a city wall 15 km (9 miles) in circumference. It was, like many towns on this coast, a center of Pythagorean philosophy visited by such luminaries as Plato and Aristoxenes. Today the city, with its ancient and modern quarters separated by a canal on the waterfront, is the home of Italsider, one of Europe's most important iron works.

Taranto's **Museo Nazionale** is the second most important museum in southern Italy, rivaled only by the Museo Archaeologico in Naples for the splendor of its antiquities. The collection includes Greek and Roman sculpture and a wonderful series of Roman floor mosaics including a compelling fragment depicting a lion and a boar fighting. Rooms V-VIII contain one of the most complete collections of ancient ceramics in Apulia. Of particular interest are the many protocorinthian ointment boxes decorated with geometric and human figures; the corinthian vases, of which the museum has one of the largest collections in the world; a rare Laconian cup of the 6th Century BC with a design of radiating fishes; and numerous attic black- and red-figure vases.

Of interest in Taranto's old city is the church of **S. Domenico Maggiore**, founded by Frederick II in 1223, rebuilt in 1302 by Giovanni Taurisano, and much altered in Baroque times. Taranto's

Castel del Monte.

Duomo contains fine mosaic floors and antique columns from pagan temples.

For those willing to persevere, a fascinating side trip is 21 km (13 miles) from Taranto to the nearby town of **Massafra**, known for its early Christian cave churches hewn into the sides of a deep ravine that snakes through the center of the town. The **Chiesa-Crypta di San Marco**, located at the bottom of an unmarked staircase off the Via Scarano just below the Ponte Nuovo, preserves a fine fresco of St. Mark. The buzzing of the flies and the interesting odors that rise from the bottom of the gorge only enhance the mysterious freshness of the rock painting. The more extensive series of churches gathered under the name **Capella-Cripta della Candelore** must be visited with a guide (apply to the Polizia Urbana in the Piazza Garibaldi). It is best to arrive early as guides are unavailable during the *mezzogiorno.*

From Massafra by back roads (37 km [23 miles]) or from Taranto by superstrada (22 km [14 miles]) you can move on to **Grottaglie**, a hilltop town where Apulian potters compete to produce the ceramic pitchers, plates, bowls and cups available in gift shops across the region. The visitor may watch the meticulous and speedy potters at work creating the decorative spaghetti plates for which the town is known throughout Italy.

Baroque Lecce

Lecce is known for its profusion of Baroque houses and churches. The city owes its appearance to the malleable characteristics of the local sandstone, which is easy to carve when it first comes out of the ground but hardens with time. Intensive building in the 17th and 18th centuries created an architectural uniformity unique in Southern Italy. Churches drip with ornate altars and swirling columns that give the effect of classicism gone berserk. Outside, shadeless streets meander past curving yellow palaces bright with bursts of bougainvillea.

At the center of town, in the cobblestoned **Piazza S. Oronzo**, stands a single Roman column stolen from its mate in Brindisi. The pair originally marked the southern terminus of the Via Appia from Rome. A bronze statue of Saint Orontius, patron saint of the city, once stood on top of the column, but was taken down in 1985 to protect it from disintegration

A fine example o Leccian Baroque: Palazzo de Governo.

from smog. The partially excavated remains of a Roman amphitheater dominate the southern half of the square.

Leece's harmonious **Piazza Duomo**, just off the **Corso Vittorio Emanuele**, is framed by the facades of the Duomo, the **Palazzo Vescovile** and the **Seminario**, all built or reworked in the 17th Century. The Duomo actually has two facades: the lavish one facing the Corso, with its statue of Saint Orontius, and the more austere (and older) one facing the Palazzo Vescovile. The altars inside the Duomo, carved with flowers, fruit and human figures, are typical of the ornate local style.

Bright Basilica

The most complete expression of Leccian Baroque is the **Basilica di Santa Croce**, whose exuberant facade sports a balcony supported by eight grotesque caryatids. The bright interior has an overall restraint that unifies the different designs of its chapels. A chapel in the left transept contains a series of 12 bas-reliefs by the local artist Francesco Antonio Zimbalo showing the life of San Francesco di Paola.

Leece's modern and informative **Museo**

Provinciale, just outside the old city, is built around a spiral ramp reminiscent of the Guggenheim Museum in New York. In the archaeological section, attic black-and red-figure vases are nicely arranged around a central core containing bronze tools and suits of armor. The picture gallery, on the third floor, contains paintings by various southern Italian artists including the great Calabrian, Mattia Preti.

The rewards of travelling in Apulia, as in its neighbors Basilicata and Calabria, always include the pleasure of ending a day on the beach. Apulia has the longest coastline of any region in Italy, a fact which has made it peculiarly attractive to foreign invaders from the ancient worshippers of Zeus to the sun-worshippers of the present day. Lecce is within easy reach of beaches at far-famed **Gallipoli** on the Ionian and **Otranto** on the Adriatic seas.

In the peace and the wave-song of the pristine Apulian sands you could lie dreaming for many months, lost in reveries on the passage of so many heroes through these parts, from wily Odysseus to broad-minded, gallant, brooding Frederick II.

azza del uomo, ecce.

CALABRIA AND BASILICATA

"Your Calabrian is strangely scornful of luxury and even comfort; a creature of few but well-chosen words, straight-forward, indifferent to pain and suffering, and dwelling by preference, when religiously minded, on the harsher aspects of his faith. A note of unworldliness is discoverable in his outlook on life."

— Norman Douglas

Calabria is closer in spirit than any other region in Italy to the Italy of Byron and Shelley — the land of mouldering ruins, vine-clasped and ignored, that inspired the romantic thoughts of 19th Century travellers. The region is fast changing, to be sure. The completion of the *autostrada* from Salerno to Reggio di Calabria, governmental support of housing and industry, and vast improvements in the quality of hotels have begun to lure both northern entrepreneurs and foreign tourists to this long isolated part of Italy. No major city is now without its *Zona Industriale*, no village without its rebellious, adolescent roars of motorcycle engines at night. But the tourist industry is still young here. Foreign faces are few and far between, and what efforts have been made to exploit the region's cultural and artistic resources have done little to alter the picturesque traditions — and not so picturesque poverty — of its inhabitants. Much of Calabria's heritage still lies buried among the roots of olive trees.

The landscape of the region is dominated by its backbone of mountains that descend in fantastic foothills to the sea. Only nine percent of the territory consists of flat land. It was from the sea that Calabria's first invaders, the Greeks, came in the 8th Century B.C., crossing the straits of Messina from Sicily; and it is fitting that also from the sea has come Calabria's most celebrated reminder of those early settlers, the awesome **Bronze Warriors** discovered by fishermen off Riace in 1972. These two colossal Greek statues, thought to have been lost overboard from a ship sailing between Calabria and Greece, have, after two millennia on the Ionian sea bottom, also had to withstand a recent tug-of-war between Calabria and jealous museums in the north. Today they are installed, to the relief of local authorities, in the **Museo Nazionale della Magna Graecia** in **Reggio di Calabria**, where they can be seen alongside numerous other hoary Greek antiquities from across the region.

The coastline just north of Reggio was first described by Homer in Book XII of the *Odyssey*, the earliest — and most hair-raising — navigational guide to the Tyrrhenian sea. Here lurked the infamous monster Scylla, whose "six heads like nightmares of ferocity,/with triple serried rows of fangs and deep/gullets of black death" did away with six of Odysseus's best men. (Robert Fitzgerald.) Nowadays the Rock of Scilla provides the foundation for a youth hostel. Modern **Scilla** has an excellent view across the Straits of Messina. Farther north, **Palmi** is worth visiting for its ethnographic museum, containing an extensive collection of terrifically ugly ceramic masks designed to ward off the evil eye. The only way to find this museum is to drive to the center of town and politely ask a policeman. **Tropea**, suspended from a cliff over one of the many fine beaches that line the shore, is perhaps the most picturesque town on the coast. The old town has a beautiful Norman **Cathedral** containing, behind the

receding ages, the ilds of the ila Massif, alabria. eft, a lady om the lbanian ommunity f San emetrio orone. ight, a reek ronze (in e Archaeogical useum of eggio alabria) ragged up om the sea.

high altar, the *Madonna di Romania*, a portrait said to have been painted by Saint Luke.

Saints and Brigands

Highway 111 is the loneliest road in Calabria. It twists across the central mountain chain following what is believed to be an ancient trade route connecting **Gioia Tauro** on the Tyrrhenian with **Locri** on the Ionian sea. For many kilometers no human habitation intrudes upon its memories of the fierce brigands who once ruled the woods through which it passes. From the **Passo del Mercante**, the road's highest and loneliest point, one can see both seas in either direction. From here the road descends to the beautiful town of **Gerace**, situated on the hump of a nearly inaccessible crag. It is best to visit Gerace in the evening, and on foot, to appreciate the romantic sunset views from the grassy ruins of its castle. It is said that in the 10th Century, the city's inhabitants survived an Arab siege by subsisting on a ricotta cheese made from mother's milk. In still earlier times, a miracle-working saint, San Antonio del Castello, is said to have caused a spring of pure water to appear in a cave in the cliff that surrounds the castle. The imprint of the saint's knees, they say, can still be seen in the floor of the cave .

Gerace's **Cathedral** is the largest in Calabria. It was begun in 1045 on top of an older church — now the crypt — containing fragments from still older times including columns from the Greek settlement at **Locri**, a Roman sacrificial altar and numerous Byzantine frescoes. Gerace is a city of many layers, justifying the popular phrase, "if you know Gerace, you know Calabria."

The famous **Cattolica** at **Stilo**, one of the best-preserved Byzantine churches in existence, reminds us that in medieval times Calabria's rugged interior was a vibrant religious center. The tiny church, built on a square floor plan with five cylindrical cupolas, clings to the flank of Monte Consolino, just above Stilo, like a miniature castle overlooking its town. Its bright interior is adorned with frescoes and marble columns whose ornate capitals have been turned upside down to symbolize the triumph of Christianity over paganism.

Another important religious center farther inland is the Carthusian monastery at **Serra San Bruno** (visiting hours

Scilla, whe
Odysseus i
reputed to
have sailed

11–12, 4–5, women not admitted). In this peaceful sanctuary — reconstructed around the ruins of an earlier abbey destroyed by earthquake in 1783 — 16 bearded, white-robed monks live out their lives according to the rules of silence, solitude and poverty prescribed by the founder of their order, Bruno of Cologne, in the 11th Century. The monks eat no meat, a discovery that pained Norman Douglas, who stated that he himself would tend to "pray more cheerfully with a prospect of *Dejeuner à la Fourchette* looming ahead." To compensate for their abstinence from beef, however, the monks make an excellent cheese, available in grocery stores in the town.

Where Shepherds Wander

Of Calabria's four great mountain clusters — the Aspromonte, the Sila Piccola, the Sila Grande and the Sila Greca — the **Sila Piccola**, in the middle, is the most pleasant to visit. Among its dense pine groves and cool mountain meadows shepherd boys still wander with their flocks in an alpine atmosphere that is truly refreshing after the dry heat of the coast. The twisty road up from **Catanzaro** climbs

A Byzantine church at Stilo.

first to **Taverna**, a serene town on a hillside whose name suggests that it was once a way-station on the mule-track up into the mountains. Here was born, in 1613, the Baroque painter Mattia Preti, who left Calabria at the age of 43 to become one of the most influential painters in Naples. The church of **San Domenico**, just off the main square, contains the best of Preti's local work; paintings of his may also be seen in the churches of **Santa Barbara** and **San Martino**.

The few "tourist villages" that have been developed in the piney vastness of the inner Sila have done little to offset the sense of isolation one feels driving along its empty, winding roads, where gates are thrown down to bar vehicular passage when the snow gets too deep in winter. Even the **Lago Ampollino**, a manmade lake created earlier this century to promote tourism and create electricity, lacks the noisy crowds one usually expects to find at even the most remote of Italian vacation spots. Here, nature rules the day.

San Giovanni in Fiore, the biggest town in the Sila, is beautiful less for its overall appearance, which is rather grim, than for the austere, black-and-purple costumes of its women, which seem straight out of the middle ages. More compelling architecturally is the lovely hilltop town of **Santa Severina**, famed for its medieval scholastic tradition. Attached to the cathedral is an 8–9th Century Byzantine Baptistry of circular design, built originally as a martyrium, or shrine for the sacred relics of martyrs. Once this building stood privately and neatly alone. One of its four "arms" or entranceways was removed in the 16th Century to make room for the abutting cathedral sacristy. At the entrance to the town, the Byzantine church of **San Filomena** (the woman across the street keeps the key) has a cylindrical cupola of Armenian inspiration, and three tiny apses that would seem to anticipate Romanesque designs. The long central Piazza Vittorio Emanuele, leading to the locked **Castello**, is lined with venerable palaces dating from the 11th century.

A city worth visiting for its memories of former inhabitants is the seacoast town of **Crotone**, corresponding to the ancient Croton, founded by Greeks in 710 BC. Here the mystical mathematician Pythagoras came up with his theorem about right triangles, much to the annoyance of modern school-children, and taught the doctrine of *metempsychosis*, in which the soul is conceived as a free agent that, as John Donne later imagined, can as easily attach itself to an elephant as to a mouse before briefly inhabiting the head of a man. The English novelist George Gissing conceived some of the most amusing passages of his *By the Ionian Sea* before dying here in 1901, and the inimitable Douglas, during his lengthy sojourn in the "flesh-pots of Cotrone," speculated that the cows he encountered wandering along the beach might very well be "descendants of the sacred cattle of Hera." The modern town, on its crowded promontory, has little else to offer the tourist other than an excellent wine from the nearby village of **Melissa**, a small archaeological museum and indifferent hotels.

Northern Calabria and Basilicata

Steamy **Cosenza** is a very flat, very modern, very large city surrounding an old town on a hill. Its quite beautiful Gothic cathedral, in the old town, carries the distinction of having been consecrated in the presence of Frederick II in 1222. In the **Tesoro dell' Archivescovado** behind the Cathedral (apply to the marriage office) is stored a Byzantine reliquary cross that Frederick II donated to the church at the time of its consecration. The partially ruined **Castello** at the top of the old town unfortunately seems as if it may be permanently *in restauro*.

When Douglas visited the Albanian village of **San Demetrio Corone** in 1911, he was told by the amazed inhabitants that he was the first Englishman ever to have set foot in the town. The modern visitor may feel equally unique as he confronts the curious stares of barbers, policemen, shopkeepers and women in bright Albanian dresses.

The Albanians first fled to Calabria in 1448 to escape persecution by the Arabs, and are today the largest ethnic minority in the region. They possess their own language, literature and dress, and their own Greek Orthodox bishop. Isolated as San Demetrio is in the back hills of the Sila Greca, it was once one of the most important centers of learning in Calabria, the site of the famous Albanian College where the revolutionary poet Girolamo de Rada taught for many years. Today the college buildings stand empty and in disrepair, and it is only with the greatest effort that the visitor can convince the local police chief to telephone the gentle-

The Sassi (dwellings dug into the hillside) at Matera.

man who keeps the key to the little church of **Sant' Adriano**, just inside the College. One's work is amply repaid, however, by the Norman font and wonderful mosaic pavement inside.

On the Ionian coast overlooking the sea stands lonely **Rossano**, home of the famous **Codex Purpureus**, a rare 6th Century Greek manuscript brightened by 16 colorful miniatures drawn from the gospels and the Old Testament. This extraordinary book can be seen in the **Museo Diocesano** beside the cathedral. At the top of the grey, stone town stands the Byzantine church of **San Marco**, with five domes and a breathtaking view across the adjacent valley.

Basilicata is the poorest and most underdeveloped region in southern Italy, yet it is a land of considerable historical and sociological interest with a remarkably varied landscape. Its beaches on both the Tyrrhenian and Ionian coasts are among the finest in the south.

Matera, the second largest city after **Potenza**, presents perhaps the most unsettling example of the clash between the prehistoric and the modern in Southern Italy. Until quite recently, people in Matera literally lived in caves. Their rock-cut

dwellings, called **Sassi** by local inhabitants, date back to Byzantine times when they were originally built as churches. In later years, overcrowding caused many of the churches to be converted into homes where humans and livestock crowded together in unsanitary dankness, watched over by Byzantine frescoes painted onto the rock.

To visit the Sassi, it is best to hire one of the boys who will crowd around your car as soon as you enter the town. They are just as knowledgeable as and a great deal less expensive than the official tourist guides. The church of **Santa Lucia**, in the main part of town, contains the two most famous frescoes in Matera, the Madonna del Latte and San Michele Arcangelo, both dating from the second half of the 13th Century. Nearby, the Apulian Romanesque Duomo has a striking rose window. Across the valley, built into a hillside covered with wild thyme, is the church of the **Madonna delle Tre Porte**, with an exquisite fresco of the Virgin.

Venosa, in northern Basilicata, was the birthplace of both Horace and Manfred. Here lie the remains of **La Trinità**, a Benedictine abbey begun in the 11th Century and never completed. The structure, built of stones from an earlier Roman temple on the site, is a topless treasure trove of inscriptions, portals, sarcophagi and frescoes romantically situated in a grassy park surrounded by olive trees. **Melfi**, just to the west, has a fine Norman castle containing the **Museo Nazionale del Melfese**, with interesting archaeological finds. Here Frederick II promulgated his *Constitutiones Augustales*, the just code of laws for which his regime is still remembered by local inhabitants.

Of the many beautiful coastal towns in Basilicata, **Metaponto** on the Ionian sea is best known for its **Tavole Palatine**, a Doric temple dating from the 6th Century BC, with 15 standing columns. The Greek city of Metapontum was founded in the 7th Century BC and is today an active archaeological center with an excellent antiquarium. **Maratea**, over on the Tyrrhenian coast, rivals Ravello in Campania for its pleasant streets and its breathtaking views over the sea. Above the abandoned medieval town (Maratea Superiore) rises an odd, monumental statue of The Redeemer, designed in 1963 by the sculptor Bruno Innocenti. The nearby resort town of **Acquafredda** has a charming and very friendly hotel called the Villa Chieta, just above a beach.

SICILY

"This timeless Grecian Etna, in her lower-heaven loveliness, so lovely, so lovely, what a torturer!... How many men, how many races, has Etna put to flight? It was she who broke the quick of the Greek soul. And after the Greeks, she gave the Romans, the Normans, the Arabs, the Spaniards, the French, the Italians, even the English, she gave them all their inspired hour and broke their souls."

— D. H. Lawrence

Nature and history have made Sicily a land of considerable and striking contrasts. The greatest island in the Mediterranean Sea, located smack in the middle of it, Sicily was for centuries the center of the known world. Its peculiar geographic position made the island vulnerable to attacks by foreigners, but at the same time helped to make it a meeting-place of Mediterranean civilizations, a bridge between East and West. This happened during the Greek colonization (8th-3rd Century BC), the Arab invasions (9th–10th Century) and the Norman dominations (11th-12th Century). These were Sicily's great epochs, when commercial towns were founded and developed along the sea. In fact, foreigners mostly stopped at the coastal areas, because of the difficult, mountainous terrain inland. Sicily's volcanic features, represented by Mt. Etna and the Eolie Islands testify to her recent geological origin. The island sometimes suffers violent earthquakes, but the lava has also made the plain at the foot of Mt. Etna immensely fertile.

The island's current state of underdevelopment compared to the rest of Italy has other reasons. First of all, the lands' organization is still feudal and unproductive in the interior, while the coastal zones, even if very productive, are not able to sell off their citrus fruit production because of foreign competition. The same thing happens with industrial products, especially sulfur and oil. Sicilian people have been forced to emigrate en masse both to northern Italy (Milan and Turin) and to foreign countries (Germany, Belgium, Switzerland). And when they find work, they are often hired to do the worst jobs.

Preceding pages, Bagheria near Palermo. Below, mosaics from Piazz Armerina.

Charms of the Ionian Coastline

A ferry-boat, goes from Villa San Giovanni in Calabria to **Messina** in half an hour. Usually the traveller arriving at Messina is surprised at finding himself in a modern city with low buildings and wide avenues; the surprise becomes astonishment because of the wonderful scenery offered by the **Peloritani Mountains** surrounding the city from the back and sloping down towards the sea.

Why does a city, founded in the classical age by Greek settlers and developed mostly between the 15th and the 17th centuries, not present its original aspect anymore? The answer lies in a fateful morning in the year 1908, when terrifying earthquake jolts, followed by a violent seaquake, shook the city and razed it almost totally to the ground. After that disaster many discussions were held about whether the city should be rebuilt or not, but at last in 1911 people decided to give birth to a new Messina.

But, even if it is difficult to find traces of the ancient Messina which Cicerone described as *civitas maxima et locupletissima* (a great and wealthy city), an unhurried traveller can take a walk along Via Garibaldi and see the church of **SS. Annunziata dei Catalani** (12th Century) and near it the **Duomo**. In spite of all reconstructions, this church still preserves its medieval structure, dating back to the period of the Norman splendor, when Messina was enriched with beautiful monuments and fortifications because of its strategic importance for the island.

The **Museo Regionale** too, on the coastal road leading to the **lighthouse**, is worth visiting to admire the *Polyptych of S. Gregorio*, a great masterpiece by Antonello of Messina, the city's most famous artist (15th Century). After a stop at **Billè** in **Cairoli Square** to taste a Sicilian sweet, keep driving along the Ionian coast through luxuriant vegetation in the direction of **Taormina**.

In the Shadow of Etna

After 45km (28 miles), the road winds to a town that perhaps is the essence of the idea of Sicily. "It is the greatest work of art and nature!" exclaimed Goethe in his book *Italian Journey*. And in fact **Taormina** has no middle tones, knows no grays and no restful colors. Its beauty is made up of light, color and sea. Lying on a short terrace of the coast against a mountain,

Taormina slopes down a cliff "as if it had rolled down there from the peak" (Guy de Maupassant). At its shoulders the village is embraced by the enormous, sometimes puffing Etna.

Climb the hillock to the **Greek Theater**, Taormina's most famous monument, celebrated by many writers because of its magnificent position. Built in the 3rd Century BC and almost completely remade by the Romans, it shows the ability of the Greeks to choose a setting where nature would enhance art.

Besides the theater, Taormina has two other distinct areas: the coast and the old town, each with its own peculiarity and role. The jagged coast reveals nature at its most dramatic: a reaching out of rocks, layers and spurs segmented by creeks, ravines, inlets. **Corso Umberto**, that cuts through the center of the **Old Town**, is the place for shopping, for walking up and down, for stopping at bars crowded with people from all over the world. Here the foreigners dominate, but Taormina can absorb the "different" into its own dimension, which is still that of a village. You can see this village in its churches (for example the harmonious and massive **Duomo**) or in the family residences

ne luxury
nd superior
osition of
e Jolly
otel at
aormina.

(**Palazzo Corvaia**, **Palazzo Ciampoli**, **Palazzo Duca di S. Stefano**) which bear witness to noble stock, with their mullioned windows, marble tracery, scrolls and swollen balconies.

Sicily's Smokestack

Leaving Taormina, Highway 18 follows the coast. The landscape is dominated by **Mt. Etna**, the majestic volcano (3.323m./10.959 ft) with its snow-capped peak. It is one of the few volcanos almost perpetually active; it takes up an area of 1,337 sq km (516 sq miles), its perimeter is 165 km (103 miles) long and presents a slope interrupted by about 200 cones, smaller craters, accumulated layers of lava, gashes and valleys. Etna's history is a series of more or less ruinous eruption, from that of 396 BC, which stopped the Carthaginians, to the latest of 1981 which destroyed part of the cableway and forced geologists to reconsider the necessity of taking drastic measures against the giant mountain.

In the fruitful plain stretching from the southern foot of Mt. Etna rises the great and beautiful city of **Catania**. It was an important Greek and Roman colony and suffered from the various dominations that succeeded in the island. Destroyed twice by violent earthquakes (in 1169 and 1693), in 1669 the city was covered by lava which even advanced into the sea for about 700 meters. Catania is the economic center of the richest area of Sicily: its development is based mainly on the growth of citrus fruits, wineries and vegetables, but also on commercial and industrial enterprises. This is why it has been named the "Milan of the South."

The city feels modern with an urban plan characterized by wide streets designed in the 18th Century by G.B. Vaccarini. Catania's main axis is **Via Etnea**, where people usually gather and walk up and down window shopping. At the beginning of this street there is **Piazza dell' Università** surrounded by 18th Century buildings (to the right, the **Palazzo S. Giuliano** to the left the noble **Palazzo dell' Università** and a few steps farther the **Chiesa Collegiata** with its elegant facade). But Catania's Baroque soul is better tasted in the smaller **Via dei Crociferi** in which churches and monastic buildings open like wings of a theater. The street is covered by a wonderful arch, it too Baroque, that links the **Great Badia** to the

A lava flow on the slopes of Mount Etna

184

Little Badia of the Benedictines. Another landmark in the history of the Baroque style is the church of **S. Niccolò**, which can be reached from Via dei Crociferi. This is the greatest church of all Sicily, whose sight makes an impression on the visitor with its unfinished facade looking like a portent of decay. Be sure to go up to the cupola from where one can have a wide view of Mt. Etna and of Catania. Passing near the **Teatro Romano** any visit to the city would be incomplete without seeing **Castello Ursino**, erected by Federico II di Svevia (1239-1250) and then restored on several occasions. At last, you can rest in the garden of **Villa Bellini**.

Town of Tyrants

The trip continues in a land of ancient civilization, from the wide plain of Catania to the very famous **Syracuse** (Siracusa) through landscapes of classical beauty, counterpointed by archaeological remains. Built in 734 BC by a group of Corinthian farmers who settled on the small isle of **Ortigia**, Syracuse developed so rapidly that in a short time it began to establish new colonies along the Sicilian coast. In 485 BC, when it had become a rich town and an appetizing booty, it was conquered by the tyrant Gelon. From this moment Syracuse enjoyed its greatest political, economic and artistic magnificence, becoming one of the most important centers of the Mediterranean. Many a time it defeated the Carthaginians, Etruscans and even Athenians until it ruled over almost all of Sicily. After short and turbulent periods of democratic regimes, there were a series of more or less enlightened tyrants: the most famous of them were Gerone, Trasibulo and Dionislio. Great monuments and public works testify to the epoch's glory and wealth; at **Ortigia**, the ancient, but still vivacious heart of town, you can admire some exceptional temples: **Tempio di Apollo** (7th-6th Century BC), and the grandiose **Tempio di Athena** (5th Century BC) which, in a later epoch, was transformed into the **Duomo**.

When you leave Ortigia across the **Ponte Nuovo** and toward that part of town called Neapolis (i.e. new town) you can visit the **Teatro Greco**, the greatest in Sicily and one of the greatest in the Greek world (138 metres [452 feet] in diameter). Here, during the months of May and June a series of high quality classical per-

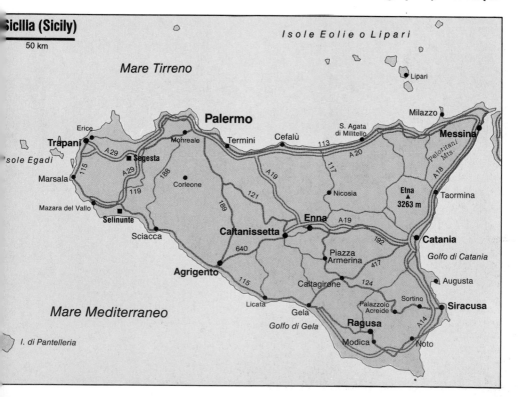

Sicilia (Sicily)

50 km

Mare Tirreno

Isole Eolie o Lipari

Lipari

Milazzo

Palermo

Erice

Trapani

Isole Egadi

Segesta

A 29

Mohreale

Termini

Cefalù

S. Agata di Militello

113

A 20

Messina

Peloritani Mts.

A 18

Marsala

115

A 29

188

Corleone

A 19

117

Nicosia

Etna 3263 m

Taormina

Mazara del Vallo

119

121

189

Selinunte

Enna

A 19

Catania

Sciacca

Caltanissetta

192

Golfo di Catania

640

Piazza Armerina

417

Agrigento

115

Caltagirone

124

Augusta

Licata

Gela

Palazzolo Acreide

Sortino

Siracusa

Mare Mediterraneo

Golfo di Gela

Ragusa

A 14

I. di Pantelleria

Modica

Noto

formances are held.

Near the theater there is the area of the **Latomie**, large ancient excavations for building stones. Later the latomie were used as prisons for those sentenced to hard labor. In the **Latomia del Paradiso**, there is an odd artificial cave known as **Dionisio's Ear**; inside the echo is prodigious, even a whisper becomes a scream which the walls send back and amplify. This phenomenon permitted the tyrant Dionisio, who was very suspicious, to listen to prisoners talking.

If you relish the ancient legends, stop at the **Aretusa Fountain** (back in the Ortigia). The beautiful nymph, in order to escape from the river Alfeo, jumped into the sea and was transformed into this spring.

Leaving Siracuse, a good destination is the small town of **Noto**. It stands out from the slopes of a hill, on the side of the **Iblei Mountains**, furrowed by a long and straight road which widens out at regular intervals with wonderful scenes of inclined squares. Here the Spanish Baroque architecture triumphs; it is in the churches, in the palaces, in the monasteries, in the squares and in the flights of steps, built with stones of deep gilded color. Noto's most interesting monument is the **Monas-**

tery of SS. Salvatore, a triumph of pilaster strips, adorned windows, loggias, terraces and bell-towers. Its strangest palace is **Villadorata**: a classic facade with Ionic columns and Baroque balconies with lions, cherubs, medusae and monsters.

Sicily's Harsh and Imposing Heart

From the coast, it is possible to go on an interesting excursion to the bare stretches of Sicily's inland to the reddish sulfur mines through lands strewn with vividly colored bushes and little villages grouped on the hills. One of these is **Piazza Armerina**, famous almost all over the world for its Roman **Villa del Casale**, dubbed by Giacomo Caputo "the eighth wonder of archaeology." This is a complex construction, built in the 3rd-4th Century AD when the great noble families of the Roman Empire sought relief from the menaces of social agitations and took shelter in the country. The villa has a series of extraordinary mosaics, the work of African artists, representing hunting scenes, imaginary creatures, natural landscapes; an entire ancient world seems to come to life before your eyes.

The harbor at Syracuse

Land of the Gods

From the neglected landscapes of the mine area, you arrive at the solar beauty of **Agrigento**, dubbed by the Greek poet Pindar as "the finest town of the mortals." The symbol of the city is a group of superb temples, so magnificent that it fills a valley. The origins of Agrigento (Akragas for the Greeks) go back to 581 BC. The 5th Century marked the apogee of the town (in that epoch the chief temples were erected), which was later conquered by the Carthaginians and by the Romans. Its importance diminished under the successive Byzantine and Arab domination, but grew again with the coming of the Normans. To the "ancient town" belong the following monuments, that are connected by the amazing "archaeologic promenade": the **Tempio di Giove Olimpico** (480 BC), the **Tempio di Giunone**, with its impressive view of the valley, the **Tempio della Concordia** (one of the best preserved temples in the world), the **Tempio di Ercole**, the **Tempio di Castore e Polluce**.

Compared to its old magnificence, the modern town is insignificant and the only points of interest are the **Duomo** (11th Century) and the Gothic church of **S. Maria dei Greci**.

The temples of **Selinunte** can be seen from afar, on a promontory between a river and a plane in the middle of a gulf with no name. The massive and slender columns lift up to the skies from a sea of rocks that crush the dark red earth. Selinunte looks like a puzzle made of stone pieces: columns divided into many trunks, chipped capitals, and white and gray cubes are all heaped one on another, as if a giant hand had mixed the pieces to make the reassembling of the original image more difficult. However the ruins' language is clear: it reveals libraries, warehouses, court-houses, temples — all of which testify to a prosperous ancient town developed in the middle of fertile lands. Amid the stones "selinon" grows, that wild parsley which gave the name to the powerful Greek colony. Selinunte was destroyed in its attempt to expand at the expense of Segesta: in 409 BC, 16,000 citizens of Selinunte were slayed by the Carthaginians.

To complete the plunge into the past, go to **Segesta**, Selinunte's rival in the 5th Century. In spite of the frequent destructions resulting from wars between the Greeks and the Carthaginians, an impos-

...uin of a ...eek ...mple, ...elinunte.

ing **Temple** in Doric order has survived till this moment. It stands on the side of an arid and wind-beaten hill and it is propped up by 36 columns. A few hundred meters farther up is the **Theater**, constructed in the 3rd Century on the top of Mount Barbaro and from which one can enjoy a splendid view on the **Gulf of Castellamare**.

The Conca d' Oro

Closed by a chain of mountains, the Conca d' Oro, an evergreen valley that widens as it approaches the sea, is still irrigated and cultivated according to old customs. The valley is dominated by **Monreale**, which was founded in the 11th Century around the famous Benedictine Abbey bearing the same name. Adjacent to the monastery, there is the cathedral, a masterpiece of the Norman age. The church owes its fame to the mosaics, probably made by a troupe of artists coming from the Eastern Empire. The mosaics represent the world's history, from the creation to the Apostles, in a golden splendor which dies away into gray giving a tone of "sad brightness" summed up by the gesture and in the glance of the huge *Pantocrator Christ*. To pass from

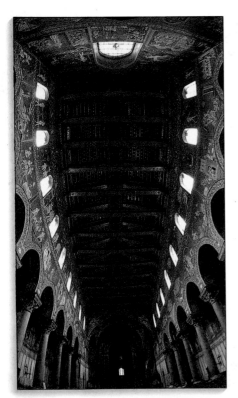

the Cathedral to the cloister is to move from East to the West. Here, the beauty is seen in the 109 groups of capitals whose sculptures show an unusual freedom in execution, typical of the Romanesque style.

After having relished the view on the Conca d'Oro from the church's terraces (180 steps), you can go on to **Palermo**, chief town and port of Sicily, situated at the bottom of a wide bay enclosed to the south by Capo Zafferano and to the north by Mount Pellegrino, which Goethe described as "the most beautiful promontory in the world."

When you first arrive, it is difficult to understand why Palermo has been celebrated as an extraordinary meeting-place of cultures. You will see only miserable cabins and desolate old buildings. But be patient and set out to discover the city without preconceived ideas.

The best place to start an itinerary in Palermo is from the high oasis of the **Palazzo dei Normanni**. Inside are the **Capella Palatina**, and **La Sala di Re Ruggiro**, both encrusted with mosaics of eastern influence. From there, follow the former **Cassaro** (nowadays **Corso Vittorio Emanuele**), the city's oldest thoroughfare, where little fantasy is needed to relive the picturesque and busy commercial life of Mussulman and Norman times. Now its appearance bears the mark of manneristic art: in the upper part there is the cathedral, a mixture of styles, from Spanish Gothic to Baroque.

Corso Vittorio Emanuele goes down to the **Quattro Canti**, in the center of the old town, a brisk cross-road cut by **Via Maqueda**, the other axis of Palermo. Here Sicily's Baroque soul dominates in the four monuments decorated with fountains and statues. Another beautiful fountain is in nearby **Piazza Pretoria**. A few steps further bring one into the Norman period, when Palermo was defined by the geographer Idrisi as the "town which turns the head of those who look at it." Here are two churches: the **Martorana**, decorated with Byzantine mosaics and **San Cataldo**, which preserves three strange little domes painted in red. A curiosity: the nuns of the church of Martorana are famous, because they cooked for the first time the savory Martorana's fruits, marzipan fruit-shaped sweets.

Between Via Maqueda and the Palazzo dei Normanni extends the **Albergheria Quarter**. Next to the desolate facades of new buildings, it is still possible to dis-

Mosaic adorned interior of the Duom Monreale.

cover old Palermo, near an open market in the quarter's center. Isolated by an artificial oasis of green, there is the small church of **S. Giovanni degli Eremiti**, a masterpiece of medieval architecture. Its five Moorish domes recall the 500 mosques that once characterized the town, as described by the traveller Ibn Hawqal in the 10th Century. The south eastern quarter of the old town, called the **Kalsa**, shows signs of a long existence, which has reduced the buildings to crumbling houses. But age old tampering does not hide the underlying massive structure of the **Palazzo Chiaramonte**, also called the Steri. Not far from here, the church of **S. Maria della Catena** is a synthesis of Gothic and Renaissance art. Taking a walk along **Via Alloro**, one arrives at the **Palazzo Abatellis**, built in the 15th Century and now restored to house the **Galleria Regionale della Sicilia**.

Have a little rest in the park of **Villa Giulia**, a good example of Italian garden, planted in 1777 with rigorous symmetry. Close by is the **Orto Botanico** which offers exotic plants, water-mirrors, rare trees among which Goethe loved to rest. Your visit of the town continues along the Marina, a promenade along the seaside, which

leads to the **Cala**, the old port. No longer used as a port, the Cala remains a picturesque shelter for its gaily-colored fishing boats, a delight for the seeker of local color. The actual center of Palermo is situated in **Via Ruggero Settimo** and in the first part of **Viale della Libertà**. Here are the best shops, several book stores, a lot of movie theaters, but few bars, because the Palermitan is not used to the life of Italian coffee-shops.

Palermo's picturesque and difficult life is still seen in the food market of the **Vucciria**, a triumph of colors, lights, sounds and voices and in the **Zisa** palace, built in the 1150 by Guglielmo I, which remembers the time when Palermo was almost the world's capital.

Along the Tyrrhenian Coastline

Along the intense blue Tyrrhenian sea the road is full of flowers and bordered by luxurious citrus-groves and olive-trees. The visitor threads his way through a winding road from which he can catch only a glimpse of **Cefalù**. A full panorama of the town, possible only from the sea, is extraordinary. One sees a little town clinging to a promontory at the foot of an

enormous rock and, to the west, a beautiful sandy beach crowded with bathers and tourist hotels and services. Cefalù's fame is due both to its natural beauty and to its medieval charm, created mostly by the Cathedral.

Eolie Islands

The Sicilian experience must end with a taste of adventure. And the best place for this is an archipelago of seven little isles emerging in front of the **Gulfo di Patti**: **Isole Eolie** or **Lipari**. Their name is indeed charming, recalling to mind Aeolus who, in Greek mythology, is the king of the winds. To the nature loving tourist, the Eolie offer the charm of the four elements, air, water, earth and fire moulded in forms of rare attraction.

Vulcano, the first to which you arrive on the ferry boat, was where Rossellini filmed his movie *Vulcano*. **Lipari**, the largest and most populated island, is the most complex geologically and the richest historically. Its pumice beach has the only white dazzling sand in the whole archipelago. Then **Salina**, the highest, the greenest, the only one which has springs of water, shows the elegant and gentle outline of her two symmetrical volcanos.

Panarea, with her little white houses surrounded by a luxurious vegetation, is a smiling land that disguises her volcanic birth. This is the most exclusive isle, a refuge for rich tourists and their luxury yachts.

Stromboli, on the other hand, is the "black giant" always restless, one of the few volcanos in the world that is constantly active. Landing at Stromboli always feels like a ritual, as if an almost religious deference toward "him," the volcano, were necessary. At a distance of five, 15 and even 25 minutes apart the distant rumbles of the explosions can be heard in the isle's silence. Stromboli is nothing more than lava, ash and scoriae. It is the youngest of the seven "sisters," born only 40,000 years ago.

The visitor to **Filicudi** and **Alicudi**, has to forget modern comforts, for there is neither electricity nor running-water. Despite such inconveniences, Filicudi and Alicudi are a paradise not only for divers and fishers (the depth contour is very rocky and irregular so that destructive trawling is impossible), but also for people who love open-air life, quiet and solitude.

Left, mosa in Palace of the Normans Palermo. Below, dancers a a church festival in Palermo.

MAFIA

To people living in Northern Italy the word "mafia" conjures up violent images of *lupara*, the shot-gun used by the Sicilian underworld, and of corpses dripping with blood. The common prejudices come from a folkloric idea: the Mafia is Sicily, a rural world, the Middle Ages. On the contrary, today's Mafia is a modern business.

The origin of the Mafia is wrapped in mystery. We are not even sure of the word's etymology. It might come from the Arabic *mu'afàh* literally (protection, but also meaning beauty, skill, ability and safety). That derivation explains, the nature of the mafia as a private and spontaneous management of society, based on a brave man watching over the weak and the fearful, who rely on him and accept his undiscussed authority over them. Mafia can also be thought of as a popular feudalism founded on audacity, and arrogance instead of military power or land possession.

There are different points of view on the exact beginning of the history of this behavior. Capuana and Pitrè give a positive judgement, dating it back to the end of the 12th Century, when a secret sect opposed the misrule of the emperors. This interpretation was supported by the Sicilian puppet theater, because the heroes of this kind of performance act like a bold Mafia member, contributing to the acceptance of Mafia by people of humble birth.

There is no question that Mafia's roots go deep into the feudal age, when the landowner gave parts of his land for cultivation to the peasant farmers. Mediators (named *gabellotti*) acting in their own interest, made farmers accept hard working conditions and low wages for farmhands and so dissuaded the owner from direct control of his land. These *gabellotti* became very powerful and, under Spanish domination the government entrusted them with the task of fighting against brigands. This kind of rural army sometimes persuaded the robbers to give back the spoil in exchange for freedom from persecution. The mediator obtained prestige and remuneration from both sides. He was named "man of honor" and people referred to him with similar problems.

When Italy was finally unified, in 1860, the particular culture of Sicily clashed with the other cultures of the nation. The feudal structure of the Sicilian economy made it difficult for the island to be included in a society beginning an industrial transformation. The farmers were deceived in their hopes of revolution and redistribution of land. The old land-owners were successful in preserving their power through their support of the new Parliament's political structure. They thought that "it was necessary that everything changed so that everything could remain the same" (as an aristocratic Sicilian writer, Tomasi di Lampedusa wrote in his novel *The Leopard*).

Sicily with all her natural resources was taxed severely to support northern industry. The impatience of the Sicilian people showed itself in open rebellion. For about 10 years the army had to quell the violent guerrillas. In its desperation to defeat them, the government used the influence of the *gabellotti* and so increased the strength of these individuals beyond that of the state itself. The people, deprived of the necessities of life, believed the *gabellotti* could provide something better.

When Fascism arrived the suppression of elections deprived the Mafia of its most important control of the political process. It has been said that the clash between Fascism and Mafia was really a struggle between two kinds of Mafia, the traditional version and that of the state. It was at this time that many Sicilian bosses emigrated to the United States, where the Mafia had already been known since the beginning of the century as "Black Hand." During this period the "mustache Petes," linked with Sicilian bosses (as demonstrated by the murder of Joe Petrosino), organized the clandestine immigration of Italians to New York, Chicago and New Orleans. After World War Two, the inquiries of Senator Kefauver caused the deportation from the United States of the most famous bosses. Upon returning to Italy, they imported and applied sophisticated methods of crime. Together with the "old mafia," there was now a "new mafia" that specialized in racketeering, smuggling, cigarettes and drugs and, during the building boom of the 1950s, in construction-site speculation.

SARDINIA

You may approach **Ólbia** (one of Sardinia's three main harbors) when the sun is sinking on the horizon and shooting light across the painted green, cobalt, grey and gold waters of the gulf, or when marvelous stars are sparkling and flashing over the silent, night-dark, land-locked harbor. It's the same setting — with different light conditions — for the first scene of a trip in a forsaken, forgotten, prehuman world. At your left the magnificent terrifying mass of rock of **Isola Tavolara** is standing out humanless, unapproachable, wild, treeless, sloping down into the sea. Behind the big hump of Tavolara island rises another hill, **Isola Molara**, almost like a wall with a flat top, a narrow long plateau, looking like a stone age ramp. You feel dizzy while the ship is rushing along in the powerful glow of the sunset or slipping carefully between the dark, lustrous waters of **Golfo Avanci**. For you, now, there is no escape.

The island of **Sardinia** (Sardegna) is the relic of a land that emerged from the sea more than 600 million years ago when the Italian peninsula wasn't yet formed and a larger Sea covered much of Europe and Africa.

No other Italian region has a richer geological history in such a limited space. A trip through Sardinia is essentially an environmental trip. The island is more attractive, and less spoiled than almost any other Italian region. The landscape of continental Italy is the typical setting of a 19th Century painting (fresh streams, ruins of ancient aqueducts, elegant little figures arranged in theatrical attitudes) or it may be the slightly more stylized setting of a Renaissance painting (soft Tuscan hillsides dotted with cypresses and gay cheerful cottages). Sardinia's landscape is a completely different thing: when it's not extraordinarily dramatic and bewitching, but only ridges of moor-like hills, burnt by the sun, running away into the distance, it's still a strange, moving, disturbing landscape. It's another world, a lunar scenery, a prehuman place that is yet worn out like the end of the world, out of time and space.

North of Olbia lies the region of **Gallura** with its tormented granite profile, its continuous alternation of hills and sloping mountains rounded and chiseled in the most varied forms; picturesque rocks towering like inaccessible castles on a background of pastures and bleeding cork-trees. The east coast of Gallura, the **Costa Smeralda** or Emerald Coast, is a rocky shore of granite covered with splendid Mediterranean bush and indented by pure, white beaches. A beautiful panoramic road winds along the coast from Golfo Aranci up to the wide bay of **Cala di Volpe** — where an elegant hotel in the modern Mediterranean style overlooks the bay. Farther north you reach the Capriccioli and the famous beach of **Romazzino**, from whence you can make an excursion to the nearby islands of **Mortorio** and **Soffio** with their enchanting little coves. On the way to **Porto Cervo** — the most elegant resort of the coast, a meeting place for the international jetset — one skirts **Golfo Pero**, a large bay with wide, empty beaches. After Porto Cervo you reach **Liscia di Vacca, Baia Sardinia** and **Porto Quato**, all pleasant beach resorts.

Palau, a small town with a resident population of NATO officers, is also the terminus for a ferry boat that services the **Isole Maddalena**. Among these islands is **Caprera**, where Garibaldi spent his last

Woman wearing a traditional costume in Sardinia.

years. His house is now a museum, the second most popular museum in Italy after the Uffizi in Florence. Another worthwhile excursion from Palau is to **Porto Raphael** with its villas, its beautiful gardens and its famous *piazzetta* protruding onto the beach. The promontory of **Capo d'Orso**, famous for the granite bear carved on its top by the wind, is nearby.

The most stunning of the granite rocks on Sardinia are to be found west of **Santa Teresa di Gallura**, near lonely **Capo Testa**, at the beach of **Calla Spinosa**.

Barbagia, the most impervious and internal region of Sardinia, the heart of the island in a historical, and cultural as well as geographic sense, offers a unique spectacle. Its imposing Dolomitic tablelands, its green heights of pine woods, its massive walls and its granite amphitheaters seem at the frontier of the world.

In this inaccessible region, easy to defend but difficult to conquer, the Carthaginians, the Romans and later rulers of the island left few traces of their presence. It was here, safely sheltered from foreign raiders, that a population of shepherds developed a fierce, proudly closed and isolated society, which even recent history has done little to transform. Here there

are no urban centers of interest nor artistic achievement of great merit; once again, the natural landscape with its solitary and wild feature prevails. But the most genuine aspects of Sardinia are here: ethnic arts and crafts, local cuisine, big traditional festivals, and the splendid costumes still worn daily in various places.

Driving south of **Dorgali** up to the **Sopramonte**, an immense uninhabited mass of rock with caves, canyons, woods and wild animals, one can see one of the most important natural environments in Europe. It's an enormous array of uncontaminated nature where trees, animals and men live in full liberty in a setting which retains the flavor of times gone by.

Besides the harsh peaks and secluded villages, the Barbagia also includes a vast eastern seafront. The most interesting segments of this coast are the **Golfo d'Orosei** and the shore of the **Ogliastra** region. The former winds through 40 km (25 miles) of white limestone walls that reach as high as 500 meters. Rarely does the Mediterranean offer a shore that is so wild, harsh and constantly surprising. To see the wonders of this coast, start at **Cala Gonone**.

A trip farther south will lead to **Santa Maria Navarrese**, another corner of paradise from which you can enjoy a stupendous view of the island of Oglisastra. Next stop should be the famous cliffs of **Arbatax**, hovering rocks of burning porphyry on a background of the intense azure of the sky and the transparency of purple on the sea. To reach the coast take exits off State road 125.

The Campidano

Typical of the south coast of Sardinia is the wide, picturesque, shallow bay called the **Golfo degli Angeli**, at the head of which looms the steep, lofty, golden town of **Cagliari**, the island's capital. Beyond the white pyramids of the local salt factories begins the vast, hospitable, fertile **Piano di Campidano**, flourishing with trees and crops. It's a long hallway — once a sea channel — bordered by ancient masses of rocks, that extends to the bay of Oristano. It's the only plain in Sardinia. The prevailing landscape is almost African: colors are strong and precise.

In the extreme southwest of the island is the wild region of **Sulcis** with its black rocks fringing into a restless sea, sparkling with foam. It is the most ancient chunk of all the Italian territory.

Map of Sardinia showing: I. Asinara, Golfo dell'Asinara, La Maddalena, I. Maddalena, Palau, I. Caprera, Costa Smeralda, I. Mortorio, Castelsardo, Soffi, Porto Torres, Olbia, Golfo Aranoi, Tempio Pausania, Sassari, Alghero, Ozieri, Siniscola, Bosa, Macomer, Nuoro, Dorgali, Cala Gonone, Golfo di Orosei, Oristano, Aritzo, Santa Maria Navarrese, Arbatax, Barumini, Sarnassi, S. Priamo, I. di S. Pietro, Iglésias, Cagliari, S. Antico, I. di S. Antica, Teulada, Golfo di Cagliari, 50 km. **Sardinia**

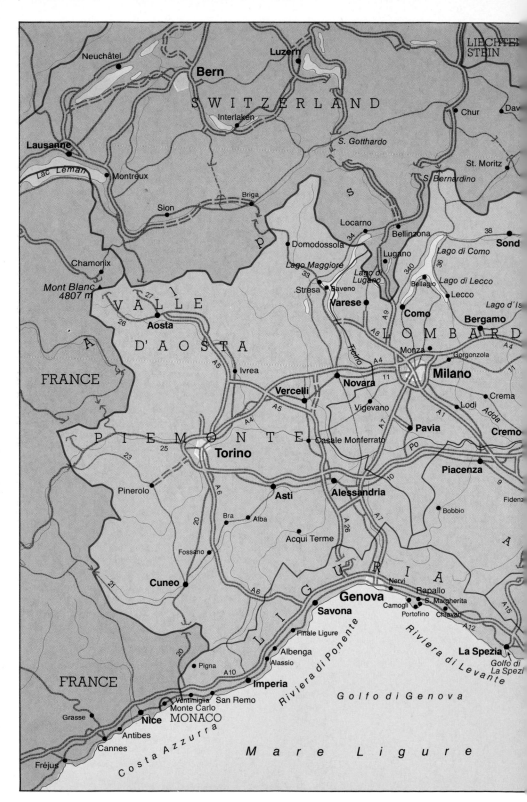

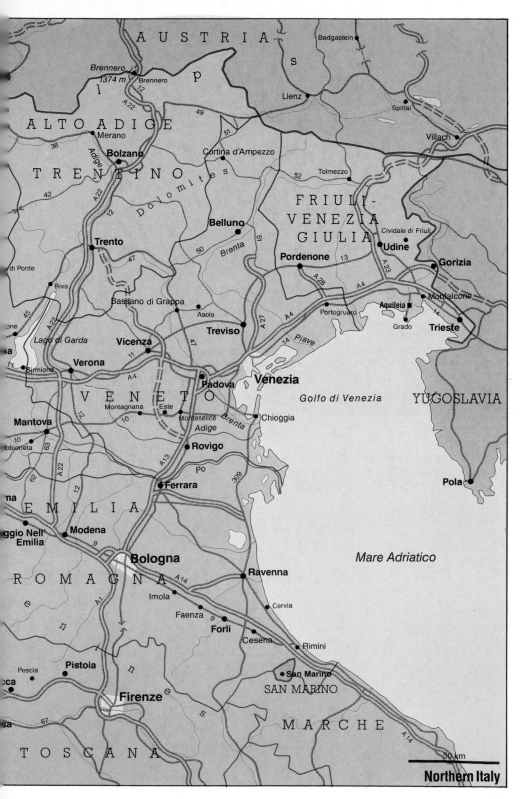

Northern Italy

THE NORTH

Above all the sense of going down into Italy — the delight of seeing the North melt slowly into the South — of seeing Italy gradually crop up in bits and vaguely latently betray itself — until finally at the little frontier Village of Isella where I spent the night, it lay before me warm and living and palpable (warm, especially) — all these fine things bestowed upon the journey a delightful flavor of romance ... Down, down — on, on into Italy we went — a rapturous progress thro' a wild luxuriance of corn and vines and olives and figs and mulberries and chestnuts and frescoed villages and clamorous beggars and all the good old Italianisms of tradition.

— Henry James (from his *Letters*, vol. I, ed. Leon Edel)

For centuries most travellers arrived in Italy from the North. They crossed the mountains from Switzerland or France and often, if physically rugged and romantically minded, as was the young Henry James, they made part of the journey on foot. The result was that Italy gradually came into focus for them, as they left behind the cold North and made their way south from the Lake District onto Milan. From there the celebrated cities of the Poe valley beckoned the visitor all the way to the Adriatic.

If at all possible, this is still the best way to see Northern Italy. Don't rush through, with your eyes on the train schedule and your mind checking off each town you have "done." See fewer cities, but see them well. Each one is so ancient, so rich in legend and art that it merits weeks. After all, this is the Italy of Shakespeare — *Romeo and Juliet*, (Verona), *The Taming of the Shrew*, (Padua). It is the Italy of Medieval communes and Renaissance princes. The great families — the Visconti in Milan, the Gonzaga in Mantua, the della Scala in Verona, the d'Este in Ferrara — are still remembered for the vile intrigues and artistic triumphs of their courts. (Best literary insight into the Renaissance in the North: Ariosto's *Orlando Furioso*.)

Our text goes onto the eastern shore where Venice and Ravenna sparkle with the gold of Byzantium; and to Padua and Bologna jammed with university students since the Middle Ages; and then to Florence, the final destination of all lovers of Renaissance Italy. The city is perfectly preserved and literally bursting with painting, sculpture and the ghosts of Dante's *Divine Comedy* (more recommended reading).

The people in the North, though generally less intrusive than the more gregarious southerners, are always pleased to answer questions and make suggestions. Especially in the smaller towns, the natives will spare a moment to give a stranger a little known fact or their personal opinion about some character who has been dead for half a millennium. And quite possibly that native, you will notice, bears more than a slight resemblance to the figures in the 15th Century frescoes of the *Duomo*. In these regions the past is always present.

MILAN AND LOMBARDY

Beneath is spread like a green sea
The waveless plain of Lombardy,
Bounded by the vaporous air,
Islanded by cities fair

— Shelley

From the heights of the central Alps to the low-lying plains of the Po Valley, the province of Lombardy is remarkably diverse. Contrasts abound in this land named for the Longobards, one of the barbarian tribes that invaded Italy in the 6th Century. There are small atmospheric cities famous for their beauty since the Renaissance; there are the incomparable vistas of the Italian lakes jutting into the heart of a steep mountain range, and the delights of rides through fertile farmlands and fields of gently swaying poplars.

Above all there is one of Europe's great metropolises — **Milan** (Milano) — center of business and high fashion, home to Da Vinci's *Last Supper* and the world's premier opera house, La Scala. The Milanese themselves are prosperous and polite, pleasant enough to the visitor but too preoccupied with their own lives to stare inquisitively at foreigners. The female tourist will receive little of the unasked-for attention that either torments or delights her farther south. Milan's reserved northern European flavor made it, according to Henry James, more "the last of the prose capitals than the first of the poetic." But there is poetry in Milan despite its modernity and efficiency.

There is no better place to begin a tour of Milan than at its spiritual center, the **Duomo**, called by Mark Twain " a poem in marble." This gargantuan Gothic cathedral, (third largest church in Europe) was begun in 1386 but not given its finishing touches until 1813. Decorating the exterior are 135 pinnacles and over 2,245 marble statues from all periods. The "Madonnina," a beautiful four-meter (13-foot) gilded statue graces the top of the Duomo's highest pinnacle.

The British novelist, D.H. Lawrence called the Duomo "an imitation hedgehog of a cathedral," because of this pointy intricate exterior. But inside, the church is simple, majestic, and vast. Five great aisles stretch from the entrance to the altar. Enormous stone pillars dominate the nave, which is big enough to accommodate 40,000 worshippers. In the apse three large and intricate stained glass windows attributed to Nicolas de Bonaventura, shed a soft half-light into the area behind the altar. The central window features the shield of the Viscontis, the ruling family of Milan during the 13th and 14th centuries. It was Duke Gian Galeazzo Visconti, the most powerful member of his family, who authorized the building of the Duomo.

A gruesome statue of the flayed St. Bartholomew, carrying his skin, stands in the left transept. In the right transept there is an imposing 16th Century marble tomb made for Giacomo di Medici by Leone Leoni after the style of Michelangelo.

The crypt contains the tomb of the Counter-Reformation saint Charles Borromeo. This 16th Century Archbishop of Milan epitomized the Lombardian virtues of energy, efficiency and discipline. Ascetic and rigorously self-denying, he expected no less from his flock, and his virulence led to frequent battles with the lay authorities, when, for example, he tried to curtail dancing, drama and sports.

The roof of the Duomo reveals a more playful side of the Milanese. Here is a

special world, a roofless treasure cave where adorned pinnacles seem like stone stalagmites, and carved rosettes are the jewels scattered on the cave's floor. The view is spectacular; on a clear day you can see the Alps. Directly below, the piazza is full of life. Pigeons wheel in flight and cluster around generous bird lovers who are tossing them crumbs. Crowded trams criss-cross the piazza, and hurried citizens, who seem even from above to be more businesslike than those of other, less efficient Italian cities, stride along.

Come down into the **Piazza del Duomo** where Milan's many worlds meet. The large equestrian statue that stands at one end is of Italy's first king, Victor Emmanuel II (namesake, you will notice, for major boulevards in cities throughout Italy). On two sides the piazza is lined with porticos, where Milanese of all ages and styles love to gather. To the north is the entrance to the **Galleria Vittorio Emanuele**, the world's oldest and most elegant shopping mall. Its four-storey arcade is full of stores, offices, bars and restaurants, but before you sit down to watch the world go by, be forewarned, the cafes are predictably pricey.

At the other side of the Galleria is **Piazza della Scala**, site of the famed **La Scala** opera house. Built between 1776 and 1778, the theater suffered serious damage during Allied bombings in World War Two, but has since been carefully restored. Here Verdi's *Otello* and *Falstaff*, and Puccini's *Madama Butterfly*, were first performed. (Puccini certainly did not benefit from Lombard self-control, his work was greeted by catcalls and worse.)

The interior of the opera house is elegantly shabby. The walls are covered in slightly worn red damask and trimmed with gilt. Crystal chandeliers provide light for about 3,000 fans.

The **Museo Teatrale alla Scala** next door is a treasure trove for opera buffs. Memorabilia include original scores by Verdi, Liszt's piano and portraits of plump primadonnas and beefy tenors. Follow the via Verdi from La Scala to the **Palazzo di Brera**, home of one of Italy's finest art collections. Paintings of the 15th to 18th centuries are especially well represented in the **Pinacoteca di Brera**. Some famous works included in the collection are Mantegna's horrifying *Dead Christ*, Caravaggio's *Supper at Emmaus*, the recently restored 15th Century *Madonna and Saints* by Piero della Francesca,

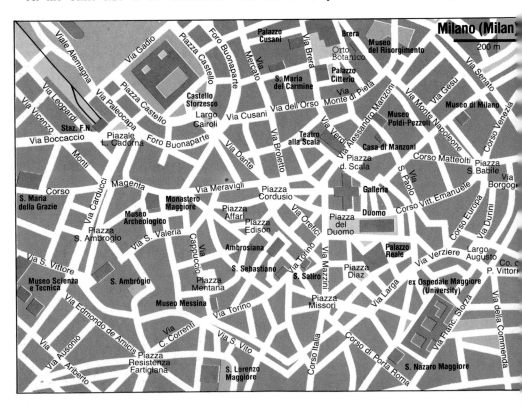

and Raphael's beautiful *Marriage of the Virgin* (lo Sposalizio), a masterpiece of his Umbrian period. Currently, the Pinacoteca is being restored and renovated, so some works have been temporarily moved to the **Palazzo Reale**, south of the Duomo.

A Despot's Dwelling

Off the Piazza del Duomo is Via Mercanto. From there Via Dante leads to the **Castello Sforzesco**, stronghold and residence of the Sforza family, the despotic rulers of Milan in the 15th Century, (*sforza* means strong in Italian.) The greatest of the Sforzas was Francesco, a mercenary general who became the fourth Duke of Milan. To design his stronghold, Francesco employed a local architect, Giovanni da Milano, but the decoration of the principal tower was undertaken by Filarete, a Florentine architect. In what was the residential part of the castle, the Corte Ducale, you can find today a magnificent collection of sculpture, including Michelangelo's *Rondanini Pietà*.

Three blocks west of the castle stands the church of **Santa Maria delle Grazie**, begun in 1466 but expanded by Bramante (in 1492), who also built the exquisite cloister. Next door, **Cenacolo Vinciano**, once a refectory for Dominican friars, is home to Leonardo's famous Last Supper (1495-1497). Because Leonardo did not use the proper fresco technique the painting is considerably damaged. The ongoing restoration cannot completely counteract the effects of time and dampness.

But despite the fact that the Last Supper is considerably faded, to visit it remains a powerful and moving experience. The work is far larger than expected, approximately nine meters (30 feet) long and 4.5 meters wide. Only some of the expressions on the faces of the disciples can be discerned but the careful composition of the work remains completely clear. On either side of Jesus sit two groups of three figures, linked to each other through the gestures and glances of the individual apostles. What is being captured is that horrifying moment when Jesus says: "One of you will betray me."

From Santa Maria delle Grazie proceed to the **Church of Sant' Ambrogio** on Via Carducci. This is the finest medieval building in Milan. To enter, you must step down from the modern street level, and cross an austere atrium. The church is

azza del
Jomo.

dark and low, but strangely compelling in its antiquity. Originally founded between 379 and 386 by St. Ambrose, then bishop and later patron saint of Milan — it was he who converted St. Augustine — the basilica was enlarged first in the 9th Century and later in the 11th. The brick-ribbed square vaults that support the galleries are typical of Lombard architecture. For a gruesome glimpse of the past, venture down into the crypt where the skeletal remains of St. Ambrose lie, along with those of two early Christian martyrs.

Down Via San Vittore from the basilica is the **Museo Nazionale della Scienza e della Tecnica**. Although the large section devoted to applied physics will probably be of interest only to specialists, everyone will enjoy the huge room filled with wooden models of Leonardo's most ingenious inventions; some of them bear a curious resemblance to modern machines.

Return in the direction of the Duomo to find the **Biblioteca Ambrosiana**, a library founded by Cardinal Federico Borromeo and built by Lelio Buzzi in 1607-1609. It now houses a small but exquisite collection of paintings from the 15th through the 17th centuries. Most notable among the works are Leonardo's *Portrait of a Musician* in Room 8 as well as Caravaggio's *Basket of Fruit* in Room 11.

Fashion Avenue

For a break from sightseeing and a glimpse of a lively and important part of Milanese life, stroll down the **Via Monte Napoleone**, which extends off Corso Vittorio Emanuele between the Duomo and Piazza S. Babila. This is the most elegant shopping street of Milan, the fashion capital of Italy.

If you have time on your visit to Milan, two more churches are worth a visit. In the Via Torino, near the Piazza del Duomo, stands **San Satiro** built by Bramante between 1478 and 80. Inside, the architect cleverly used stucco to create a trompe-l'oeil that makes the church appear to be far larger than it actually is. **San Lorenzo Maggiore**, quite nearby on Corso di Porta Ticinese, attests to this modern metropolis' great antiquity. The basilica was founded in the 4th Century and rebuilt in 1103. Martino Bassi restored it once again between 1574 and 88, but its octagonal shape and many beautiful 5th Century mosaics are original.

More modern fac of Milan.

Certosa di Pavia

An easy day trip from Milan, or a stop over on a longer journey south is the **Certosa** (charterhouse) **of Pavia**. This world-famous church, mausoleum and monastery complex founded in 1396 is a masterpiece of the Lombard Renaissance complete with relief sculpture and inlaid marble. The interior of the church is Gothic in plan, but highly embellished with Renaissance and Baroque details. Inside stand the tombs of Ludovico Visconti and his child-bride Beatrice d'Este. Their bodies are not actually buried there, but life-sized effigies atop the tombs portray them in all their life-time splendor.

Behind the Certosa is a magnificent Great Cloister where Carthusian monks, who had sworn vows of silence once lived in the individual cottages that line the sides of the elegant courtyard. Each cottage is two storeys high with two rooms on the ground floor and a bedroom and loggia above. The monk in seclusion in his cottage had his food delivered to him through the small swing portal at the right of his doorway.

Nowadays Pavia seems like a charming country backwater, but between the 6th and 8th centuries it served as the capital city for the Lombards. Pavia's fame was augmented when in 1361 the university was founded, and to this day it remains a prestigious center of learning.

On the Via Diacono in the old center is the church of **San Michele** consecrated in 1155. Here the great medieval Lombard leader Frederick Barbarossa was crowned king of Italy. Look for the carefully sculpted scenes of the battle between good and evil above the three doorways. Inside, San Michele is plain and somber; only the columns are highly decorated with fine, detailed sculpture.

Eclectic and Electric

To reach the **Duomo** follow the Strada Nuova from S. Michele. A strange sight will greet you, for this cathedral is an awkward mixture of four centuries of architectural styles. The basic design is Renaissance (Bramante and Leonardo worked on it). But the immense cupola was a late 19th Century touch and the facade was put on in 1933. The rest of the exterior is unfinished.

If you continue on the Strada Nuova you will arrive at the **Università**, where

Certosa di Pavia.

17,000 students currently attend classes. One of Pavia's most famous graduates is Volta, the physicist who discovered and gave his name to volts. His statue stands in the left-hand court of the university complex.

At the end of the Strada Nuova sits the **Castello Visconteo**, an imposing square fortress built between 1360 and 1365. Today, the castle is home for the Museo Civico. Included in the museum's collection are many fine Lombard-Romanesque sculptures and remnants of Roman Pavia — inscriptions, glass and pottery.

Go west from the castle, to reach San Pietro in Ciel d'Oro, a fine Lombard-Romanesque church. San Pietro is smaller than S. Michele, but otherwise quite similar. A richly decorated Gothic arch at the high altar is said to contain the relics of St. Augustine.

Before leaving Pavia have a bowl of the hearty *zuppa alla pavese* first concocted by a peasant woman for Francis I of France. The King was about to lose the Battle of Pavia (1525) to the Spanish when he stopped for a bite to eat at a nearby cottage. His hostess wanted her humble minestrone to be fit for a king so she added toasted bread, cheese and eggs.

Cremona

Two hours drive from Pavia lies the city of Cremona, world famous center of violin making and a pleasant market town on the banks of the Po River. The greatest of Cremonese violin makers was Antonio Stradivari (1644-1737) whose secret varnish formula may account for the beautiful, unique sound of a Stradivari violin. Some of these glorious instruments are on display at the 13th Century **Palazzo del Comune** on Corso Vittorio Emanuele and the modern International School of Violin Making nearby.

The **Duomo** at Cremona is a beautiful pink marble structure in the Lombard-Romanesque style. Although it was consecrated in 1190, it was not completed until much later. The fine rose-window above the entrance, dates from 1274. Inside the church, 17th Century tapestries of the life of Samson surround some of the heavy columns.

Mantua

Because **Mantua** (Mantova) lies on a peninsula in the Mincio River, surrounded by a langorous lagoon on three sides, it is sometimes called *piccolo Venezia*. But history, rather than geography, has given the city a more resonant name: "Ducal Mantua," because from 1328 to 1707 the enlightened, but nevertheless despotic, Gonzaga family ruled over the town from their somber fortress.

Mantua has always had a slightly musty medieval atmosphere about it. Wandering through the cobblestoned streets at night, the visitor might imagine being challenged by a couple of comic bravoes from a Shakespeare play, or happening upon one of the trysts between the unfortunate Gilda and the philandering Duke of Mantua in Verdi's *Rigoletto*. The city's history goes back even further than the Renaissance to the time when a simple peasant woman dreamed that she would give birth to a laurel bough, and soon produced the greatest of Roman poets: Virgil, who always looked on Mantua as his home town.

During the Renaissance, the Gonzaga court was one of the bright lights of Italian culture, especially under the influence of the Marchioness Isabella D'Este (1474-1539). This greatest of Renaissance women modeled her life on the text book of courtiers and ladies, Castiglione's *Cortegione*, (sort of a cross between a Pla-

Portrait of Isabella d'Este by Leonardo d Vinci.

tonic dialogue and Emily Post). She gave Castiglione a palace in Mantua. Nor was her patronage limited to literary geniuses, since she also hired Raphael, Mantegna and Giulio Romano to decorate the **Reggia dei Gonzaga (Palazzo Ducale)**. This royal blue-stocking left behind a correspondence of over 2,000 letters. But it is in the Palazzo Ducale that she left the strongest impression of herself. You can visit some of its more than 500 rooms.

Particularly worth seeing are the nine tapestries in the **Appartamento degli Arazzi** that were done in Flanders from drawings by Raphael. The **Camera degli Sposi** (the matrimonial suite) is decorated with frescoes by Mantegna that depict scenes from the lives of the Marquess Ludovico Gonzaga and his wife Barbara of Brandenburg.

Across town is **Palazzo del Te**, the Gonzaga summer residence. Designed by Giulio Romano in 1525, this palace is delicate and charming. Many rooms are decorated with frescoes of summer scenes and there is a lovely garden, though linden trees (tigli) that gave the palace its name are long since gone.

The **Duomo** of Mantva, located near the Reggia, has a Baroque facade added in 1756. Inside, the cathedral has a pleasant Renaissance design and stucco decoration by Giulio Romano, the architect of Palazzo del Te.

Also worth a visit is the **Basilica di Sant'Andrea** in Piazza Mantegna. The Florentine L.B. Alberti designed most of Sant'Andrea starting in 1472, but the dome was added in the 18th Century. Inside, Sant'Andrea is at once simple and grand. The frescoes that adorn the walls were designed by Mantegna and executed by his pupils, among them Correggio.

Bergamo

If you wish to escape from the hot stillness of "the waveless plain of Lombardy," there is no more restful or picturesque town than Bergamo, too often bypassed as tourists race along the autostrada between Milan and Venice. Bergamo is, in fact, two cities: **Bergamo Bassa** and **Bergamo Alta**. The modern Bergamo Bassa, though pleasant and spacious, is less dramatic than its parent town which rises upon a rough-hewn crag. Beneath its shadow, runs **Via Pignola** lined with elegant palaces of the 16th-18th centuries.

ooftop view
er
ergamo.

But the real treasure of Bergamo Bassa is the **Accademia Carrara**. Where else but in Italy can you find, in a small city, a collection of paintings that the grandest metropolis would be proud to have? It seems to happen by chance, in this case, the good taste of the 18th Century Count Giacomo Carrara. And there's no need to line up or push to look at paintings by Pisanello, Lotto, Carpaccio, Bellini and Mantegna since the museum is deserted except for the cordial guards.

If you're not fond of mountain climbing take the creaking funicular to Bergamo Alta, a fairytale fortified village built in a warm brown stone. The local inhabitants keep their ancient town in beautiful condition. Best place to appreciate them (and it) is the central **Piazza Vecchia** — a good spot to stop for a lunch of the local specialty *polenta con gli uccelli*. The piazza is flanked by the 17th Century **Palazzo Nuovo** and the 12th Century **Palazzo della Ragione**. Beyond the medieval building's arcade is the small **Piazza del Duomo** packed with ecclesiastical treasures: the Romanesque **S. Maria Maggiore** and the Renaissance **Colleoni Chapel** (designed by G.A. Amadeo who contributed to the Certosa di Pavia). The chapel

was dedicated to the Bergamesque condotierre Bartolomeo Colleoni who did so well for the Venetians that they rewarded him with an estate in his native province which, at that time, was under Venetian rule. Music lovers will want to visit the **Istituto Musicale Donizetti**. The overworked composer was born in 1797 in Bergamo to a seamstress mother and pawnbroker father. He died here 51 years later and quite insane, having composed close to 70 operas.

The Lakes

The Italian lakes have long been a retreat for romantics, and today they are also a playground for the rich, as well as the destination of hundreds of thousands of tourists and honeymooners from all over the world. But despite their popularity, the lakes have lost none of the charm and natural beauty which attracted writers from Pliny the Younger to Shelley, Stendhal and D.H. Lawrence to their shores. "What can one say of Lake Maggiore, of the Borromean Islands, of the Lake Como, except to pity people who do not go mad over them?" wrote Stendhal.

The westernmost lake, **Lago Maggiore**,

The Baroc interior of the Duom Bergamo.

has a special attraction: the Borromean Islands, named after their owners, a prominent Milanese family which included a cardinal, a bishop and a saint. **Isola Bella**, the most romantic of the three, was a desolate rock with a few cottages on it until the 16th Century when Count Charles Borromeo III decided to civilize the island in honor of his wife Isabella. With help from the architect Angelo Crivelli Charles designed the splendid palace and gardens. **Isola dei Pescatori**, is, as the name suggests, a fishing village. Another Borromeo palace, and elaborate botanical gardens decorate **Isola Madre**. All three of the islands are serviced by ferry boats from the main lakeside towns.

The most famous, and liveliest settlement on the shores of Lago Maggiore is **Stresa** (put on the literary map by Hemingway's *A Farewell To Arms*). In the town itself, and on its outskirts you will find many beautiful villas. Two of them adjoin the landing stage: The **Villa Ducale**, residence of the philosopher Antonio Rosmini (1797-1855), and the **Villa Pallavicino**, remarkable for its fine gardens. From Stresa it's a short drive to the summit of **Monte Mottarone**, from where you can get a stunning view of the Alps, the Lake, and the town below.

Baveno, northwest of Stresa is a small quiet town near the islands and the site of many villas, among them the **Castello Bianca** where Queen Victoria spent the spring of 1879. The drive south from Stresa to **Arona** along the Lungolago is very pretty. The road is tree-lined, the views of the lakes and islands spectacular. Arona itself is a rather unremarkable resort town, but it does contain a number of attractive 15th Century buildings.

Lago di Como is the most dramatic of the lakes. At many points the shore line is a sheer cliff, and the Alps appear like a wall at the north end of the lake. **Como** itself is a thriving industrial town. Silk weaving, which for many years was confined to homes and small workshops in Como, has been concentrated into several factories.

A pleasant spot in Como is the **Giardini Pubblici** overlooking the lake. In the midst of these gardens stands the Tempio Voltiamo, a classic rotunda that is home for many of Volta's experimental instruments. It's an easy walk across the town to **Santa Maria Maggiore**, Como's 14th Century marble cathedral. The intricately carved portal is flanked by statues of the two Plinys, among the earliest admirers of

Lake Como's splendor. "Are you given to studying, or do you prefer fishing or hunting or do you go in for all three?" the younger Pliny asked a friend and boasted that all three activities were possible at Lake Larius (Como). And 2,000 years later, Como still offers the athlete sports, the harried city dweller relaxation and the poet inspiration. Most people come here to unwind. But should man's artistic achievements tempt you to interrupt your meditations on nature from a boat or a hotel balcony, then drive to the outskirts of Como. The 11th Century **Sant'Abbondio** will throw you back to Como's pre-resort days, when it was a pious and prosperous medieval village. Chances are you'll have this solemn Lombard church to yourself. The moving frescoes of the life of Jesus, in the apse, are worth the trip.

Although the distance between the two cities is not great, it takes an hour of driving on narrow, twisting roads to reach **Bellagio** from Como. Going by public boat from Como's pier is more pleasant. Bellagio sits on the point of land that divides Lago di Como into three parts. From here you can see the entire expanse of the lake and enjoy a spectacular view of the Alps. "Sublimity and grace here com-

*illa
Carlotta,
ake Como.

bine to a degree which is equalled but not surpassed by the most famous site in the world, the Bay of Naples," wrote Stendhal in the *Chartreuse de Parme*. The Frenchman set the opening scenes of his novel in the **Villa Carlotta** (across the lake from Bellagio) where he had been a guest. Today the Villa is open to the public and its idyllic gardens provide the perfect setting for a picnic lunch.

Lecco, a pleasant city at the southeast end of Lago di Como, is famous as the setting of *I promessi sposi* (*The Betrothed*), a 19th Century novel which is a classic of Italian literature, and a revealing piece of social history. The author, Alessandro Manzoni, was a native of Lecco and a political activist instrumental in bringing about Italy's unification. Visitors can explore his childhood home, the **Villa Manzoni**.

Among the more antique attractions of the city is the **Basilica** with its fine frescoes from the 14th Century depicting the Annunciation, the Deposition and the life of San Antonio. The oldest monument in the city is the bridge spanning the Adda river, the **Ponte Azzone Visconti**, built in 1336-38.

Lago di Guarda, is the cleanest and largest of the Italian lakes. Nowadays it is particularly popular with Northern European tourists, who come to boat, water-ski and swim.

On the shores of this lake is a garish remnant of the fascist era — **Il Vittoriale** — the home of the flamboyant Italian poet and patriot Gabriele D'Annunzio. Located in **Gardone Riveria** Vittoriale is more than a house, it is a shrine to D'Annunzio's dreams of Italian imperial triumph. Included in the estate is the prow of the warship Puglia which has been built right into a hillside. In the auditorium, the plane D'Annunzio flew during World War One is suspended from the ceiling. Mussolini subscribed to all of D'Annunzio's ideas whole-heartedly, and accorded him a place of honor in fascist Italy.

From Salo and Gardone Riveria it takes no more than an hour to reach **Sirmione**, a medieval town built on a spit of land extending out into the lake. A castle, the **Rocca Scaligera**, dominates the town's entrance. It was originally the fortress of the Scaliger family, rulers of Verona, and it is said that they entertained the poet Dante here. Across town, at the peninsula's end are the ruins of a Roman villa.

Belagio, Lake Com

LIGURIA

"There is nothing in Italy more beautiful to me, than the coastroad between Genoa and Spezia."

— Charles Dickens

Liguria, a narrow strip of coastline sandwiched between sea and mountains, curves and twists in an east-west arch from the French border to Tuscany. Known as the Italian Riviera, the region is favored by a year-round mild climate, excellent beaches, and the dramatic Maritime and Ligurian Apennines which plunge in sheer cliffs or slope gradually to the sea. It is an area of sudden contrasts, not merely between rocky shores and deep green-blue water, but between cosmopolitan resorts and isolated villages, bustling ports and quiet inlets.

Genoa rises above the sea like a great theater whose tiers are elegant palazzi and whose pit is a noisy, strong-smelling port, the most important in Italy. La Superba, as the city was known in her heyday, rose to prominence between the 11th and 15th centuries, growing fat off trade with the East, and economic and cultural control of Liguria and Corsica.

Immediately behind the docks, the lower city begins. Here streets are ancient and narrow with twisting alleys called *carugi* — nowadays lined with exotic shops. The afternoon *passeggiata* in Genoa takes place on the elegant **Via Luccoli**, a *carugio* of slightly wider proportions than most. As you stroll along with the prosperous Genoese, decide whether Mark Twain was right to consider the Genoese women the most beautiful in Italy.

Not far from the dock that serves large luxury liners, is the **Stazione Principe,** an open and airy building facing a small square with a striking statue of Christopher Columbus, the most famous Genoese of all time. From the station follow the Via Balbi, an avenue lined on both sides with Renaissance palazzi. Stop at 10, the 17th Century **Palazzo Reale,** famous for its mirror gallery and its art collection housed on the second floor.

Continue toward the center of the city on Via Balbi until it becomes **Via Garibaldi.** This street splits Genoa in two; to your right are the twisting alleys of the old town, and to the left are the newer sections on the hillside. Number 11 Via Garibaldi is one of the most magnificent of Genoese palaces: **Palazzo Bianco.** This 16th Century structure was originally white, but the stone has darkened considerably with time. The facade is Baroque, part of a remodeling job done on the palace in the early 18th Century. Inside, an art collection features many extraordinary works by Flemish masters.

Across the street is the **Palazzo Rosso;** in this case time has wrought few changes in the color. Enter this palace to see the beautiful courtyard. Most of the other Renaissance residences on Via Garibaldi are privately owned and can only be admired from the outside. The Romanesque Gothic **Cathedral** (12th to 14th centuries) was, according to legend, founded by St. Lawrence in the 3rd Century. History dates the building to 1118. One of the Gothic portals bears a relief sculpture of the Roman saint's gruesome martyrdom. While being burned alive he is said to have taunted his tormentor: "One side has been roasted, turn me over and eat it."

The doors open onto a severe interior, simply decorated with black and white marble in the central nave and galleries. At the end of the left nave is the entrance

t the arborside, enoa.

to the **Treasury**, a museum of the cathedral's artifacts. Among the sacred relics of the church is a basin of green Roman glass, that according to tradition was used at the Last Supper. Many believe it to be the true Holy Grail.

The Doria family who ruled Genoa in the Middle Ages, built their houses and a private church around the **Piazza San Matteo**, two blocks behind the cathedral. All the buildings on this small, elegant, piazza have black and white facades.

To reach another fine Genoese church proceed from the cathedral down Via Chiabrera to Piazza Embriaci. Follow the precipitous Salita della Torre degli Embriaci up to **Santa Maria di Castello**, an elegant church with a complex of chapels, courtyards and gardens attached. This was once the site of a Roman camp, and several Roman columns have been incorporated into the Romanesque design of the central nave. The chapel to the left of the high altar is the home of a miraculous crucifix. Jesus' beard grows longer, it is said, each time there is a crisis in the city.

When you're tired of the churches and palaces head down to the bustling waterfront for a plate of *trenette* with *pasta alla genovese* — a pungent sauce of basil, garlic and strong cheese.

The Italian Rivieras

Flanking Genoa on either side are two famous and beautiful coasts; each offers ample doses of sand, sun and sea, but they are quite different. The **Riviera di Ponente**, stretching from Genoa to the French border, is the longer of the two, and the one with more popular resorts. The **Riviera di Levante** has an abundance of cliffs and rocky promentaries, plus a large naval port at La Spezia.

Heading towards France from Genoa, the first city you will pass is **Savona**, a port and industrial center. With the exception of a small Pinacoteca on Via Quatda Superiore, Savona offers little of interest to the tourist. The town of **Finale Ligure**, a half hour farther on is a more inviting place. Visit the **Church of San Biagio**, with an octagonally shaped Gothic bell tower adjoining.

The most important town on the Riviera di Ponente, from the artistic and historic point of view, is **Albenga**. The Romans founded a port on this site in 181 BC, but over the centuries the coastline San Rem

has shifted so today the old center is a kilometer from the beach. Surrounding the town is a well-preserved medieval wall and three large 17th Century gates. The cathedral of **San Michele** dates back to the 5th Century. Even older are the Roman aqueduct and the ruins of a Roman amphitheater. In addition to its historic monuments, Albenga offers fine facilities for swimming and boating.

The nearby resort of **Alassio** has long been popular with celebrities and ordinary Italian tourists alike. The **Cafe Roma** in the center of town has a wall —the **Muretto** — decorated with tiles bearing the signatures of, among others, Ernest Hemingway, Sophia Loren and Sir Winston Churchill.

Imperia was once two separate seaside towns: Oneglia and Porto Maurizio. It was Mussolini's idea to unite the two and name the city after a nearby river. The **Corso Matteotti**, a wide boulevard with magnificent views of the coast, links the two town centers. **Oneglia**, in the east, is the more industrial and modern sector — a center of olive oil and pasta production. A large church, **San Maurizio**, towers over the narrow streets of **Porto Maurizio**.

The Edwardian Age lives on at **San Remo**, a large, international resort, that was once a glittering gathering place for the European aristocracy. Although there is a sense that San Remo's best days have passed, the city offers two enjoyable diversions: walking along the famous palm-lined promenade; and gambling at the casino. Near the tourist office at the city's center is an authentic **Chiesa Russa** recognizable by its dome and its gilded cross, that was built by a colony of exiled Russian nobles in the 1920s.

The gateway to France is at **Ventimiglia**, a center of flower cultivation and a pleasant city with a fine medieval quarter. The major architectural attraction is the 11th Century **Cathedral**. Of great natural beauty are the **Giardino Hanbury**, located in the village of Mortola, about 6 km (four miles) from Ventimiglia. Here can be seen the living flora of five continents.

Riveria di Levante

Among the eastern suburbs of Genoa is **Quarto dei Mille**, famous as the starting point of Garibaldi's daring 1,000-man expedition that liberated Sicily and led to the unification of Italy. Nearby **Nervi** is the oldest winter resort on the eastern

coast. Here you can take hot sea baths, or follow a three-km (two-mile) cliff walk which is the city's pride.

After Camogli, take the branch off the main road that leads to **Portofino** by the way of **Santa Margherita** and **Paraggio**. Of these three resorts, Portofino is by far the most interesting. A tiny waterfront village of extraordinary, concentrated beauty, it was discovered by millionaires after World War Two. Once, only fishing boats docked in the narrow, deep-green inlet, edged on three sides by high cliffs, that is now home for innumerable yachts. Part of Portofino's attraction is its small size. There are no beaches, and few large shops and restaurants. The pleasures of the port are visual — the reflection of brightly painted houses in the clear water, the ragged edges of stone heights against the brilliant blue of the sky.

Rapallo is a family-style resort, with a large beach and many moderately priced hotels. Other attractions include the 17th Century **Collegiate Church** with its interesting bell-tower, and the 16th Century church of **San Francesco**, which houses several fine paintings by Borzone, a local artist. Nearby **Chiávari**, a wealthy shipbuilding city, once had close links with South America; in the municipal museum is a collection of Inca relics.

The Gulf of La Spezia has been praised so often by poets — Dante, Petrarch, Byron and Shelley — that it is often simply called Golfo dei Poeti. On its western point the elongated orange and yellow houses of **Porto Venere** stretch up the precipitous mountain. The resort atmosphere here is friendly and relaxed as natives exchange gossip and tourists stroll alongside the pungent harbor, home to boats with names such as "Vergilia" and "Byron." Anglophiles and romantics must make a pilgrimage to the grotto — now littered with cigarette packages, drink containers and barely clad lovers — from where the virile Lord Byron started his famous swim across the Gulf to visit Shelley in **Casa Magni**. If you take the 20-minute boat ride to **Lerici** you will appreciate what a formidable swimmer and devoted friend the poet was! Shelley, alas, had less luck against the waves when his ship sank off the coast. The plaque on Casa Magni commemorates the tragedy in the purplest Italian prose: "... Sailing on a fragile bark he was landed by an unforeseen chance to the silence of the Elisean Fields."

The seafro at Portovene

PIEDMONT AND VALLE D'AOSTA

*"If it is not so Italian as Italy it is at least
more Italian than anything* but *Italy"*

— Henry James

Piedmont (Piemonte) may strike today's
visitor, as it did James, as not very Italian.
The bordering nations of France and
Switzerland have contributed much to the
cultural life of this most north western
region. Moreover, the Alpine scenery of
Piedmont, especially in the dramatic Valle
d'Aosta is different from that to be found
elsewhere in Italy. But the particular
Piedmontese twist on basic Italian life and
custom is not unappealing. It is as if the
cool mountain breezes have had a calm-
ing effect on the population. After visiting
Piedmont, you might better understand
how it happened that a Piedmontese king,
Victor Emmanuel and his crafty Piedmontese advisor, Cavour, guided Italy to
independence.

Turin (Torino) the capital of Piedmont,
is a genuinely Italian city, but its proximity to France and its century-old ties to the
neighboring country give it a strong
French flavor. During the Middle Ages, it
was part of a Longobard duchy, but in the
16th Century it became the capital of the
French province of Savoy. Following the
Risorgimento it was the capital of United
Italy from 1861 to 1865.

Today Turin is headquarters for some
of Italy's most successful industries
including the **Fiat** and **Lancia** automobile
works. It is also a center for the chemical
and candy industries, metal working, and
industrial design. But the factories of
Turin are far from the city's gracious center, where wide streets cross at right angles
and where there are many beautiful
squares, gardens and parks for a visitor to
languish in, soaking up the sun and the
spirit of this most modern of Italian cities.

The center of civic life in Turin is the
fashionable **Via Roma**, an arcaded shopping street that connects the main railroad
station with **Piazza Castello**, a huge rectangular Renaissance square planned in
1584. In the center stands **Palazzo
Madama**, a 15th Century castle that now
houses the **Museo Civico di Arte Anchio**
(Museum of Ancient Art). Included in
this museum's collections are copies of the
famous Book of Hours of the Duc de
Berry, illustrated by Jan van Eyck.

Another fine building giving onto the
Piazza Castello is the Baroque church of
San Lorenzo, once the royal chapel. The
royal residence was the 17th Century
Palazzo Reale, in the nearby piazza of the
same name. From the balcony of this
palace, Prince Carlo Alberto declared
war on Austria in March 1848. In the
same square is the **Armeria Reale** (Royal
Armory).

Behind the Palazzo Reale, in **Piazza
San Giovanni** are the **Duomo** and **Campanile**. The former is a Renaissance construction designed by the Tuscan Meo del
Caprino; the campanile is the work of the
Baroque architect. Of far greater interest
is the chapel behind the cathedral —
Capella della Si Sindone (Chapel of the
Holy Shroud) — a work of Guarino Gua-
rini. On the altar is an urn said to contain
Christ's shroud. This relic is exhibited
only on rare occasions, and pilgrims come
from all parts of the world to take part in
the ceremony. For four centuries the
royal house of the Savoys owned the
shroud, but on his death in 1983, the
exiled king Umberto left the relic to the
Vatican. It will, however, remain in Turin.

The Piedmontese capital may seem an
unlikely center for the study of Egyptian

view over
urin with
ıe Mole
ntonelliana
n the right.

art, but there is a rich **Egyptian Museum** housed at the **Palazzo dell' Accademia delle Scienze**, off via Roma. The same palazzo also contains a good picture collection on the second floor in the **Galleria Sabauda**. There are several beautiful Flemish and Dutch works, and many paintings by Piedmontese masters.

For a taste of France, visit the agreeable **Parco del Valentino**, on the bank of the Po, which contains miles of paths, a Botanic garden and the **Castello del Valentino**, a 17th Century palace built in the style of a French chateau. In 1884, Turin was the site of a great international exhibition for which the **Borgo Medioevale** (a pseudo-medieval town), which sits in the park, was erected. It is not surprising that the automobile capital of Italy should have a fine museum of cars. One can spend hours in the **Carlo Biscaretti di Ruffia Museo dell'Automobile**, whose display includes the earliest Fiat, the Itala that won the world's longest automobile race (between Peking and Paris in 1907) and an elegant Rolls-Royce Silver Ghost.

Across the Po, a small hill, the **Monte dei Cappuccini**, is crowned by a Capuchin church and convent. After visiting here it is possible to take a bus or the rack railway to **Superga**, where you can visit the **Basilica di Superga**, a "great votive temple" (Henry James) by Juvarra that houses the tombs of the kings of Sardinia and the Princes of Savoy. This basilica sits on a high hill that commands a splendid view of the semi-circle of the Alps around the Turin plain.

Valle d'Aosta

For anyone who wishes to get away from the city, the beautiful Alpine valleys of Piedmont have much to offer in both winter and summer. During July and August the thrills of winter sports give way to the calmer delights of hiking and touring in an area with glaciers, hilltop castles, clear mountain lakes and streams, pine forests and green meadows.

The most striking part of this area is called Valle d'Aosta. In 1947, this valley acquired political autonomy and became a region in its own right. Here rise Europe's highest mountains: Mont Blanc, Monte Rosa, and the Cervino (Matterhorn). The capital **Aosta**, was an important city in Roman times and has many interesting Roman ruins. Roman walls surround the city, and the ruins of the

The automobil museum i Turin.

Roman Theater, in the northwest corner of Aosta, include the well-preserved backdrop of the stage. Emperor Augustus, nicknamed Aosta the "Rome of the Alps," and it is the Arch of Augustus that guards the main entrance to the city.

From Aosta's medieval period, the cathedral remains, along with several smaller churches. Among the latter group, the church of **Sant' Orso** (outside the walls on Via Sant' Orso) is the most interesting. The architecture is a strange mix of Gothic and Romanesque. St. Orso, who converted the first Christians in the Valle d'Aosta, is buried beneath the altar. Be sure to visit the cloister, which dates back to the 12th Century and is known for its unusual carved pillars. Each carving represents a different scene from the history of Christendom.

In the valley southeast of Aosta are many castles worth exploring. The ones at **Fénis** and **Issogne** are the most interesting. Both were used as residences and fortresses. The Lord of Verrès, Giorgio de Challant built the castle at Issogne in 1497 and 1498. Today you can stroll through the former seigneurial apartments with a collection of tapestries, jewelry and furniture.

Southeast of Turin the landscape of Piedmont is one of rolling hills, and long valleys. In some ways it is reminiscent of Tuscany, and like Tuscany it is an excellent wine-growing area. From Turin head toward **Alba** along the autostrada. If you have time, make a stop at **Bra** to see a fine baroque church, **San Andrea**, and an attractive Gothic building called the **Casa Traversa**. The small town of **La Morra**, 10 km (six miles) from Bra is surrounded by hills where one of Italy's greatest wines, Barolo is made. Between La Morra and Alba is the castle of **Grinzane Cavour**.

Alba has long been a favorite with gourmets. It sits at the center of an area where white truffles are found. These treats are a principal attraction at the city's October fair. Alba also has a fine late 15th Century Gothic cathedral, with a 16th Century inlaid wooden choir.

For more taste treats proceed to **Asti**, a city at the center of a valley that produces Asti Spumante and other famous wines. The city's Gothic cathedral is a splendid edifice with three ornate portals and circular openings above. The nearby baptistery of San Pietro, dating from the 12th Century, is the most interesting of the city's medieval monuments.

cobbled
reet in
osta.

VENICE

*I stood in Venice, on the "Bridge of
    Sighs;"*
A Palace and a prison on each hand:
I saw from out the wave her structures rise
*As from the stroke of the Enchanter's
    wand:*
*A thousand Years their cloudy wings
    expand*
Around me, and a dying Glory smiles
*O'er the far times, when many a subject
    land*
Looked to the winged Lion's marble piles,
*Where Venice sat in state, throned on her
    hundred isles!*

           — Byron

Already when Lord Byron arrived in
1817 "la Serenissima," "the Queen of the
Adriatic" had been in decline for many
centuries, "her palaces," as Byron who,
nonetheless, doted on her noted, "crumbling to the shore."

Admitting with the historians that
Venice has been on the skids since the
League of Cambrai in 1509, she remains
the most spectacular urban display in the
annals of tourism. Nor is she a trap only
for tourists, but also for poets and painters, novelists and playwrights, and esca-
pists of all sorts. (Just a few of the writers
who have found the city irresistable:
Proust, James, Waugh, Hemingway,
Mary McCarthy.) Nor can any city claim
a more prolific or talented group of home
town painters from Giorgione and the
Bellinis, through Carpaccio, Titian, Tintoretto, Veronese, Tiepolo, Longhi, Cana-
letto and Guardi.

Perhaps it is the sense of precarious-
ness, of infinite possibility, that hovers
over these 100-odd islands connected as in
some fabulous genetic chain by dozens of
delicate bridges that lead the visitor on
from one wonder to the next. There is the
sense that once one turns one's back on
their vibrant glory these bits of land that
legend says were first inhabited by
Romans fleeing the hordes of Attila will
indeed crumble away, disappear like a
mirage into the nacreous Adriatic as if by
some celestial conjuror's trick.

And yet Venice has stood there — there
is evidence everywhere of its spectacular
history — for well over a thousand years.

Most tourists have heard descriptions,
seen pictures or read books about Venice

Preceding
pages, the
annual
carnival of
Venice wit
the Bridge
Sighs in th
backgroun
Below, the
lion symbc
of Venice.

222

before actually reaching the city, but for all the most feverish imaginings arriving in Venice still has to be a revelation. Only by actually seeing the city can one believe it, and appreciate its uniqueness.

At the heart of Venice stands the vast **Piazza San Marco** with its pigeons, its trippers, its band concerts. At one end, crouching like some enormous dark vegetable inviting us to explore its inconceivable innards, is the great **Basilica di San Marco**, its five deep arches, its shimmering mosaics — some splendid, some not so splendid — its onion domes, genuine; its bronze horses, not (the real ones, thought to have adorned the hippodrome in Constantinople, are now sequestered in the Basilica's **Museo Marciano**).

The Basilica is named for the evangelist St. Mark whose remains were recovered, or stolen, depending on your perspective, by the Venetians from Alexandria in the 9th Century. The then ruler of Venice, Doge Guistiniano Participazio, first built a church on this site to house those remains. The original church burnt down 100 years later and was replaced by the huge, ornate edifice we see today.

The basilica's interior, in the shape of a Greek cross, was probably inspired by the Church of the Apostles in Constantinople. Above the columns of the four naves are the women's galleries where the ladies used to sit separately, as was the custom in orthodox churches in the east. The sumptuous atmosphere of the interior is created by the decoration of the walls: marble slabs cover the lower part, while golden mosaics adorn the upper reaches. These mosaics, found everywhere in the basilica, follow a complicated iconographic plan. For a brief explanation, join one of the tour groups that regularly circle the church. The mosaics are also the reason why St. Mark's is sometimes called 'Basilica d' Oro' — church of gold.

Among the many great works of art to be seen at the Basilica, Titian's *Last Judgement* over the north aisle should not be missed. Nor should you overlook the *Pala d' Oro* a gem-studded gold and enamel altarpiece of great antiquity (part of which is supposed to have been painted by St. Luke) that now stands behind the main altar. Visit the marble Chapel of the Crucifix off the north aisle. It's remarkable for its sharp, high roof and ornate, oriental wooden crucifix that hangs above the altar.

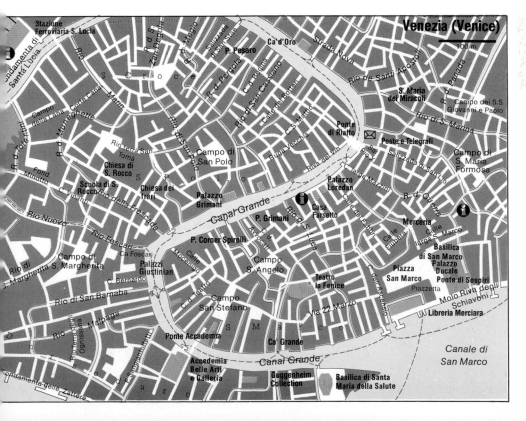

Two famous towers flank the Basilica. On the right is the **Campanile**, a faithful replica of the original tower that collapsed in 1902. Inside, an elevator, or, for the strong, a stairway, carries you up 300 feet (100 meters) to the top for a sweeping view of the city and lagoon area. The tower to the left of St. Mark's is Coducci's intricate **Torre dell'Orologio** (clock tower) designed in 1496. Two bronze mechanical Moors strike the hours.

Opposite the bell tower is the **Piazzetta San Marco**. On the right, if you face the water, is the 16th Century **Libreria Sansoviniana**. Palladio, one of Italy's most famous architects a century later, considered this structure with its fine-sculpted arcades and detailed figures, one of the most beautiful buildings since ancient times. Today it houses an archaeological museum; a national library; and the Venetian 'Old Library,' a collection of treasures from the city's golden years.

At the seaward end of the Piazzetta stand two large 12th Century columns topped with statues. On one is a winged lion, the symbol of Venice, and on the other is St. Theodore, who was the original patron of the city.

The Doge's Domicile

The **Palazzo Ducale** (Doge's Palace) borders the Piazzetta on the left. Once it was the official residence of Venice's rulers and chief magistrates. Today "the vast and sumptuous pile," as Byron wrote, convinces the visitor, far more eloquently than words ever could of the pomp and power of the Doge's city at its prime. The pink and white marble horseshoe clings like a magnet to the Basilica of San Marco. Inside all three wings unravel in endless grandiose rooms and halls. (One, the **Sala del Maggior Consiglio** was large enough to accommodate all of Venice's patricians at one time.)

The art collection housed here gives a foretaste of the treasures scattered prodigally throughout the city, particularly works by two Venetian giants, Tintoretto and Veronese. One painting, *The Paradise* by Tintoretto, is claimed to be the largest oil in the world. Veronese is best represented by *The Rape of Europa*.

Adjoining the palace is the former ducal prison. Once a prisoner had been tried and convicted in the palace, he was led across a slender covered bridge to his cell. Since it was here that a prisoner

Palazzo Ducale.

would catch his last glimpse of freedom, the bridge was nicknamed **Ponte dei Sospiri** (Bridge of Sighs). Whatever its grim purpose, the bridge has a delicate and romantic air, and today is favored by young lovers, who believe if they kiss under this bridge, their love will last.

Back in Piazza San Marco, you should be ready for a coffee break, at one of the many open-air cafes. The most famous is the **Café Florian**, which in the days of the Austrian occupation of Venice was a gathering place for local patriots. Across the way, **Quadri's** is equally comfortable and elegant.

The Watery Way

The **Grand Canal**, what James called "the great street of Venice," winds for more than two miles through the city. This splendid, shimmering S-shaped thoroughfare is lined on both sides by pastel-colored palaces in every style from Gothic to Neoclassical to Baroque, built from the 14th to the 18th centuries.

The best way to see the Grand Canal is from a boat. If you're feeling flush hire a gondola at San Marco Station (to the right of the cathedral). Thomas Mann, who said the gondolas of Venice were "black as nothing else on earth except a coffin," nonetheless found their seats "the softest, most luxurious, most relaxing in the world." For a cheaper, noisier, less comfortable ride, the public vaporettos (line 1) travel the same route.

Coming from San Marco, **Santa Maria della Salute** is on the left. To the enamored James the church was "like some great lady on the threshold of her saloon ... with her domes and scrolls, her scalloped buttresses and statues forming a pompous crown, and her wide steps disposed on the ground like the train of a robe." On the right bank opposite is the **Ca' Grande** a three-storey Renaissance residence, now the office of the city magistrate. Opposite is the **Palazzo Venier dei Leoni** which today houses a vast collection of modern art (Jackson Pollock in Venice!) assembled by the late Peggy Guggenheim. When the American playgirl millionairess was living there, the nude equestrian statue by Mario Marini in the courtyard on the canal was rumored to have a removable penis.

The first bridge that spans the canal is the **Ponte dell'Accademia** named for the nearby **Galleria Accademia**, a baroque

an Marco.

structure on the left. Enter its slightly musty innards to find the greatest concentration of Venetian masterpieces anywhere. Painters represented include: the Bellinis, Giorgione (*The Tempest*), Carpaccio, Titian, Tintoretto, Tiepolo. Another gallery, specializing in 18th Century art, is housed in the **Ca' Rezzonico**, (farther down on the left bank), where the poet Robert Browning died in 1889.

Wagner was staying at the second of the two Gothic **Palazzi Giustinian** on the left bank when he composed the second act of *Tristan and Isolde* during 1858 and 1859. Next door is the **Ca' Foscari**, also a 15th Century building in the Venetian Gothic style. The economics department of the city University now occupies this palace.

Several palaces on the right after the Sant' Angelo boat station are of particular interest. The **Palazzo Corner-Spinelli** was built during the early Renaissance in the Lombardesque style by Coducci. The **Palazzo Grimani**, now the court of appeals, is a Neoclassic masterpiece by Sanmicheli. Venice's most famous bridge the **Ponte di Rialto** arches over the canal at this point. It has two rows of shops built into it. Three pathways give pedestrians access to the shops. The architect of the Rialto was Antonio da Ponte, who oversaw its construction between 1588 and 1592.

The most beautiful Gothic building in Venice, the **Ca' d' Oro** appears on the right a little way beyond the bridge. The architect responsible was Matteo Raverti. The **Palazzo Pésaro**, an enormous Baroque building, stands nearly opposite. Longhena, architect of many 17th Century structures in Venice, designed this palace which now houses the **Galleria d'Arte Moderna**. Before you reach the railroad station at the end of the Grand Canal you will pass the **Palazzo Vendramin Calergi**, where Wagner died in 1883.

It is impossible to list all of Venice's architectural treasures or to summon up all of the the ghosts from her brilliant past. The greatest experience the city offers visitors is the personal discovery of tiny squares or narrow, silent canals. There are a few spots, however, that should not be overlooked.

Canal Tunes

Lovers of grand opera should not miss **La Fenice**, Venice's jewel-box opera house. Two of Verdi's most popular tune-

Rialto Bridge.

226

ful works — *La Traviata* and *Rigoletto* —were first performed here. According to opera legend, Maestro Verdi did not give either the tenor or the orchestra the music to "La Donna e Mobile" until just before the opening of *Rigoletto*, so convinced was he that if the catchy tune got out before the premiere, every amateur tenor in Venice would be warbling it, and claiming it as his. Verdi did not misjudge the song's popularity, and gondoliers to this day will sing it to paying passengers.

The **Mercerie**, Venice's busiest shopping street, begins just beyond the clock tower of Piazza San Marco. It leads north and west. Off to the right is the route to **Santa Marià dei Miracoli**, one of the loveliest Renaissance churches in the city. Lombardo constructed this delicate edifice in the 1480s. Inside, the walls and choir are covered with rich marble. The Doges were buried in the nearby Gothic church of **Santi Giovanni e Paolo**. In the Campo SS Giovanni e Paolo is Andrea del Verrocchio's stunning bronze equestrian statue of the fierce Condottiere **Bertolomeo Colleoni**. Turn left off the Merceria and head for the Campo Sant' Angelo, you will find the church of **Santo San Stefano**. This early Gothic church

has an elegant and elaborate brick facade. Use the Ponte dell' Accademia to cross the Grand Canal. Once on the other side it's quite a long walk to **San Sebastiano**, but the destination is worth the trip. This is a high Renaissance church filled with interesting paintings, many by Veronese.

Also on this side of the Grand Canal is the **Scuola Grande di San Rocco**. The main facade by Scarpagnino is asymmetrical, intentionally so. Inside, other unusual works of art abound. See Tintoretto's paintings of New Testament subjects, especially his crucifix, of which Henry James wrote, "surely no single picture in the world contains more of human life; there is everything in it, including the most exquisite beauty. It is one of the greatest things of art...."

Opposite is the church of **Santa Maria Gloriosa dei Frari**, called simply the Frari. Inside, the church reveals some of the best works of Venetian artists, including an exquisite Madonna by Giovanni Bellini, and Titian's sublime *Assumption*.

Island Excursions

There is much to see off the main islands of Venice. The lagoon area was

ondola ith ondolier.

settled unevenly, and as a result there are relics of many eras within a short boat ride of the city.

The island of **San Michele** is occupied by Venice's cemetery and the church of **San Michele in Isola**, built (1469-1478) by Coducci. Although both the church and cemetery are interesting they are not the most important sites in the lagoon.

Murano is the island you will next come to if you are heading out from Venice. Actually, Murano sprawls over five islands and is crisscrossed with canals that make it look like a mini-Venice. This is the center of Venice's glass-blowing industry. The local **Museo Vetrario** has many examples of beautiful glasswork, and the main street of Murano — the **Fondamenta dei Vetrai** — is lined with glass-blowing shops that offer constant free demonstrations. (You will, however, be encouraged to buy the products.)

The lace industry of Venice is headquartered at **Burano**, the next stop on the route out. Innumerable little shops on the island sell lace handkerchiefs, shawls, bedspreads, and blouses. The prices are far better than on the mainland.

Torcello, the furthest island out, is also the least populated and the most interesting. It was the site of the original settlement in the Venetian lagoon. At one time in the 7th Century, over 20,000 people lived here. Torcello was abandoned after the river Sile silted up, creating malarial marshes.

The magnificent Byzantine cathedral of Torcello was built in the 7th Century. Mosaics of the virgin and saints decorate the apses, and on the west wall is a mosaic of the Last Judgement. The sight of these mosaics alone is worth the entire 90-minute boat ride to Torcello.

This leaves to the enterprising visitor the exploration of the **Lido**, where Mann's unfortunate Koming Von Aschenbach loitered too long and contracted plague; or of **Harry's Bar**, the favorite hangout of Hemingway, where the drinks are named for great artists of Venice's past; or of the **Giardini Pubblici**, where, if it happens to be an even-numbered year, the **Biennale di Venezia** — an international exhibition of modern art — is held in a multitude of pavilions; or of the dozens of grand and not-so-grand hotels from the ultra fashionable Cipriani, Gritti and Danieli to the back street pensione where British remittance men and American teachers eke out their allowances.

The island Burano.

VENICE ENVIRONS

"Fair Padua, nursery of Arts" was how Shakespeare described the city of Italy's second oldest university, where Renaissance Englishmen came to "suck the sweets of sweet philosophy;" where (perhaps) even earlier, Chaucer met Petrarch and learned from him the anti-feminist tale of "Patient Griselda;" where Dante and Galileo lectured; and where, in at least one instance, in the mid-17th Century, a learned woman earned her doctorate. (Though most famous of Padua's daughters is without doubt Shakespeare's shrew, Katherina.)

Padua

But long before the university was established in 1222, Padua (Padova) was an important Roman town, believed by Virgil to have been founded by the brother of the Trojan King Priam after the fall of Troy, though in fact a settlement of pre-Roman tribesmen. (The Roman historian Livy was born in the nearby hills and was always proud to call himself a Paduan.)

Padua is also a gathering for the faithful. Every June, pilgrims come from all over the world to honor St. Anthony of Padua, a 13th Century itinerant preacher whose spell-binding sermons packed the pews in churches throughout Italy. The **Basilica di S. Antonio**, built over his remains between 1232 and 1307, celebrates his sanctity with works by Donatello, Sansovino, Menabuoi. Venetian influence is evident in the church's design. Byzantine domes, an ornate facade and two high, thin bell towers give the exterior an eastern appearance. The interior, despite its Gothic plan, also has many Byzantine decorative details. The Chapel of St. Anthony, where the revered tomb lies behind the altar, is a 16th Century design by Briosco.

In **Piazza del Santo**, to one side of the basilica, stands a famous equestrian statue of Erasmo da Narni, called *Gattamelata*, by Donatello. This sculpture of the great Venetian condottiere is believed to be the first great bronze cast in Italy during the Renaissance. Also in the piazza is the **Oratorio di San Giorgio**, originally a private mausoleum for the

Donatello's Gattamelata.

prominent Soranzo family. The oratory is completely decorated with beautiful frescoes of the lives of the saints by Altichiero and Avanzo. On the corner of the piazza is the entrance to the **Museo Civico** which houses paintings by Bellini, Titian and Giorgione, among others.

The via Belludi leads to another notable square, the **Prato della Valle**. A small park at its center is reached by crossing one of the four stone bridges over a circular moat. In the park itself is a circle of statues: famous past citizens of Padua.

The city centers around the crowded **Piazza delle Erbe**, one of the three market squares. Here stands the **Palazzo della Ragione**, called locally **Il Salone**, a massive medieval structure. The interior is one vast hall, decorated with fine frescoes and housing a large wooden horse copied from Donatello's bronze masterpiece.

Behind Il Salone is a large coffeebar, **Caffè Pedrocchi**, famous throughout Italy as a gathering place for intellectuals. During the Risorgimento, liberals from the nearby university would meet here to discuss the founding of the new nation.

From here it is only a short walk through **Piazza dei Signori** to Padua's **Duomo**. Although the cathedral was designed by Michelangelo, many alterations in the master's plans were allowed and the result is rather disappointing. The most interesting corner of the church is the frescoed Baptistry.

Miser's Madonna

To the north of the university lies the **Cappella degli Scrovegni**, also called Madonna dell'Arena, because of the nearby ruins of a Roman amphitheater. Enrico Scrovegni commissioned this richly decorated chapel in 1303 to atone for his father's sinful miserliness and usury. It contains a cycle of frescoes that depicts the history of Christian redemption from the immaculate conception of the Virgin Mary through the Last Judgement. The panels are considered Giotto's masterpieces; his style marked a turning point in western painting because he gave the human figure more physical solidity and emotional depth than it had had since ancient times. "In my opinion," wrote Giorgio Vasari in the 17th Century, "painters owe to Giotto, the Florentine painter, exactly the same debt they owe to nature, which constantly serves them as a model and whose finest and most beautiful

A view ove the city of Vicenza.

aspects they are always striving to imitate and reproduce ... it was Giotto alone who, by God's favor, rescued and restored the art, even though he was born among incompetent artists." (Translated by George Bull.)

It is lucky for art lovers that the Arena Chapel escaped the fate of the nearby **Erimatani** whose apse, covered with precious Mantegna frescoes, was bombed during World War Two. That was the greatest loss of art the Italians suffered during the last war.

Vicenza

Andrea di Pietro, nicknamed Palladio, the most prominent architect of the Italian High Renaissance, lived and worked for most of his life (1508-1580) in Vicenza. At that time, the gentry of the city were rich, and eager to decorate their city with new buildings. They gave Palladio many opportunities to use his talents. As a result there is hardly a street in central Vicenza not graced by a Palladian villa despite the fact that 14 of Palladio's buildings were destroyed during World War Two.

In **Piazza dei Signori** at the city's heart,

stand two of Palladio's master-pieces. The **Basilica**, his first major work, is not a church but a remodeling of a Gothic courthouse, called basilica in the Roman sense of the word — as a place where justice is administered. Palladio's elegant design features two open galleries, the lower one with Tuscan Doric columns and the upper one with Ionic columns. Facing the basilica is the **Loggia del Capitanio**, a later Palladian work with a far more ornate style. This building was commissioned in 1571 to honor the victory at Lepanto — an occasion which called for the garish details and the triumphant balustraded windows.

The city's **Duomo**, with a Gothic design, stands two blocks behind the Basilica. It was badly bombed during World War Two but has been completely rebuilt. The interior is unremarkable. A Palladian cupola tops the roof.

North of the duomo is **Corso Palladio**, the city's main street, lined with many fine villas. The architect never lived at number 163, the so-called **Casa del Palladio**. He built this house for one of the city's merchants. With its classic lines and precise, geometric proportions, it is a typical example of Palladio's work. Another

Palladio's Olympic Theater, Vicenza.

excellent specimen of the Palladian style is the **Palazzo Chiericati**, in the Piazza Matteotti, at the end of Corso Palladio. This beautiful building houses the city's art collection. Tintoretto's *Miracle of St Augustine* and several fine works by Flemish artists are on permanent exhibit.

Palladio was not the only famous architect to work in Vicenza. The younger Scamozzi, who learned much from Palladio, is famous in his own right. **The Palazzo del Comune** on the Corso Palladio, is Scamozzi's work and reflects his strict interpretation of classical architecture. But, in general, he was less innovative than his master.

The finest example of Scamozzi's and Palladio's joint work is the **Teatro Olimpico**, said to have been the first covered theater in Europe when it was built between 1580 and 1582. Palladio died before its completion; for that reason Scamozzi took over. The theater is a wood and stucco structure with a permanent stage set of a piazza and streets in perfect perspective. In 1585, the first play performed here was Sophocles' *Oedipus Tyrannus*. The theater is still in use today.

Monte Bérico, a forested hill visible from all parts of Vicenza, is well worth a visit. Take a bus from the Piazza Duomo, or walk for approximately one hour to reach the basilica that crowns the top of the hill. This is the **Madonna del Monte**, a 17th Century rebuilding of a chapel that commemorated the site of two apparitions of the Virgin. The final section of the approach is covered by a portico with 150 arches and 17 chapels. Inside, the basilica is spacious and airy. Of the works of art most notable is a *Pietà* by Montagna to the right of the altar.

During World War One, the mountains beyond Vicenza were the scene of many great battles. The **Piazza e della Vittoria** a few yards from the church, is a memorial to all the Italians who died near here. Farther down hill is the **Villa Rotonda**, a famous belvedere built by Palladio, with a distinctive circle within a cube design.

Verona

This city of Romeo and Juliet is built almost completely in the distinctive local pink marble. Verona has a rosy hue, as if the sun were constantly setting. In actuality, there is nothing faded about this modern industrial center, now at the peak of its glory. What was once a thriving

Bridge over the Adige, Verona.

Roman settlement is today one of the most prosperous and elegant cities in Italy.

The **Piazza Brà** is where Veronese gather day and night to talk, shop and drink. They sit or stroll in the shadow of the glorious 1st Century Roman **Arena**, the third largest such structure in existence. It seems large today, but it was once even bigger. The highest fragment, called the Ala, reveals the arena's original height. The Veronese have taken an interest in the arena's preservation since the 16th Century. It is often used for city fairs and, in summer, for opera.

The Roman Forum of Verona was located in what is now **Piazza delle Erbe**, off the **Via Mazzini**. This large open space has a quirky beauty due to the variety of *palazzi* and towers that line its sides. Among the most impressive is the Baroque **Palazzo Maffei**, next to the **Torre del Gardello**, the tallest Gothic structure in the square. The palace, with the attractive double arched windows on the corner of **Via Palladio** is the medieval guild house — **Casa dei Mercanti**.

The adjoining **Piazza dei Signori** is more formal than its neighbor. The **Palazzo della Ragione** stands on the border between the two squares. It's a massive structure with heavy exterior decoration; but the interior courtyard has a delicate Gothic stairway. Opposite this palazzo rises the **Loggia del Consiglio**, considered the finest Renaissance building in the city. Nearby are the tombs of the Scaligeri, dedicated to the della Scala family, the one-time rulers of Verona. The high monuments have been elaborately sculpted in the 14th Century style.

In Verona — and only in Verona — Romeo and Juliet are actual historic figures. What is now a rather seedy bar on the Via delle Arche Scaligeri, was allegedly once the **Casa Romeo**. Juliet's house is better maintained, Number 23 via Cappello, near Piazza Erbe, is a compact medieval townhouse complete with balcony. It is also possible to visit Juliet's purported final resting place. The "tomb" is several kilometers out of the center on the Lungadige Capuletti.

If your taste runs to the Gothic, head for **Sant' Anastasia** which, behind its brick facade, houses a magnificent painting by Pisanello of St. George, as well as frescoes by Altichiero and Turone. Verona's **Duomo** is nearby. Inside is Titian's *Assumption of the Virgin*.

The **Castelvecchio** on the Adige is a reminder of one of the grimmer chapters in "fair Verona's" history. The castle was begun in 1354 by the hated tyrant Can Grande II della Scala so that he might shut himself up safely if a rebellion occurred. As it turned out, he met his end, not at the hands of the mob but through the treachery and ambition of his own brother, who stabbed him. As elsewhere in Italy, this fortress, whose closets are crammed with skeletons, is now a very pleasant museum with paintings by Veronese, Tiepolo, Bellini and other artists of the Veneto.

A Saint

But in addition to a benevolent or malevolent ruling family, an Italian city must have a patron saint, and Verona is no exception. Little is known about S. Zeno, a 4th Century holy man, though it seems he was a fisherman. His most famous miracle involves this occupation and is depicted by Nicolas Pisano on the porch of the **Basilica di S. Zeno**, Verona's most beautiful church. The story goes that the saint was fishing one day when he saw an unfortunate man being pulled into the Adige by crazed oxen. St. Zeno made the sign of the cross, exorcised the devils and the man continued safely on his journey. The bronze doors of the church are of splendid workmanship though the artists who created the slightly crude, but emotionally powerful scenes are unknown.

For an explanation of these panels and all the art on and in the church, you should buy the little explanatory booklet from the bookshop; it is well worth the 2,000 lira (1984).

And a Prophet

Although S. Zeno and the Arena are Verona's most important monuments, there is no question that most people are drawn to Verona because of those luckless star crossed lovers, Romeo and Juliet. In recognition of the terrific publicity Shakespeare has given their city, the Veronese often perform his plays during the summer months in their **Teatro Romano**, an ancient construction of perfect proportion and superb acoustics. Perhaps you'll be lucky enough to see *Romeo and Juliet*. The bereaved Montague's closing speech has certainly proved prophetic: "That while Verona by that name is known,/ There shall no figure at such rate be set/ As that of true and faithful Juliet."

MOUNTAINS

Since Cortina d'Ampezzo was chosen as the site of the 1956 Winter Olympics, it has been a world-renowned center for winter sports. Facilities for skiing and skating abound, as do luxury hotels and elegant boutiques. The spectacular natural setting makes Cortina a pleasant place to visit in summer, too.

The sights of Cortina are the mountains that ring the town. Cablecars can take you to the top of **Tofano di Mezzo**, where you will enjoy a view of the entire Adige Valley. Cablecars also reach the peak of **Tondi di Faloria**. Here several trails fan out from the drop-off point. Following them, it is possible to explore the whole summit area.

The **Olympic Ice Stadium** off the Corso Italia is the best spot for skating. To find out about local skiing visit the Tourist office in the piazzetta San Francesco.

Trentino Alto Adige

This region is actually two separate, culturally distinct provinces. In the south, the area around the capital **Trent**, is predominantly Italian-speaking. The northern district centered at **Bolzano** is largely German-speaking, and includes that section of the eastern Alps known as the Dolomites. Neither of these provinces was part of the Italian unification of the 1860s and 70s. They were only brought under Italian sovereignty in 1919 as part of the peace settlement at the end of World War One.

The Dolomites

The craggy irregular peaks of the **Dolomites**, and the broad, lake-filled valleys that separate them make for a year-round vacation paradise. In winter, tourists frequent the region for skiing, skating and sleighing; in summer they come for the cool clear air, unspoilt mountain villages, and some of the best climbing on the Continent. The mountains are divided into the following groups: to the west of Trent is the Brenta Range; to the east of Bolzano are the Catinaccio, Sella and Marmolada groups; and surrounding Cortina d'Ampezzo are the Tofane, Tre Cime di Lavaredo, and Antelao. Each

Cortina d'Ampezz nestling ir the Dolon range.

group has its own major ski centers. Near Trent try **Folgaria** or **Brentonico**, near Bolzano: **Alta Venosta** or **Colle Isarco**.

For 18 years, between 1545 and 1563, Europe's attention was focused on the small and charming Italian city of Trent — site of the Council of Trent. This clerical meeting called by the Catholic church hierarchy to discuss the growing threat of Lutheranism, was a bastion of conservatism. Today, Trento is home to Italy's most modern and advanced university, famous for its active and radical social sciences division.

The most interesting buildings in Trent are its **Duomo**, a 13th and 14th Century cathedral built in a severe Romanesque-Gothic style, and the **Castello del Buonconsiglio**, (Castle of Good Counsel), the moated residence of the prince-bishops who ruled the city for centuries. This castle now houses two museums: one of war relics from Napoleonic times to World War Two, and the other of local artwork.

All around Trento are beautiful valleys and plains. To the southeast of the city is the plain of **Lavarone**, an area of deep forests, wide meadows, lakes and caves full of stalactites and stalagmites. To the north are the **Paganella** mountains, which some people consider the most beautiful in all Italy.

To reach Bolzano from Trento take the road through the complex of valleys known as the *Giudicarie*. This is a slightly longer route but the scenery is certainly well worth it.

Bolzano

Everywhere in **Bolzano** one witnesses the clash of two cultures. The city is located on the sunny southern side of the Alps along the great passageway leading to the Brenner Pass. For over 2,000 years this has been the main route between the German North and the Latin South. To its many German speaking residents, the city is **Bozen**. Street signs are in both languages, and parents can send their children to either German or Italian public schools.

Interesting churches include the Gothic **Duomo**, and **Chiesa dei Francescani**. Travel to the north end of town to see the **Castello Roncola**: the main hall is decorated with 14th Century frescoes of King Arthur.

elow, a
ow-topped
rt
nerging
om the
ountain
nes.

FRIULI-VENEZIA GIULIA

Since the 2nd Century BC, when the Romans took over the northeast corner of what later became known as the Italian peninsula, Friuli-Venezia Giulia has been a victim of foreign invasions. The Visigoths poured into the area in 403 AD; Attila the Hun — who here earned his nickname "the Scourge of God" — took over in 452; and in 489 came Theodoric and the Ostrogoths. Many of the region's most gracious modern towns, including Cividale, started out as Barbarian outposts. Venice conquered most of Friuli in 1420, and though strong Trieste managed to hold out against the Venetians, she needed the help of the Dukes of Austria to do it. Once the Austrians had gotten a foot in, they stepped in the rest of the way, kicking out the Venetians and ruling from the 18th Century until the unification of Italy.

Of all Friuli's foreign invaders, however, perhaps the most well-known is a certain young Irishman who arrived in **Trieste** in March, 1905. James Joyce may not be Trieste's favorite son — he was constantly in debt, often drunk, and given to shouting in the theater — but the city managed to overlook the oddities of his restless, self-appointed exile enough to provide him a home for the following 10 years. Here Joyce's wife, Nora Barnacle, gave birth to their two children, and here Joyce finished *Dubliners*, wrote the final draft of *A Portrait of the Artist as a Young Man*, and conceived the design of his great novel *Ulysses*.

Today the city — divided, like so many Italian cities, into the Città Nuova and the Città Vecchia — has an air of faded elegance. Once Venice's rival for trade on the Adriatic; later the gateway to the sea for the massive Austro-Hungarian empire, Trieste is now a port without a hinterland, a city that history left behind.

In the Città Nuova, long, straight avenues flank a "Grand Canal" where tall ships once anchored. Southwest of the canal is the **Piazza dell'Unità d'Italia**, said to be the largest piazza in Italy. Life in Trieste is centered on the waterfront, and the waterfront is centered at the Piazza dell'Unità, where cafés provide pleasant roosting spots from which to eye the passing scene. At the head of the Piazza stands

Trieste on the Adriatic

the ornate **Municipio**, of 19th Century Austrian inspiration. At the foot of the Piazza, across the railroad tracks, stretches the long quay or *Riva*.

It is behind the Municipio that one enters the narrow, winding streets of the **Città Vecchia**. Stairs by the **Teatro Romano** (closed to visitors) ascend steeply to the 6th Century **Cattedrale di San Giusto**. The two basilicas that originally stood side by side here were combined into a single four-aisled structure in the 14th Century.

At the top of the hill here — also named San Giusto after the city's patron saint —rises a 15th Century Venetian **Castello**, with a sweeping view of the city and the harbor. The **Museo Civico** inside the castle has exhibits of early weapons plus a small art collection.

On your way back down the hill, you may want to stop at the **Museo di Storia ed Arte**, which features relics from the various invaders and inhabitants of Friuli-Venezia Giulia: Roman sculpture and engravings, prehistoric vases, Lombard jewelry. Also worth a visit is the Basilica of **San Silvestro** on the hillside, dating from the 12th Century.

The turn of the century brought the Art-Nouveau style to Trieste. The most interesting example is the odd **Arena Edena**, at 35 Viale XX Settembre. The Arena now houses the city's off-track betting office.

For a last glimpse of Trieste, a city halfway between east and west, stop at **San Spiridione**, located near the canal. This Greek Orthodox church boasts more than 100 icons.

Seven km (four miles) west of Trieste is the seaside town of **Barcola**. There, the **Castello Miramare** once of the home of Archduke Maximilian, brother of the emperor Franz Josef of Austria, sits on a promontory overlooking the waves. Built between 1856 and 1860, this residential fortress is a strange mix of a neo-classic linear style with mock medieval details. The interior is now a museum honoring the ill-fated archduke, who later became Emperor of Mexico and died in front of a revolutionary firing squad.

The Romans based their Northern Adriatic fleet at **Aquileia**. The sea has receded in 2,000 years — today Aquileia is a small town several miles inland. The many Roman remains include ruins of the once-vast harbor, dating from the 1st Century AD. Aquileia was also a grand city in the early middle ages. The best remnant of that time is the **Basilica**, with its beautiful mosaic floor.

Though off-the-beaten track for most tourists, **Udine** has an appealing style all its own. Echoes of Venetian rule are everywhere: the 16th Century **Castello** that towers over the city was built as the residence for Udine's Venetian governors. The area around it was the only part of Udine that was seriously damaged in the great earthquake of 1976. The castle is still undergoing repairs and restoration and is closed to the public (1985). At the foot of the castle hill, lining the monumental Piazza della Libertà, are elegant buildings, Venetian in style. Along the north end is the graceful **Porticato di San Giovanni**, built in 1523. Across the piazza is the **Loggia del Lionello**, the city hall constructed in the 15th Century. The design of this colorful building shows a distinct Venetian influence. The masonary is layered pink and white, and the windows and arches have the pointed tops typical of the Venetian style.

And here Tiepolo, the greatest Venetian painter of the Baroque, did some of his best work. The city's **Duomo** on the via Vittorio Veneto has three chapels decorated by him in glorious golds and pinks.

the neo-classical church of ant' ntonio by e Grand anal, ieste.

EMILIA–ROMAGNA

"At night we were again in Bologna, of which we had not seen the gloomy arcades for two years. It must be a dreary town at all times: in a rain it is horrible; and I think the whole race of arcaded cities, Treviso, Padua, and Bologna, are dull, blind, and comfortless."

— William Dean Howells

Natives call it the "Kansas" of Italy. In Emilia-Romagna the winters are cold, wet and foggy, and the summers long and hot. This climate and the rich soil of the Po Valley make Emilia-Romagna one of the country's most prosperous farming regions. But in addition to its wealthy present, Emilia Romagna has a rich cultural past. The Via Emilia, a road first built by the Romans, cuts through the center of the region, and strung out along it are several beautiful cities — Rimini, Bologna, Modena, Parma and Piacenza — all first founded by the Romans as way stations along the road from the Adriatic to the interior. The other major cities of

Emilia-Romagna, Ferrara and Ravenna, are off this main thoroughfare. In the Renaissance, Ferrara was home for the Este family whose court was a center of culture and learning. Ravenna was a great international center from the 4th to 8th centuries first as the last capital of the Western Empire then as the seat of the Byzantine Emperors.

Bologna

Bologna, the capital of Emilia-Romagna, is a city of half a million people famous for its university, its sausage, its Communist party and its beautifully preserved historic center. Many of Bologna's old buildings are of a soft orange-red brick and most have marble or brick porticoes attached on the street side. In rainy weather it's possible to walk for blocks in the center of Bologna and never get wet.

The old city revolves around two huge adjoining squares, the **Piazza Maggiore** and the **Piazza Nettuno**. On the east side of the Piazza Maggiore stands **San Petronio**, the largest church in Bologna. Originally the competitive Bolognese had hoped to make this edifice even bigger than St. Peter's in Rome, but church

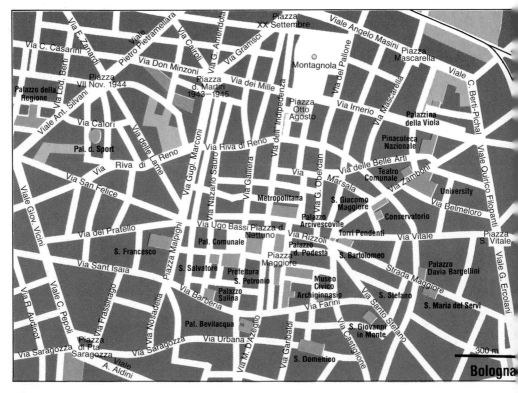

authorities decreed that some funds must be set aside for the construction of the **Archiginnasio** nearby. San Petronio is still imposing. The design is by Antonio di Vincenzo, and although construction began in 1390, the facade is still unfinished. The completed sections are of red and white marble and decorated with reliefs of scenes from Biblical history.

The interior of San Petronio is simple but elegant. Most of the bare brick walls remain unadorned. In the fifth chapel on the left is a spectacular 15th Century altarpiece of the Madonna and saints by Lorenzo Costa. At the east end of this aisle is a museum which includes interesting plans for the completion of the facade and the enlargement of the church. Cross over to the south aisle, where in the eighth chapel are to be seen intricately carved inlaid stalls by Raffelle da Brescia.

Behind San Petronio is the Archiginnasio, now home of the municipal library but once an important building of the university. The world's first lessons in human anatomy were given at Bologna University, and upstairs at the Archiginnasio is an actual 17th Century anatomical theater.

The Piazza Nettuno has many attractions. At its center is the **Fontana del Nettuno**, a 16th Century fountain with bronze sculptures of the muscle-bound god Neptune surrounded by cherubs and mermaids. On its west side is the Majestic **Palazzo Comunale**, a medieval building remodeled in the Renaissance by Fieravante Fieravanti. The bronze statue above the gateway is of Pope Gregory XIII, a native of Bologna. To the left is a beautiful terracotta Madonna by Nicolò dell 'Arca.

From Piazza del Nettuno follow the **Via Rizzoli**, a picturesque street lined with cafes, down to the **Piazza di Porta Ravegnana**, where you'll find yourself at the foot of the **Due Torri**, or "Leaning Towers" of Bologna. In medieval days 180 of these towers were built by the city's aristocratic families; now only a dozen remain. Legend has it that the two richest families in Bologna — the Asinelli and the Garisendi — competed to build the tallest and most beautiful tower in the city. If this story is true, then the Asinelli won, for the Torre Garisenda was built with a weak foundation and could not be finished. For safety's sake it was shortened between 1351 and 1360, and is now only 48 meters (157 feet) high and leans more than three

Preceding pages, view over Bologna. Below, news and gossip in Piazza Maggiore, Bologna.

meters (10 feet) to one side. The Torre degli Asinelli is still standing at its original height of 97 meters, but it too leans, more than a meter, out of the perpendicular.

The **Strada Maggiore** leads east from the two towers along the original line of the Via Emilia to the **Basilica di San Bartolomeo**. Inside, look for an Annunciation by Albani in the fourth chapel of the south aisle, and a beautiful Madonna by Guido Reni in the north transept. Farther down the Strada Maggiore is **Santa Maria dei Servi**, a well-preserved Gothic church that was begun in 1346 and enlarged later in the 14th Century.

The **Basilica di Santo Stefano** — a complex of churches all dedicated to St. Stephen the martyr is located off the Via Santo Stefano. Of the several churches, the most interesting is the polygonal **San Sepolcro**, where San Petronio, patron saint of Bologna, is buried near the striking Romanesque pulpit. To the left is **Santi Vitale e Agricola**, the oldest church of the group, a 5th Century structure containing several Roman capitals and columns. In San Sepolcro is the entrance to the 12th Century **Cortile di Pilato**, "Pilate's courtyard," and beyond this open courtyard is the church of the **Trinità**, a dark, 13th Century building.

Bologna's **University**, the oldest in Italy, an institution founded in the 11th Century and famous in its early days for the revived study of Roman law, is located on **Via Zamboni**. Petrarch attended classes here, as did Copernicus. For many centuries, the university had no permanent quarters. Today, although various faculties are spread about the city, the university's formal center is the 16th Century **Palazzo Poggi**.

Past the university on the left is the **Pinacoteca Nazionale**, home of an interesting and varied collection of Italian painting. Although the emphasis of the Pinacoteca's collection is on the development of Bolognese artists from the Middle Ages through the 1700s, also included are a number of fine Renaissance works by artists who were not natives. Look out for works by Vitale da Bologna, (especially the painting of St. George and the Dragon), and Frederico del Cossa and Ercole de' Roberti of the Ferrarese school. And on no account miss Raphael's great *Ecstasy of St. Cecilia.*

South and west of the Piazza Maggiore, Bologna has more architectural treasures to offer. Follow the **Via Ugo Bassi**

Bologna is the "sausag capital" of the world.

242

west to **Piazza Malpighi**. On the west side of this Piazza rises **San Francesco**, constructed between 1236 and 1263, with a design of French Gothic inspiration. The larger of San Francesco's two towers and the surrounding decorative terracotta are the work of Antonio di Vincenzo. Though badly damaged in the war, the tower has been skillfully restored. Inside, San Francesco is pretty and bright.

From San Francesco walk southeast to reach **Palazzo Bevilacqua**, a 15th Century building in the Tuscan style. Here, the Council of Trent met for two sessions after fleeing an epidemic in Trent. Nearby **San Domenico** is a church dedicated to the founder of the Dominican order. The tomb of St. Dominic stands in a chapel off the south aisle.

Bologna has earned many epithets, "La Dotta" (the learned one), "La Turritta" (the turreted one), and finally "La Grassa" (the fat one), for here the rich cooking of Emilia-Romagna reaches its height. So when you have had your fill of history and architecture, it is time to eat. Specialties, besides the obvious baloney sausage, are mortadella sausage, tortellini, and the tagliatelle, said to have been invented for the marriage feast of Lucrezia Borgia and the Duke of Ferrara. These long, light-colored noodles were inspired by the bride's lovely locks. The Bolognese dress their tagliatelle with *ragu*, known in its watered down state as "meat sauce," but here in its home town forms an incredibly thick blend of beef, ham, vegetables, cream and butter.

Modena and Parma

Since the Romans conquered Modena in the 2nd Century BC, the city has thrived. In the past, the sources of Modena's wealth were the rich farmland of the Po plateau that surround it, and its position on the Via Emilia. This famous Roman road still runs through the center of Modena, but the city has new riches; the auto factories where Maserati and Ferrari sports cars are manufactured.

Modena's massive and magnificent Romanesque **Duomo** sits right off the Via Emilia. The building dates back to the end of the 11th Century when Countess Matilda of Tuscany, then ruler of Modena, decreed that a cathedral should be built worthy of receiving the remains of St. Geminiano, the patron saint of the city. Matilda commissioned Lanfranco, the greatest architect of the time, to design the cathedral.

The partly Gothic, partly Romanesque bell tower that stands to one side is the famous **Torre Ghirlandina**. In this tower is housed a bucket that was stolen from Bologna in 1325 and sparked off a war between the two cities. The Italian poet Tassoni immortalized the incident in his celebrated poem *La Secchia Rapita* (The Stolen Bucket).

Strolling around Modena one is apt to see the smartly-dressed students of the **Accademia Militaire**, Italy's military academy which is housed in a 17th Century palace at the center of Modena. Another Modenese palace, **Palazzo dei Musei**, contains an interesting art collection and the **Biblioteca Estense**, the library of the Este family, dukes of Modena as well as Ferrara. On permanent display in the library are a number of illuminated manuscripts, a 1481 copy of Dante's *Divine Comedy*, and the stunning Borso d'Este Bible which contains 1200 miniatures of the Ferrara school of the 15th Century.

If you think Parmesan cheese is just for sprinkling over pasta, you are missing a wonderful treat. True *Parmigiano* (as opposed to the sawdust you buy pre-

University students sitting by the Neptune Fountain, Bologna.

grated in supermarkets) can be sliced and eaten just like any other cheese. There is no better place to become a connoisseur of this hard sharp-flavored cheese than here at its source. **Parma**, a pleasant, medium-sized city that, thanks to nearby mountains, has a cooler, fresher climate than other spots in the muggy Po Valley.

The history of Parma is full of interesting personalities. Napoleon's widow Marie Louise (Maria Luigia to the Parmesans) was ceded this city after her husband's death, and despite her reputation of being overly fond of the opposite sex, she did much for Parma. She built roads and bridges, founded orphanages and other public institutions. It was she who started the picture gallery in the 16th Century **Palazzo della Pilotta**. Hanging there are four great canvases by Emilia's master painter, Correggio, whom Bernard Berenson called "too sensuous." However, the main esthetic attraction of Parma is the **Duomo** and adjoining Baptistry. Even in this region famous for Romanesque churches, Parma's 11th Century cathedral stands out, for its nave and cupola are decorated with splendid frescoes by Correggio. Contemporaries gushed over these masterpieces: Titian said that if the dome of the Cathedral were turned upside down and filled with gold it would not be as valuable as Correggio's frescoes. Vasari wrote of the *Assumption*, "It seems impossible that a man could have conceived such a work as this is, and more impossible still, that he should have done it with human hands. It is extraordinary in its beauty, so graceful is the flow of the draperies, so exquisite the expression on the faces." (Text ed. by B. Burroughs).

The Baptistry is the work of Benedetto Antelami, who built this octagonal building in the rich red Verona marble and then sculpted the reliefs that adorn both the interior and the exterior.

In the dome of **San Giovanni Evangelista**, another splendidly sensuous Correggio fresco can be seen. It depicts St. John gazing up at heaven where the rest of the apostles are already sitting with Christ.

If you are driving northwest on the Via Emilia toward Piacenza, consider making a quick stop in **Fidenza** to see another glorious Romanesque cathedral. Just beyond Fidenza is the turn off for the little town of **Roncole**, where you can visit the humble cottage in which Giuseppe Verdi, the titan of Italian opera, was born and spent his early youth.

In the revolutionary year of 1848, when Prince Charles Albert of Savoy called for Italians to join together under his leadership and form an independent nation, the citizens of **Piacenza**, by way of a plebiscite were the first to respond. This vote of rebellion was a remarkable event in Piacenza's otherwise peaceful history. Situated at the point where the Via Emilia meets the Po, Piacenza has been a lively trading post and farmer's market since 218 BC. Although nothing remains of the Roman period, Piacenza is the site of many fine medieval and Renaissance buildings.

At the center of the city is the massive **Palazzo del Comune**, called "Il Gotico." This town hall was built during Piacenza's "Communal Period" (approximately 1200–1400) when the city was an independent and important member of the Lombard League that defeated Emperor Frederick II of Hohenstaufen in his bid to conquer Italy completely. "Il Gotico," begun in 1280, is a remarkably well-preserved building of brick, marble and terracotta. In front of it stand two massive Baroque equestrian statues of Piacenza's 16th Century rulers, the Farnese dukes. On the left is Duke Alessandro Farnese, and on the right Duke Ranuccio, his son.

At the end of the Via Venti Settembre stands Piacenza's Romanesque **Duomo**. Although rather gloomy on the inside, the cathedral is worth a visit for the frescoes on the columns near the entrance. These depict saints, who are meant to appear as if they were standing amidst the congregation.

Ferrara

A prosperous modern market-town on the banks of the Po River, Ferrara seems at first glance to be peaceful and provincial. But the city also has a colorful history and treasures to delight any visitor. In the southern part of the city is a well-preserved medieval town, and to the north are long broad avenues lined with Renaissance palazzi and their carefully groomed gardens.

The Este family ruled Ferrara from the late 13th Century until 1598. At the ducal court the Este surrounded themselves with poets, scholars and artists and at the same time insured that lively commerce and trade kept Ferrara wealthy. The Renaissance was the city's golden age, and is echoed in all its major monuments.

Dominating Ferrara's skyline is the huge medieval **Castello Estense**. Because of its moats, draw-bridges and towers, the castle looks like something off a Hollywood set. The interiors are disappointing, but it is possible to visit the dungeons, a must for fans of medieval romance and adventure.

Two blocks behind the castle is Ferrara's 12th Century cathedral. Among the noteworthy paintings in the Duomo and adjoining museum: Cosimo Tura's *San Giorgio* and his *Annunciation* and Jacopo della Quercia's *Madonna della Melagrana.*

Across from the Duomo is the **Palazzo del Comune**, a medieval building with a beautiful Renaissance staircase. The piazza in front of this town hall is the center of life in modern Ferrara. The passagiata is a daily event here. Not all Ferrarese are on foot, however, bicycles are the rage in this town without hills.

The beautiful **Palazzo di Schifanoia**, one of the Este's summer residences, is on the other side of the medieval section. Many of these streets south of the cathedral are lined with fortified houses. And stretching across the **Via delle Volte**, a narrow street near the Po, are several ele-

gant arches. At the Este palace, climb the steep stairs to the Salone dei Mesi, a large, high room decorated with colorful frescoes of the months of the year. These lively works were executed for the Duke of Borgo d'Este by various masters of the Ferrarese school including Ercole de' Roberti.

Down Via Mellone from Schifanoia, is another smaller Este palace, **Palazzo di Ludovico il Moro**, designed completely by the famous Ferrarese Renaissance architect Biagio Rossetti. Although the plan of the building is actually simple and stark, the elaborate decoration gives the palazzo an ornate effect.

North of the Duomo, Ferrara is a city of broad avenues. Along one of the prettiest of these streets, Corso Ercole D'Este, stands Rossetti's **Palazzo dei Diamanti** a large Renaissance structure with a unique facade. The diamond, emblem of the Este family is repeated there 12,600 times.

Rimini

Today Rimini is two cities: the old Medieval and Renaissance town, and the ultra-modern beach resort a mile distant. In the skyscraper hotels that line Rimini's

te Castle, rrara.

seashore, you are more likely to hear German or English spoken than Italian, but the old center retains its native charm despite the constant influx of tourists and money.

The infamous ruler Sigismondo Malatesta has left his mark everywhere in Rimini. It was this anticlerical patron of art who presided over the transformation of a 13th Century Franciscan church into one of the most spectacular Renaissance buildings in Italy. The **Tempio Malatestiano** is considered more a personal tribute to Sigismondo's mistress Isotta degli Atti, (who later became his third wife), than a church. But perhaps that is what Sigismondo intended since he and the church authorities were never the best of friends. Pope Pius II even went so far as to excommunicate the violent and sensual Sigismondo, and to condemn him publicly to hell.

Sigismondo had better luck with women and artists than with religious types. He was patron for such great artists as Piero della Francesca and Leon Battista Alberti, among others. It was Alberti who designed the exterior of the Tempio. (He found inspiration in the Roman Arch of Augustus that still stands at the gates of Rimini).Note the wide classical arches on each side of the entrance. The interior rebuilding was supervised by Matteo de Pasti, and although the simple single-nave plan and wooden-trussed roof of the original Franciscan church remain, the side chapels (some added and others only redecorated) are opulent and intricate in design. Immediately on your right as you enter is Sigismondo's tomb, decorated with his initials intertwined with Isotta's. This insignia, which looks vaguely like the dollar sign, recurs often throughout the church.

To the left of the Tempio is the **Piazza Tre Martiri**, named in honor of three Italian partisans hung there by the Nazis in 1944. The piazza is also the site of the ancient Roman forum, whose columns now support the porticoes of the two eastern buildings.

Walk out of the piazza along **Corso di Augusto** for four blocks. At the end of the corso stands the **Arco di Augusto**, dating from 27 BC. With this archway the Romans marked the juncture of the Via Emilia and the Via Flaminia, their primary road north from Rome to the Adriatic.

Not part of Emilia-Romagna or even of

The beach Rimini ge little crowded.

Italy, **The Republic of San Marino**, 27 km (17 miles) from Rimini, has been an independent state for more than sixteen centuries. The tiny state thrives today on tourism and the sale of seemingly innumerable commemorative postage stamps. Most of San Marino's 61 sq km (24 sq miles) of territory are on the slopes of Monte Titano. From the summit, you can enjoy a panoramic view of the capital, San Marino (of Rimini) and the sea. Within the town walls, the church of **San Francesco** and the adjoining **Pinoteca** are interesting sites.

Ravenna

When the unstoppable Barbarians overran Rome in the 5th Century AD, Ravenna benefitted, gaining the honorable rank of Capital of the Western Empire. This Adriatic port town continued as capital under the Ostrogoths, and the barbarian leaders Odoacer and Teodoric also ruled their vast dominions from here. Later, when the Byzantine emperor Justinian reconquered part of Italy, he too made Ravenna his seat of power, liking it not only for its imperial tradition under the Barbarians but also,

and perhaps more importantly, for its direct sea links to Byzantium.

Under Justinian's rule the Ravenna we know today began to take shape. New buildings arose all over the city, including a handful of churches that are among the wonders of Italian art and architecture. There is no preparation, in their simple brick exteriors, for the brilliant mosaics within. It is these mosaics that make modern Ravenna, if no longer Capital of the Western World, at least a capital of the western art world. No visitor to Italy should miss them.

Start with **San Vitale**, the city's great 6th Century octagonal basilica, famous for the mosaics in its choir and apse. These "monuments of unaging intellect," as W.B. Yeats put it, immediately draw the eye with their marvelous colors, and their intricate detail that manages to suggest even the flesh and bones beneath the garments of human figures. Bright ducks, bulls, lions, dolphins, a Phoenix intertwine with flowers and oddly angled corners of buildings to frame Old Testament scenes and portraits of Byzantine rulers with a humor and exactitude reminiscent of the Nile scenes in mosaics from Pompeii. There is a sense of eternal color

and freshness here, an unalterable brightness of startled birdsong that, as Yeats wrote, might "keep a drowsy emperor awake."

Old Testament scenes in the lunettes of the choir include (left to right) Jeremiah and Moses on Mount Sinai; two scenes from the life of Abraham, including Abraham's hospitality to the angels (with Sarah in the background) and the Sacrifice of Isaac; Isaiah and the life of Moses; and the offerings of Abel and Melchisedech. In the dome of the apse a purple-clad and beardless Christ sits on a blue globe flanked by archangels and, at his far sides, Saint Vitalis and Bishop Ecclesius. Christ hands the saint (Ravenna's patron) a triumphal crown while the bishop (who founded the church in 521) carries a model of the structure as it finally appeared many years after his death. Below stretch imperial scenes of Justinian with his courtiers and Theodora, his beloved wife, with hers.

San Vitale is not the only place to see mosaics in Ravenna. Nearly every church contains a pristine example of the art. Just north, another set may be seen at the **Mausoleo di Galla Placidia**. This interesting lady was born a Roman princess, sister to Emperor Honorius, but after she was captured by the Goths, she intelligently married their leader, Athaulf and ruled with him. He, however, soon died, and she next married a Roman general whom she bore a son. This son became Emperor Valentinian III. As Valentinian's regent, and a woman with connections in the highest barbarian circles, Galla Placidia played a powerful role in the world of "the decline." The building that houses her tomb has a simple exterior but inside the walls, floors, and ceiling are completely covered with decoration. Overhead the Cross floats in a star-strewn sky. Above the doorway, Christ appears as the Good Shepherd, surrounded by lambs, and opposite is St. Lawrence with his gridiron. Round about appear the apostles and the evangelists.

Through the gate that lies between San Vitale and Galla Placidia are two Renaissance cloisters that now house the **Museo Nazionale**. The museum includes, as one might expect, many mosaics as well as other relics from Ravenna's past. There's glass from San Vitale to see and also fabrics from the tomb of St. Julien at Rimini.

A pleasant walk along Via Fanni, Via Barbiani and left onto Via d'Azeglio leads to Ravenna's **Duomo** — originally constructed in the 5th Century but redone in the Baroque style in the 1730s. Far more attractive than the cathedral itself is the adjoining **Battistero Neoniano**, a 5th Century octagonal baptistry that was once a Roman bath house. The interior combines spectacular Byzantine mosaics with marble inlay from the original bathing establishment.

Across Piazza Cadutti from the cathedral complex is **San Francesco**, another 5th Century church almost completely redone in the Baroque style. To the left stands **Tomba di Dante**, not a remarkable building architecturally, but of great historic interest. The author of *The Divine Comedy* was exiled from his home in Florence for his political outspokenness and found refuge in Ravenna in 1317. He spent the remaining four years of his life here, putting the finishing touches to his great work. His latin epitaph, carved in 1327, may be roughly translated as follows: "The rights of monarchy, the heavens and infernal lakes of the Phlegethon that I visited I sang, as long as mortal destiny decreed. But my soul was taken to a better place and reached its creator among the stars. Here I lie buried, Dante, exile from my birth-place, a son of Florence, that loveless mother." The poignant epitaph was written by one of his contemporaries.

After Dante's death, the repentant Florentines would dearly have loved to honor their famous son with a splendid tomb, but proud Ravenna refused to give up the poet's remains. The battle over the bones continued for hundreds of years. At one point in 1519, it looked as if Ravenna would lose. The powerful Medicis of Florence sent their representatives to Ravenna with a papal injunction demanding the relics. The sarcophagus was duly opened, but the bones were not inside! Someone had been warned of the Florentine scheme, and had removed the bones to a secret hiding place. They were not found again until 1865. The bones now rest within the sarcophagus that is on display.

Down the Via di Roma from the troubled tomb is another church full of beautiful mosaics: **Sant Apollinare Nuovo**. The scenes are of processions, one of virgins and the other of martyrs who appear to be moving toward the altar between rows of palms. Above, the decorations depict episodes from the life of Christ.

San Vitale Ravenna.

248

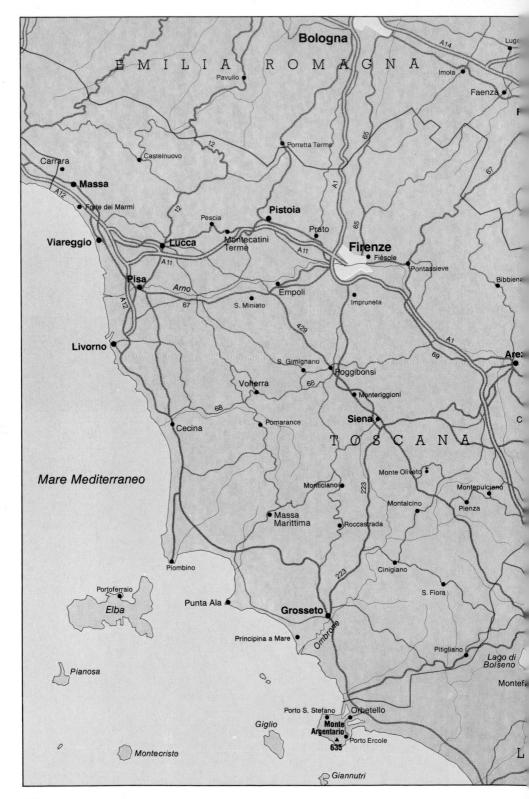

Tuscany, Umbria and The Marches

30 km

venna

Cervia

A 14

Bellaria

sena

Rimini

Riccione

Cattolica

S. Marino

Pesaro

SAN MARINO

Fano

Urbino

Fossombrone

Senigallia

73

A 14

Ancona

Ostra

polcro

Pergola

Iesi

S. Maria di Porto Novo

Sirolo

Numana

Osimo

Città di Castello

M A R C H E

76

Cingoli

Recanati

Gubbio

Fabriano

Macerata

Civitanova Marche

Umbertide

Tolentino

77

Perugia

Camerino

Fermo

Assisi

3

go simeno

Spello

75

A 14

Marsciano

Foligno

Amandola

S. Benedetto

Porto d' Ascoli

Montefalco

Ascoli Piceno

U M B R I A

Vettore

▲

2478 m

4

Todi

Norcia

Arquata

Roseto d. Abruzzi

Spoleto

Teramo

3

A 14

Terni

Montereale

Pescara

Narni

79

80

Penne

terbo

Tevere

A B R U Z Z I

A 1

Rieti

Cittaducale

17

L'Aquila

I O

A24

17

Mare Adriatico

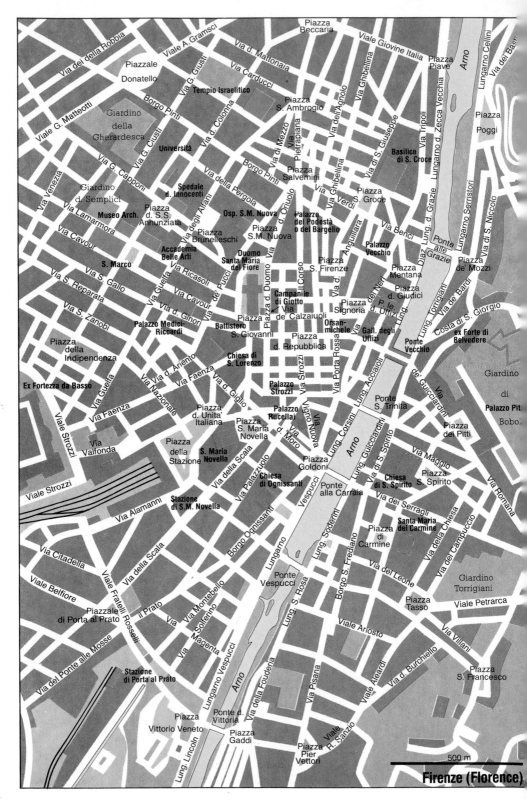

Firenze (Florence)

FLORENCE AND TUSCANY

Girt by her theatre of hills, she reaps
Her corn, and wine and oil – and Plenty
leaps
To laughing life, with her redundant
Horn.
Along the banks where smiling Arno
sweeps
Was modern Luxury of Commerce born,
And buried Learning rose, redeemed to a
new Morn.

— Byron

Tuscany, Goethe observed, looks like Italy should. Fortunately for today's visitors, not much has changed in the two centuries since the German poet was himself a tourist in *Toscana*. Although the city of Florence, capital of the region, is often shrouded in an acrid haze of smog, in most of the rest of Tuscany the air and light are still pure and soul-lifting. Urban sprawl has stayed at a minimum, and Tuscan cities and towns quickly give way to wondrous countryside. On arrival here, every fantasy from your days as an armchair traveller will be satisfied. The steep hills of the eastern and central part of the region, latticed by olive orchards and vineyards, are if anything more beautiful than in the photo books. The coast, especially near the town of Grosseto, is warm and inviting. And everywhere there is history, from the Etruscan stronghold of Fiesole to the Roman colony of Volterra to the Renaissance splendor of Florence.

The Good Life

The feel of Tuscany is quintessentially Italian as well. Although the citizens may be a bit more reserved than their neighbors farther south, they are still open and friendly. Despite the millions of tourists who pour through their towns every season, somehow the Tuscans have managed to hold onto a firm sense of themselves. They live comfortably, and joyously, amid the history and natural beauty of their surroundings. And they feed on the land's bounty, through some of the region's heartiest foods. Not to be missed are *bistecca alla fiorentina*, a huge grilled steak, cooked with nothing but a little olive oil and served with lemon wedges. *Cacciucco*, or fish stew, is the gastronomic legacy of Livorno, on the Mare Tirreno, and a host of wild game, from birds to boar, can be found in the marshlands of the Maremma, along the southern coast. Then, of course, there is chianti, the ruby-red Tuscan wine with its stout but smooth quality that goes so perfectly with Italian food.

In short, Tuscany offers the best of Italy. The *lingua Toscana* is the purest dialect in the country. Birthplace of the Renaissance, Tuscany produced the first humanist, Petrarch, and, in Macchiavelli, the first truly modern political mind. In science, art and architecture, Galileo, Michelangelo and Brunelleschi all came to their full flowering here. The ultimate Renaissance man, Leonardo da Vinci, was born in a hamlet near Florence. A feast for the senses and the intellect as well, Tuscany cannot help but please.

Even it you didn't know that Florence (Firenze) was the birthplace of the Renaissance, you could guess it. The city is imbued with a sense of harmony and grace, dignity and serenity. Surrounded by gentle hills dotted with villas and villages, Florence is marked by the tranquil and unobtrusive course of the Arno through the city's jumble of umber-colored, red-roofed buildings. The scale is small, manageable on foot: human, in the best Renaissance tradition. Unlike the Rococo femininity of Paris or muscular strength of Manhattan, Florence calls to mind the ordered graciousness of London or the quaint bookishness of Boston. It is not simply a man's town, but a gentleman's town, full of shop windows displaying handsome leather wallets, silk ties and old architectural prints in burled wood frames. Florence is, after all, associated with some very famous men — Dante and Donatello, Ghiberti and Galileo, Macchiavelli and the Medicis, and San Giovanni (Saint John the Baptist), the patron saint honored every June 24 with a sportsmanly football game in medieval costume, topped off with fireworks.

Florence's apparent order and dignity rests on a history of strife. The city was born when a fissure in Etruscan tribes occasioned some members to leave the Fiesole hill and settle by the river. A Roman encampment followed, leaving behind the via Romana — the old Roman way — and the name, *Florentia*, meaning, prophetically "destined to flourish." Goths and Byzantines and Lombards followed, then clashing Guelphs and Ghibellines, warring Blacks and Whites, and the deadly Black Plague that, taking no sides,

receding
ages, the
owd
agerly
waiting the
art of the
alio.

wiped out half the city in the 14th Century.

Birth of the Renaissance

And despite the appearance of harmony and balance, Florence holds its surprises. Approaching the center of the city, the **Piazza San Giovanni**, you file through sober streets lined with buildings presenting a stern and defensive face. Suddenly, there's the **Duomo** with its 19th Century facade of marble — green from Prato, pink from the Maremma, white from Carrara — as festively and floridly worked as a bake shop cake; there's Giotto's delicate **Campanile**, similarly decorated; and the octagonal **Baptistry**, dating from the 9th Century, with its glittering mosaics in the interior and its famous gilded bronze doors outside. If it is possible to pin the birth of the Renaissance on a date, place or event, it is here, at the baptistry. The north doors are the result of a contest in 1401 between Ghiberti and Brunelleschi: first in a series of public works commissions that fueled and financed the Renaissance. Winner Ghiberti's later east doors are the ones so magnificent Michelangelo dubbed them "the Gates of Paradise."

Brunelleschi countered with his own "first" — the first great architectural feat of the Renaissance — and it looms over his rival's doors: the gigantic dome of the **Duomo** (Santa Maria del Fiori), the first massive dome since antiquity (construction began in 1420). The interior of the Duomo is also noted for its size (10,000 Florentines could fit in for Savonarola's sermons), much of its art having been moved to the **Museo dell' Opera del Duomo** behind it.

The museum, set up specifically to house works of art, seems an aberration in a city where art, history, science and literature are inextricably woven into city life. Even Florence's great museums functioned first for other purposes: the **Uffizi** was an office building; the **Pitti** Palace a private residence; the **Bargello**, a prison. Places of worship saw other service: the church of **Orsanmichele**, just south of the Duomo, was once a granary — you can see the grain shoots on the columns inside — and its exterior is studded with sculptures of the patron saints of various guilds.

Nowhere was art more a part of everyday life than at **San Marco**, to the north of

Brunelleschi's dome of Florence's cathedral.

256

the Duomo. The church is unremarkable; the cloistered convent is a marvel. Every monk's cell is adorned with a Fra Angelico fresco — a tranquil *Visitation*, a tender *Annunciation* — for the quiet meditation of its inhabitant. At the end of the corridor is the religious zealot Savonarola's room from which he was dragged in 1498 ultimately to be burned at the stake, just as he had previously exhorted the burning of books in his Bonfire of the Vanities. It is also at San Marco that, with Florence's gift for incongruity, you'll find Europe's first public library.

Near San Marco is another first — the first outdoor architectural accomplishment of the Renaissance — the graceful loggia of the **Ospedale degli Innocenti** (Foundling Hospital), designed by Brunelleschi and built in the 1420s. With its touching della Robbia tondos of babies wrapped in swaddling clothes, the loggia is far-removed in spirit from its famous next-door neighbor: Michelangelo's towering statue of *David* (1501–4) in the **Galleria dell' Accademia**. The original of all the copies you see about town, David stands proudly in his own rotunda, bathed in light, the focal point of a long hallway lined with Michelangelo's un-

finished *Slaves*. The setting is splendid; here is the Renaissance ideal; here is man at his noblest.

The Florentine Renaissance was dominated by the Medici family, rulers and patrons of the arts from the 1300s to the 1700s. Heading back towards the Duomo are two monuments to their influence. The commission for the **Palazzo Medici-Riccardi** on Via Cavour was supposed to go to Brunelleschi, but Cosimo Medici feared his design would be too grand and alienate his populace. The resulting edifice, by Michelozzo, is marked by its solid classicism and by a tiny interior chapel frescoed by Benozzo Gozzoli to show the Journey of the Magi: in reality, the faces are those of Medicis. At the nearby church of **San Lorenzo**, with Brunelleschi's measured, mathematical interior, are the Medici's private chapel, crypt and library, masterful examples of Michelangelo's skill at sculpture (the statues of *Dawn* and *Dusk, Night* and *Day* on the tombs in the New Sacristy, 1520–34) and architecture (the sweeping staircase of the **Biblioteca Laurenziana**, 1524–34).

Outside San Lorenzo, the bustle of the street market, purveying old clothes, new clothes, leather goods and trinkets,

otticelli's ewly leaned *Primavera*.

quickly dispels the stateliness within. The proceedings reach their pitch inside the big cast-iron **Mercato Centrale** — two floors stocked with sides of wild boar, fresh herbs, porcini mushrooms, tripe, tomatoes, squid, eel: a cornucopia of food stalls.

If San Lorenzo is the church of the Medicis, **Santa Maria Novella**, to the west, near the train station, houses the private chapels of the powerful Strozzi and Rucellai families. (The patrons' homes — the impressive **Palazzo Strozzi** and Alberti's **Palazzo Rucellai** are, naturally, in the neighborhood.) In Santa Maria Novella's peaceful cloister are the frescoes of the Spaniards' Chapel, depicting Catholic life; in the church's apse are the graceful frescoes of Domenico Ghirlandaio (1485-90). Commissioned by Giovanni Tornabuoni, a prominent Florentine, to show the lives of the Virgin and St. John the Baptist, they also provide a valuable look at contemporary city life at its most elegant and refined.

Tornabuoni Chic

The **Via Tornabuoni**, heading towards the river, is lined with the great names in Italian fashion: Ferragamo and Gucci, Armani and Valentino. Nearby is more modern-day Florence: the **Piazza della Repubblica**, built in the 19th Century, with a parking lot in its middle, surrounded by open-air bars.

A piazza of truly historical dimensions is close at hand: the **Piazza della Signoria**, with its crenelated and towered **Palazzo della Signoria**, or **Palazzo Vecchio** (1299) — the town hall that inspired others of its kind throughout Tuscany. The mood at this center of civics and politics is majestic yet sinister: here is the underbelly of Florence's history. The spot where Savonarola was burned at the stake is marked on the Piazza's stone pavement; Ammannati's **Neptune** fountain is sneeringly dismissed as "ruined marble"; the bordering **Loggia dei Lanzi**, where Swiss lancers stood guard, displays sanguinary statues of rapes and beheadings; and the Palazzo's **Salone dei Cinquecento** — one of the largest public assembly halls anywhere — is frescoed with scenes of bloodshed and battle.

Behind the Palazzo, a similar-looking tower holds equally sinister associations, for this is the tower of the **Bargello**, the prison that's now the National Sculpture

The Ponte Vecchio.

Museum. Bells tolled here when an execution took place. Up the steps of the Bargello's evocative courtyard are masterpieces of Renaissance sculpture: Donatello's early marble *David* and later bronze *David* (a saucy youth and the first free-standing nude statue since antiquity), his *St. John, St. George, Marzocco* (the city's heraldic lion), and Brunelleschi's and Ghiberti's competing panels for the Baptistry doors.

One of the great museums of the world stands just next door to the Palazzo Vecchio: the **Uffizi** Gallery, designed by Vasari in 1554 as a government office building. Long, broad, windowed corridors lead to galleries holding highlights of the history of art, from 13th-Century Cimabues to 17th-Century Rembrandts, with the finest and largest collection of Renaissance art anywhere in between — room after room of Raphaels, Lippis, Titians and Botticelli's exquisite and much-loved *Birth of Venus* and *Primavera*.

To see Michelangelo's tomb, along with Machiavelli's and Galileo's, head to the east, to **Santa Croce**. Behind what everyone delights in calling a horrible new facade, Santa Croce's interior is splendid, with a floor that's a jigsaw puzzle of marble tombs, chapels frescoed by Giotto with his solid, voluminous figures, and, off the cloister, Brunelleschi's gem of Renaissance design, the **Pazzi Chapel** — small in scale, pure in line, restful and rational in spirit, and tremendous in its impact on the history of design.

Jewelers' Bridge

Bridging the Arno is the famous **Ponte Vecchio**, lined with jewelers' shops since 1593 (its goldsmith heritage is honored by a bust of Benvenuto Cellini in its center) and the only bridge not to have been bombed into oblivion during World War Two. The Ponte Vecchio will take you to the **Oltrarno**, the other side of the Arno, where the atmosphere is often more like that of a country village than a major city. Nowhere is this better felt than at the **Piazza Santo Spirito**, in front of Brunelleschi's noted church of the same name, with its benches and trees and lazy little open air market. Nearby is the church of **Santa Maria del Carmine** with revolutionary frescoes by Masaccio: breakthroughs in three-dimensional space (*The Tribute Money*) and human emotion (the poignant *Adam and Eve*, expelled from Paradise).

The Oltrarno contains another of the world's great art museums, the 15th Century **Pitti** Palace: squat and stern on the outside, gilded, lined with silks, and hung with chandeliers — and great paintings — in its interior galleries. The collection scattered through opulent state apartments is vast, ranging from antique vases to Titians, Raphaels and Rubens. The setting is dazzling, and the feeling that of viewing a private collection at the gracious invitation of the resident royalty.

The grandiose formality of the Pitti enhances the innate intimacy and charm of the 11th Century church of **San Miniato**, perched on a nearby hill. A veritable jewel, with its intricately carved pulpit, its zodiac-inlaid floor, its della Robbia vaulted chapel, and the touching cemetery on its grounds, San Miniato is one of the best-loved churches of Florence. Walk down the hill to the **Piazzale Michelangelo** for one of the world's finest views: the hills of Fiesole and Bellosguardo, cradling the whole of Florence — from Santa Maria Novella in the West, to Santa Croce in the east, from Brunelleschi's great dome to the Palazzo Vecchio's slender tower — spread out before you in all its glory.

The Church of San Miniato rises gracefully above Florence.

Florence Environs

Three excursions outside Florence are often recommended: Prato, Pistoia and Fièsole.

In **Prato**, see the rich heritage of fresco master Fra Filippo Lippi (1406-1469). In midlife, the cleric Lippi fell in love with Lucrezia Buti, a novice nun. She served as the model for many of his Madonnas and Salomes, and the two lovers eventually produced a son, Filippino (1457-1504), an artist in his own right. The elder Lippi's legacy can be seen in the Prato **Duomo** especially in frescoes of the Banquet of Herod, Salome's Dance and scenes of St. Stephen and St. John. Here too is the **Cappella del Sacro Cingolo**, a chapel said to contain the girdle of Mary. As legend has it, the Virgin appeared in a vision before the Apostle Thomas, handing him her girdle as proof to the doubting saint of the resurrection of Christ and her own assumption.

The residents of Pistoia had such reputations for violence that the first handguns in Italy were named after the daggers, or *pistolese* they often carried. Remnants of the city walls are impressive, as are the Gothic **Palazzo del Comune** and the della Robbia terracottas on the facade of the Duomo. But both Prato and Pistoia are heavily industrialized, and in truth are worth a visit only for true art buffs. Given the choice of a trip to either town or an extra half-day in Florence, by all means choose the latter.

On the other hand, leap at an opportunity to visit Fièsole. For centuries the Etruscans and the Romans made this hilltop city south of Florence a major garrison in the region. On the **Piazza Mino da Fièsole**, once the site of a Roman forum, is the **Duomo**, with works by sculptor Mino da Fièsole. Head left of the church up the steep hill for a spectacular view of Florence — literally all of the city laid out at your feet. Farther up, on a small landing just to the right, is the tiny, austere church of **Sant' Alessandro**, built on the site of a temple to the Roman god Bacchus. On top of the hill is the monastery of **San Francesco**, with small, lovely cloisters and monk's cells. Swing down through the cool, leafy public gardens to the archaeological site, where there is a trove of Etruscan and Roman treasures, including a perfectly restored Roman *teatro*, or amphitheater, the ruins of a bath and temple and a small museum.

To the southeast of Florence, through some of the most forested and mountainous terrain of Tuscany, is **Arezzo**. Behind severe defensive walls, the city, with its steeply-pitched, dark and narrow medieval alleyways, presents a forbidding face. Indeed, Arezzo strategically positioned to command all passes of the central Apennines, was once a Roman stronghold. Even the city's world-renowned attraction — the church of **San Francesco**, smack in the center of town — is surprisingly plain. Its unadorned facade of umber brick, and its stark nave, offer no clue to the beauty and delight lurking just behind the altar: the *Legend of the True Cross* frescoes by Piero della Francesca (1416-1492). They trace the story of Christ's cross from its mythic beginnings as the tree that proffered sinful fruit to Adam, to its rediscovery by St. Helena. Scholars toast these frescoes for their geometric approach to anatomy, and mathematical handling of spatial arrangements. Ordinary travellers are more often enchanted simply by their humanity.

Arezzo's **Duomo** pales in comparison. Up the sloping via Cesalpino to the north east, adjacent to the pleasant **Passeggio del Prato** park, the Duomo, built between the 13th and 16th centuries, sits behind an unremarkable 20th Century facade. Inside you'll find a few high points: impressive tombs, brilliant stained glass windows by early master, Marcillat, a Piero della Francesca fresco of Mary Magdalen, and in a side chapel, charming della Robbia terracottas.

The church considered an Arezzo landmark is **Pieve di Santa Maria**, built between the 12th and 14th centuries and standing midway between the Duomo and San Francesco on the **Corso Italia.** No matter about directions: you'll have no trouble finding it — its tall campanile is pierced by 40 bifora windows, earning it the nickname "the tower of 100 windows." The church itself vaunts a delightful facade — three tiered loggias — that make it a prime example of Pisan-Lucchese Romanesque architecture.

Santa Maria forms one of the boundaries of the **Piazza Grande** — an intimate, quiet, sloping square undeserving of so imposing a name. It is surrounded by medieval buildings, many still with their wood balconies, and many housing antique shops. The square itself is the site of a popular antiques fair the first Sunday of every month, as well as a colorful joust in the 12th Century costume the first Sunday in September. The Renaissance also stakes a claim along one flank of the square, with native son Giorgio Vasari's stately loggia, reminiscent of his design for the Uffizi in Florence. You can visit Vasari's own home, the immensely ornate **Casa di Giorgio Vasari** in the north of -town, on the Via Vente Settembre. Other favorite sons: the poet Petrarch, the writer Pietro Aretino, the artist Spinello Aretino, and a man known simply as Guido d'Arezzo — the inventor of the musical scale and the inspiration for the city's annual international choral festival.

Siena

Enter Siena and step back to the Middle Ages. Not to the dark side of the era, when plague, pestilence and war were the lot of the common man; no, Siena's spirit is more that of Camelot. Sitting along the edge of the steeply sloping **Campo**, or square, you can almost see the knights on horseback and hear the trumpets blare. Formed by the confluence of the three hills on which Siena is built, the chevronshaped square is divided into nine sections, commemorating the beneficent rule of the Council of Nine "Good Men" who governed Siena from the mid-13th through the early 14th centuries, a period of exceptional stability. (Traffic is barred here, as it is in most of the central city.)

Twice a year, on July 2 and August 16, the Sienese faithfully recreate their medieval heritage in the *Palio*, a sumptuous pageant-cum-horserace around the Campo. This is no mere tourist event; the residents of the city's *contrade*, or districts, pack the square as their representative horses and riders career around the Campo, and the rider who wins the race and the *Palio*, a heraldic banner, becomes an instant local hero.

At the base of the square is the **Palazzo Pubblico**, with its crenelated facade and waving heraldic banners. Erected in the early 14th Century, it housed the offices of the city government. At its left corner is the slender tower fondly called the *Mangia*, or wastrel, after an early bellringer. Climb its more than 500 steps, and get a panorama of the city.

The modern functions of the Palazzo Pubblico reflect perfectly Siena's links to — and respect for — its past. Although bureaucrats still toil in parts of the Palazzo as they have for nearly seven

sole at
sk.

centuries, much of the complex has been given over to the **Museo Civico**, which houses some of the city' greatest treasures. Siena's city council once met in the vast **Sala del Mappamondo**, although the huge globe that then graced the walls has disappeared. What remains are two frescoes attributed to the medieval master Simone Martini: the majestic mounted figure of *Guido Riccio da Fogliano* and, opposite, the *Maesta*. (The *Maesta* is signed in Simone Martini's own hand, but in recent years a nasty squabble has broken out among art historians about the authenticity of the *Guido Riccio*. Some now theorize that a smaller fresco recently uncovered below the huge panel may be Simone Martini's original, and that the *Guido Riccio* was in fact, executed long after the artist's death.)

In the **Sala della Pace o Dei Nove** is Ambrogio Lorenzetti's sweeping *Allegory of Good and Bad Government*. Intended as a constant reminder to the city fathers of their responsibilities, it depicts the entire sweep of medieval society, from the king and his court to the peasants working the tiered hillsides outside the city walls.

Exiting again to the Campo, head up the hill via one of the winding streets to **Piazza del Duomo**. The facade of the vast striped cathedral is a festival of green, pink and white marble, which will help prepare you for the stunning black-and-white geometric patterns of the interior. Take special care to study the 15th and 16th Century marble inlaid paving of the Duomo, which depicts allegories and scenes from the New Testament. (Unfortunately, many are covered most of the year to protect them from heavy traffic.) Off the left nave (and requiring an admission fee) is the decorative **Libreria Piccolomini**, built in 1495 to house the personal papers and books of Pope Pius II. The frescoes by Pinturicchio show scenes from the life of the pope, and in the center of the room is the famous "*Three Graces*," a Roman copy of a Praxiteles sculpture.

For those with more time, Siena boasts two other important museums: the **Museo dell' Opera Metropolitana** or Cathedral Museum, at the left and to the rear of the Piazza, and the **Pinacoteca** (Picture Gallery) **Nazionale**, in the Palazzo Buonsignori on the Via San Pietro, about two blocks left of the Campo. The Cathedral Museum's main attraction

Sunset enhances the earthy tones of buildings Siena.

is the entire room devoted to the works of Duccio, including his moving *Maesta*.

Pisa

To the northwest of Siena, directly west of Florence, is the city of the Leaning Tower. In the 12th Century, when Florence was still caught in the upheaval of the Middle Ages, Pisa was at her apex. Situated on the banks of the Arno just 12 km (7.5 miles) from the Ligurian Sea, the city was a major trading capital, with close ties to ports in the Middle East and beyond. But Pisa's heyday was to last only a brief moment; by 1300 the younger, more vital cities of the region had begun to pass her by. Nature was no less unkind: in the 15th Century Pisa's harbor filled with silt, and the once bustling port became barely navigable. Although it remained a commercial center, Pisa's glory days were over. Nearly five and a half centuries later came the cruelest blow: massive destruction during World War Two.

Fortunately, the centerpiece of Pisan culture, the spectacular **Piazza del Duomo**, remains intact. Also known as the **Campo dei Miracoli**, or the Field of Miracles, it is exactly that: a magnificent cluster of white marble religious buildings whose "Pisan style" incorporates both the European and Eastern architectures which Pisan merchants and sailors were exposed to during their travels.

Nowhere is that influence more obvious than in the **Duomo**. It was the first cathedral in Tuscany to use the dark and white striped marble facade, a pattern copied in dozens of the region's other churches. As you enter, linger at the bronze doors, which depict scenes from the life of Christ and the Holy Virgin. Inside, the pattern of the facade is continued, soaring skyward to a spectacular royal blue and gilt ceiling. The cathedral contains two important works of art: Giovanni Pisano's intricate pulpit, and, to the right of the chancel, Andrea del Sarto's *Saint Agnes*.

Directly in front of the Duomo is the Baptistry, which contains Nicola Pisano's lovely pulpit. To the left is the **Campo-santo**, or holy field. Don't neglect to visit this walled cemetery; as legend has it, the earth for the burial ground was brought back by crusaders from the Hill of Calvary.

Then, of course, there is the **Campanile**, better known as the Leaning Tower.

e Duomo,
ena.

Begun in 1173, the structure had started to list by the time the third storey was completed. According to some accounts, it was here that Pisa's most famous son, Galileo, disproved Aristotle's theories about the acceleration of falling objects by dropping different-sized balls from the belfry. True or not, the tower's real notoriety comes from its amazing slant. It is now nearly 15 feet out of plumb, and tilts a little more every year despite efforts to firm up the ground underneath. The 294-step climb to the top is for the sturdy of limb. And only the strong-hearted should venture out onto the top loggia; at that point there is only a slender rail between you and the earth below.

Unfortunately, that's about it for Pisa. As you can see from the top of the tower, much of the rest of the city is of post-war vintage. The area around the Piazza del Duomo has one of the largest collections of tourist gewgaw stands anywhere in Tuscany. Unless you're in the market for a model of the leaning tower — available in any size from three inches to three feet tall — you'll be well advised to continue your journey.

A neighbor of Pisa, just to the north, is **Lucca**. Its 16th Century walls, redesigned in the early 19th Century to include a lovely tree-lined promenade at the crest, serve as a perfect introduction to the serene beauty of the city within. Thanks to them, Lucca was protected from any siege; consequently, its historic center is perfectly preserved. There you'll find landmarks diverse in appearance and history — from a medieval maze of alleyways to the Roman grid-like arrangement of passageways, from Renaissance loggias to Rococo facades. Even the views outward from the top of the walls offer dramatic contrasts: from fertile plains to the Apuan Alps. These disparate elements combine, to give Lucca a distinctive look among Tuscan towns. In flavor, it is, arguably, prettier, wealthier, more feminine, more aristocratic, and rather more Northern European. Beneath red-tiled roofs, buildings are frequently brick, white or cream. The campanile of churches and palaces often crowned with crenelations — even trees — rise slender and delicate against the sky; the palaces themselves are more ornamented and open, less fortress-like.

Lucca flourished in the Middle Ages as a banking and merchant center, known principally for its beautiful silk. Today,

Romanes‹ cathedral Pisa with ‹ celebratec tower.

the city is said to produce the finest olive oil in the world. The center of town, the **Piazza Napoleone** (the city was a Napoleonic principality), fronted by the ducal palace, contains a monument that embodies Lucca's character: a statue of Marie Louise de Bourbon, the proud, and elegant duchess who later ruled Lucca.

To the east of the Piazza is **San Martino**. The **Duomo's** assymetrical facade — re-designed in the prosperous 12th and 13th centuries, when many churches were enlarged and enriched — reflects the influence of Pisa's Duomo. Inside, a filigree of slender pillars reveals glimpses of star-studded ceiling, gold against deepest blue. In the center of the nave is native son Matteo Civitali's gilded **Tempietto** which houses *The Sacred Countenance*, a wooden crucifix that legend claims was carved by Nicodemus on a cedar of Lebanon. Another jewel: Iacopo della Quercia's tomb of Ilaria del Carretto Guinigi (1408), the beautiful young wife of Paolo Guinigi (a name you see a lot around town; he was a ruling noble), touchingly guarded for eternity by the faithful dog at her feet.

To the north of the Piazza Napoleone, **St. Michele in Foro** symbolizes another piece of city history: its founding as a Roman colony in 180 BC. On the site of the old forum, the church boasts a facade that's a prime example of Pisan-Lucchese architecture. (You'll also see the feral and floral designs said to have been inspired by the city's silks.) Continuing the forum's tradition as the seat of government is the **Palazzo Pretorio**, the former town hall and the city's major Renaissance building, begun in 1492 by Matteo Civitali. Not far, on **Via de Poggio**, you'll discover the house where another famous son, Giacomo Puccini, was born in 1858.

A block from the forum, the Via Fillungo leads past the **Torre dell' Ove**, a clock tower that has ticked off the hours since 1471 — to the **Anfiteatro Romano.** Here, an oval of medieval homes embraces the perimeter of what used to be the 2nd Century Roman amphitheater.

Nearby, you'll find the dazzling gold mosaic facade of the church of **San Frediano**. Inside, there's a beautifully sculptured 12th Century baptismal font. In the church's "backyard": the gingerbread **Palazzo Pfanner** (1667), with its fountain and statue-studded 18th Century garden. Other *palazzi* to see are the **Villa Guinigi** (Paolo's old home), directly to the east of

nce
ucca's
oman amphi-
eater, now
piazza
ssuming
e same
ape.

the city and the site of the Museo Nazionale di Villa Guinigi, and the **Palazzo Mansi**, housing the Pinacoteca, straight across town to the west. Its 18th Century Wedding Room gives new meaning to the expression "gilding the lily."

Right outside Lucca are more delightful villas — the royal **Villa Reale**, the sculpture-studded **Villa Torrigiani**, the fresco-filled **Villa Garzoni** — all, testaments to Lucca's wealth, nobility and beauty.

The Seacoast and Hill Towns

If you don't want to see another duomo, and *palazzi*—and the crowds—begin to take a toll on spirit and body, then head west from Lucca for Tuscany's coast. But hurry: at the rate things are going, the sunbathers on the Tyrrhenian Sea beaches will soon be packed elbow to elbow. Not that this is exactly virgin fishing-village territory; the glories of the so-called "Tuscan Riviera" have been known to a tiny European *cognoscenti* for years, and the good word is leaking out fast.

Farthest north are the older resorts of **Viareggio**, **Forte dei Marmi** and **Livornio**. The Lucchese nobility has vacationed here for centuries and Shelley's body washed up on the shore at Viareggio after he was shipwrecked in 1822. Now the beaches are overdeveloped, and jammed the entire summer. For those with plenty of time and a desire to get away, take the ferry from **Piombino** to the **Isola D'Elba**, Napoleon's place of exile, which is dotted with fishing villages and spectacular rocky beaches.

If you want to stick to the mainland, however, hit the coast of the province of **Grosseto**, beginning somewhere around the resort of **Punta Ala**. Founded in 1960, this is the place to go if you want to be pampered and are willing to pay the price.

Those looking for something a little less glitzy, should push even farther south. Grosseto itself is an inland commercial and industrial center, but spread out from it like the spokes on a wheel are some of the least-known, most attractive beaches on the coast. There's no nightlife in the tiny town of **Principina a Mare**, but the beaches are not mobbed and in the cool of the evening you can hear the nightbirds call. At **Monte Argentario**, a peninsula linked to the coast by three slender roadways, visitors can have their choice of an upscale resort or a working port with all the comforts of home. The former is

Jet-set re of Port' Ércole.

266

Port Ercole, on the south side of the peninsula, long a favorite of artists and increasingly a stop-off for the jet set. On the northern coast is **Porto Santo Stefano**, where there are fewer posh shops and beautiful people.

There is a long stretch of Tuscany, a triangle from Grosseto to Pisa to Arezzo, where the name of every town seems to start with "mont": Monteriggione, Montalcino, Montepulciano, Monticiano. Since *monte* means mountain in Italian, the pervasiveness of these names gives a good clue to the nature of the region.

The famous hilltowns of Tuscany have their similarities. Almost without exception, they are surrounded by defensive walls or ramparts hollowed out with arched and sometimes turreted *portas*. The *portas* accommodate the exits and entrances of the "main" streets, paved with stone, one car — or donkey cart — wide (many towns do not permit cars inside the walls and parking lots are often found by the *portas*). Off the main street, which often runs the length, or spine, of the town, is a labyrinth or medieval passageways, twisting up steps and under archways. Near the center of town is, frequently, the main *piazza*, with a big stone well, a church designed by da Sangallo, say, and frescoed by the likes of Benozzo Gozzoli, introducing a bit of Renaissance light and classicism into the prevailing mystical medieval mood.

Looking at **San Gimignano**, northwest of Siena and considered one of the country's best-preserved medieval towns, you can see immediately a feature vital to every hilltown: the tower. Tuscans like to say that St. Gimignano's skyline resembles Manhattan's, even though a mere 13 of the original 70-plus towers remain. Practically every family had a belfry from which to hurl stones at its enemies. Families competed to build the highest tower; to state, in a rather obvious fashion, their supremacy in power and prestige.

Pienza, located the other direction outside Siena, is another jewel: small, charming, and historically significant. Pienza is the earliest example of Renaissance town planning. Pope Pius II (né Aenea Silvius Piccolomini) was born in 1405 in Pienza (then called Corsignano). As Pope, he enlisted the services of Bernardino Rossellino to rebuild the medieval village in his honor. The main street leads straight to Pius' showpiece: the **Piazza Pio II**, and its little **Duomo**, flanked by palaces, a Bishop's Palace, and the **Palazzo Piccolomini**, which looks like a miniature *Palazzo Rucellai*. Across the piazza is the **Palazzo Comunale**, which, with its little crenelated tower, looks like a tiny version of Florence's Palazzo Vecchio.

Nearby **Montepulciano** is another miniature Renaissance city with a 14th Century town hall also reminiscent of Florence's Palazzo Vecchio ... and with one of the great wines of Italy, *Vino Nobile di Montepulciano*. Neighboring Montalcino is noted for its powerful *Rocca* (fortress) and its rival wine, *Brunello di Montalcino*.

The drive to **Volterra**, not far from San Gimignano, lets you fully appreciate the term "hilltown." The 520-meter — (1,700-foot) — hairpin climb to the city walls can be as exhilarating — or as dizzying — as a trek up Pisa's Leaning Tower. Some visitors feel that the **Balze**, or cliffs, viewable to the northwest of town are worth seeing; you might get equally breathtaking views from any position on the ramparts. Volterra, one of the bigger hilltowns (pop. 15,000) offers even more possibilities for meandering through lovely piazzas and parks, climbing, all the while, towards the **Piazza dei Priori** with its **Palazzo dei Priori** the oldest such building in Tuscany.

an imignano's edieval kyline.

UMBRIA

"Two of Italy's greatest saints — Francis, and Clare lived their lives in this little region. In my religion we believe that wherever a holy man passes, he leaves a bit of his holiness behind. The energy of these saints is still very much a part of the hills here."

So an Italian-born convert to Indian mysticism explains the startling perfection of Umbria and the Marches. Whether your opium is Sai Baba or Christ or Buddah or Marx, Umbria and the Marches will move you. The country is, quite simply, sorcerous. Brochures proclaiming this area to be "The Green Heart of Italy" do not exaggerate. The hillsides and valleys of endless green are, more precisely, an array of greens: the silver green of the olive groves, the black green of the cedars and cypruses, the blue green of the durum wheat, the emerald green of the vineyards. In the spring the green is splattered with poppies, cornflowers, Apenninian eidelweiss. In the autumn the oaks and chestnuts turn brilliant amber, and the vineyards, deep mulberry.

The people of these two provinces have observed the verdure through the centuries from towns built at the top of whichever hill afforded the best vantage for spotting advancing armies, and for hailing arrows down on same.

The towns of the region were primarily self-governing free communes from the 11th to the 15th centuries, jealously guarding their liberty from neighboring duchies. As long as security depended on literally being on top of things, walls maintained these towns' boundaries as well as their independence. The people built up, slapping layer upon layer, city upon city. An Umbrian or Marchean town from a certain angle reveals Italian history in the strata of silt: a prehistoric cluster of huts supporting an Etruscan necropolis supporting a Roman village supporting a medieval commune. Archaeology is omnipresent and obvious.

After centuries of battling and rebuilding, the hilltowns lolled into a dreamy stasis. Only in the last 50 years or so have the towns begun to seep through chinks in their antique walls, and creep down the mountainside.

The conjuction of earth and stone and spirit has produced a people with quiet charm and dignity — and insularity and scepticism for things foreign. An architect from Assisi is dismayed by the people's "narrow-mindedness and provinciality. It is impossible to do anything without everybody in town knowing about it." On the other hand, an aspiring magistrate, also from Assisi, finds the distinguishing characteristic of the locals to be their "equilibrium. They are reserved — the interior life is more important than the exterior. They have the self-respect of real, honest people." Whether you agree with the professional or the student depends on how appealing you find the simple life. Umbria and the Marches are for the *viaggiatore* who wants to drift away from noise and haste, cradled in drowsy hills crowned by streets dark enough to respect secrets, old enough to appreciate mysteries.

Perugia

The sun around which orbit the other towns of Umbria was christened Perusia. One of the 12 city-states of Etruria, in the 6th Century BC; it fell into Roman hands 300 years later. During the Middle Ages,

ft, race of
e three *Ceri*
Gubbio.
ght, St.
ancis –
nbria's
st-loved
n.

it spent most of its time fighting neighboring free communes, finally challenging Papal forces around the turn of the 16th Century during the infamous salt wars when the Perugians refused to pay Pope Paul III's tax on salt. To this day, Perugians bake saltless bread — crisp, no butter — to dip in a glass of Torgiano.

If you collar a native Perugian — of which there are plenty about — he will sadly point to Benetton and Emporio Armani, admitting Perugia's local artisans and curiosities have been driven hence by big-city chic. Those things which gave Perugia her particular flavor are being eroded by creeping cosmopolitanism. But if you're not a purist, Perugia's piquant juxtapositioning of old and new can be pleasant.

The **Piazza IV Novembre** is the epicenter of the city, freshened and serenaded by the 13th Century **Fontana Maggiore**. The pigeons and people gather on the steps of the Gothic **Cattedrale San Lorenzo** to preen, chatter, flirt, and above all assure themselves that everyone else is doing likewise.

Sweeping down from the piazza is the **Corso Vannucci**, choked with pedestrians day and night. On the right hand is the **Palazzo dei Priori** or **Town Hall** (13th to 15th Century). Up its steps is the **Sala dei Notari**, painted at the end of the 13th Century and since restored.

In the same building is the **Galleria Nazionale dell' Umbria** containing an extensive collection of Romanesque and Gothic church masterpieces and a comprehensive collection of the most important of the many artists who lived in Umbria. Francesco da Rimini, Fra Angelico, Piero della Francesca, Pinturicchio, painted the same hills that can be seen from the gallery's windows.

Across the Corso Vannucci is the **Collegio del Cambio** (15th Century), distinguished by frescoes of Perugino and his school, and by 17th Century inlay woodwork.

The rest of the Corso Vannucci is best appreciated at night. Relax in one of the cafes on the street and watch the students watching you. Stop at the end of the Corso in the **Giardini Carducci** to enjoy the second best view in Perugia: the hills twinkling under the stars.

Near the **Arco Etrusco**, through whose ancient masonry run cars and bicycles, is a long staircase atop which is the best view in Perugia. From this vantage you can

Perugia under a rainbow.

map out your strategy for visiting Perugia's architecturally unique and various churches: **San Angelo**, a 5th or 6th Century circular church; **San Domenico**, a Gothic cathedral; **San Pietro**, built in the 10th Century, housing works by Perugino: and **San Francesco** which adjoins the 15th Century **Oratorio di San Bernadino**.

And yes, you *can* go through the Perugina chocolate factory, about 10 km (six miles) outside of the town; however you *must* make reservations at least several weeks in advance. If you can't get in to see them making chocolate *baci* (kisses), try a visit to the wine museum, about 16km (10 miles) away in the town of **Torgiano**.

Assisi and Gubbio

There is no place quite like Assisi. Yes, it is one of the few places in Umbria full of foreign tourists, and mercantilism can never be far behind. However, the sight, as you approach Assisi, of the dome of **Santa Maria degli Angeli** piercing the perpetual Umbrian haze, and of the shadows lengthening across the valley revealing the contours of the hills, makes the rest of the world seem blissfully far away.

Inside the town, a nun might open an automatic garage door set in a 13th Century wall, while a monk passes in berry-brown robes, hardly making a sound in his soft sandals.

The streets are almost too postcard perfect: cascades of flowers fall from wall sconces, alleyway gardens hoard every scrap of sunlight, the smell of roses and wood smoke permeates the air. The **Basilica di San Francesco** is perfectly situated for sunsets. The facade of the cathedral, designed by a military architect, is, like the saint it commemorates, beautiful in its poverty, in its paucity of folderol. There is something about this particular vista that imparts a sense of order and optimism and sanity in the universe. It bespeaks a purposeful spirit at work.

Chronologically, a tour of Assisi begins with the **Roman Forum** beneath the **Piazza del Comune**. The forum's aboveground vestige is the **Tempio di Minerva**, whose interior has been revamped in an unfortunately gaudy manner. In the northeast sector of town, the **Anfiteatro Romano**, where live naval battles were staged, has been topped by homes that follow its original oval structure.

The **Rocca Maggiore**, grim and immo-

ssisi.

bile above the town, destroyed and rebuilt, was part of a string of towers guarding Assisi. The **Duomo** (12th Century, dedicated to San Rufino) is best appreciated for the imagination of its exterior details; its interior was revamped in 1571.

Chiesa **Santa Chiara**'s pink and white exterior is supported by wing-like buttresses that are decidedly feminine in their generous curves, their airiness and strength. The chapel houses the 12th Century crucifix supposed to have spoken to Saint Francis. In an adjoining chapel hang the tunics of Saints Francis and Clare.

Return to the basilica of San Francesco and enter the **Chiesa Inferiore** with works by Simone Martini, Pietro Lorenzetti, Cimabue and Giotto. In contrast to the lower church's half-light, the **Chiesa Superiore** is bright with light streaming through the 13th Century French stained glass. There is a crucifix by Cimabue and a delicately inlaid choir. Of course, the ravishing feature of the upper basilica is the cycle of 28 frescoes by or in the style of Giotto — (the final four are attributed to Giotto's school).

Gubbio clings to the mountainside by its 14th Century fingertips. Above the town (walk or take the funicular up Mt. Ingino) rises the jewel of the **Basilica di San Ubaldo** wherein lie the remains of the saint in stately, if somewhat grisly splendor. Legend has it San Ubaldo intervened in a battle against Perugia, gaining a decisive victory for the badly outnumbered Gubbians. The basilica also displays the three immense Ceri which the sturdy men of Gubbio race up the hill in an orgiastic celebration of the saint's day every May 15.

Like the **Camignano** that flows through town, Gubbio sparkles sluggishly, but surely. Every empty street is more beautiful than the last, your head will be constantly turning this way and that so as not to miss a sequestered garden or an ancient alleyway. Always eager to assist a visitor, the people of Gubbio are quite conscious of the loveliness of their town, and will always ask if Gubbio "*ti piace?*" A merely ecstatic "Si" should suffice.

Unfortunately many of Gubbio's externally beautiful churches tried to out-gild one another's interior spaces during the 16th Century. The churches' clean-line facades belie the busyness of decoration inside. The 13th Century **Duomo** is one

Madonna by Filippo Lippi in the cathedral Spoleto.

outstanding exception: its interior is as uncluttered and pretty as its exterior.

Across a small passage from the cathedral is the **Palazzo Ducale** begun in 1476 by Federico da Montefeltro, Duke of Urbino, inspired by the palace in that town. The Ducal Palace's rooms sport frescoes and interesting architectural features.

The outstanding element of Gubbio's skyline is the belltower of the **Palazzo dei Consoli** (14th Century). The Palace's Great Hall houses a quixotic collection of medieval paraphernalia and is sided by a high staircase that affords some remarkable acoustic effects. Up the staircase are the famous **Tavole Eugubine**: seven bronze plates upon which a purposeful and precise hand has translated the ancient Umbrian language into Latin.

Spoleto

Spoleto does not have the spectacular location of other Umbrian towns, but, there is excitement — a sophistication unspoiled by cosmopolitan pretention. Who else but the most relaxed cognoscenti would put a Calder sculpture at the train station?

Browse through the art postcards in the **Piazza del Mercato** and have a look in the windows along the **Via Arco di Druso** at the racks of *fettucini* dangling suggestively over scores of black truffles dozing unsuspectingly in rich, heavy oil. Shop the best of Umbrian artists and artisans along the **Vias Fontesecco and A. Saffi**. There is sure to be a symphony or a *bocce* tournament or a troupe of German filmmakers breezing into town — both announced and not. Not only during the renowned Festival of Two Worlds, held here in June to July, but also the rest of the year, Spoleto fairly hums with arts to amuse.

The people hereabouts have always enjoyed good entertainment as the **Teatro Romano** will attest. In a worse state of disrepair is the **Rocca del Albernoz**, once the castle of Lucretia Borgia. The rocca is best seen from the outside; this is easily done as you walk across the mind-boggling span of the 13th Century **Ponte delle Torri**.

Spoleto's most outstanding treasure is the **Duomo** (12th Century). The medieval porch is surmounted by a rose window. The cathedral floor has an intricate herringbone and spiral Romanesque design.

xterior of
he cathedral
t Spoleto.

The chapel to the right was decorated by Pinturicchio. The apse is ablaze with Filippo Lippi's final work, the coronation of an exquisite Madonna surrounded by a rainbow and an arc of angels.

On the north side of the stairs leading to the Piazza del Duomo is the jewel-like 12th Century **Chiesa Sant' Eufemia** whose chaste perfection contrasts with the cathedral's perfect grandeur. Note Sant' Euphemia's massive stone throne behind the altar.

Todi

The lovely view from the **Piazza Garibaldi** is enhanced by the fragrance of a garden beneath. Nearby the Piazza is the grand **Piazza Vittorio Emanuele** or **Piazza del Popolo**. Facing the **Duomo** is the **Palazzo dei Priori** (13th Century). To the right up the imposing stair are the **Palazzi del Capitano** (14th Century) and **del Popolo** (13th Century). The former in the Gothic style with a bay of triform windows. The latter in the Lombard style resting on an impressive network of pillars.

At the head of the square stands the Duomo which was begun in the early 12th Century. The Gothic campanile, built a hundred years later, strays from the church's fine Romanesque style.

The Duomo's entrance wall is decorated by a Faenzone fresco. To the right is a 16th Century Giannicola di Paolo painting of the Madonna enthroned. The interior is softlit by some of the finest stained glass in the region.

A constitutional around the hill brings you to the **Chiesa di San Fortunato**. The structure was built in stages during 200 years of architectural revolution beginning in 1292. The exterior shows its seams in a not unattractive way. On the facade of San Fortunato, the central portal's sculptures deserve an up-close examination of their tiny, whimsical depictions of humans and beasts. Take a moment to appreciate the row of palaces down the lefthand side of the stairs as you descend.

The interior affords a great sense of expanse; the eggshell whiteness of stone enhanced by the abundance of light contrasts with the deep sable of the carved choir and the formidable pillar-mounted lectern. Belowstairs, Jacapone, the Franciscan poet reputed to have written the "Stabat Mater" is buried.

Through the **Parco della Rocca**, replete

Todi, class Umbrian hilltown.

with good views, and on down the mountain the **Tempio di Santa Maria della Conzolazione** is perched on a little shelf of green. The structure was designed by Bramante and constructed between 1504 and 1607. The altar may seem to some a bit too much, but the space is light and airy, the intricate sunburst of stones on the floor, a marvel of geometrics.

Orvieto and Urbino

The hill which supports Orvieto is volcanic in origin, therefore porous, therefore in danger of bringing the city down as it crumbles. There is a city noise ordinance — largely neglected — to prevent such an occurrence.

After climbing up serpentine curves and through narrow streets, cars burst into the unexpected and exquisite expanse of the **Piazza del Duomo**. With any luck, the hour will be late afternoon as the sun is glittering off the tesserae of the 14th Century cathedral's astonishing facade. The cathedral's steps are always generously littered with Orvietans, soldiers garrisoned down the street and visitors.

The cathedral was begun Nov. 15, 1290 to house relics of the miracles of Bolsena

mbrians
e among
e most
served of
alians.

(1263): principally a chalice-cloth onto which blood flowed from the host during a celebration of the mass. Although the original architect is a matter of some debate, by its completion in the late 14th Century the Duomo's construction required the input of legions of architects, sculptors, painters and mosaicists. The result is amazing. The Lorenzo Maitani-designed facade is bolstered by zebra horizontals of basalt and travertine. Inside, the black and white stripes point up the curvilinear arches. The wall of the apse is decorated by scenes from the life of the Virgin begun by Ugolino di Prete Ilario and completed by Pinturicchio and Antonio Viterbo during the late 14th Century. To the left of the altar is the **Cappella del Corporale** painted by Ugolino and assistants, depicting the miracles of Bolsena. To the right is the Cappella Nuova whose decoration was begun by Fra Angelico in 1447, completed finally by Luca Signorelli at the turn of the next century. The frescoes feature lurid scenes of hellfire with a deep contextual nod to Dante.

The **Via Duomo** and the **Corso Cavour** are both generously equipped with examples of Orvietan ceramics — whose simple, medieval designs are some of the prettiest in the region — elegant restaurants, chic clothiers, and purveyors of unique Orvietan wood sculptures. To the right off the Corso Cavour is the **Palazzo** and **Piazza del Popolo** (the latter now a parking lot). Straight ahead are the **Palazzo Comunale** and the **Chiesa di S. Andrea** in the **Piazza della Republica**. To the left is the **Old** or **Medieval Quarter**, easily the most charming part of town with its antique walls hung with pots of tumbling geraniums, high-walled gardens and the songbirds they attract, and tiny cave-like workrooms of Orvietan artisans.

On the east side of town sinks **Pozzo di S. Patrizio (St. Patrick's Well)**, remarkable for its dampness and tourists. We suggest a postcard instead of a descent. Bypass the well and continue down the hill to the **Necropoli del Crocifiso del Tufo**, a group of Etruscan tombs unearthed in a field of clover and buttercups. One section was constructed in the 6th Century BC, the other, two centuries later. Inside are the resting couches of the husband and wife with ample space for their gold and silver and several bottles of white wine. After a visit to the tombs, sample said *vino bianco*, evanescently crisp, inordinately cheap. You'll understand why for the past 26 centuries Orvietans have insisted on being buried with at least three large bottles.

It could not be mere coincidence that a patron of the arts such as Duke Federico da Montefeltro constructed one of the great treasures of cinquecento architecture in the Marchean hills. **Urbino** is an aerie of a town whose golden buildings are set high amid a spectacular enfolding of mountains. Urbino is one of the few hill towns not ringed by unsavory intrusions of modernity. The original old city remains almost completely "unimproved" perched at the tops of its two peaks.

The **Piazza del Popolo** is a tourist center by day: postcard hawkers and taxis. By night some of the University of Urbino's 16,000 students recline here on the steps, in the cafes, or stand in the street and discuss politics, the latest foreign film, last night's poetry reading. The facades are old; the faces are young. The contrast exemplifies the relaxed symbiosis that exists between Urbino's walls and the lives they enclose.

The Duke and his contemporaries felt man was the center of the universe — a significant break with previous philosophy. The courtyard of his **Palazzo Ducale** is paved with a hub and its radiating spokes of marble to symbolize man's central position. The building itself is part palace, part fortress: a graceful, secure nest in the rarefied Marchean air for the Duke to feather with marvelous works of art. **Galleria Nazionale delle Marche**, now housed in the palace, has several fine works by Giovanni Santi, and one by his son, Raphael. Also remarkable is the trompe l'oeil inlay work in the Duke's study. The palace was the vision of the Duke and his architect, Laurana. Begun in 1444, it was completed by Francesco di Giorgio Martini in 1482. The impressive interior is also noteworthy.

The **Duomo** in the **Piazza Duca Federico** has been over-rococoed inside, but do explore its museum's eclectic if eccentric collection of 17th Century glass and ceramics and religious objects among the forgettable paintings.

The **Fortezza Albernoz** is just the place to appreciate how the cityscape to the south is unchanged over these 500 years, or for appreciating the landscape beyond the **Monumento a Raffaello** to the north, dotted with hayricks and villas.

Down the stairs from the fortezza is the house where Raphael spent his first 14

View over Urbino in the Marches.

years. The middle-class house contrasts with the ducal splendor. There is a beamed kitchen with arcane fittings. Outside in the courtyard is the stone upon which the Santi's padre et filio, ground their pigments.

Walk through the **Oratorio di S. Giovanni Battista** (St. John's Oratory) for the 15th Century Salimben's studies of John the Baptist.

Ancona

Ancona is a mishmash of fishing town, port city, cosmopolitan pretentiousness and internationalism. By trying to be so many things to so many people it fails to successfully provide enough of the amenities to satisfy anyone seriously involved with history, commerce, fashion or culture. It is a place to visit for the day while you are staying at one of the beaches on the Adriatic.

Atop the town is the **Duomo San Ciriaco** (12th Century), built on the site of a pagan temple, its portal borne on the backs of a brace of handsome lions. The inside is disappointing. Down the hill is a string of structures including Arco di Traiano and l'Arco Clemantino, all

behind a **Napoleonic tacade**.

The most chic shops and offices are found in the shadowy **Merchants Arcade** bounded at one end by **Santa Maria Della Piazza**. The Church's fanshaped tympanum depicts medieval beasts interspersed with Della Robia inlays Inside, the church has thankfully not been fussed with, a single crucifix adorning the back wall. single crucifix adorning the back wall.

The **Fonatano Calanno** has been removed from its original site and remounted carefully so that its 16th Century bulging-cheeked elves still spout water.

To the north of Ancona is **Fano**, a picturesque seaside town, more manageable than the crowded port, with pretty oceanview cafes, a sandy and a stony beach, and a medieval quarter interesting enough to beguile the hours not spent by the sea.

To the south of Ancona are the towns of **Portonovo** and **Sirolo** on the **Riviera del Conero**. The former town has a lovely 11th Century Romanesque church, **Santa Maria di Portonovo**, set in the woods overlooking the Adriatic, and also an 18th Century watchtower. The latter town has a Franciscan convent said to have been founded by the saint himself in 1215.

ow and
nt,
bled
eets and
row alleys
Jrbino.

ITALIAN FOOD

Halfway through his dinner with Trimalchio Petronius receives the final main course: ". . . a calf was brought in on a two-hundred pound plate: it was boiled whole and wearing a helmet. Following it came Ajax, slashing at the calf with a drawn sword like a madman. Up and down went his arm — then he collected the pieces on the point of his sword and shared them among the surprised guests ... I looked at the table, already there were trays of cakes in position, the center of which was occupied by a Priapus made of pastry, holding the usual things in his very adequate lap — all kinds of apples and grapes ... every single cake and apple needed only the slightest touch for a cloud of saffron to start pouring out ... naturally we thought the dish must have some religious significance to be smothered in such an odor of sanctity ..."

Today's gustatory pilgrims will find it blessedly difficult to locate the specific ingredients and culinary techniques immortalized by Petronius in *The Satyricon*. Nonetheless, those fortunate enough to feast within the fragrant boot of Italy can be comforted in the knowledge that an all consuming attitude towards the art of eating continues to flourish throughout the nation. Though Petronius wrote his description shortly after the death of Christ, meals are indubitably being prepared with commensurate passions at this very instant. Above all else, Italians preserve a sense of the meal as a kind of high communal religious theater. Part of the piety derives from affording each dish — each *substance* — its due appreciation. Dinner is at once a drama to be witnessed in stages with mounting surprise and delight, and, a sacrament to be shared in affirmation of bonds by blood or love. While French Cuisine lavishly costumes and furnishes the elements of its national cooking drama, for Italians, the meal is a spectacle of life itself — a celebration less of man's art, than of nature's wondrously bountiful providence.

Much of the explanation for France's smoothly saucy, grandiosely appareled fare in contrast to the naked splendor of Italian cuisine lies in the relative fecundity of their national soils. While France is far from being the farmer's inferno, Italy appears to have been picked as Vicar for Vegetable Heaven. After

Preceding pages, eating al fresco in Positano. Left, a cat looks for scraps at an outdoor restaurant.

making pulp of Mexico, Cortes returned to the Old World laden with numerous pagan foodstuffs. Among them was a humble, fleshy yellow sphere smaller than a ping-pong ball. In 1554 Italians presumptuously dubbed this fruit "Pomo d' Oro," or "Golden Apple." Two hundred years of exposure to sensualizing Italian atmospheres converted these jaundiced cherries to huge, lush *bulges* in deep ruby hues; moreover, their relatively demure taste transformed into a veritable flavor odyssey — piquant, seedy, and titillatingly sweet — all at the same time! Nor is the tomato alone in

reaching its true potential only on Italian earth — where else are the bright, beading emerald grapes — where the scrumptious, bawdy squashes! The proudly pornographic peppers! The ontologically supreme onion. Bursting sunset peaches! Omnipotent olives.

Even the most subtle and complex Italian cooking seeks to combine ingredients so that each organic flavor can be savored intact. Rather than attempting to discover the common note shared by a number of different foods, then blending those foods so as to make that single note embody all their essences at once, Italian cooks seek to sustain a maximum quantity of *individual* tastes. Harmony in Italian cuisine is invariably polyphonic. This total dependence on the countryside's natural flora and fauna makes the concept of an Italian national cuisine highly treacherous. In reality, Italy's cooking varies sharply from region to region; even within a particular region, geographical diversity frequently schisms people's eating habits. In Italy, availability is everything.

A Savory Past

Until the Renaissance, the history of Italian cooking largely corresponds with Italy's military fortunes. In the 9th Century Islamic Arabs invaded Italy: though they brutally desiccated the land, Arabs brought some cooling recompense to the palate; they introduced Italy to Persian sherbets and icecreams. Two hundred years after the Arabs exited, Italy

today. Food preparation became a fine art. Bartolomeo Sacchi, Vatican librarian, composed a highly sophisticated cookbook entitled *De Honesta Voluptate ac Valetudine* (Concerning Honest Pleasures and Wellbeing); within three decades the volume ran through six editions. Florentine merchants devoted huge sums to the establishing of schools for promotion of culinary knowledge. Solidification of the Venetian Spice Route assured the whole of Italy that *all* dishes might waft with fragrances as opulent as those pervading a pasha's palace. New cooks created the marvelous pastries for which we almost proudly diet today: macaroons, frangipane, panettone and pere ripiene. Conquistadors bombarded the Old World with its first potatoes, pimentoes and, of course, tomatoes.

abandoned its own shores to crusade in the land of the Saracens. Their return was sweetened by the presentation of sugarcane which they had discovered in Tripoli. Refined, they referred to it as "Indian Salt" and used it as simply one more condiment for meat and vegetables, not suspecting for almost another whole century its natural affinity for dessert. Sometime in the late Middle Ages pasta appeared. Nobody knows exactly how it was invented, but the legend of Marco Polo having brought it back from Cathay is firmly refuted by references to pasta occurring in a cookbook composed in 1290 — some five years before Marco Polo returned.

In the Renaissance, cooking developed into much the same form that our mouth waters for

Renaissance Italians cooked with the passion of its finest painters. The gorgeous fruits of this labor gave the world its first fully developed cuisine. When Catherine de Medici married Henry, she brought with her to France the *Italian* cooks who laid the foundations for French Cuisine. At least until the time that Catherine's father-in-law Francis I became obsessed with Italian cooking, the French had virtually no cuisine whatsoever. Even Larousse Gastronomique honors Italy as the Mother Cuisine.

Above, about to cleave an enormous tuna in Palermo, Sicily. Right, a Venetian woman picks the freshest fish from an outdoor market.

Regional Flavors

The most important characteristic of modern Italian cuisine is that it does not exist! Instead of one cuisine Italy offers the world more than 20! Politics and geography are primarily responsible for Italy's range of cooking styles. Because Italy only became united about a century ago, each different state has been eating by itself for most of its existence. Distinctive culinary identities evolved as naturally as particular painting styles or costumes. Even more influential than political boundaries were natural variations in soil type, climate and proximity to the sea.

But the single inescapable territorial distinction is that between the North and the South. There are two important culinary differences from almost middle. One scholar asserts that every Italian culinary state produces a different type of pasta. Depending on how one rolls out the terms for separate classification, several conflicting figures can be arrived at for the final count of pasta varieties. However, by most accounts, 600 types seems a fairly conservative estimate!

As for fish, between the Adriatic and the Tyrrhenian, Italy hauls in well over 700 million pounds of fish a year, (the diversity in crustaceans alone threatens pasta's title to most types). And the varieties of wine positively flood pasta right out of the ring! Italy bottles more sorts of wine than any other nation. Recently, Gianni Bonacina wrote a three volume encyclopedia called *Lo Stivale in Bottiglia* (*The Boot in a Bottle*); he listed 3,811

between the two regions: northerners eat flat pasta shaped like a ribbon; southerners eat round pasta shaped like a tube. Northern noodles are known as pasta Bolognese; they are usually prepared at home with eggs and eaten almost immediately. Southern noodles are not noodles at all, but are known as macaroni. They are manufactured in factories without eggs and purchased dry. The second difference between North and South concerns the lubrication used for cooking. From Emilia-Romagna north, Italians butter almost all pots and pans. South of Bologna olive oil sets off the chef's sizzle.

Even if butter and oil go a long way towards sliding north off south, they offer little help chopping east from west or mincing middle different wines and was able to provide descriptions establishing the basis for every distinction. However, there are Italian wine makers who mock Bonacina's figure, not because he exaggerated so monstrously, but because he underestimated so provincially. Certain professors of Italian viticulture claim to have identified as many as 5,000 different types of wine. If there are so many varieties, drinking a different bottle every night, it would take almost 15 years to sample all of Italy's wine cellar.

Everywhere in Italy it is the number of foodstuffs which most impresses the hungry imagination. Spices from saffron to sage; superb fruits and vegetables in each season and every region. (Ravenna has been famous for producing the world's best asparagus practically since the time of Romulus and Remus!)

Italy also produces some of the finest meats in the world. Tuscany's Chianina cattle are pure alabaster in color and grow to weigh 4,000 pounds. After being slaughtered, Chianina steers ideally become the noble *bistecca alla fiorentina* — a recipe in which you marinate the steak in a little olive oil, wine vinegar and garlic, then rapidly broil it, needing to do no more than showcase the beef. Game birds abound: warbler, bunting, lark and pheasant, each takes his place in the menus of those regions where he has sung, flown and been shot down for hundreds of years.

With such a stupendous catalogue of ingredients, it is no wonder that Italy, unlike France, has never found it necessary to sauce its national specialities. Complexity of flavor-

ing is left to nature — the eating habits of animals, the soil and climate of plants.

Of all Italy's provinces, Rome has the most festivals. And Rome's cuisine comes nearest to sustaining a feast atmosphere. Suckling pigs and suckling lambs are two of the most succulent Roman specialties. Romans thrive on *gnocchi* — big bulbous lumps of *farina* mixed about with butter, eggs, nutmeg and a mouthwatering rapid-melting Parmesan maelstrom. Rome still produces wines that the Caesars drank. The following tale tells of the origins of one of the more popular varieties, Est Est Est.

When Henry V was to be coronated in 1110, a German cardinal named John Fugger felt it necessary to travel to Italy. He loved wine and consequently sent ahead of him a simple ste-

ward, Martin, to taste the wine. Wherever Martin quaffed a good wine he scratched Est across the tavern door. In this way Cardinal Fugger would be guaranteed his daily chugger. The cardinal arrived in Rome when he came across a doorway on which was scrawled Est Est Est (It is, It is, It is). Cardinal Fugger rushed forward and at once tripped over the body of the dead drunk Martin. It seems the hasty cardinal was well rewarded because he ended by spending the rest of his days in the neighborhood of that tavern (today called Montefiascone). After his master's death, Martin had the following epitaph engraved upon Cardinal Fugger's gravestone (still to be seen nearby the bar): "It is. It is. Because of too much it is here Jo De Fuk my Lord is dead."

Emilia the Fat

Emilia–Romagna has splendid natural resources. Moreover, the entire province has always had one of the world's best road systems insuring rapid distribution of ingredients sought after in one corner and available in another. Romagnans have perfected the art of making sausage. Bologna, the capital of Italian cuisine, lies in the heart of Emilia–Romagna, and from there *Mortadella* dubbed by one connoisseur "the noblest of pork products," issues. Mortadella is made from finely hashed pork, wildly spiced, then forced into a casing made from suckling pig skin.

Wonderful fish abound in Emilia–Romagna. Alpine streams make the Adriatic significantly less salty and cleaner than most oceans. So Italians are able to consume *Rombo*, "the pheasant of the sea," and *Gobies*. The latter's Latin name Gobius Pagenellus (little pagans) derives from another interesting culinary legend. It is said that when St. Anthony of Padua came to Rimini in 1221 he preached a sermon for which all the fish, save the Gobie, lifted themselves from the water.

"If the first father of the human race was lost for an apple, what would he not have done for a plate of *tortellini*?" So asked an unnamed poet, and visitors to Bologna who taste the city's all characteristic pasta. Legends as to tortellini's origins abound. The most generally accepted version gives credit for the invention to the young cook of a wealthy Bolognese merchant. The merchant's money enabled him to win the hand of one of Italy's most beautiful women. But the merchant's jealousy caused him to hide his wife away from the eyes of the entire city. One day, his cook happened to walk in upon the beautiful wife while she slumbered naked. Since he knew he could never have a more intimate knowledge of the lovely lady without risking his life, he resolved to create a dish that would pay tribute to her pulchritude. So it was that the wealthy merchant ended up being served with a high mound of pasta moulded in the shape of his wife's navel.

Lombardy is polenta country; it is also famous for having the most modern methods of food production in Italy. Paddies produce more rice than in any other European country and the famous *Risotto a la Milanese* does justice to the native grain. Florentine specialties are beef, beans and Chianti. Naples is the place to eat pizza baked over wood in a brick oven. Sicily produces the most delicious pastries. The list is endless!

Despite the boggling diversity of regional dishes, Italy's cuisine is tied together by a single national attitude towards eating. Because important event of the day, the one opportunity to unite with all other family members and share adventures.

Italians are also unified by the way in which they eat. Though the foodstuffs composing each course may differ greatly, all regions eat their particular specialties in a remarkably similar order. The first course consists of a pasta, a rice dish or soup. The second course follows, often complementing or elaborating the theme begun by the first. Perhaps, if the first course was tortellini filled with parsley and ricotto, the second would be something relatively light — a sauteed chicken dish with lemon and a little bit more parsley to recall and resonate the first course's theme. The second is usually enhanced by at least one, and sometimes as many as two or three vegetable side dishes.

meals are a primary means by which the Italians celebrate life, their feelings for one another and their gratefulness to the land, Italian meals, even at their most festive, retain an element of piety. One way in which the Italians demonstrate their devotion to any repast, however humble its contents, manifests itself in the *time* Italians spend at the table. In most parts of Italy work stops for a full two hours at midday. During that time, everyone from the poorest to the richest, is expected to go home and eat. Often the midday meal is the most

Left, proprietor of 12 Apostoli in Verona gingerly lifts pastry lid off salmon. Above, interior of 12 Apostoli is decorated with frescoes.

Funghi trifolati (mushrooms sauteed with garlic and parsley) might still more enrich the sensory symphony already begun with the tortellini and poultry. Afterwards, a light green salad is ordinarily served to cleanse the palate. It prepares the happy belly for the sweet grand finale — anything from an exotic pastry (*dolce*) to one of Italy's many cheeses served with fruit. Needless to say, each course is washed down with ample quantities of wine from the big 5,000 Roster mentioned earlier.

But wherever and whatever you eat in Italy remember that Italian cooking is nothing less than a call for man to explore his relation to the natural world, to celebrate the fertility of the land with the fertility of his own imagination.

TOWARDS AN ITALIAN LOOK

At the dawn of the Italian look one finds not a group of refined stylists of international renown but a bunch of patriots fighting for Italy's independence and unity. One hundred and fifty years ago, when Milan was still under the hard rule of the Austro-Hungarian empire, those patriots launched a program of National Fashion. Their idea, which had not esthetic but political and economic foundations, was to put an end to the importation of German cloth and, at the same time, to revive the old Italian traditions in design and fabrics against the prevailing fashion of the French style. Why waste money abroad when corduroy was still produced in Genoa according to an ancient tradition of craftmanship?

That was the time when women still wore crinolines and fashion meant ladies fashion, for mens dress had already made its great "renunciation," in the early 19th Century, giving up color and ornament, and limiting itself to the dull uniform of the three-piece suit (jacket, trousers and waistcoat). The only possible expression of originality was in the excellent quality of the material and in the cut, following English styles.

Another characteristic of the Italian style of the time was the flaming red shirt of the *Garibaldini*, the 1,000 men (*i mille*) of the army of the revolutionary leader Giuseppe Garibaldi. These red shirts — actually a sort of tunic —were originally designed to be worn by Argentinian butchers at work. Owing to trade difficulties between Buenos Aires and Montevideo, Uruguay, where the shirts had been made, their stock remained unsold. Garibaldi, who happened to be there momentarily off duty, was given a good price. The red color also fitted his Republican cause: the red flag was the banner of revolution.

The Twentieth Century

In Milan in 1906 an intelligent seamstress, Rosa Genoni, made a new attempt to launch an Italian fashion to counteract the persistent influence of French *couture* in Italy. Finding inspiration in Medieval and Renaissance paintings, and in Greek and Egyptian art, she put together a whole series of patterns which brought her the admiration of the French

Left, runway model in Milan show. Editors from magazines around the world crowd Italy's fashion capital during the showings of the spring and fall collections.

themselves. Botticelli's *Primavera*, Giotto, Pisanello, Fra Angelico and even frescoes in the catacombs were among the sources of her inspiration. Actress Lyda Borelli, later to become Countess Cini, and other elegant ladies used to wear Genoni's dresses for cocktail parties, theaters and horse races. Signora Genoni also contributed to the trend towards simplicity in fashion by launching her *robes fourreau*.

In the years following the end of World War One a further and unhappy contribution to the building up of an Italian style was made. It was the fascist black shirt, worn by Mussolini and his followers after the *Arditi*, a sort of storm trooper employed by the Italian army during the war. Later on, during the Fascist regime, the black shirt was matched by *orbace* (a fabric from Sardinia) black trousers and shining black boots.

Fascist fashion for women was slightly more varied. In 1930 Mussolini's beloved daughter Edda married handsome Count Galeazzo Ciano. Maria Jose of Belgium married the Crown Prince, Umberto di Savoia, a look-alike for Hamlet. Both brides wore Italian wedding-dresses, and Maria Jose, according to Mussolini's directions in favor of Italian homemade products against the "perverse Parisian chic," did not open her 80 trunks full of marvelous French lingerie and parures.

The rich Italian ladies were not allowed to buy French dresses or Italian imitations of French dresses. What the Italians could do was to copy Renaissance portraits of Belle Dames or, if democratic minded, peasant costumes of every part of Italy. Their embroideries, jewels, and eclat of contrasting primary colors — black, red and white — were especially attractive, though the rural humor and diversity of those Madonna-dresses looked rather unsuitable for modern young women in Milan or Rome.

The underprivileged Fascist woman was not slim, nor could she diet, since her first duty was to procreate children for her country's sake. She had to wear dresses made from the newly found synthetic fibers including rayon and a loathsome fabric called *lanital*. Lanital was Mussolini's answer to the fact that Italy's national annual production of wool was far less than demand. Since he did not want Italy to have a negative balance of trade, he encouraged the development of lanital as a wool substitute. Unlike other synthetics, it was not made from vegetable substances, but from an animal product, casein, the milk residue left behind after butter is made. Lanital had many unfortunate qualities: it smelled, and if wettened it grew in size and then stiffened. Rich ladies laughed at the thought of having it in their wardrobes, but the witty graphic designer Brunetta Mateldi remembered how lanital could be very economical. She would buy a sweater of lanital, hang it up for a few days, and it would become a dress of quite an elegant length. The futurist poet, F.T. Marinetti even wrote a poem about lanital, but nothing could change the fact that lanital had an awfully rancid smell.

When Italy occupied Ethiopia, a shopkeeper in Milan had the idea of printing Mussolini's speech for the occasion on a scarf. Many fashion critics were delighted, even the American magazine *Harper's Bazaar* which said: "These days, women want to carry their faith right up front where everyone can see it."

As soon as Italy entered World War Two against the Allies, the press invited everyone to become familiar with a new fashionable object: the gas-mask. Gas masks came in several different styles and sizes for men, women and children. They were to be worn whenever one detected a strange aromatic smell like that of garlic, mustard or geraniums. Magazines published drawings of how a woman could wear a gas mask without messing up her hair too much. The masks could also be worn hanging from the neck, across the chest, and, by the most daring of women, around the waist like a trophy.

The magazines soon undertook another political purpose. They supported Mussolini and the Pope, Pius XII, in the former's condemnation of bourgeois life, and especially women who imitated the style of American movie stars with their slim trousers, turbans and painted fingernails. And nothing was worse than women who smoked.

On Feb. 12, 1951, Florentine Marquis Giovanni Battista Giorgini, who had operated as an antique dealer on the American market during the war, set up a memorable fashion show of the Italian *haute couture* in his beautiful house in Florence. This event was to remain a turning point in the history of modern Italian fashion. For this kermess he gathered not the already well-known Italian houses who were working along French patterns, but new and

adventurous young stylists: Jole Veneziani, with her gorgeous fur coats that found inspiration in the theater and her strange gold and embroidered eyeglasses; Carosa — Princess Giovanna Caracciolo — with her exquisitely aristocratic outfits that blinded one like the strong reflected sun in the bay of Naples: Princess Simonetta Colonna who revolutionized the usual schemes of the feminine figure with help from Alberto Fabiani, the sculptor of a silhouette which displayed a lightness never

From left to right: Garibaldi's red shirt; Sorella Fontana's black dress, modeled here by Eva Gardner, was worn by Anita Ekberg in Fellini's *La Dolce Vita*; ruffled feathers look; and Pucci bathing suit seen before; the Fontana sisters, expert dressmakers whose white, full skirts and little straw hats were soon seen as far away as Hollywood; and Germana Marucelli, the greatest vestal of the plastic values of the Florentine art.

The reaction of the few American buyers and journalists attending the show convinced Giorgini that the moment had come to launch the Italian style throughout the world. Upper class women gave up the French look and those of the middle class followed suit. They went to their seamstresses with the latest fashion magazines under their arms showing the pictures of the Florentine models: sloping shoulders, floating coats, rows of buttons, scarves, knots, ribbons and collars up to the chin, high stiletto heels and tiny cloches which made the head look small and shrunken. The

Pucci, the Florentine aristocrat, passionate sportsman and multi-decorated war pilot, who had now turned to the making of exclusive boutique articles in astonishing colors. His shirts and scarves were a landmark.

The Roaring Sixties

The Italian economy was going full blast when in 1960 *The Financial Times* of London awarded the lira an "Oscar" for its fine performance. The new prosperity spread wealth widely through the population. At the same time, women working in factories and offices wished to look better and more sophisticated. Stylists and textile managers worked together to meet the new demand for fashion. The results in the fashion industry were revolution-

image was that of a calyx with a pistil at the top.

New buyers joined the pioneers. *Life* and *Time* called up to get the tickets and to know what the voltage was for their lighting equipment.

In 1953 the fashion show moved to the Sala Bianca of Palazzo Pitti, the famous palace designed by Brunelleschi in 1440 for the magistrate Luca Pitti who wanted to vie with the Medicis. The new stage was now a 30-meters-long platform covered with light-beige moquette, around which fashion editors from all parts of the world crowded themselves.

By 1952 there had already been a first swoop of Italian fashion over the United States. This was the triumph of the existing style of Emilio

ary. The *prêt-a-porter* became more and more common to meet the demands of among others, American department stores who wanted well designed clothes at more affordable prices than those customary in haute couture.

But there were blows to come. In 1966, the mini-skirt, soon followed by hot pants, arrived from England. Italian men of every age were flabbergasted. Then, in the second half of the sixties, student riots started in Berkeley, Paris, Milan and Rome. In search of new ideals, young people rejected their conformist fathers along with the tie and the grey flannel suit. They wore costumes of the rebel: blousons noires, the mimetic shirts of Cuban barbudos, tight jeans, red scarves, leather jackets and pilot and Eskimo coats for fighting the police in the streets. In order to show their restiveness against any form of coercion, including fashion which is imposed from above, they dressed casually (or they pretended to to so) according to the idea that "fashion is not fashionable any more." They believed everyone should organize his own image. "To dress oneself must be a fact of self-security and self-knowledge, not an adjustment or an act of obedience imposed by others," said Fiorucci at this time. There was no longer one fashion which prevailed, but many different ones co-existing.

To describe what happened to fashion in the 1970s is impossible. Stylistic trends were fragmented, the lines and shapes of dresses changeable. One had the impression that the latest fashion didn't exist and that nothing ever really went out of fashion. The figure of the *haute-couturieur* as a dictator vanished. The mini-skirt co-existed with the midi- and the maxi-. The style of dressing young was the only consistent theme in fashion. More than any other designer, Fiorucci rode the wave of the "young" style. A parallel phenomenon in fashion was "revivalism" (Walter Albini), whereby the looks of past decades were tried on once more.

The effect of the liberalization of morals continued to be seen. Fashion which accepted the mini-skirt and the hippy style and the gypsy look (particularly popular with feminists) all in the name of looser mores, gave way to the Nude Look. Garments were designed to show off and reveal various parts of the body. And towards the end of the decade, as the emphasis on sex differences in clothing diminished, unisex came to the fore.

At the end of the cultural and esthetic earthquake of the 1960s and 1970s the man seemed to be the one who gained the possibility of wider expression through clothes. After more than a century of grey-suit conformity men re-discovered their taste for color, ornament and originality, which in earlier centuries had been right and habit.

Fashion is in fashion again. Stylists are held in the same esteem as great artists and designers. The mythical figure of the couturier seems to have come to life again. The Fendi sisters have designed the costumes for Fellini's movies and the furs for Ken Russell's *Boheme*; Krizia, the radical chic Milanese stylist who launched the hot pants in the 1960s, entertains Michelangelo Antonioni, Francesco Rosi (her brother-in-law), and Andy Warhol in her intellectual parlor and sponsored a tour of the most prestigious Italian State theater (the Piccolo Teatro di Milano) to Los Angeles for the Olympics; Gianni Versace designs costumes for Bejart; a big textile concern from Turin sends Lorin Mazeel on the podium to conduct in Bologna; fashion shows are held in the Brera Gallery in Milan with a background of Burri's masterpieces; Renato Guttuso, the official painter of the Italian Communist party, the charismatic interpreter of Italian socialist realism, designs scarves and fabrics for stylist Nicola Trussardi; the Missoni, husband and wife, — whose sweaters are in the collection of the Metropolitan Museum of Modern Art, at Dallas Museum and in Bath's Museum of Costume (England) — design Luciano Pavarotti's costumes for *Lucia di Lammermoor*; Giorgio Armani dresses John Travolta; the University of Parma organizes a retrospective exhibition of Sorelle Fontana; and Valentino promotes a "Valentino's award" to men of culture.

Italian fashion is a leader among Italian exports with higher figures than either cars or chemicals. Krizia and Missoni clothes sell best in the United States, as well as those made by Saint Laurent. Valentino, Coveri, Nino Cerruti and other Italian stylists are no longer strangers on the Paris scene. The Revlon Research Center has recently produced an atomic proof capsule which will not be opened until year 2453. Its contents consist of about 50 items selected to characterize today's life for either future generations or creatures coming from other worlds. Among these items there are a miniature of the Concord, a cassette with the voice of Maria Callas, a tie made by Gucci and a purse made by Fendi.

But what is the essence of Italian fashion today? No simple answer to that question exists, not because Italian fashion is currently in crisis but because it is going in so many different directions at once. Italian fashion today is in a period of transition. Constant movement from style to style is yielding rich and creative results. Today's fashion enjoys a close two-way relationship with street innovation and advances in the arts, especially the visual arts.

One thing is clear: the Italians have a wonderful ability to play with materials and forms. It's always the same old art of the pastry-cook, the baker, the ice-cream maker, the green-grocer, the Holy Child crib makers (*presepi*) in Naples, the marzipan maker in Sicily. This is the core of the art of the fashion stylist; and it matches perfectly with the Italian drive and effort of expressing through their clothes a whole range of feelings of pleasure connected to their body. With fashion they can transform into body gratification what they have achieved on the social and economic level.

Krizia is one of Italy's most popular designers today.

ITALIAN FILM

Italian cinema has always flickered between monumental spectacles and unabashedly intimate emotions. Before the outbreak of World War One, Italian directors had already filmed *The Romance of a Poor Young Man* and several versions of Bulwer-Lytton's monumental novel *The Last Days of Pompeii*. Roberto Rossellini, patriarch of neorealism, launched his career filming for Benito Mussolini a patriotic panegyric on dashing navy pilots. Paolo Pasolini documented nihilist delinquents demolishing one another atop heaps of Roman ruins, in *Accattone* (1961), then piously scripted *The Gospel According to St. Matthew (1964)*. Focusing at the sensory extremities, Italian cinema appears to be a remake of the national character.

Melodramatic factionalism in Italian government has caused the country's film to be particularly susceptible to ideological framing. The challenge for Italy's filmmakers has always been to produce motion pictures which portray both the absolutism of national political attitudes and the ambivalence of human characters. The best Italian films show individuals who can sustain both feelings of spellbinding nostalgia and acute awareness of their immediate surroundings. Italian neo-realism influenced the whole world with its physical images of what it feels like to live.

When the Alberini-Santoni production company released *La Presa di Roma* in 1905 the Italian feature film was born. The subject is the 1870 rout of the Pope by Garibaldi's troops. In its most famous scene, Bersaglieri rallies his inexhaustible forces to breach the wall at Rome's Porta Pia. Because so much of it was shot on location, *La Presa di Roma* anticipates both the dominant currents in Italian film history: realism and historical spectacle. Indeed, many of the films made in the first decade appear prophetic of the themes which occupy Italian cinema to this day.

However, unlike America or France, Italy produced nothing of lasting merit until the second decade of the 20th Century. As a result, Italian cinema skipped several steps in the evolution of international cinema. In England, America and France, a gradual realization of cinema's artistic potential compelled early directors to associate themselves with vaude-

Left, Marcello Mastroianni, Italy's most sophisticated leading man, in Fellini's *8½*. above, early Italian heart-throb, Maciste, had a cruder appeal for audiences.

ville and music halls. Consequently, in these countries, motion pictures connoted "low entertainment." Since Italian cinema did not pass through the carnivalian stage, film-makers did not risk dismissal as "fairground mentalities." Italy's first feature filmmakers were the most learned and aristocratic in the world. As early as 1914 the critic Papini declared Italian cinema to be a "cerebral cinema." At that time most other countries still imagined that film would ultimately be employed solely as a tool for scientific research. Film was amusing only because it was a novelty. In Italy it had already

become a way to express the meaning of life.

Early Extravaganzas

In the 1910s two directors, Enrico Guazzoni and Piero Fosca revolutionized Italian films. The historic and histrionic tastes of the two directors perfectly complimented Italy's burgeoning nationalism. Both men thrived on glorifying the martial exploits of the ancient Roman macho masses. But Guazzoni's significance derives as much from his commercial innovations as from his conceptual ones. *Quo Vadis?* (1913) the film which established his reputation, was promoted as enthusiastically for the quantity of its footage as for the quality of its scenes. Rolling in at a full ten reels, *Quo*

Vadis? ran for two hours and was easily the longest film to date from Italy and one of the longest yet anywhere. Guazzoni backgrounded his cast of togaed thousands with the world's first gargantuan sets. Guazzoni shrewdly limited distribution to first-class theaters. In New York, *Quo Vadis?* received the first socialite sparkled premiere. The glamor of Guazzoni's openings led to their being credited with the initiation of the star system. His marketing perspicacity enabled future producers to command unprecedented financial backing. However, *Quo Vadis?* itself hides any complexity of character in extra busy sets and costumes; an escapist addiction to costume drama haunts Italian cinema to this day.

Piero Fosco's contribution is more aesthetic and, ultimately, more influential than that of

being mere ciphers. Maciste — prototype for all future film strong men — tempers his pectoral flexes with a surprisingly silly sense of humor; Scipio, the romantic hero, is capable of oddly prolonged sulking fits. D.W. Griffith, the American director whose film *Birth of a Nation* is often considered the most influential film in history, was directly influenced by *Cabiria*. It was from Italy that Hollywood acquired the foundation for its epic attitudes.

After the successes of *Quo Vadis?* and *Cabiria*, a diverse section of the populace became awakened to film's potential. Industrialists perceived at once the possibility for a new financial hunting ground. Also intrigued was the aristocracy which has produced many of Italy's best filmmakers. (Luchino Visconti, first generation neorealist, was the scion of an

Guazzoni. His grand opus, *Cabiria* (1913), details the adventure of virtuous maidens, strong men, gruesome villains and romantic generals during Rome's conquest of Carthage in the Punic Wars. Elephants dexterrously career down Alpine zigzags; virgins weep; muscle men bend iron bars; armies pursue; dictators gesture; virgins weep; crowds scatter; lovers unite. Fosca originated a number of practices which advanced film's effectiveness — allowing cameras to glide across a vast scene, arranging for live orchestras to play music at each screening — Most importantly, *Cabiria* made it possible to envision epics which would not exclude individuals. Though many of Cabiria's characters are based on stock types, astounding details save them from

ancient Sicilian aristocratic family; a Roman Countess provided Rossellini with the money to begin filming *Roma Città Aperta*.) The fealty of the nobility to Italian cinema has been offered as one explanation for the high production standards of early Italian cinema. While directors in France and the United States were still pinning up painted backdrops, Italians hired the nation's finest architects to design and construct full scale sets. Furnishings in historical dramas were often borrowed from the collections of actual descendants of

Above, Roman orgy in early historical spectacle, *Quo Vadis?* Right, Anna Magnani a housewife who resists Nazis in neo-Realism's masterpiece Rossellini's *Open City*.

the depicted heroes. Butler actors had been acting as actual butlers since boyhood. When aristocratic background figures were necessary to provide the proper atmosphere, authentic aristocrats were invited to make the grandest guest appearance of all time.

Tragically, this so-called Golden Age of Italian cinema hardly had time to prove its glitter was genuine before the fascists came to power. Mussolini supervised the organization of several institutions to regulate cinema, so convinced was he of the power of the medium.

The Direzione Generale per la Cinematografia became an official department of the ministry of Popular Culture. In addition a sezione cinematografica was added to Banco del Lavoro. Directors who established their ideological credibility were eligible for up to 60

Neo-Realism

In 1944, while the Germans were still in the process of departing from Rome, Roberto Rosellini made *Rome Città Aperta*, a film which even today unnerves audiences with its refusal to falsify. The film follows the lives of several resistance workers. Every scene, except Gestapo headquarters, was shot on location. *Roma Città Aperta* has a rough visceral throb that was revolutionary for the time. Some sequences seem to be documentary footage; actors never exaggerate; the camera jerks and twists; shots break off suddenly without conventional aesthetic purpose. Yet despite the unprecedented, relentless immediacy, *Roma Città Aperta* has a complex symbolic structure. Each character is as much a representa-

percent state financing. Particularly patriotic endeavors, like *Scipio Africano* might receive total backing. If the government was pleased with the final film, producers were excused from making any repayment.

The final blow to creative competition was dealt by the newly formed Ente Nazionale Importazione Pellicole Estere (National Body for Importation of Foreign Films). The state decided which films could be imported into Italy. Once permitted to be shown, a film had to be dubbed into Italian. (To this day it is virtually impossible to see a foreign film in Italy still in its original language.) Unable to compete economically, Italy's better directors went into hibernation. Motion pictures metamorphosed into military cheerleading.

tive of some larger element in contemporary Italian society, as he is a discreet, complete individual. Pina (Anna Magnani) is almost unbearably vivid as an agonized mother when she leads a mob of matriarchs to plunder exploitative bakeries in the neighborhood. However, it is known from Rossellini's notes that the different traits that make up Pina's character were intended to highlight those conditions which were most universal for Italian housewives during the war.

Roma Città Aperta elevates squalid drug addicts, priests, German lesbians and Austrian deserters to levels of general symbolic import without sacrificing their unique personalities. The nationally shared revulsion for further rhapsodies on imperialist conquest made possible a film which imbued actual existence with formalist grace. Federico Fellini, who helped Rossellini write the script for *Roma Citta Aperta*, summarized the atmosphere following World War Two that produced neo-Realism:

"We discovered our own country ... we could look freely around us now, and the reality appeared so extraordinary that we couldn't resist watching it and photographing it with astonished and virgin eyes."
(from *Patterns of Realism* by Roy Arms).

For the next six or seven years, Rossellini, along with De Sica, Visconti and Lattuada developed a cinema characterized by rapid, seemingly spontaneous juxtaposition. Neo-Realism remains the core of what is considered modern in film.

Neo-Realism was a result of the remarkable societal union Italy achieved just after World War Two. Confusion concerning the future did not undermine the almost unanimous conviction that fascism was wrong. Neo-Realist directors spoke from and for an Italy which could confess, if not to chaos, at least, to contradictions. But as the Cold War set in, Italian cinema again began to schism. The government accused the best neorealists of purposefully blackening Italy's image to make it open to Communist invasion. The worst neo-Realists fixated only on those quainter aspects of Italian poverty, such as washing clothes and eating pasta which traditionally found substantial "Tourist by Talkies" audiences abroad. Most directors returned to making motion pictures about how much fun it was to have money.

Partially because Italy always takes its cinema so seriously, all films must accept some political responsibility. Even the silliest costume drama implies an advocation of escapism and hence, support of the *status quo*. Thus, Italian cinema's greatest virtue, a faith in the power of film to communicate human essentials, also breeds its worst failing, a tendency to sacrifice individuals to party interests. Mussolini's filmmakers' numerous epics on Scipio Africanus had no interests in Scipio as an actual human being. They presented him to satisfy the nationalist desire for glory in Italy's contemporary African invasions. Scipio was interesting only as a "type" for Mussolini. But directors cannot conform their human subjects to an ideology without betraying the emotional breadth that defines the Italian character. In this context, fascist directors grabbing through history for Imperialist gusto are no worse than degenerated neo-Realists prostrating themselves before overestablished icons of the slum's heartbreak. Fat matrons gathering laundry from endless lines while undershirted men beat bare tables with hairy fists in between chugs from straw-covered chianti jugs are no more inherently real than stalwart legions marching into Apish Carthaginians waving spears from above the swirling trunks of elephants. Rather a fidelity to reality's irrepressible digressiveness lies at the heart of what is best in Italian film.

Following the Cold War, new economic prosperity excited another resurgence of Italian film. This time the directors were Fellini, Antonioni and Rosi. Because the moral crisis facing these directors was an international crisis of faith, rather than the specifically Italian experience of fascism, their films seem less dependant on a particular time period, than do those of De Sica and Rossellini. Questions of belief in God eclipse debates about finite political systems. In many ways Federico Fellini can be viewed as the triumphant culmination of neorealist philosophy. In so far as neorealism refuses to limit one film to one style and one message Fellini has remained a consummate neorealist. His characters are constantly torn between the desire to realize their true selves and the urge to conform to superficially seductive societal institutions. Fellini's heroes swing wildly between the lust to be like no one and the lust to be like everyone. They do not hesitate to remember being bathed by their mothers or to confess a desire to be an emperor hosting a bloody, gaudy, sexy orgy.

Fellini's most autobiographical work, $8\frac{1}{2}$ stars Marcello Mastroianni (Fellini's favorite male actor) as a director about to begin his greatest opus. Gradually it becomes apparent that Guido has no idea what his grand opus should be about despite the fact that he has hired Europe's most prestigious stars to act in his film and has promised all of them the roles of their lives! Sometimes Guido remembers his parents, his poor childhood, the obese whorish woman who taught him and his classmates to do the samba, at other times he chases after a beautiful woman in white. Full of ambiguity, oscillating drunkenly between reality and dream, spontaneity and steady linear narration, $8\frac{1}{2}$ celebrates the fact that life can be loved even though it cannot be controlled. This effort to represent the whole of life without reducing it to an inferno has always been the object of Italy's most creative filmmakers. Fellini succeeds because his heroes fall in love constantly and against all reason with everything from Christ to clowns, but nonetheless passionately and with the entirety of their irreducible beings.

Right, Federico Fellini on the set.

296

OPERA

"These are the laws of the musical theater," the composer Giacomo Puccini said of his art, "to interest, to surprise, to move." Of himself, he once commented, "I have more heart than mind." In these characteristics lies the tremendous appeal, of Italian opera. The form is sensual and lush, appealing more to our emotions than to our intellect. The subtleties exist, especially in Verdi's more difficult late works, yet opera's overriding effect remains emotional and sensual.

Rossini, Donizetti, Bellini, Verdi and Puccini head up the list of those composers whose music is performed again and again throughout the world. The bookends of Italian opera's best days stand clear: on the one side the 1815 production of Rossini's classic *opera buffa* (comic opera), *Il Barbiere di Siviglia*; on the other, the posthumous 1926 opening of Puccini's last and unfinished opus, the romance of *Turandot*. Between the two lay more than a century of operatic triumphs. The course of 19th Century Italian opera marked a cultural flowering of tremendous proportions.

And yet there is much more to the story of Italian opera than those few dozen classics which live on along with the names of the giants who composed them. By the wayside, hundreds of other operas lie lost or forgotten, their makers relegated to the backroom of musical trivia. Also important, looking beyond matters of artistic merit, is the vital sociological and political role that opera has played in modern Italian society. In a world bereft of television, cinema, or organized athletics, opera provided the spectacle upon which to focus everyday social life. Opera was, up until very recently, an institution whose significance transcended the bounds of mere entertainment.

For an art form that is popularly conceived of as "classical," opera is really a relatively new phenomenon. Its roots are traced from the traditional Italian mystery plays, the *maggi*, and from the madrigal comedies of the early 16th Century. An intellectual and historical rationale for the new form emerged from scholarly discoveries that Greek drama had and should be set throughout to musical accompaniment. In the early 1580s composers, poets, and noble literati gathered in the Florentine salon of the Count of Vernio, to discuss the

potentials for musical reform. The new style of composition was first put to the test by Jacopo Peri with a 1597 private production of *Dafne*, the score of which no longer survives. Peri also staged the first public showing of an *opera in musica* (literally, "work in music"), a performance in Florence of *Euridice* to mark the marriage of Maria de' Medeci to Henry IV of France in 1600.

Where these first works amounted to little more than dramatic recitals with a skeletal musical accompaniment, the operas of Claudio Monteverdi (1567-1643) exploited more fully the new medium by employing an orchestra of 39 brass, wood, and stringed instruments. Monteverdi's *Arianna* "visibly moved the entire theater to tears" at its first performance in 1608; but it is his *La favola d'Orfeo* (1607) that is generally acknowledged to be the first operatic masterpiece.

Quick to secure a foothold as fashionable entertainment, opera soon found regular venues throughout the Italian peninsula, and indeed in major cities throughout Europe as a whole. The first public opera house, the Teatro di San Cassiano, opened in Venice in 1637. By 1700 Venice had 17 theaters in which opera was performed. From there opera's popularity exploded. Almost 2,000 original compositions were first (and often last) produced in 18th Century Italy, an incredible feat for a society that had had no institutional entertainment at all only a few hundred years before.

With those kinds of numbers, of course, it was impossible to maintain the standards we are accustomed to in opera today, and in fact opera's first 200 years were plagued by artistic inadequacies. Many felt as did the French intellectual Charles de Saint-Evremond, who found opera "a bizarre thing consisting of poetry in music, in which the poet and the composer, equally standing in each other's way, go to endless trouble to produce a wretched result." Italian composers soon resorted to clichéd musical formulas and conventions. The aesthetic erosion was obvious to many: witness Venetian composer Benedetto Marcello's satiric tract: *The theatre à la mode, or, The Secure and Easy Method of Composing and Performing Italian Operas.*

Rowdy Audiences

If the quality of operas had fallen to an abysmal low, most 18th Century Italians didn't seem to mind, for they flocked to the houses

Left, portrait of Verdi in the Museum of La Scala, Milan.

night after night for hours of social frolicking. "Every small town, every village has a theater," remarked one contemporary. "The poor may lack food, the rivers may lack bridges, the sick unprovided with hospitals ... but we may be sure that the idle will not want for a Coliseum of a kind." The comparison to the ancient Roman circus seems altogether apt. In the theaters the middle and upper classes gathered to eat, drink, and gamble. The operas themselves were often mere sideshows.

Opera houses were all constructed on the model of the early Venetian theaters. A horseshoe of box tiers loomed over the *platea* (the "pit," or orchestra) in an auditorium of not unimpressive size. The original San Carlo in Naples, for instance, was 30 yards long and almost 20 yards high, with a stage covering

nobility.

In the pit, on the other hand, one found mostly middle class merchants and professionals. "Cultured ladies did not sit there," wrote the English singer Michael Kelley, noting that box holders were want to spit and litter from their perches. The unpleasantness of the *platea* was notorious. As one papal inspector bemoaned of his bailiwick, "Complaining about the discomfort and the filth of our theaters would be simply a repetition of what the whole world has already been saying, to our disgrace."

Opera goers were a generally rowdy bunch. The theaters provided the only forum in which Italians might publicly display a playful exuberance; not coincidentally, attendance reached its peak each year during the carnival season,

some 10,000 sq feet. "The King's Theatre," wrote Englishman Samuel Sharp of San Carlo, "upon first view is, perhaps, almost as remarkable an object as any man sees in his travels."

Theater boxes, which one could buy, sell, mortgage, or sublet as with any other piece of property, were much sought after by local elites. Each box enjoyed a private dressing room and often a balcony curtain with which to ensure complete privacy (or refuge from a bad performance). Those patrons most prominent on the social ladder ordinarily opted for the second tier, where the royal box, if there was one, would be situated; the higher one went, the lower the prestige. As a rule, however, boxes were held only by members of the

which ran from the day after Christmas until Shrove Tuesday. Such unruliness was wholly illegal — the various governments of the politically fragmented peninsula enacted statutes against everything from curtain calls to excessive applause — but the boisterous audiences always seemed to get their way. In Milan, for example, a law against clapping before the sovereign's lead was circumvented by choruses of coughs or nose-blowing. Fearing, with some justification, that outbursts would evolve into full-fledged riots, the authorities in Rome went

From left to right: animated 19th Century audience in Naples' San Carlo Opera House; composer Vincenzo Bellini; and self-portrait by Gaetano Donizetti.

so far as to install a flogging block outside the Teatro Valle, although its use was apparently more symbolic than actual.

Some performers would undoubtedly have preferred a more harsh enforcement of such laws. When opera patrons had the spare moment to look up from the roulette or dining tables in their box, they were not famed for their generosity. Charles Dickens, after an excursion to Genoa, noted the "uncommonly hard and cruel character" of Italian audiences, who seemed "always to be lying in wait for an opportunity to hiss." Listeners seated in the *platea*, known to follow librettos closely by the light of their own candles, would yell out "brava, bestia" ("bravo, you beast") upon catching a singer in a botched line. Overworked *prima donnas* might be showered not

dramatically towards that ideal, "to interest, to surprise, to move." All three born within the span of a decade, they took a hackneyed form and infused it with vitality, so that it was towards Italy that Europe once again looked for operatic innovation. All three shared much in style, artistic and personal; and their meteoric careers followed many of the same paths and detours.

Rossini is probably most celebrated for his productions of *Il Barbiere di Siviglia* and *Guillaume Tell*, Donizetti for the tragic masterpiece *Lucia di Lammermoor, and the Daughter of the Regiment*, Bellini for the *semi seria* work *La Sonnambula*, for *Norma* and for *I Puritani*. These operas remain today part of standard repertories everywhere.

The three shared a small-town background.

with roses and flattering sonnets jotted on handkerchiefs but rather with radishes and leeks, traditional symbols of ridicule. After an opening night gone awry, a local theater organizer (the *impresario*) could come home to find his windows smashed out with stones. As Italian opera moved into its golden age, some of these nightclub-like excesses disappeared, but even the premiere of Puccini's *Madama Butterfly* (1904) met with catcalls and whistles of derision.

Opera's Golden Age

It was with the 19th Century composers Giocchino Rossini, Gaetano Donizetti, and Vincenzo Bellini that Italian opera moved

Rossini and Bellini were both sired by provincial musicians, and, though Donizetti was not, he was clearly exposed to song and composition in his childhood. Each enjoyed tremendous success at an early age; if a laggard is to be found it would be Bellini, whose operatic debut came when he was all of 22 years old. Each faced the gargantuan appetites of demanding impresarios and the finicky tastes of leading performers, and each responded with a remarkable ability to produce works in the space of a few weeks time. Each followed gold and glory to extended residences in Paris and elsewhere in Europe. Finally, and tragically, all three spent most of their artistic talent too quickly. Bellini and Donizetti died young, the latter a crazed syphillitic. Rossini's last triumph came before he turned forty.

Not surprisingly, there developed a fierce and jealous rivalry among the three. Upon hearing that Signor Rossini had composed *Il Barbiere di Siviglia* in 13 days, Donizetti shrugged proudly and concluded, "No wonder — he is so lazy." At one point, Bellini saw in the other two no less than a villainous plot to subvert his artistic opportunities. "Rossini decided to have Donizetti commissioned also," said the third, speaking of engagements in Paris, "because in that way, set up against me, he would suffocate me, exterminate me, with the support of Rossini's colossal influence." As the three faced decline, they were reconciled, and it is only fitting that they should have been followed by a lone great, Giuseppe Verdi, the brightest light of Italian opera.

distinguished career. From then on, Verdi saw success after success, highlighted by *Rigoletto* (1851), *Il Trovatore* (1853), *La Traviata* (1853), *La forza del destino* (1862), *Don Carlo* (1867) *Aida* (1871), and *Otello* (1887). With premieres in London, Paris, St. Petersburg, and Cairo, along with those in the theaters of Italy, Verdi was a composer of true international stature.

It was a reputation well deserved. His sharp, almost brutal dynamism freed Italian opera from the last vestiges of long-empty conventions. His productions, refined yet fresh, "had nothing to do with theories," wrote one critic, "it is the voice of nature speaking in the idiom of art." The English composer Benjamin Britten sang his praises most eloquently: "I am an arrogant and impatient listener, but in the case of a few composers, a very few, when I hear a

Verdi was born in 1813 (the same year as German composer Richard Wagner) in Le Roncole, a small village 12 miles from Parma. His father was a semi-literate peasant, and the Verdis had no history of talent, musical or otherwise. It looked as if Giuseppe's experience as the local church organist would go to waste when in 1832 he was denied admission to the prestigious Milan Conservatory. But persistance was his natural response to the early rejection, despite frequent self-doubts, and in Verdi's case the persistance paid off. Although his first two productions, *Oberto* (1839) and *Un giorno di regno* (A One-Day Reign, 1840) met with lackluster receptions at La Scala premieres, rave notices for the epic *Nabucco* (1842) marked only the beginning of a long and

work I do not like I am convinced it is my own fault. Verdi is one of those composers."

In at least two important respects, the context in which Verdi thrived was more suited to artistic success than those in which his predecessors had labored. Composers were, first of all, no longer subject to the whip of their *impresari*; their fortunes now hinged with large publishers such as Ricordi and Lucca, who were much less interested in volume than in quality. Late in his life, Verdi looked back on the 1840s and 1850s, during which he had pro-

From left to right: famous 20th Century tenor Enrico Caruso (right) on stage; Giacomo Puccini; curtain call at La Scala, Milan.

duced one or two scores a year, as his "time in the galleys," although that workload would have constituted a veritable vacation to an 18th or early 19th Century composer. Secondly, Verdi refused to tailor his works to the whims of individual singers, something no composer had dared do in the past. Verdi's independence extended into his personal life. In a very conservative and religious society, Verdi openly lived with his mistress, the soprano Giuseppina Strepponi, for more than a decade before taking her to the altar in 1859.

If Verdi was permitted such artistic and personal freedoms, he was still constrained by the political realities of his day. Censorship was an omnipresent artistic impediment in an Italy dominated by foreign powers, much to Verdi's irritation. Dictated revisions were often trivial,

historical works were charged with analogies to the Italians' plight, allusions not lost upon native audiences. A dear friend of Count Cavour, Verdi served at his bidding in the new chamber of deputies for a short time after unification. On his death in 1901, Verdi was mourned not only as a composer but also as a patriot.

Although operas of fine quality continue to be composed today, the golden age of Italian opera drew to a close with the career of Giacomo Puccini. Others contended for the mantle of Verdi; Puccini had the advantage of the blessing of the old man himself. "Now there are dynasties, also in art," lamented rival Alfredo Catalani, "and I know that Puccini 'has to be' the successor of Verdi ... who, like a good king, often invites the 'crown prince' to

as when the exclamation "Dio" ("God") had to be replaced with the less offensive "Cielo" ("Heaven"). (Bellini had faced a similar problem. His opera *Bianca e Fernando* was opened as *Bianca e Gernando* because the original name happened also to be that of the King of Naples.) Other times, the censor tried to rip the heart from a work with scores of senseless changes. Scrutinizing an early manuscript of *Rigoletto* butchered by the Austrian authorities, in which, among other things, names and localities were changed wholesale and the title character was not allowed to be a hunchback, Verdi could only exclaim, "Reduced in this way, it lacks character, importance, and finally the scenes have become very cold."

Verdi was himself an ardent nationalist. His

dinner!" A dynasty it may have been, but one clearly based more on merit than on anything else. *La Bohéme* (1896), *Tosca* (1900), and *Madama Butterfly* (1904) are among this crown prince's many contributions to the art of opera.

From Monteverdi to Puccini, Italy remains, of course, the best place to sample the operas of the great Italian composers. Such grand old houses as La Scala in Milan, San Carlo in Naples, the Teatro Comunale in Florence, and La Fenice in Venice, and the many others that maintain an old-world elegance — all provide an incomparable backdrop of authenticity. No visitor should miss the opportunity to enjoy the art where it began, and where it has flourished.

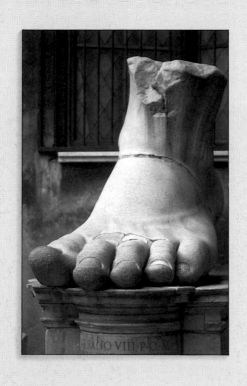

TRAVEL TIPS

GETTING THERE

BY AIR

In recent years, air traffic to and from Italy has increased greatly, and Italian airports are often inadequate in view of the demands of foreign travelers. Italy has 29 main airports, but only two of them are International Airports: Roma Fiumicino and Milano Malpensa. Roma Ciampino is a landing field for some charter flights.

For information and reservations, look under "Linee Aeree" in any telephone directory's Yellow Pages.

Leonardo da Vinci Airport Fiumicino is located 35.5 km southeast of downtown Rome. It is the fourth busiest airport in Europe. Built in 1961 in expectation of 6 million passengers a year, these days about 14 million arrive annually. Waiting rooms, baggage-rooms and loading bridges are inadequate.

Transportation to and from Fiumicino is provided by the ACOTRAL bus every 15 minutes from 6 a.m. to 9.30 p.m. Fare for the 45 minutes ride is L. 5,000. The downtown bus terminal is at Stazione Termini. Taxi fares average L. 50,000 to and from the city's center by yellow taxis. Do not take unofficial taxis which can ask you for about L. 100,000 or more.

Milano Malpensa Airport is 46 km from the center of Milan. Buses to Malpensa leave from the bus terminal at Stazione Garibaldi (Viale Sturzo) or at Stazione Centrale two and a half hours before flights. Fare for the 45/50 minute ride is L. 6,000. By taxi, the fare is about L. 60,000.

Roma Ciampino is a dowdy military airport where charters usually land. From here, the ACOTRAL bus will bring you to the Subaugusta stop on subway line A, which will take you to Termini, the Spanish Steps, or the Vatican. Taxis charge about L. 35,000.

TRAVEL ESSENTIALS

VISAS & PASSPORTS

All travelers require a passport for entry into Italy. Visitors coming from Common Market countries (M.E.C.) need not have a visa or a passport; an identification card valid for foreign travel is sufficient.

People from Eastern countries need a visa acquired from an Italian Embassy in their own country. Tourists from the U.S.A. do not need a visitor's visa unless they stay in Italy for more than three months. Drivers must carry civil liability accident insurance and a valid international green insurance card, which can be bought at the border.

MONEY MATTERS

The use of American-dollar traveler's checks is advised, because, when lost or stolen, they can be replaced. Traveler's checks are as acceptable as cash in big hotels or in tourist areas.

Most merchants, however, will not change money, so it is best to have this done at the airport, especially if you arrive on a weekend, when banks are closed. Unlike in the U.S.A., every bank in Italy will change foreign money.

The exchange rates fluctuate with the world market. Current rates are published in the press or can be obtained from banks. At time of press, the official exchange rate was US$1 to about L. 1380.

CREDIT CARDS

Many restaurants, hotels and shops honor Visa, American Express, Diner's Club and Carte Blanche credit cards, but stores and gas stations usually do not accept credit cards instead of cash.

TIPPING

Tipping is not the norm in Italy, but in better restaurants and hotels it is appreciated for courteous and efficient service.

In nearly every restaurant, the service charge is included in the bill and may be indicated as *"servizio e copreto"* or only as *"coperto."* Remember that you are obliged to ask for the fiscal receipt which you must preserve at least until 100 meters distant from the restaurant.

WHAT TO WEAR

In recent years, Italians have been particularly obsessed with appearance and fashion. But even in the most sophisticated cities, the streets are filled with tourists and natives dressed in everything from ultra-high fashion to the most casual wear. Only first class restaurants require jackets and ties for men. Just remember that neither women nor men can enter churches or Catholic museums dressed in shorts, or in a shirt with uncovered shoulders.

Unless you are going to visit the mountain areas, the moderate climate makes heavy clothing unnecessary. A light jacket will be adequate for evening in the summer. If you plan to spend time in the sun, be careful to use sunscreen lotions.

CUSTOMS

Inspection of cars and baggage takes place at Customs. The temporary duty-free importation of the following articles is permitted:

a) personal jewelry, two cameras and 10 rolls of film; one small movie camera and 10 rolls of film; one record player and 10 records; one tape recorder; one portable radio in your car; one portable T.V.; one pair of binoculars; one bicycle; two pairs of skis; two tennis rackets; camping equipment and food supplies for personal use; not more than 200 cigarettes and other maximum quantities of tobacco, alcoholic beverages and cigars.

b) souvenirs, gifts or non-commercial articles for a maximum value of L. 400,000.

c) pack units or walkie-talkies with citizens' band are to be declared at Customs, where they will be duty sealed.

There is no restriction on the amount of foreign currency (or credit cards or traveler's checks, if issued abroad in foreign currency) a visitor may bring into Italy.

A maximum of L. 200,000 per person (including children), may be brought into and taken out of Italy.

Foreign currency for a value of up to one million lire may be taken out of the country. If you want to export foreign currency over this limit, you must ask the customs police for a special declaration form (V2) and fill it out, declaring the amount of foreign currency you are bringing into Italy. This form must then be exhibited at Customs upon leaving Italy.

GETTING ACQUAINTED

GOVERNMENT & POPULATION

About 58 million people live in this democratic republic with a Western-style economy. Parliament and Government bureaucracy are based in Rome, the capital city.

TIME ZONES

There is one time zone through the country – 1 hour ahead of Greenwith Mean Time (GMT). From late April until the end of September, time is advanced one hour to give extended daytime through the summer.

During Standard Time periods, when it is noon in Rome, it is . . .

1 p.m. in Athens and Cairo
2 p.m. in Moscow and Istanbul
4.30 p.m. in Mumbei (Bombay)
6 p.m. in Bangkok
6.30 p.m. in Singapore
7 p.m. in Hong Kong
8 p.m. in Tokyo
9 p.m. in Sydney
1 a.m. in Honolulu
3 a.m. in San Francisco and Los Angeles
5 a.m. in Chicago

6 a.m. in New York and Montreal
8 a.m. in Rio de Janeiro
11 a.m. in London
noon in Bonn, Paris and Madrid

CLIMATE

The climate is generally temperate but the weather changes according to latitude and altitude. There are three main kinds of climate: 1) in the mountainous areas (Alps and Apennines), winter is long and cold, summer is short and cool. Even for summer visits, you are advised to bring sweaters and light boots; 2) in the Pianura Padana (Milan), the climate is characterized by harsh winters and sultry summers; 3) in the rest of Italy, the winters are mild and lukewarm and the summers aren't hot and dry, being tempered by the sea-breeze, more along the Tyrrhenian coastline than along the Adriatic. Summers can be torrid in the south, on the islands, along Sicily's African seaside and in the interior lands.

CULTURE & CUSTOMS

In Italy it is courteous to use such typical expressions as:
"*per piacere*" or "*per favore*" (please) when you ask for something;
"*grazie*" (thanks) as in the English expression "yes, thanks" (*sì, grazie*);
"*prego*" (you are welcome) when somebody says "*grazie*" to you, as in the English "you're welcome." The word may also be used to say "pardon."

BUSINESS HOURS

Shops are open for business in the morning from 9 to 12.30 a.m. and in the afternoon from 3.30 or 4 p.m. to 7.30 or 8 p.m. In areas serving tourists, hours are generally extended beyond those listed above. Shops close one day a week, usually Monday (or Monday morning only). Some close on Saturday. Everything is closed on Sunday.

Banking hours are 9 a.m. to 1.30 p.m. from Monday to Friday. Some banks are open in the afternoon from 3 p.m. to 4 p.m.

Shops and banks close during holidays.

HOLIDAYS

Capodanno – January 1
Lunedì dell'angelo – the day after Easter
Anniversario della Liberazione – April 25
Festa del Lavoro – May 1
Assunzione S. Vergine – August 15
Ognissanti – November 1
Immacolate Concezione – December 8
Christmas – December 25
S. Stefano – December 26

In addition, some cities have a holiday to celebrate their own patron saint.

FESTIVALS & SEASONAL EVENTS

The Italian Calendar is packed with special events, some linked to festivities of the catholic church, others to cultural activities or commercial fairs. Here are suggestions:

Festival dei Due Mondi di Spoleto, from late June to early July, offers opera, theater, concerts, ballets and exhibitions each year. At Spoleto, near Rome.

Biennale. A large exhibition of international art, held every even-numbered year in Venice.

International Film Festival also in Venice, at the Lido, each year toward the end of August.

Carnevale. This period of festivities preceding Lent (February and March) has been reinstated by Venice.

Fair of Rome. This national industrial exhibition takes place in late May or June.

Festa di Noiantri. During the latter half of July, this great pagan feast, involving plenty of music, fireworks and eating, is celebrated in Trastevere, one of the oldest quarters of Rome.

Frast of St. John and Gioco del Calcio are held in Florence on June 24 and 28. The Gioco del Calcio (Soccer game) is a very rough traditional soccer game played by men wearing 16th-century costumes.

Fiera Internazionale di Milano is held in late April and is one of the most important in the world.

Read also section on "Music and Dance."

COMMUNICATIONS

POSTAL SERVICES

Post office hours are usually 8 a.m. to 1.30 p.m., but every town has a main post office open throughout the day. Postage rates are as follows:
– letters inside Italy are L. 450 for the first 20 grams, L. 900 for 50 grams, and so on;
– postcards inside Italy are L. 400 for the small, L. 450 for bigger;
– letters to foreign countries are L. 800; postcards to foreign destinations are L. 600.

Besides post offices, stamps may be purchased from tobacco shops, where you can ask also for the zip-codes of Italy.

The post office can also provide such services as *raccomandata* (registered), *espresso* (express) and *via aerea* (air mail) to speed up delivery.

You can receive mail addressed to Pôste Restante, held at the Fermo Posta window of the main post office in every town, picking it up personally with identification.

A very fast delivery service, CAI-post, is also provided by the post office to send important documents almost all over the world in 24/48 hours.

Remember that you do not have to line up to post your mail: you can simply post it in the red letter-boxes near the tobacconists or at the station.

TELEPHONES & TELEGRAMS

Public telephones are almost everywhere in Italy, but especially in the bars, which serve as telephone centers. From some of them you can call a "*scatti*" (ring first, pay later). Otherwise, you need the "*gettone*" (a token which costs L. 200).

From public telephones it is possible to makes local and long distance calls. The payment can be made, according to the telephone's kind, by tokens (*gettoni*) and/or L. 100 and L. 200 coins.

If you have no small change or no tokens, it is best to make international and collect calls from the public telephone offices (PTP). PTP (posto telefonico pubblico) offices in the major cities are:

Rome: ASST piazza San Silvestro or at Termini
Milan: ASST piazza Edison, in the post office; ASST Stazione Centrale; SIP, Galleria Vittorio Emanuele
Florence: ASST Palazzo delle Poste, v. Pellicceria; SIP, Stazione S. Maria Novella
Venice: at the main post office, Fontego dei Tedeschi, by Rialto
Naples: At the train station and in the Galleria across from San Carlo.

Local calls cost L. 200, except in Torino and a few other cities where they cost L. 200 every nine minutes.

Long distance call rates vary, according to the distance and the call's hour. Rates decrease after 6.30 p.m. and after 10 p.m., before 8 p.m., on weekends and on holidays.

Check the directory for all local and other numbers or call Information at 12 if you are calling from a private telephone. It will cost 3 "*scatti*."

For numbers outside where you are, dialing must be preceded by "0" and then the area code, which you can obtain from Information. There is no fee for calling in this case. The area codes of main cities are: Rome (06), Milan (02), Florence (055), Venice (041), Turin (011), Naples (081).

SIP (Società Italiana per l'Esercizio Telefonico) will take telegram messages if you call from a private phone by dialing 186. Otherwise, you can send telegrams and telex from the post offices.

EMERGENCIES

SECURITY & CRIME

In the last few years, the biggest threat to public safety, terrorism, has been repressed to a great degree. But the government is still fighting against the Mafia. For tourists, the major problems are pocket-picking, bag-snatching and robbery. It is advisable to have insurance coverage against these.

In the large cities there is sometimes danger of purse-snatching or robbery, but usually Italians are unsuspicious and friendly. Police are always armed.

Observe these simple rules: don't linger in non-commercial areas after dark, don't carry all your cash with you, use credit cards and traveler's checks.

Never leave your luggage unattended. Most hotels provide a storage service. Never leave your money or jewelry in your hotel room, but put them in the hotel's safe-deposits. Always turn in your room key at the desk when going out.

The difficulties encountered by women traveling in Italy are often overstated. However, they should not walk in deserted areas alone. During the day they usually have to put up with much male attention, especially in the south. If this is often annoying, it is rarely dangerous.

When you need the assistance of a police officer, dial 112 (or 113).

One final note: If driving, lock your car and never leave luggage, cameras or other valuables inside.

MEDICAL SERVICES

In cases of real need, such as medical aid or ambulances, you can dial 116, or the Public Emergency Assistance number, 113. These numbers and their services operate on a 24-hour basis, and the number 113, in the principal cities, will answer in the main foreign languages. You can also call the number 112 for the Carabinieri Immediate Action Service.

The Italian National Health Service operates through the Local Health Units (U.S.L.). So, if you need medical assistance, you have to go to the Health Unit in the city or place where you are. The addresses and telephone numbers of the Local Health Units are found in the directory under "Unità Sanitaria Locale." Information about the nearest hospitals and the name of a physician can be obtained by dialing 116.

In case of illness, accident or even childbirth, citizens of Common Market (and of countries with other ties to Italy, such as Brazil, Monaco, Spain and Yugoslavia), must obtain in their country of residence the E-111 form. This form is to state that the bearers are registered in their national health service, in which case they have the right to the same assistance offered to Italian citizens. Citizens of other countries must pay for medical assistance and medicine at the current fees, so health insurance is recommended while traveling in Italy.

Most hospitals have a 24-hour emergency room called "Pronto Soccorso."

GETTING AROUND

DOMESTIC TRAVEL

By Air: The major centers – Rome, Milan, Florence, Venice, Naples – and towns of touristic interest are connected by flights provided mostly by Alitalia Airlines. Smaller airlines are ATI, Alisarda (to and from Sardinia) and Aligiulia. Flying in Italy is expensive compared to taking the train, but it can be useful for long distances.

For detailed information, you can contact your nearest travel agent or Alitalia offices.

Remember that infants under 2 years, accompanied by an adult, have a 90 percent discount; children over two years and under

12 have a 50 percent discount, and young travelers of 12 years to 21 have a 30 percent discount. If you leave on Saturday and return by the following Sunday, you have a 30 percent discount on all Alitalia and ATI domestic services.

BY RAIL

The cheapest and fastest way to travel in Northern and Central Italy is the train. Sometimes it can be difficult to get from one middle-sized city to another but you can always ask at the "Uffici Informazione F.S." in the main railway stations. Check their number in the directory under "Ferroive dello Stato."

Italian trains are divided into several categories: 1) *Locale* is the slowest and stops almost everywhere; 2) *Diretto* is faster than locale, but pretty slow; 3) *Espresso* is the most convenient and relatively quick; 4) *Rapido* is the best and fastest, but you have to pay an additional charge depending on how many kilometers you have to cover. Some of the *rapido* type have only first-class fares and obligatory reservations. These are called TEE (Trans Europe Express). Now there are also IC trains, i.e. Intercity, and airconditioned Eurocity trains which are faster trains connecting Turin, Milan, Venice, Trieste, Genoa and Ventimiglia. They offer reasonable regularity, efficiency and comfort.

Every other train has two different fares: first and second class. The difference between them is limited to the comfort of the seat.

You can buy a ticket at the station or at every F.S. Travel Agency without paying taxes. It is also possible to buy some rail passes, like Rit-Rail Inclusive Tour to travel all around Europe, or Inter Rail for young people under 26. Throughout Italy, there is the Italian Kilometric Ticket which is good for 20 trips amounting to 3,000 km. This can be used for two months by as many as 5 people alone or together. A first class kilometric pass costs L. 207,000, second class L. 115,000 if bought at Italian train stations.

F.S. also provides an efficient service between the Continent and Sicily and Sardinia, but it is advisable to book in advance.

BUSES

Each province in Italy has its own inter-city bus companies and each company has its own fares and lines. It is almost impossible to list them all. For information, check the "Tuttocitta" or ask the EPT offices. It is worthwhile to take buses, especially when you are going to the mountainous interior, because usually buses are cheaper and faster than the train. The ARPA bus line in the Abruzzo is especially efficient, and much faster than the trains.

Rome: The bus system (ATAC) is still cheap, but not so fast and efficient. Buses run frequently throughout the city, but the traffic makes them go slowly and sometimes they are extremely crowded. The ticket costs L. 400 and is available at bars, tobacco shops and some newsstands. The ticket is good only for one ride.

Maps of bus lines are sold at the ATAC Information Office on Piazza Cinquecento in front of Termini station; check also Tutto Città for detailed maps of each zone of Rome.

Milan: Bus and tram service (ATM) is fast and efficient. Tickets, which must be purchased in advance at tobacconists and newsstands, cost L. 500 and are good for 70 minutes of transportation.

Florence: ATAF is the city bus company. A ticket costs L. 400, can be used more than once within an hour's time limit, and is sold at bars, tobacconists and some newsstands. The ATAF Office at Piazza del Duomo 57r will give you a free bus map, but the best transportation in Florence remains simply your feet.

Venice: In this labyrinthine city, it is necessary to buy a good map and walk on foot. There is no bus service, of course; but you may sometimes take motor-boat buses called *vaporetti*. Buy tickets before getting on or pay a surcharge. *Vaporetti* are normal (accelerato) or faster and cost L. 1,200/ 1,500. Usually tourists use lines 1 or 2 (both ply the Canal Grande and go out to the Lido) and 5, the Circolare, which circumnavigates the city in both directions. A 24-hour pass costs L. 8,000.

Naples: Buses (L. 400) run everywhere and are the only public tranportation available along the waterfront. They are generally packed during rush-hour. Due to the traffic's intensity, taxis are not much faster than buses and are much more expensive.

SUBWAYS

Rome: The Metropolitana (subway) is good for longer hauls, even if it is not enough for the rapidly increasing traffic of Rome. There are only two lines: line A covers an 18-km route through the center of the city, from Ottaviano near the Vatican to the eastern edge of the city, just past Cinecittà (Anagnina); line B runs south to the suburbs and beaches (Ostia). The lines intersect at Termini. The fare on each is the same as for the buses, but you cannot use the same ticket, because it is managed by ACOTRAL. There is a special ticket, called Big, which permits travel by both bus and subway for one day on every line (fare is L. 2,800).

Milan: The Metropolitana Milanese (MM) is the best subway in Italy. MM has two lines (1 and 2) which serve almost all the city and the hinterland. Usually tourists get on line 1, which runs south from near the Stazione Centrale through the Piazza del Duomo and west beyond Piazza Santa Maria della Grazie. Tickets are sold at coin-operated machines in each station and cost L. 500, enough for 70 minutes of transportation, if you stay above ground. A L. 2,500 ticket is available for a day on all forms of transport.

Naples: The fast, clean and frequent Metropolitana (L. 400) connects the Stazione Centrale at one end of the city with Mergellina on the other, with only three stops in between. Funiculars (Funicolare Centrale, Funicolare di Chiaia, Funicolare di Montesanto) run up the steep Vomero hill. The Circumvesuviana commuter line runs from the Stazione Centrale around the Bay of Naples, via Ercolano (Herculaneum), Pompeii and Castellemmare di Stabia, to Sorrento. There are two lines and it is important to check that you are on the right one. For complete information, check the monthly tourist publication *Qui Napoli*, available at the tourist office in the train station and at major hotels.

TAXIS

Transportation by taxi is not a convenient alternative to public buses or subways. But it could be necessary sometimes. In that case, you can call for a taxi by dialling the following telephone numbers:
– in Rome, Radio Taxi 3570, 3875, 4994 and 8433;
– in Milan, 6767
– in Florence, 4390 and 4798
– in Naples, 364-444, 364-340
For the other towns check the Tutto Città (first page) or the Yellow Pages.

Fares are calculated by meters and taxi drivers are obliged to show you, if asked, the current list of additional charges. Extra charges are for night rides, luggage, station pick up and the like. It is a general rule to leave a small tip rounding off the fare to the nearest L. 1,000.

WATER TRANSPORT

There are a great many ferryboat and hydrofoil speedboat lines that offer connections between the mainland and Italy's many islands both large and small.

The services run by the State Railways, the Tirrenia, Grandi Traghetti, Trans Tirreno Express and Nav.Ar.Ma. provide all connections with Sicily and Sardinia.

Many other lines connect the peninsula with the smaller islands. Here is some basic information regarding some ship lines.

State Railways: Civitavecchia-Golfo Aranci (Sardinia): departures many times a day for passengers with autos. The crossing takes nine hours.

Tirrenia lines: Civitavecchia-Olbia; Civitavecchia-Cagliari, both direct and via Arbatax. These connections with Sardinia are daily for passengers and cars, with both day and night runs. Tirrenia line also runs Genoa-Porto Torres, Genoa-Cagliari, Naples-Cagliari, all to Sardinia, with an average crossing time of 12 to 15 hours.

Trans Tirreno Express: Leghorn-Olbia, particularly during the high season.

Grandi Traghetti: This line offers connections from Genoa to Porto Torres (about 11 hours) and from Genoa to Palermo (22 hours) both for passengers and cars.

Nav.Ar.Ma: This lines offers a ferry service from Piombino (Tuscany) to the island of

Elba and to Bastia (Corsica).

Toremar-Siremar-Caremar: Toremar offers connections with the Tuscan island (Elba, Giglio) while Siremar runs to the Aeolian islands and Caremar has runs from Naples to the Naples Gulf islands (Capri, Ischia).

Alimar-Aliscafi SVAV: This is a hydrofoil speedboat line which connects Naples and Palermo, via Ustica, in only five hours.

Adriatic: This is another shipping line which can carry passengers and cars from Venice, Trieste, Ancona, Pescara, Bari and Brindisi both to Adriatic and foreign ports. For further information about schedules and fares, ask the various travel agencies and/or the EPT offices.

PRIVATE TRANSPORT

Driving Safely

The speed limit in the cities is 50 km per hour (about 30 mph), while on Italian Highways (*Autostrade*) it is posted along the road. *Autostrades* are fast and uncrowded (except in summer), but Italians sometimes drive faster than the speed limit.

Pay attention to street signs advising no-parking because police are strict on illegal parking and will call a tow truck for vehicles found in no-parking areas. You'll need plenty of cash to bail your car out. Try to park in a garage for the night: it will be a little expensive, but much surer.

In the south, especially in Naples where parking is a nightmare, cars may be left with some degree of safety with the official car parkers, who wear white caps. Never leave a car under the guardianship of somebody who is not wearing a white cap; he may be only guarding his right to steal. Never leave valuables in a car.

Hitchhiking is forbidden on the *autostrade* and is not advised for women traveling alone, especially in the south.

When traveling into the mountain areas during the winter months, it is advisable to call 194 for road conditions. At times, chains will be required on the tires.

CAR RENTALS

Major car rental firms such as Avis, Hertz and Europcar are represented in most cities and at all airports. Agencies are listed in the directory's Yellow Pages under "Autonoleggio." Basic charges range from L. 35,000 to L. 70,000 per day and are based on time plus kilometer. Usually they include a sole insurance coverage, but ask for details about insurance coverage for the renter and all passengers. Rentals may be charged through an Avis charge card or other major credit cards.

The renter must be over 21 and must be in possession of a valid driver's license. Foreign travelers may need to produce an international driver's license.

WHERE TO STAY

HOTELS

Italy offers elegant and luxurious hotels together with inexpensive hotels often called *Albergo* or *Pensioni-Soggiorno*.

The Grand hotels are particularly expensive, but well-suited to the international traveler. Hotels in the luxury and expensive categories usually have every comfort and their staff will help you to find seats at sporting events as well as tours, telex, theater tickets and airline reservations. These hotels are often attractive landmarks in themselves and are recommended for the sophisticated traveler as well as for businessmen.

The rates of these large hotels range from L. 100,000 to L. 250,000 per night, double occupancy (about 50 to 125 U.S. dollars), but rates vary from season to season. Be sure to call or write beforehand to verify and make reservations.

Then there are the smaller hotels, which are a good alternative. These are not always cheaper, but each of them offers basic comfort and good service. The rates of these small hotels range from L. 40/50,000 to L. 150,000 per night, double occupancy.

The listing below offers only a very small selection of the Grand hotels and small hotels in Italy; there are so many hotels in the cheaper categories that choosing among them is almost impossible for this section on travel tips. Your travel agent or the EPT offices in Italy can give you more complete information.

ROME

Grand Hotels

Le Grand Hotel, via Vittorio Emanuele Orlando, 3, tel: 4709. Located between the railway station and via Veneto area. This formal, dignified hotel belongs to the CIGA chain and, like all the others, is very well run and stylish. Expensive.

Hassler-Villa Medici, piazza Trinità dei Monti, 6, tel: 6792651. Ideally located at the top of the Spanish Steps, this hotel is definitely meant for an elite clientele. Particularly beautiful is the roof garden restaurant, with its view of the city. Expensive.

Cavalieri Hilton, via Cadlolo, 101, tel: 3151. At the top of the hill of Monte Mario. Another resort hotel in Rome, offering a beautiful swimming pool, tennis-courts and more. Expensive.

Excelsior, via Vittorio Veneto, 125, tel: 4708. Preferred by the Americans, this grand hotel has for almost a century been a meeting-place of actors, actresses and society people. Expensive.

Eden, via Ludovisi, 49, tel: 4743551. Close to Villa Borghese. Quiet and intimate, with excellent service and a roof garden restaurant. Expensive.

D'Inghilterra, via Bocca di Leone, 14, tel: 672161. Very old-fashioned, with old furniture and old traditions. Ernest Hemingway, Anatole France and Alec Guinness have all stayed here. Very good location in the center of the shopping area. Moderate to expensive.

Parco dei Principi, via G. Mercadante, 15, tel: 841071. Modern, with a swimming pool, on edge of Villa Borghese. Moderate.

Lord Byron, via G. De Notaris, 5, tel: 3609541. Close to Villa Borghese, this first-class small hotel looks like a private club. Only 47 rooms, but a good restaurant (Le Jardin). Moderate.

Forum, via Tor de' Conti, 25, tel: 6792446. In the middle of the Imperial Forum, this charming hotel is a bit out of the way, but offers a beautiful view of Rome from its roof garden. 82 units. Moderate.

Raphael, largo Febo, 2, tel: 6569051. Close to Piazza Navona and near the Senate and the Chamber of Deputies, this hotel attracts many Italian politicians. The service is good, but not excellent. Moderate.

Jolly, corso d'Italia, 1, tel: 8495. The usually high-quality Jolly service, as in the other hotels of the chain.

Small Hotels

Gregoriana, via Gregoriana, 18, tel: 6794269 or 6797988. The attraction here is the decor, which is reminiscent of art deco, with room letters by the 1930s fashion illustrator Erte. Only 19 rooms and no restaurant. Moderate to inexpensive.

Nazionale, piazza Montecitorio, 131, tel: 6789251. Near the Chamber of Deputies, this is another central hotel famous for former guests, including Simone de Beauvoir and Sartre. 78 rooms. Moderate.

Columbus, via della Conciliazione, 33, tel: 6565435. A second-class hotel near St. Peter's, with ancient furniture and 107 rooms. Inexpensive.

Dinesen, via di Porta Pinciana, 18, tel: 4754501. This small hotel is charming for its position, just behind Via Veneto and next to Villa Borghese. Inexpensive.

La Residenza, via Emilia, 22, tel: 6799592. Just off the busy Via Veneto, this is a small, quiet hotel with only 27 rooms. Inexpensive.

Margutta, via Laurina, 34, tel: 6798440. Near piazza del Popolo, this hotel has no restaurant and only 21 rooms, but it is still fairly nice.

Fontana, piazza di Trevi, 96, tel: 6786113. In a restored 13th-century monastery next to the Trevi Fountain, with a beautiful rooftop bar. Inexpensive.

MILAN

Grand Hotels

CIGA. This chain runs four of the best hotels in the city:

Hotel Principe di Savoia, piazza della Republica, 17, tel: 6230. Located north of the Cathedral, this is a classic deluxe hotel, with great service. 298 rooms. Expensive.

Palace Hotel, piazza della Republica, 20, tel: 6336. Close to the railway station, in front of the Principe di Savoia, this very comfortable hotel was recently renovated in an ultra-modern style. Expensive.

Duca di Milano, piazza della Republica, 13, tel: 6284. The hotel is in the same league with the two hotels above.

Diana Majestic, viale Piave, 42, tel: 203404. CIGA style.

Excelsior Gallia, piazza Duca d'Aosta, 9, tel: 6277. Luxury category, a historic hotel located close to Stazione Centrale, near the air-terminal and business center. Expensive.

Milano Hilton, via Galvani, 12, tel: 6983. Contemporary. Decorated in a provincial/modern style. Located in the new commercial center of the city. Expensive.

Executive Hotel, via Don Luigi Sturzo, 45, tel: 6294. American-style, with first-rate service and a good restaurant. Expensive.

Francia Europe, corso Vittorio Emanuele, 9, tel: 708301. Centrally located, near the shops. Quiet and comfortable. Closed August. Moderate.

The JOLLY HOTEL chain has two hotels in Milan:

Jolly Touring, via Tarchetti, 2, tel: 665653. Top class comfort and expensive.

Jolly President, largo Augusto, 2, tel: 7746. Excellent and expensive.

Small Hotels

Marino alla Scala, piazza della Scala, 5, tel: 867831. Friendly, small and comfortable, this hotel is next to La Scala and thus is much frequented by artists and opera lovers. Moderate.

Antica Locanda Solferino, via Castelfidardo, 2, tel: 656905. This is a scrumptious hotel, with old-fashioned furniture and atmosphere. From the rooms' windows, you can look out on the Brera quarter. The service is good, but not excellent. Inexpensive.

Pensione Kennedy, via Tunisia, 6, tel: 200934. A clean and small pensione in a convenient location. Inexpensive.

FLORENCE

Grand Hotels

Excelsior Italiae, piazza Ognissanti, 3, tel: 294301. Luxury category. The only CIGA in Florence. The hotel overlooks the Arno, which you can admire from the terrace restaurant. Expensive.

Villa Medici, via II Prato, 42, tel: 261331. With its huge bedrooms, its roof garden restaurant and its swimming pool, the hotel offers everything your heart could desire, including a good location near the railway station. Expensive.

Grand Hotel Villa Cora, viale Machiavelli, 18, tel: 2298541. Luxury category. Located on the hills of Florence. Built by the Baron Oppenheim in a Neo-classic style, the place is famous for having hosted Eugenia di Montijo, the widow of Napoleon III, and the rich Baroness Von Meck, patroness of Tchaikovsky and Debussy. The hotel offers a quiet atmosphere, a huge park and a pool. Expensive.

Savoy, piazza della Republica, 7, tel: 283313. In the heart of Florence, the hotel is classic in style and service. Many rooms are decorated in Venetian style. Expensive.

Hotel de la Ville, piazza Antinori, 1, tel: 261805. Quiet and elegant, located in the center of Florence, next to Via Tornabuoni. Good service and comfort. Expensive.

Small hotels

Hotel Regency, piazza Massimo d'Azaeglio, 3, tel: 245247. This is the right place for people who like quiet and comfort. The hotel offers a charming garden, beautiful furniture, a gourmet restaurant and a central position. Expensive.

Lungarno, borgo San Jacopo, 14, tel: 264211. This modern hotel overlooks the Arno between Ponte Vecchio and Ponte Santa Trinita. Moderate.

Beacci Tronabouni, via Tornabouni, 3, tel: 212645. This small delightful pensione is built on the most elegant street in Florence. Inexpensive.

Pensione Bencistà, Fiesol, tel: 59163. A little bit out of the city, between Fiesole and San Domenico, this small hotel in a 15th-century villa is small and simple, with no phones in the rooms, but it is quiet and rates are inexpensive. Closed from November to mid-March.

Pensione Annalena, via Romana, 34, tel: 222402. Located across the Ponte Vecchio, just beyond the Pitti Palace, this elegant little place offers a lovely Florentine experience at inexpensive prices.

Castello di Gargonza, 52048 Monte San Savino, Arezzo. tel: 847021. A restored country hamlet in the Tuscan hills between Arezzo and Siena. Visitors stay in modernized 13th-century cottages. The place has been meticulously restored. Excellent restaurant. Moderate.

VENICE

Grand Hotels

Gritti Palace Hotel, campo Santa Maria del Giglio, 2467, tel: 26044. Luxury category. Extremely comfortable, located in a 15th-century palace on the grand canal that belonged to the Doge Andrea Gritti. Hemingway, Winston Churchill, Herbert von Karajan and Greta Garbo all stayed here. The service is perfect, the cuisine refined and the position charming. Very expensive.

Danieli Royal Excelsior, riva degli Schiavoni, 4196, tel: 26480. This CIGA Hotel is also rich with memories of the important men and women who spent the night here: George Sand, Alfred de Musset, Dickens, D'Annunzio, Wagner; kings, princes, stars... The incredible front hall is an attraction in itself, and the rooms are magnificent. The roof garden restaurant has a wonderful view of the Laguna. Of course, expensive.

Europa & Regina Hotel, San Marco, 2159, tel: 700477. In front of the Church of the Salute, with rooms overlooking the Canal Grande, this old hotel has been tastefully redecorated. The service is first-class. Expensive.

Excelsior Palace Hotel, Lungomare Marconi, 41, Lido di Venezia, tel: 760201. Another CIGA hotel, perhaps the first among luxury hotels in Italy. It looks like a castle, with a great number of huge rooms and incredible service. It has a private beach, always clean; a night-club, tennis courts, gardens, golf-links and even a theater. Very expensive.

Cipriani, Isola della Giudecca, 10, tel: 85068. A great invention by Giuseppe Cipriani: from here piazza San Marco and the Palazzo Ducale seem to be different. It offers big and comfortable rooms, a swimming pool, gardens and flowers together with a refined but simple cuisine.

Locanda Cipriani, Isola di Torcello, tel: 730150. Only 6 rooms (!) very, very exclusive, with a homey atmosphere, on a little island far from the noisy center of Venice. Expensive.

Grand Hotel des Bains, Lungomare Marconi, 17, tel: 765921. This CIGA hotel brings to mind Thomas Mann and Mahler's Fifth Symphonie – in a word, "Death in Venice." It is located on the sea, and has every comfort. Expensive.

Small hotels

Monaco and Grand Canal, San Marco, 1325, tel: 700211. First category. Located where the Canal Grande flows into the Laguna. Very intimate and comfortable. The rooms are perhaps a little bit small and sometimes noisy, but there is good service. Moderate.

Saturnia International, Calle Larga XXII Marzo, 2398, tel: 708377. A very romantic hotel, near piazza San Marco, in a 16th-century palace. Intimate and comfortable, at moderate prices.

Flora, Calle Larga XXII Marzo, 2283/A, tel: 705844. A small but delightful hotel (only 42 rooms) with a garden. Quiet and comfortable. Inexpensive.

TURIN

Villa Sassi, Strada Traforo del Pino, 47, tel: 890556. Located on the hill of Torino, the hotel is an 18th-century villa, in the middle of a great park, with only 12 bedrooms, excellent service and great comfort. Very exclusive and expensive.

Jolly Hotel Principi di Piemonte, via Piero Gobetti, 15, tel: 532153 or 591693. The most central hotel in Torino. Very comfortable, with excellent service. Expensive.

Jolly Hotel Ambasciatori, Corso Vittorio Emanuele, 104, tel: 5752. Favored by businessmen. It is in a good position, with good service. The hotel hosted the Rolling Stones in 1982. Expensive.

City, via F. Juvarra, 25, tel; 540546. A small, comfortable hotel of the first category, close to the station of Porta Susa. 40 bedrooms. Moderate.

TRIESTE

Duchi d'Aosta, via dell'Orologio, 2, tel: 62081. This hotel is small but very charming, with big, well-furnished rooms, an excellent restaurant (Harry's Grill), efficient service and a central position. Expensive.

Savoia Excelsior Palace, Riva del Mandrachio, 4, tel: 7690. First category, 154 rooms and every comfort. Expensive.

Jolly, Corso Cavour, 7, tel: 7694. Jollystyle, the usual great service and comfort. Expensive.

GENOA

Colombia Excelsior, via Balbi, 40, tel: 261841. CIGA-style: luxury category, close to the railway station, in an *art nouveau*-style palace, with big, comfortable rooms and excellent service. Expensive.

Bristol Palace, via XX Settembre, 35, tel: 592541. First category. Despite its modest entrance, this is a well-furnished hotel – particularly the dining-room, which is decorated in the Louis XVI style. Good service. Moderate.

Savoia Majestic, piazza Acquaverde, tel: 261641. First category, comfortable, good service, in a central position. Expensive.

Plaza, via M. Piaggio, 11, tel: 893642. This hotel was a small villa before being transformed into comfortable lodgings in an ideal location close to piazza Corvetto.

BOLOGNA

Royal Carlton, via Montebello, 8, tel: 554141. This big hotel, close to the railway station, is extremely comfortable but a little anonymous. Excellent service. Expensive.

Jolly, piazza XX Settembre, 2, tel: 264405. Close to the station and the Alitalia terminal. Large and comfortable. Moderate.

Grand Hotel Elite, via Aurelio Saffi, 36, tel: 437417. Very modern and comfortable, with one of the best restaurants in Bologna. Expensive.

RAVENNA

Jolly, piazza Mameli, 1, tel: 35762. Excellent, like the others of the Jolly chain. Restaurant. Expensive.

Bisanzio, via Salara, 30, tel: 27111. Close to the most important monuments in Ravenna, modern and comfortable, with simple rooms and a good service. Moderate.

Villa Bolis, via Corriera 5-Barbiano, località Cotignola (Ravenna), tel: 0545-79347. A quarter of an hour away from Ravenna, in the middle of the sweet country of Romagna, lies this Perfect British countryclub hotel, with swimming pool, tennis courts and excellent cuisine. Moderate.

UMBRIA AND THE MARCHES

La Rosetta, piazza Italia, 19, Perugia, tel: 20841. A good hotel of the second category, with a new and an old part. In the summer, come here to eat in the courtyard under pergolas and palms, fine service. Moderate.

Subasio, via Frate Elia, 2, Assisi, tel: 812206. The columns of this hotel link to the church of San Francesco, the terraces command a wonderful view of the town and countryside. Many famous people have stayed in this hotel, including the king and the queen of Belgium, Charlie Chaplin, James Stewart and Marlene Dietrich. Good rooms and service. Moderate.

Umbra, vicolo degli Archi, 6, Assisi, tel: 812240. Its location close to the piazza del Comune makes this the most central hotel in Assisi. Though small, the rooms are comfortable and the restaurant is very good. Moderate.

Piero della Francesca, viale Comandino, 53, Urbino, tel: 4570. Fine hotel. Moderate.

Le tre Vaselle, Torgiano Perugia, tel: 982447. A few kilometers from Perugia. This delicious small hotel in an ancient villa owned by Giorgio Lungarotti, one of the most famous wine-collectors in Italy. This hotel has pleasant atmosphere and great cooking. Expensive.

ABRUZZO

Duca degli Abruzzi, via duca degli Abruzzi, 10, L'Aquila, tel: 28341. A second category hotel that happens to be very well run. From the restaurant there is a wide panorama. Moderate.

Esplanade, piazza 1 Maggio, 46, Pescara, tel: 292141. Old-style hotel with recently modernised interior. Excellent views. Right across from the beach. Moderate.

MOLISE

Skanderbeg, via Novelli, Campob Asso, tel: 93341. The best in town, comfortable. Moderate.

LIGURIA (THE RIVIERA)

Grand Hotel Diana, via Garibaldi, 110, Al Assio, tel: 42701. First category, open from April till October, with good service, a swimming-pool and a terrace-garden at moderate prices.

Royal, corso Imperatrice, 74, San Remo, tel: 79991. Luxury category. Gardens filled with flowers, palms and terraces surround this classic hotel with big comfortable rooms which overlooks the sea or the hills. Expensive.

Grand Hotel Londra, corso Matuzia, 2, San Remo, tel: 79961. First category. Old, quiet and pleasant. Close to the Casino. Moderate.

Grand Hotel Cap Ampelio, via Virgilio, 5, Bordighera, tel: 264333. Ideally located on the hill of Bordighera, this refined hotel has a splendid view over the sea and coastline. Expensive.

Grand Hotel del Mare, via Aurelia a capo Migliarese, Bordighera, tel: 262201. First category, overlooking the sea, preferred by adults for its quietness, its comfort and its beautiful rooms. Expensive.

La Riserva, A Castel d'Appio, Ventimiglia, tel: 39533. This is a small place with a wonderful view of the Riviera dei Fiori and the Costa Azzurra. The rooms are comfortable and the service is homely, but courteous. Moderate.

Cenobio dei Dogi, via Cuneo, 34, Camogli, tel: 770041. First category. This hotel, in a wonderful spot overlooking the sea, is surrounded by a splendid park. It is known for its beautiful rooms, fine restaurant, salt water swimming-pool and solarium, its private beach and its nightclub during the summer. Expensive.

Imperial Palace, via Pagana, 19, Santa Margherita Ligure, tel: 88991. Luxury category. This is a big hotel in the classic tradition, surrounded by a tropical garden. Old-fashioned decor, big rooms and excellent service. Expensive.

Splendido, Portofino, tel: 69551. Luxury category. This hotel is a peaceful oasis along a street lined with olive-trees, with a splendid view of the Portofino promontory and every comfort. Expensive.

Grand Hotel dei Castelli, via alla Penisola, 26, Sestri Levante, tel: 41044. In front of the church of S. Niccolò, very quiet and pleasant, surrounded by a big park overlooking the sea. An elevator descends to the private beach. Excellent service. Expensive.

NAPLES

Excelsior, via alla Penisola, 26, Sestri Levante, tel: 41044. A CIGA hotel. Just across the street from the Castel dell'Ovo, with a wonderful view of the Gulf of Naples. Expensive.

Vesuvio, via Partenope, 45, tel: 417044. Another top hotel just down the street from the Excelsior, with more moderate prices.

Jolly, via Medina, 70, tel: 416000. This modern high-rise has a roof-garden restaurant with great views of the city. Moderate.

Parker's, corso Vittorio Emanuele, 135, tel: 684866. Located in a 19th-century palace with casual decor, this first category hotel is far from the sea on the hill of Posillipo. Good service. Moderate.

APULIA

Palace Hotel, via Lombardi, 13, Bari, tel: 216551. Modern, big, comfortable. Moderate to expensive.

Jolly, Ia Giulio Pietroni, 15, Bari, tel: 364366. A new, comfortable and quiet hotel in the Jolly style. Expensive.

President, Ia Salandra, 6, Lecce, tel: 51881. A top class hotel with good service. Expensive.

CALABRIA

Grand Hotel Excelsior, piazza Indipendenza, Reggio di Calabria, tel: 25801. First category. Very comfortable rooms and good service. Moderate.

Grand Hotel San Michele, on the S.S. (Strada Statale) 18 at Cetraro (COSENZA), tel: 91006. It is a sheer drop from this hotel to the sea, and the place is located in a wonderful park. The hotel offers all the comforts (tennis courts, swimming pool and elevator to the beach).

SICILY

Grand Hotel Villa Igiea, Salita Belmonte, 1, Palermo, tel: 543744. Located near the Lido di Modello, under the Monte Pellegrino, this hotel was built by the architect Basile in the Liberty style for don Ignazio Florio, a famous Sicilian shipowner. The outside looks like a Norman palace, but the interior is richly decorated with flowers. The terraces and the big park, with a swimming pool overlooking the sea, complete a suggestive whole. Very expensive.

Jolly, Foro Italico, 22, Palermo, tel: 235842. Big and modern, this hotel offers the top-class comfort and service of all Jolly hotels. Moderate to expensive.

Jolly Hotel dello Stretto, corso Garibaldi, 126, Messina, tel: 43401. Every comfort, as usual, and at moderate prices. First category.

Hotel San Domenico Palace, piazza San Domenico, 5, Taormina (Messina), tel: 23701. This hotel is quite famous for its location, its park and its rooms which have extraordinary views. Expensive.

Jolly dei Templi, Villaggio Mosé, S.S. 115, Agrigento, tel: 76144. This is a modern hotel in a central location, and though the surroundings are a little bit noisy, the rooms are comfortable and the service is good. Moderate.

Villa Politi, via Politi, 2, Siracusa, tel: 32100. This hotel has an atmosphere similar to that of the hotel in Giuseppe di Lampedusa's *The Leopard*. Quiet rooms and good service. Moderate.

Jolly, corso Gelone, 43, Siracusa, tel: 64744. Close to the archaeological sites, comfortable, elegant. Expensive.

FOOD DIGEST

WHAT TO EAT

The gentle lifestyle of Italy is partly a product of its civilized eating habits: eating and drinking in tranquility at least twice a day are the norm here.

Italian breakfast is quite different from the English or American. *Colazione* usually is light and consists of *cappuccino* (coffee and milk) and a *briosche* (roll), or simply *caffè* (black and strong espresso).

Except in the industrialized cities, *pranzo* (lunch) is the big meal. It consists of *antipasto* (hors-d'oeuvre), a *primo* (pasta, rice or soup) and a *secondo*, meat or fish with a vegetable (*contorno*), or salad. Then one may have cheese and/or fruit. Italians usually drink coffee (espresso) also after lunch and/or a liqueur, such as *grappa, amaro* or *sambuca*.

Dinner is similar to lunch, but lighter. If one eats less at lunch, dinner becomes the major meal.

During summer people are used to eating ice creams or *granite* (crushed ice with syrup flavored with different fruits – known in New York as "Italian Ice"). The best ice cream in Italy can be tasted at Vivoli's, via Isola delle Stinche 7, in Florence; the *granita* is a specialty from Sicily.

Every region in Italy has its own typical dishes, so that it becomes difficult to list them all. Remember that the further south you travel, the more the food is spicy and heavy, the more the wine is strong.

WHERE TO EAT

Italy has thousands of restaurants, *trattorie* and *osterie* (in roughly descending order, from the more expensive and fancy to the inexpensive).

If you do not want to have a complete meal, you can have a snack at the bars or at *tavole calde* and *rosticcerie* (grills).

If you go to a restaurant, don't order just a salad: the waiters could look down on you! If you think a complete meal is too big for you, renounce the *antipasto*, but take a *primo* and a *secondo* at least.

The restaurants listed below have been recommended by Italian food writers and/or the authors of this guide. We categorize our restaurants by I = inexpensive (about L. 20,000); M = moderate (from L. 20,000 to 40, 000); E = expensive (about L. 40,000 or a few more). We even list some very high-quality restaurants, indicating them by L = luxurious (from L. 50/60,000 to 100,000).

RESTAURANTS

Rome

El Toulà, via della Lupa, 29/B, tel: 6781196. Closed Sat. midday, Sun. and August. Very elegant decor. The cuisine is refined and international, but the regional (Venetian) dishes are the best. An impressive wine list. Reservations necessary. Major credit cards accepted. "L"

Hosteria dell'Orso, via dei Soldati, 25, tel: 6564250. Closed Sun. and August. In a Renaissance building, between piazza Navona and the Tiber river, with a beautiful terrace and a night-club. The cuisine is international too. Try *cannelloni Hosteria, tagliolini dei Borgia, sogliola alle mandorle, tournedos Semiramis*. Wine list mostly national. Reservations. "L"

Passetto, via Zanardelli, 14, tel: 6540659. Closed Sun., Christmas and August. Classic Italian cuisine. Traditional atmosphere and good service. "E"

Ranieri, via Mario Dè Fiori, 26. tel: 679-1592. Closed Sun. Founded in 1849, the restaurant is just right for tête-à-tête dinners. Fin de siècle furniture, historic motif. "E"

Le jardin dell'Hotel Byron, via de Notaris, 5, tel: 3609541. Exquisite, elegant, first rate, in a wonderful garden. "L"

Eau Vive, via Monterone, 85, tel: 6541095. Closed Sun. and August. In a 15th-century palace managed by nuns. International cuisine, especially French. "M"

Taverna Giulia, vicolo dell'Oro, 23, tel: 6569768. Closed Sun. and August. A classic restaurant which serves food outside during the summer. Great national and Genoese cuisine. Try *trenette al pesto* (thin noodles in a sauce of fresh basil, pine nuts, garlic and olive oil), and *stinco al forno* (roast shoulder of veal). "M"

Chianti, via Ancona, 17, tel: 856731. Closed Sun. and August. Rustic *trattoria* with tavern. Great Tuscan cuisine. "M"

Carmelo, via della Rosetta, 9, tel: 6561002. Closed Sun., Mon. lunch, and August. A small and rustic seafood place. Even if this trattoria smells of salt water, it is worth visiting for a taste of Sicilian seafood and fish cuisine. "E"

Girarrosto toscano, via Campania, 29, tel: 493759. Closed Wed. Modern tavern with traditional Tuscan cuisine. "E"

Piperno, via Monte de' Cenci, 9, tel: 6540629. Closed Sun., Mon., Christmas and August. Traditional Roman *trattoria*, with romantic outside service during the summer on a little piazza in old Rome. Roman cuisine: *ravioli ricotta e spinaci, saltimbocca* etc. "E"

Checchino dal 1887, via Monte Testaccio, 30, tel: 576318. Closed Sun. dinner, Mon., Christmas and from July 15 to August 15. Authentic old-time family atmosphere, typical Roman cuisine. Reserve. "M"

Ciceruacchio, via del Porto, 1, tel: 580-6046. Closed Mon. and August. At Trastevere. Very touristy place on the lines of an old-fashioned tavern. Roman cuisine, list of local wines. "M"

Romolo, via di Porta Settiminiana, 8, tel: 5818284. Closed Mon. and August. Reserve. Trastevere ambience with a summer court. Good Roman cuisine. "M"

Colline emiliane, via degli Avignonesi, 22, tel: 475738. Closed Fri. and August. Reserve. Classic ambience, rich Emilian cuisine. "I"

Al ceppo, via Panama, 2, tel: 84409696. Closed Mon. and August. Typical restaurant with Roman cuisine. "I"

Pierdonati, via della Conciliazione, 39, tel: 6543557. Closed Tue. and August 1-15. Medium comfort, tavern. Traditional Italian cuisine, local wines. "I"

Elettra, via Principe Amedeo, 72, tel: 4745397. Closed Fri. night, Sat. and August. Crowded with regular diners, the place has a pleasant homely atmosphere and a traditional, but often varied, cuisine. "I"

Cannavota, piazza S. Giovanni in Laterano, tel: 775007. Closed Wed. and August. Crowded with tourists, very informal, Roman cuisine. "I"

La vigna dei cardinali, piazzale Ponte Milvio, 34, tel: 3965846. Closed Sat. and August 15. A nice restaurant with a beautiful summer garden. Traditional cuisine, with variations. "I"

NEAR ROME

Cinque statue, largo S. Angelo, 1, Tivoli, tel: 20366. Closed Fri. and Sun. night. Great ambience with tourist tables, plain cooking, modern furniture and, in summer, tables outside.

Antico ristorante Giudizi, piazza Cavour, 20, Tarquinia, tel: 855061. Closed Mon. In front of the Museum. Regional fish and seafood cuisine. "I"

Trattoria del Gobbo, lungoporto Gramsci, 29/35, tel: 23163. Closed Wed. Reserve. Traditional seafood. *Cívitavecchia*. "I"

Stella, piazza della Liberazione, 3, Palestrina, tel: 9558172. Modern ambience, local cuisine. "I"

La Taverna, via Nemorese, 13, Nemi (Colli Albani area), tel: 9378135. Closed Mon. Reserve. Nice and simple with a great fire-place, offering traditional cooking. "I"

Allo sbarco di Enea, via dei Romagnoli, 657, Ostia, tel: 5650034. Crowded with tourists, during the summer one can eat both meat and fish cooked in a Roman way under a bower. "M"

Belvedere, via dei Monasteri, 33, Subiaco, tel: 85531. Closed Tues. In a little hotel, this great restaurant offers Italian cooking. "I"

MILAN

Gualtiero Marchesi, via Bonvesin della Riva, 9, tel: 741246. Closed Sun. and from July 15 to August 30. Reservations necessary. The temple of Italian cuisine, the best in Italy, modern ambience. For elite people. "L"

Savini, galleria Vittorio Emanuele, 11 close to piazza Duomo, tel: 8058343. Closed Sun. and August. Reserve. In the living-room of Milan, with an exquisite decor, ultraprofessional service and classic Italian cuisine. "L"

Scaletta, piazza Stazione Genova, 3, tel: 8350290. Closed Sun., Mon., Easter and Christmas. Reserve. A modern ambience, with a library. International level cuisine. Very "in." "L"

Gran San Bernardo, via Borghese, 14, tel: 389000. Closed Sun. and August. Reservations necessary. A large and friendly restaurant where some of the best regional cooking is served. Try *casseoeula* (a stew of pork, sausages, carrots served with cornbread) and *polenta*. "E"

Al Mercante, piazza Mercanti, 17, tel: 8052198. Closed Sun. and August. Reserve. Friendly, overlooking the piazza. In summer you can eat outdoors under a very old loggia. "M"

Trattoria della pesa, via Pasubio 10, tel: 665741. Closed Sun. and August. Reserve. One hundred years old. Traditional Milanese cuisine is served here. "M"

Osteria al Pontell, via Mameli, 1, tel: 733818. Closed Mon. and August. Reserve. Typical Milanese *osteria*, with friendly service. "M"

Brasera Meneghina, via Circo, 10, tel: 808108. Closed Fri., Sat. lunch and August. Genuine *osteria* of old Milan, dating back to the 17th century; it preserves a fireplace and a small porch painted with frescoes, and offers outdoor dining in summer. "M"

La bella Pisana, via Sottocorno, 17, tel: 708376. Closed Sun., Mon. lunch and August, Reserve. Pleasant ambience, with a garden for summer. Padana plain cooking and fresh fish. "M"

Taverna Gran Sasso, via Principessa Clotilde, 10, tel: 6597578. Closed Sun. and August. Reserve. Kitsch restaurant, with Abruzzese cooking. "I"

Trattoria Aurora, via Savona, 23, tel: 8354978. Closed Mon. and August. This typical family-run trattoria offers Piedmontese cooking. "I"

LOMBARDY

Bixio, piazza Castello, 1, Pavia, tel: 25343. Closed Sun. dinner and Mon. 19th-century ambience and traditional cuisine. "M"

Ferrari da Tino, via dei Mille, 111, Pavia, tel: 31033. Closed Mon. and July 15 to August 15. Old-fashioned homely trattoria, regional cooking. "I"

La Pergola, via Borgo Canale, 62, Bergamo, tel: 256353. Closed Sun., Mon. lunch and August. Reserve. Located on a hill with a wonderful terrace. Known for traditional high-level cooking. "E"

Agnello d'Oro, via Gombito, 22, Bergamo, tel: 249883. Closed Mon. and January. Reserve. Good regional food in an old hotel in the high part of town. "M"

Trattoria del Teatro, piazza Mascheroni, Bergamo, tel: 238862. Closed Mon. 19th-century furniture; the food is simple, traditional, delicious. "I"

Ceresole, via Ceresole, 4, Cremona, tel: 23322. Closed Sun. night, Mon. and August. Reserve. Classic national cuisine. "M"

Cigno, piazza Carlo d'Arco, 1, Mantova. tel: 327101. Closed Mon., Tue. night and August. Reserve. In a wonderful piazza, in an ancient building, the service is as excellent as the regional cooking. "E"

Ai Garibaldini, via S. Longini, 7, tel: 329237. Closed Wed. dinner, Fri. and July. Old bourgeois style ambience, 16th-century furniture and summer terrace. Regional cuisine. "M"

TURIN

Del Cambio, piazzo Carignano, 2, tel: 546690. Closed Sun. and August. Reservations necessary. Opened in 1757, this is one of the most beautiful restaurants in Italy, with 19th-century furniture and atmosphere. For those with the highest tastes. International and national cuisine. "L"

Villa Sassi, strada Traforo del Pino, 47, tel: 890556. Closed Sun. Reserve. In a cardinal's villa, this is a restaurant for V.I.Ps, with an attached hotel (only 24 beds!). Exclusive and fancy, with superb cuisine. "L"

Ostu Bacu, corso Vercelli, 226, tel: 264579. Closed Sun. and August. Reserve. Modern ambience. Come here to taste plain old-fashioned Piemontese cooking.

La capannina, via Donati, 1, tel: 545405. Closed Sun. and August. Reserve. The ambience is rustic, as in the twin restaurant at Alba, and the food is strictly cooked in the Langarola-style (The Langhe are a part of Piemonte). Superb is the *fritto misto*. "M"

Spada reale, via Principe Amedeo, 53, tel: 832835. Closed Sun., Christmas and Easter. Reserve. Modern-style, Tuscan and Piemontese cuisine. "I"

Tre Galline, via Bellezia, 7, tel: 546833. Closed Mon. and August. Reserve. A typical old-fashioned *piola* (a meeting-place to drink wine and eat snacks); regional cooking. "I"

AOSTA AND THE ALPS

Cavallo bianco, via E. Aubert, 15, tel: 2214. Closed Sun. night and Mon., June 16 to July 15 and December 12 to 24. Reserve. 19th-century atmosphere, overlooking an 18th-century court. Good regional cuisine. "E"

AGIP, corso Ivrea, 138, tel: 44565. Closed Mon. and February. On the highway. Modern ambience, with large windows overlooking a green panorama. The food is both national and regional. "M"

Les Neige d'Antan, località Cret Perreres, Statale 406, Breuil-Cervinia, tel: 948775. Closed Mon. and September 11 to November 30 and May 3 to July 9. Reserve. This is a quiet house on a mountain, with a few bedrooms and typical Valdostana cooking, and a fine view of Mt. Cervino. Try the *fonduta*. "M"

Batezar, via Marconi, 1, St. Vinceny. tel: 3164. Closed Wed., Thur. lunch, June 20 to July 10 and December 10 to 24. Close to the Casino, with an elegant atmosphere, this restaurant offers personalized cooking and efficient service. "E"

FLORENCE

Enoteca Pinchiorri, via Ghibellina, 87, tel: 242777. Closed Sun. and Mon. lunch and August. Reservations necessary. In the 15th-century Ciofi Palace, with a delightful courtyard for dining in the open air. Superb nouvelle-cuisine, with an impressive wine collection (almost 60,000 bottles). "L"

La Loggia, piazzale Michelangelo, tel: 287032. Closed Wed. and August 1 to 15. The beautiful view of Florence will bewitch you as you indulge in international or Italian delicacies. Good service. "M"

13 Gobbi, via del Porcellana, 12r, tel: 298769. Closed Sun. and Mon. and August. Reserve. Beer-house style, but the cooking is Tuscan and Ungarian first-class. "M"

Otello, via degli Orti Oricellari, 36r, tel: 215819. Closed Tue. and August. Reserve. Typical Florentine restaurant, as is the cuisine. Try the *ribollita*. "M"

Dino, via Ghibellina, 51r, tel: 241452. Closed Sun. night, Mon. and August. Former wine store. Regional atmosphere and cooking. "M"

Omero via Pian de' Giullari, 11r, tel: 220053. Closed Tue. and August. Reserve. Also an old store, now transformed into a rustic *trattoria* with outside tables in summer. Splendid view. "I-M"

Cantinone del Gallo Nero, via S. Spirito, 6r, tel: 218898. Closed Mon. and August. Always crowded with tourists and locals, the restaurant is located in a 15th-century wine-cellar where everything is very informal. The specialty of this place is its Chianti wine collection (about 300 kinds) and the Tuscan peasant dishes, such as *crostoni, ribollita, pinzimonio.* "I"

TUSCANY

Tullio ai Tre Cristi, vicolo Provenzano, 1/7, Siena. tel: 280608. Closed Mon. and Sun. night. A 19th-century *trattoria* attached to a shrine representing the "Crucifixion." The restaurant has been managed for 40 years by the same family, who offer a Senese cusine. Try the *pici*, a kind of handmade spaghetti. "M"

Guido, vicolo Pier Pettinaio, 7, Siena, tel: 280042. Closed Mon. 14th-century style, with a big space for the kitchen, good service and traditional regional cooking. "M"

Grota Santa Caterina, via della Galluzza, 28, Siena. tel: 282208. Closed Mon. Characteristic Senese tavern. "I"

La Cisterna, piazza della Cisterna, 23, Siena, tel: 940328, San Gimignano. Closed Tue., Wed. lunch and from November to February. Reserve. In a 15th-century monastery, with a wonderful view of the turreted village. Popular among tourists.

Sergio, lungarno Pacinotti, 1, Pisa. tel: 48245. Closed Sun., Mon. lunch and January. Elegant, with great furniture and excellent regional cuisine. "E"

Da Giulio, via San Tommaso, 29 Lucca, tel: 55948. Closed Sun., Mon. and August. Just plain good food. "I"

Cecco, corso Italia, 125 Arezzo, tel: 20986. Closed Mon. and August. Hybrid place, bar and *tavola calda*, but good cooking with no pretensions. "M"

La loggetta, piazza Peschiera, 3, Cortona, tel: 603777. Closed Mon. and January. Reserve. Mellow atmosphere, with good regional cooking. "M"

VENICE

Harry's Bar, calle Vallaresso, 1323, tel: 85331. Closed Mon. and January. International, modern meeting-place, American-bar style, very refined. "E"

Antico Martini, Campo San Fantin, 1983, tel: 24121. Close to the Teatro La Fenice. Closed Tue. and Wed. lunch. Reserve. High class and intimate, with an 18th-century cafè atmosphere. Venetian cuisine. "L"

Al Graspo de Ua, San Marco, 5094, tel: 23647. Calle Bombaseri, close to the Rialto bridge. Closed Mon. and Tue. and from December 20 to January 6. The restaurant under its old wooden roof, is centuries-old, with a long tradition of excellent cooking. It is a delight for those seeking local color. National cuisine. "M"

Antica Bessetta, S. Croce, 1395, calle Savio, tel: 37687. Closed Tue., Wed. and from July 15 to August 16. Authentic Venetian *trattoria*, run by a family. Regional cooking. Try fish. "M"

Madonna, calle della Madonna, 594, tel: 23824. Closed Wed., August and January. Reserve. Close to Rialto, this is a 19th-century *trattoria*, simple and friendly. "M"

Poste Vece, S. Polo, 1608, tel: 25479. Closed Tue., Wed and from November 20 to December 20. Reserve. Near the fish market, this is an authentic Venetian *trattoria*. "I"

Antica Carbonera, S. Marco, 4648, tel: 25479. Closed Tue., Wed. and from July 15 to August 16. Recently rebuilt, but maintaining its 19th-century ambience, with good Italian cooking. "I"

VENETO

Dotto, via Squarcione, 23, Padova, tel: 25055. Closed Sun. night, Mon. and August Reserve. Classic furniture and typical Padoan cuisine. Try *pasta e fagioli* (pasta and beans) and *baccalà* (stockfish). "M"

Al Pozzo, via S. Antonio, 1, Vicenza, tel: 21411. Closed Tues. and in July and August on Sun. Comfortable belle-epoque ambience and national and regional cuisine. "M"

12 Apostoli, vicolo Corticella S. Marco, 3, Verona, tel: 596999. Closed Sun. dinner, Mon., Christmas and from June 12 to July 7. Reservations necessary. One of the best restaurants in Italy, located in an ancient building decorated with the frescoes of Casarini. "E"

Marconi, via Fogge, 4, Verona, tel: 591910. Closed Sun., Tue. dinner and August. Elegant, with new furniture; some years ago, it was simply an *osteria*. Regional classic cuisine.

FRIULI-VENEZIA GUILIA

Antica trattoria Suban, via Comici, 2, Trieste, tel: 54368. Closed Tue., August and Christmas. Reserve. Friendly and simple, with a summer bower. Good regional cuisine. "M"

Buffet Bendetto, via XXX Ottobre, 19, Trieste, tel: 61655. Closed Mon. and August. Reserve. Rustic and informal, with traditional cooking. "I"

Alla Vedova, via Tavagnacco, 9, Udine, tel: 470291. Closed Sun. dinner, Mon. and August. Reserve. Very old Friulian restaurant, with outdoor tables in summer. Good traditional cooking. "M"

TRENTINO-ALTO-ADIGE

Chiesa, parco s. Marco, Trento, tel: 985577. Closed Sun. dinner and Mon. On the first floor of a 17th-century palace with a cloister. Very elegant and refined. "M"

Da Abramo, piazza Gries, 16, Bolzano, tel: 30141. Closed Sun. dinner and Mon. In the old town-hall. Liberty-style restaurant with garden, serving good regional cuisine. "M"

BOLOGNA

Dante, via Belvedere, 2/B, tel: 224464. Closed Mon., Tues. lunch and August. In a 14th-century palace. Very elegant. International cuisine. "E"

Rosteria Luciano, via Sauro, 17, tel: 231249. Closed Wed. and August. A classic restaurant where one can sample excellent regional food. Try *tortellini* and *armonie dell'Appennino*. "M"

Serghei, via Piella, 12, in the historic center. Typical small *trattoria* with just a few tables, but good cooking, in a pleasant homey atmosphere. "I"

Birreria Lamma, via dei Giudei, 4, tel: 279422. Closed Wed. Regional cuisine, for those who are in a hurry and those who are quiet. "I"

Da Bertino e figrio, via delle Lame, 55, tel: 522230. Closed Sun. and August 1-15. Funny Emilian *trattoria*, with good cooking. "I"

Bacco Villa Orsi, località Funo di Argelato, at Km. 13, tel: 862451. Closed Sat., Sun. and August. Reservations necessary. In an 18th-century villa with a beautiful porch. Regional and international dishes. Try the roasted meat specialities.

EMILIA-ROMAGNA

Al Gallo, via Maggiore, 87, Ravenna, tel: 23775. Closed Mon. night, Tues. and February. Has a delicious *pergola* in summer. Good (not exceptional) local food. "I"

Righi-La Taverna, piazza Libertà S. Marino, tel: 991196. Closed Mon. in winter, and January. Rustic, but good food. "I"

Vecchia Rimini, piazza Ferrari, 22, Rimini, tel: 51327. Closed Mon., Tue. and August 1-15. Emphasis is on fish and seafood. "M"

Vecchia Chitarra, via Ravenna, 13, Ferrara, tel: 62204. Closed Mon. and the second half of July. Reserve. Informal restaurant with very good cooking. "M"

La Filoma, via XX Marzo, 15, Parma, tel: 34269. Closed Sat. and Sun. Refined, with 17th-century furniture and traditional cooking. "M"

Fini, piazza San Franscesco Modena, tel: 223314. Closed Mon., Tue. and August. Reservations required. Classic, elegant, but also homely, with traditional regional cuisine. Try *bolliti* (boiled meat). "E"

Da Enzo, via Coltellini, 17, Modena, tel: 225177. Closed Sat. and August. Dating back to 1912, it has been tastefully renovated. Typical Modenese cooking. "M"

UMBRIA AND THE MARCHES

Falchetto, via Bartolo, 20, Perugia, tel: 61875. Closed Mon. This restaurant serves authentic local food using the best ingredients, with no pretenses. "I"

Buca di San Francesco, via Brizi, 1, Assisi, tel: 812204. Closed Mon. and July 1-15. In a wine cellar, with a rustic atmosphere and pretty good cooking. In summer, dine outdoors. "I"

Da Remo, viale Battisti, 49, Foligno, tel: 50079. Closed Sun. night and Mon. The decor and the menu are simple, but the family that runs the place has a long tradition of fine cooking. "I"

Umbria, via S. Bonaventura, 13, Todi, tel: 882737. Closed Tues. and from December 18 to January 9. In a 14th-century building, with a delightful terrace for dining in summer, overlooking the hills. Good local food. "M"

Il tartufo, piazza Garibaldi, 24, Spoleto, tel: 40236. Closed Wed. and from July 15 to August 8. Reservations required. Quiet and dignified with well-prepared traditional cuisine. The dining room preserves a 4th-century Roman floor. "M"

Tre colonne, viale Plebiscito, 13, Terni, tel: 54511. Closed Mon. and August 1-20. Reserve. Typically rustic, Umbrian furniture and cuisine. "M"

Morino, via Garibaldi, 37, Orvieto, tel: 35152. Closed Wed. and July. Reserve. Modern. Excellent cuisine. "M"

La Badia, località la Badia, Orvieto, tel: 90359. Closed Wed., January and February. In the 12th-century SS. Severo e Martirio Abbey, along with an hotel. Panorama of the town. International cuisine. "E"

Passetto, piazza IV Novembre, 1, Ancona, tel: 33214. Closed Wed. Reserve. Elegant and exquisite. Traditional seafood cuisine. From the terrace, a view of the sea. "M"

NAPLES

Giuseppone al mare, via Ferdinando Russo, 13, tel: 7696002. Closed Sun. and Christmas. At Posillipo, right on the sea in a small port. Great seafood. "E"

La Sacrestia, via Orazio, 116, tel: 664186. Closed Wed. and August. Reservations necessary. At Mergellina, with a wonderful view back over the Gulf of Naples, in a building reminiscent of an old monastery. In summer you can enjoy typical Neapolitan food in a fresh garden. "E"

La Fazenda, via Marechiaro, 58/A, tel: 7697420, Closed Sun. and from August 15 to September 1. Reservations necessary. In a farm overlooking the Gulf of Naples and Capri, with fine Mediterranean food. In summer, the terrace-garden is open. "M"

Sbrescia, rampe S. Antonio a Posillipo, tel: 669140. Closed Mon. and August 15. Reserve. Beautiful view of the Gulf. Fresh seafood. "M"

Ciro a S. Brigida, via S. Brigida, 71, tel: 324072. Closed Sun. and August. Reserve. Classic well-known restaurant, good (not great) Neapolitan cooking. "M"

Ettore, via S. Lucia, 46, tel: 421498. Closed Sun. and August. Just plain good food in a simple *trattoria*. "I"

Giovanni, via Domenico Morelli, 14, tel: 416849. Closed Sun. and August. Reservations advised. Classic, quiet place which offers good fish and meat. "M"

Dante e Beatrice, piazza Dante 44, tel: 349905. Closed Wed. and August 20-30. Genuine Naples *trattoria*, crowded with Neapolitans. Good Neapolitan cooking. "I"

NEAR NAPLES

La piadina, via Cozzolino, 10, tel: 7717141. Closed Tue. Ercolano. Popular among tourists. Traditional cuisine. "M"

La Pigna, via Roma, 30, Capri, tel: 8370280. Closed Tue. and during the winter. The ideal place for a romantic dinner. Elegant, international and local simultaneously. Dining-room with porch and citrus orchard around it. Patio and fountain. Neapolitan cuisine with personality and flair. "M"

Ai Faraglioni, via Camerelle, 75, tel: 8370320. Closed Sun. Reserve. The island's most elegant. Dining rooms overlooks the *faraglioni* and the country. National and international cuisine. "E"

La Capannina, via delle Botteghe, 126b, Capri, tel: 8370732. Closed Wed. Reserve. Fashionable and classic, traditional seafood. "M"

Gennaro, via del Porto, 66, Ischia, tel: 99 2917. Closed Tue. Overlooking the port. Traditional fish cooking. "M"

La buca di Bacco, via Rampa Teglia, 8, Positano, tel: 875696. Closed November to March. Simple and genuine atmosphere and cuisine. "I"

Da Cicio Cielo-Mare-Terra, località Vettica, at Km. 3 via Nazionale to Sorrento, tel: 871030. Sailor's restaurant, with a splendid view of the Gulf of Amalfi. Seafood. "I"

Da Gemma, salita Fra' Gerardo Sasso, 9, Amalfi, tel: 871345. Closed Thur. Reserve. Plain cooking, summer tables on the street. Good seafood.

La Favorita, corso Italia, 71, Sorrento, tel: 8781321. Closed Wed. in winter. Time-honored restaurant, filled with strange old furniture, with a beautiful garden. Mainly seafood. "M"

Al Gambero, via Cuomo, 9, Salerno, tel: 225031. Closed Sun. and August. Reserve. Ship's furniture, regional cooking. "M"

Nettuno, via Principi di Piemonte, 1, Paestum, tel: 811028. Closed Mon. in winter. Reserve. Good view of the temples, good Italian cooking. "I"

Pascalucci, contrada Piano Cappelle, Benevento, tel: 24548. Closed Mon. Pleasant local atmosphere and cuisine. "I"

Vecchia America, Piano Cappelle, Benevento, tel: 24394. Closed Fri. Plain local cooking. "I"

ABRUZZO AND MOLISE

Guerino, viale Riviera, 4, Pescara, tel: 23065. Closed. Tue. only in winter. Modern. Terraces overlooking the sea on the elegant part of the beach. Good seafood. "M"

Venturini, via de Lollis, 10, Chieti, tel: 65863. Closed Tue. and July. Reserve. Traditional atmosphere with a terrace. Special roast game. "I"

Tre Marie, via Tre Marie, 3, L'Aquila, tel: 20191. Closed Mon. Reserve. Old-fashioned restaurant with a 17th-century fireplace and homey atmosphere. Traditional local cuisine. Try *ciufolotti* (as *primo*) and *mischietto* (as *secondo*). "M"

Duomo, via Stazio, 9, Teramo, tel: 311274. Closed Mon. Reserve. Modern, but old-fashioned local cooking. "I"

Da Emma, via Viccardi, 91, Campobasso, tel: 64617. Closed Mon. and November. Reserve. Rustic simplicity, informal atmosphere and good peasant-style cooking.

SARDINIA

Da Nicola, lungomare Vespucci, 37, S. Antioco, tel: 83286. Closed Tue., in winter and October. Modern, along the seaside, traditional cooking. Try the specialty *porchetto alla brace*. "I"

Dal Corsaro, via Regina Margherita, 28, Cagliari, tel: 664310. Closed Tue. and Christmas. During the summer, it is better to go to the restaurant of the same name located at Marina Piccola-Poetto, tel: 370295. Reserve. Great Sardinian cuisine, elegant, romantic atmosphere. "M"

Da Franco, via Capo d'Orso, 1, Palau, tel: 709310. The right place for a business meeting: refined service, terrace overlooking the little port. Mainly seafood. "M"

La Fattoria, loc, Golfo Pevero, Porto Cervo, tel: 92214. Closed Mon. except in summer. Rustic farm-house, wooden furniture, huge fireplace where meat is roasted on spits; typical Sardinian cooking. Try *zuppa quata*, *pane frattau*, *malloreddus*.

SICILY

Luraleo, via Croce, 27, Taormina, tel: 24279. Closed Tue. Reserve. Friendly, rustic, with lobsters and mussels. There is also a barbecue. Sicilian cooking, especially fish. "M"

La Siciliana, via M. Polo, 52/A. Catania, tel: 376400. Closed Sun. dinner and Mon. Elegant and classic, with a long family tradition of cooks. Offers a summer garden and good Sicilian cooking. "M"

Arlecchino, largo Empedocle, 8, Siracusa, tel: 66386. Closed Mon. and August. Reserve. Modern, first-rate service, regional cuisine; try *pasta con le sarde*.

Trieste, via Napoli, 17, Noto, tel: 835485. Closed Mon. and October 10 to 30. Classic and homely. Also a bar and *rosticceria* (grill). "I"

Villa Fortugno, street to Marina di Ragusa, km 4, tel: 28656. Closed Mon. and August. Old country farm with summer garden and good regional cooking. "M"

Del Vigneto, via Cavaleri Magazzeni, 11, Agrigento, tel: 44319. Closed Tue. and October. Overlooking the Valle dei Templi. The vineyard which gives a name to the restaurant covers part of the terrace. Excellent *caponata*. "I"

La bottle, contrada Lenzitti, 416, Monreale, tel: 414051. Closed Mon. and August to September. Farmhouse-style furniture with old barrels and classic atmosphere and cooking. "M"

Chez Pierrot, via Marco Polo, 108, Selinunte. Closed January to February. Porch overlooking the Gulf. Specialty is seafood.

Jolly Hotel, via C. Altacura, tel: 81446. Closed during the winter. Modern, belongs to the hotel bearing the same name. At Piazza Armerina. International cuisine. "M"

Tre Fontane, at Castello di Donnafugata, Ragusa, tel: 45555. Closed Fri. In a 19th-century castle in the country. "I"

PALERMO

Charleston, piazza Ungheria, 30, tel: 321366 in the winter or via Regina Elena, Mondello, tel: 450171 during the summer. Liberty-style atmosphere, excellent service. Reservations necessary. Sicilian and classic cuisine. "L"

La Scuderia, viale de Fante, 9, tel: 520323. Closed Sun. night. In the green park of "Favorita," with a summer garden in the Moorish manner. National and Sicilian cuisine. "M"

Spanò, via Messina Marina, 20/c, along the seaside, tel: 470025. Closed Mon. Traditional seafood cooking. "I"

BASILICATA AND CALABRIA

Da Mario, via XX Settembre, 14, Matera, tel: 214569. Closed Sun. Inside an old silo; the rustic furniture makes the place look like the inside of a big barrel. The cuisine is typical of Basilicata; try *orecchiette* (the ear-shaped pasta) with *rape* (turnip-tops). "M"

La Calvrisela, via De Rada, 11a, Cosenza, tel: 28012. Closed Sat. and Sun. night. Comfortable. Calabrian cuisine, heavy and spicy. "I"

Bonaccorso, via Bixio, 11, Reggio, Calabria, tel: 96048. Closed Fri. and August. Reserve. Elegant and intimate, old-fashioned atmosphere, the owner is the chef, and also happens to be an artist. Traditional cuisine, with variations. "M"

APULIA

Al porto da Michele, piazza Libertà, 3, Manfredonia, tel: 21800. Closed Wed. Classic *trattoria* with good seafood. "M"

Cicolella, viale XXIV Maggio, 60, Foggia, tel: 3880. Closed Fri. night. Sun. and August. Reserve. Elegant, with a summer terrace. The restaurant is attached to a hotel dating back half a century. Prevalently regional cuisine, with the ear-shaped pasta named *orecchiette* and fish-soup among the best dishes. "E"

Bacco, via Sipontina, 10, Barletta, tel: 38398. Closed Mon. and August. Reserve. Intimate atmosphere, very good service, national cuisine. Special fish dishes. "E"

Colombo, lungomare Colombo, 21, Trani, tel: 41146. Closed Tues. Rustic-modern with a sophisticated mussel-and-mollusc dish and regional seafood. Try the *risotto pescatora*. "M"

Ostello di Federico, Castel del Monte, tel: 83043. Closed Mon. Reserve. Close to Frederick II's famous castle, with a beautiful terrace-garden. Regional cooking. "I"

Al Gambero, via del Ponte, 4, Taranto, tel: 411190. Closed Mon. Big and well-lighted, overlooking the Mar Piccolo, with the best crawfish in Puglia. "E"

Plaza, via 140° Regg. Fanteria, 10, Lecce, tel: 26093. Closed Sun. and August. Good Pugliese cooking. "I"

Dal Moro, via Kennedy, 3, Otranto, tel: 81325. Closed Fri. Reserve. On the seashore offering a good complete meal at reasonable prices. "I"

Il Cantinone, via de Leo, Brindisi, tel: 222-122. Closed Tue. Reserve. Picturesque. Regional cooking. "I"

BARI

La Pignata, via Melo, 9, tel: 232481. Closed Wed. and August. Reserve. This is where the President of the Italian Republic, Sandro Pertini, likes to dine. "M"

Vecchia Bari, via Dante, 47, tel: 216496. Closed Fri. Reserve. The restaurant is owned by an oil depository. "M"

Gianni, via Nicolai, tel: 23524. Near the Archaeological Museum. Closed Sun. night and Mon. Reserve. A lively *trattoria* where you can watch the cook as he prepares the meal. "I"

GENOVA AND LIGURIA

Gran Gotto, via Fiume, 11/E, tel: 564344, near Stazione Birgnole. Closed Sun. and August. Reserve. Classic and elegant, with a rustic atmosphere and regional cooking. Try the *Trenette al pesto*. "M"

Antica Osteria del Bai, at Genova-Quarto, via Quarto, 12, tel: 387478. Closed Mon. and from July 20 to August 12. An historic restaurant where Pope Pius VII and Garibaldi once ate, inside a fortress overlooking the sea. Typical Genoese cuisine. "E"

Zeffirino, via XX Settembre, 20, tel: 591990. Closed Wed. Reserve. In the center of the city; modern furniture, mixed cuisine. "M"

Piro, salita Bertora, 5/R, zona Struppa, tel: 802304. Closed Mon. and August 15 to September 15. From the high vantage point of this restaurant you can admire beautiful Genova spread beneath you. This is a typical simple *trattoria*, with pretty good food. Genoese cooking. "I"

La Pergola, via Casaregis, 52r, tel: 546543. Closed Sun. night, Tue. and from August 15 to September 15. Comfortable atmosphere, regional cooking. "M"

Da Rina, Mura di via S. Agnese, 59r, tel: 294900. Closed Mon. and Christmas and Easter, August. Reserve. Traditional *trattoria*, good cooking. "M"

Giannino, corso Trento e Trieste, 23, tel: 70843. Closed Sun., Mon. lunch, July 1 to 15, December 15 to 30. Reserve. Very comfortable, high-class cooking. At Sanremo. "L"

Del porto da Nicò, piazza Brescia, 9, tel: 84144. Closed Thur. and November 1 till December 20. Reserve. The classic *trattoria* of the port, with good seafood. At Sanremo. "M"

Il pitosforo, molo Umberto I, 9, Portofino, tel: 69020. Closed Tues. and from January 1 to February 28. Reserve. Modern-style atmosphere, meeting-place for yachtsmen. International cooking. "L"

Stella, molo Umberto I, 3, Portofino, tel: 69007. Closed Wed. and from January 6 to March 3. Reserve. Marine atmosphere, regional cooking. "M"

Gambero rosso, piazza Marconi, Vernazza (5 Terre), tel: 812265. Closed Mon. and from November 7 to December 12. Close to the port. A small *osteria* worth noting for its seafood. "M"

Conchiglia, piazza del molo, 3, Lerici. Closed Wed. and from December 20 to January 10. Along the seaside, with especially fresh fish.

THINGS TO DO

As it is impossible to list every tourist attraction offered by Italian travel agencies, we will mention only the National Park areas in Italy:

Parco Nazionale del Gran Paradiso: Home of the last steinbocks and chamois in Italy, this park is the oldest in the country and is 72,000 hectares wide. Located in the Alpine zone, it is a must for nature lovers. (tel: 01-659-5704)

Parco Nazionale dello Stelvio: The biggest park in Italy (135,000 hectares), near Switzerland, rich in forests and animals. The mountains are wonderful and very high. There are plenty of hotels. (tel: 03-429-01582 or 04-737-0447)

Parco Nazionale dell'Abruzzo: Here the last brown bear in Italy lives in remote splendor in one of the highest sections of the Apennines. For information write to Parco Nazionale d'Abruzzo, via del Curato, 6, Roma. (tel: 06-654-3584)

If you would like to go hiking in the mountains, pick up the GTA (Great Trekking of the Alps), a walking-tour network of paths, with more than 80 overnight areas with shelters. Paths are marked with numerous red signs and distinctive small flags. Every stage calls for five to seven hours of hiking time at an average of about 1,000 meters in altitude.

At the overnight rest areas one finds shelters with double-decker bunks, essential services and a kitchen. The shelters are generally situated in inhabited localities, where it is possible to buy food for the next day, phone home, rest for a day, visit historical-ethnographic museums, chat with the inhabitants and also, last but not least, eat a good meal at an inn.

An itinerary can last a month, a week or a day. From the Maritime Alps to Lake Maggiore, a route stretching for 650 km that crosses five provinces with a total difference of 46,000 meters in level, the hiker crosses many splendid parks, such as the Gran Paradiso, the Orsiera-Rocciavrè, the Alta Val Pesio and the Argentera.

All the areas are open to the public from July to September.

For detailed information, call the GTA Information Office, via Barbaroux 1, Torino, tel: (011) 514477.

CULTURE PLUS

Italy has such a long recorded history that the biggest problem facing the traveler is to choose among the nation's endless cultural attractions. All main centers, most of the provincial cities and many quite small towns have museums. The theaters, galleries, concert halls and book-stores offer something for every interest.

MUSEUMS

Most museums house special exhibitions in addition to their permanent collections. Information about floating exhibitions can be obtained by calling the museum or checking the newspaper.

The museums listed below are only some of the most important in Italy, but there are many others, both in the cities listed and elsewhere. Admission prices vary frequently; seldom are they free, but they are usually cheap. Take note: if in Torino, don't miss the **Egyptian Museum** at via Accademia delle Scienze, 6 and the **Car Museum** at corso Unità d'Italia, 40.

ROME

The Vatican Museum (viale Vaticano tel: 6983333). Almost always very crowded, the Museum offers papal robes, tomb inscriptions and old maps together with the Raphael rooms, the tapestry gallery, the classical statuary, and the works of some of the most important painters of the Italian Middle Ages and Renaissance (such as Giotto, Fra Angelico, and Filippo Lippi). Don't miss the Sistine Chapel, and be sure to buy a catalogue. Open Monday through Saturday from 9 a.m. to 2 p.m. and the last Sunday of every month. From July to September it is open from 9 a.m. to 4 p.m.

National Gallery of Ancient Art (Galleria Nazionale d'Arte antica) at Palazzo Barberini, via IV Fontane, 13 and at Palazzo Corsini, via della Lungara, 10. Works from the 13th to the 18th century. Open Tuesday to Saturday, 9 a.m. to 2 p.m., Sunday 9 a.m. to 1 p.m.

Modern Art Gallery (Galleria Nazionale d'Arte Moderna) via delle Belle Arti, 131. Paintings by artists of the 19th and 20th centuries, mostly Italians. Open Tuesday to Saturday, 9 a.m. to 2 p.m., Sunday 9 a.m. to 1 p.m.

National Museum of Oriental Art (Museo Nazionale d'Arte orientale), via Merulana, 248. Bronzes, stone, pottery and wooden sculpture of the oriental civilizations. Open Tuesday to Saturday 9 a.m. to 2 p.m., Sunday 9 a.m. to 1 p.m.

Museo Nazionale Etrusco di Villa Giulia, piazza di Villa Giulia, 9. Etruscan Art collection. Open in the summer Tuesday to Sunday 9 a.m. to 2 p.m., Wednesday 3 p.m. to 7.30 p.m.; in the winter Tuesday to Sunday 9 a.m. to 2 p.m., Wednesday 9 a.m. to 6.30 p.m.

Roman Museum (Museo Nazionale Romano), piazza dei Cinquecento, Archaeological collections. Open Tuesday to Saturday 9 a.m. to 1.45 p.m., Sunday 9 a.m. to 1 p.m.

Museo and Galleria Borghese, piazza Scipione Borghese, 3 at Villa Borghese. Collections of painting and sculpture, including pieces by Caravaggio and works of Titian, Raphael and Bernini. Open Tuesday to Saturday 9 a.m. to 2 p.m. and Sunday 9 a.m. to 1 p.m.

FLORENCE

Galleria degli Uffizi, loggiato degli Uffizi, 6. Best of Italian Museums. You can see masterpieces by Botticelli, Leonardo, Raphael, Piero della Francesca, Caravaggio, Giotto and almost every other Italian and foreign artist of importance. Open Tuesday through Saturday 9 a.m. to 7 p.m., Sundays and public holidays 9 a.m. to 1 p.m.

Galleria dell'Accademia, via Ricasoli, 60. Michelangelo's works. Open 9 a.m. to 2 p.m. Tuesday through Saturday, Sunday 9 a.m. to 1 p.m.

Museo Archeologico, via della Colonna, 36. Etruscan, Greek and Roman art. Open Tuesday through Saturday 9 a.m. to 2 p.m., Sunday 9 a.m. to 1 p.m.

Museo di S. Marco, piazza San Marco, 1. Frescoes and paintings. Open Tuesday through Saturday 9 a.m. to 2 p.m., Sunday 9 a.m. to 1 p.m.

MILAN

Galleria d'Arte Moderna, via Palestro, 16. Paintings, sculptures and works of the 19th and 20th centuries. Open 9.30 a.m. to 12 noon; 2.30 p.m. to 5.30 p.m. Closed Tuesday.

Museo Archeologico. The Greek, Etruscan and Roman section is in corso Magenta, 15, open 9.30 a.m. to 12.30 p.m. and 2.30 p.m. to 5.30 p.m., closed Tuesday. Prehistoric and Egyptian art are housed at Castello Sforzesco, open 9.30 a.m. to 12.30 p.m. and 2.30 p.m. to 5.30 p.m. Closed Monday.

Museo del Risorgimento, via Borgonuovo, 23. Documents, relics, paintings, sculptures and prints of the Risorgimento movement. Open 9.30 a.m. to 12.30 p.m. and 2.30 p.m. to 5.30 p.m. Closed Monday.

Pinacoteca Ambrosiana, piazza Pio XI, 2. Paintings from the 14th to the 19th century. Open 9.30 a.m. to 5 p.m. Closed Saturday.

Pinacoteca di Brera, via Brera 28. Paintings from the 15th to the 20th century. Open 9 a.m. to 1.30 p.m. in summer; October through March 9 a.m. to 2 p.m.; Sunday 9 a.m. to 1 p.m. Closed Mondays.

VENICE

Accademia. This museum offers the cream of Venetian paintings, from the superb Bellini Madonna to Giorgione's Tempest and Tintoretto's magnificent cycle about the life of St. Mark. Open Tuesday-

Saturday 9 a.m. to 2 p.m., Sunday 9 a.m. to 1 p.m.

Collezione Peggy Guggenheim in a palazzo near S. Maria della Salute. All the major names of modern art are here. Open April to October, noon to 6 p.m., closed Tuesday. Also open Saturday 6 to 9 p.m.

THEATERS

Italian theater consists mainly of revivals of the classics, though there are a few avant-garde groups that perform in the big cities. For information on shows, ask the city's EPT (Ente Provinciale del Turismo) or check the local newspaper.

Ticket prices vary depending on the show and the playhouse. If you would like to see an Italian play, the principal theaters are: in Rome, **Teatro Sistina**, via Sistina, 129, tel: 4756841 (mainly a music hall), **Teatro Valle**, via Teatro Valle, 23 (tel: 6543794) and **Teatro Goldoni**, Vicolo de'Soldati, 3 (tel: 6561156).

A season of classical drama is held annually in July in the open-air Roman Theater at Ostia Antica.

In Milan, you can go to the **Piccolo Teatro**, via Rovello, 2 (tel: 877663) and to **L'Odeon**, via Radegonda, 8 (tel: 876320); for experimental theater, try **Teatro dell'Elfo**, via Menotti, II (tel: 712405) and the **Centro Ricerca Teatro**, via Dini, 7 (tel: 8466592).

If in Florence, you can take in an Italian production at the **Teatro Comunale**, Corso Italia, 16 (tel: 216253), at **Teatro della Pergola**, via della Pergola, 32 (tel: 272690) or at **Teatro Verdi**, via Ghibellina, 99 (tel: 296242) and **Teatro Niccolini** via Ricasoli 5 (tel: 213 282).

CONCERTS

The classical music lover will find himself right at home in Italy. Noteworthy concerts occur all year almost all over the country.

The opera season in Rome is from December to June at the **Teatro dell'Opera** (tel: 4742595) and outdoors at the **Terme (Baths) of Caracalla** in July and August. From October to May, the **Auditorium of the National Academy of Santa Cecilia** on via della Conciliazione and the **Sala dei Concerti** on via dei Greci offer first-class concerts (tel: 6790389). During the summer, there is an outdoor season at the **Basilica di Massenzio**. Concerts are held also at the **University Auditorium of S. Leone Magno** (tel: 3964777) and at the **Roman Philharmonic Academy** on via Flaminia, 118.

In Florence, the most important musical event is the International Music Festival, **Maggio Musicale Florentino**, that takes place in May and June at the Teatro Comunale, the principal opera house and concert hall. Open air concerts are held in the Boboli Gardens and in the cloisters of the Badia Fiesolana on July and August evenings. Another younger but important summer festival is **Estate Fiesolana**, which lasts from June till August. This event fills the ancient Roman theater in Fiesole and several churches in Florence with opera, concerts, theater, ballet and movies.

The very famous **La Scala** in Milan is a must for every opera fan. The opening evening (usually December 7) is the city's main cultural event. Ballets and concerts are also held here. (tel: 807041)

During the summer, parks are crowded with people enjoying a variety of outdoor cultural events sponsored by the city.

The **Teatro la Fenice** (tel: 25191) in Venice offers fine programs of music and ballet performed by guest artists. There are many other concert halls in town.

In Turin, classical music is at its peak from late August until the end of September, when **Setembre Musica**, an international music festival, takes over the town, featuring the best national and foreign performers.

Naples boasts the largest opera house in Italy, **San Carlo**, whose perfect acoustics draw performances and audiences throughout the year. Bari's **Teatro Petruzzelli** is another fine music hall in the south.

NIGHTLIFE

Nightlife in Italy follows the American and English fashions. There are many nightclubs and discos where young people gather to listen to music, dance and talk. As many of these places go in and out of popularity (or in and out of business) in the space of a few months, look for up-to-date details in local newspapers.

In recent years, Milan and Florence were tops for hip nightlife: Milan for its rock and rockabilly discos, Florence for its postmodern and new-wave style clubs.

In Rome, jazz is very fashionable, while Naples tends towards the blues. Industrial Turin is trying to forget the punk movement as it moves toward the new psychedelic music from England. Venice is not a city for nightlife, as people prefer sitting in cafes and walking through the beautiful, labyrinthine streets. Below is a list of only the more up-to-date clubs.

ROME

Alibi, via di Monte Testaccio. It is a gay disco on Tuesday nights only. On other nights it is open to all and there is a theme for dancing. New psychedelic music.

Yellow Flag, via della Purificazione, 41, tel: 465951. White new wave, including the English psychedelic music.

Black Out. Fashionable only on Fridays, when you can meet post-modern and graffiti artists.

Folk Studio, via Sacchi, 3. At Trastevere, tel: 6798269. A folk music-hall with a preference for Irish songs. Also true American country music.

Mississippi Jazz Club, Borgo Angelico, 16, tel: 6540348. An intimate club with the best Roman big or little jazz bands. Famous groups are Maurizio Gianmarco & C., Enrico Pierannunzi, Bruno Biriaco.

La Macumba, via degli Olimpionici, 19. Refuge for African, Caribbean and Latin music lovers. The rhythms are wild, with the music of Fela Kuti, Dibango and Prince.

Smania, via S. Onofrio. Offers Brazilian music, but not only samba. More fashionable is the swing of the Yemaia and of the Serpiente Latina every night.

El Trauco, via Fonte dell'Olio, 5. Is a classic place for Brazilian music.

Manuia in Trastevere, vicolo del Cinque, 56. Is a restaurant as well as a piano bar that sometimes has live Brazilian music.

Il Bagaglino al Salone Margherita, via due Macelli, 75. Offers cabaret in Italian.

Much More, via Luciani, 52. Is a disco preferred by the younger set. These days it's a little bit "out."

MILAN

Plastic. The disc jockey Nicola Guiducci chooses music for all tastes, from punk to psychedelic.

Capolinea. All big-name be-bop bands meet here. It is possible to eat while listening to the music.

Le Scimmie. Traditional good jazz. Navigli area.

Acqua Sporca. Performances of 40's-style big bands, every night. Navigli area.

La Budineria. A place for new and unknown Italian singers.

Magia. Rock groups from all over Northern Italy come here to play. Live music, but no dancing.

Rolling Stones, corso XXII Marzo, 32, tel: 733172. A "pure" disco, where big-name foreign rock singers may be seen.

Odissea, via Forze Armate, 42, tel: 4075653. Another top disco.

FLORENCE

Space électronic, via Palazzuolo, 37, tel: 293082. One of the most popular discos.

Salt Peanuts, Piazza Santa Maria Novella, 26r, open 10 p.m. to 4 a.m. This is a jazz club where bands play live. It also offers videos. Popular with foreigners.

Caffè Strozzi, Piazza Strozzi. This is a refined meeting-place popular for drinks.

Caffè Voltaire, via degli Alfani, 26r. Open every night, it is a meeting-place where friends listen to recorded music.

Yab Yum, via Sassetti, 5r, tel: 282018. Is a very popular disco in a central position.

Loggia Tornaquinci, via Tornabuoni, 6, tel: 219148. Is an elegant piano bar on the top floor of a 16th-century Medici building.

NAPLES

City Hall, corso Vittorio Emanuele. Good jazz; fusion-style; here you can rub elbows with all the great Neapolitan musicians, including Bennato, De Piscopo and Esposito.

Sensemilla, via Belle Donne. New wave club, with live music by the Italian groups Bisca, Walalla and Panoramic.

Piccadilly, via Petrarca. Beat-nights, Beatles- or Rolling Stones-style nights, and/or jam sessions with Naples' best musicians.

II Parco, via Tasso. American Funk and blues with a Neapolitan twist. It was here that the Italian artists Pino Daniele and James Senese first met success.

TURIN

The Big Club, corso Brescia, 28. New-wave disco, rock and jazz concerts.

II Santincielo at Superga, tel: 890835. Disco crowded with punk rockers.

SHOPPING

SHOPPING AREAS

Rome: The best shopping district is around the bottom of the Spanish Steps, with the elegant **via Condotti** lined with the most exclusive shops (Gucci, Ferragamo and Bulgari).

Other fashionable streets run parallel to via Condotti, such as **via Borgognona** (shops of Fendi, Gianfranco Ferrè, Gucci, and Missoni); **via delle Carrozze** or **via Frattina** (for ceramics, lingerie and costume jewelry); **via Vittoria** (where the boutique of Laura Biagiotti lies) and **via della Croce**. Most of these streets are closed to traffic. For antiques, go window shopping along **via del Babuino** (and do not miss the boutique of Giorgio Armani there) or along **via Margutta** or **via Giulia**.

Another fine shopping section is marked by via del Corso between piazza del Popolo and Largo Chigi, where **via del Tritone** begins.

Less expensive and more popular shopping streets are **via Nazionale**, near the railway station, where Fiorucci (funky and young sportswear and shoes) has his greatest shops, and **via Cola di Rienzo**.

"The other face of fashion" is represented by some open markets, such as the one in **via del Sannio** which sells new and secondhand clothes and, of course, the famous one at **Porta Portese**, open only on Sunday, where you can find almost everything. The reign of "Armani-style" secondhand clothes has become *Così è se vi pare* these last few years, in **via delle Carrozze**.

MILAN

More than Rome, Milan is the center for international fashion and manufactured products in Italy. For those with expensive tastes, the most chic and elegant streets for shopping are: via **Montenapoleone**, via **Spiga** and via **S. Andrea**, all of them near the Duomo and La Scala. These streets feature such fine stores as Krizia, Giò Moretti, Trussardi, Kenzo, Sanlorenzo, Giorgo Armani and Ferragamo. Only high-fashion women's and men's clothes are sold here.

FLORENCE

The whole center of Florence could be considered a huge shop, always crowded with tourists and well-dressed local people. Handicrafts are disappearing, leaving the place to smart and strange fashion shops. Even if it is difficult to make a choice, the most fashionable streets remain via **Calzaiuoli**, via **Roma** (absolutely "in" is Luisa), via **Tornabuoni** (Gucci and Céline), via **della Vigna Nuova** and via **Strozzi** (Neuber, Principe, Diavolo Rosa).

Ponte Vecchio is famous almost all over the world for gold and silver jewelry and some antique shops.

The area near the church of Santa Croce is full of top-quality leather goods, while for other handicrafts you can check out the city's two open markets, sprawling **San Lorenzo** and covered **Mercato Nuovo**, near piazza della Signoria.

SPORTS

SPECTATOR

Soccer:The national sport in Italy is surely soccer. Almost every city and village has its own team. The most important national championship is the "Series A" (First Division). The winner of this competition is eligible to play in a kind of European championship, the "Champios' Cup," against the top teams of other European nations.

The "Series A" championship is played from September to May, and each of the 16 teams has to play against each of the other teams twice.

The most successful Italian soccer team is the Juventus F.C. from Turin, followed by Internazionale from Milan. But many other cities are blessed with successful teams, including Verona, the surprising winner of the 1985 Championship, and Rome.

If you would like to see a game, check the newspaper to find out which team is playing, and where. Remember that it is very difficult to get tickets if the game is an important one. Prices for tickets vary according to the importance of the team, the importance of the game, and the quality of the seat you want.

CAR RACING

The second passion of the Italians is represented by cars and speed. Formula 1 races attract people interested in the sophisticated technology and in the coupling of man and car. This sport attracts mostly a T.V. audience, because it is very expensive to go around the world to see the races. But in Italy, where citizens support the red cars by Ferrari, there is always a large crowd at the Imola and Monza Grand Prix races.

OTHER SPORTS

Almost every other sport is practised in Italy, including even American football. If you are interested in buying tickets for any game, buy the pink "Gazzetta dello Sport" newspaper, where everything under the sun about sports is listed.

USEFUL ADDRESSES

TOURIST INFORMATION

General tourist information is available at the **Ente Nazionale per il Turismo** (ENIT), Via Marghera, 2/6 Rome (tel: 4971222). The ENIT also has offices on the 15th floor of 630 Fifth Avenue in New York City.

In every chief town you will find the **Ente Provinciale per il Turismo** (EPT) or the **Azienda Autonoma di Soggiorno e Turismo**. For their addresses and phone numbers, check the directory or the Yellow Pages under "Enti." Main cities have a sort of "travel tips" together with the directory named "Tuttocittà." Check that too.

Provincial Tourist Offices (EPT) of the main cities are listed below:

Rome: Main headquarters are located in Via Parigi, 5 (tel: 463748), but there is an EPT also at the stazione centrale Termini (tel: 465461) and at the airport (tel: 6011255). Main headquarters are open Monday to Saturday 8.30 a.m. to 1 p.m. and 2 to 7 p.m. and provide helpful services from sightseeing suggestions to brochures and maps of Rome and Lazio.

Milan: EPT offices are located at Stazione Centrale (tel: 206030, open in summer daily 9 a.m. to 12.30 p.m. and 2 to 6.30 p.m., in winter until 6 p.m., closed Sunday) and at Piazza del Duomo (tel: 809662, open in summer Monday to Friday 8.45 a.m. to 6.30 p.m., Saturday 9 a.m. to 5 p.m., in winter Monday to Friday 8.45 a.m. to 12.30 p.m. and 1.30 to 6 p.m., Saturday till 5 p.m.).

Florence: The EPT office is far from the center of the city in Via Manzoni, 16 (tel: 2478141, open Monday to Friday 8:30 a.m. to 1:30 p.m. and 4 to 6:30 p.m., and Saturday 8:30 a.m. to 1 p.m.). More central and efficient is the Azienda Autonoma di Turismo, via Tornabuoni, 15 (tel: 216544, open Monday to Saturday 9 a.m. to 1 p.m.).

Venice: The EPT office is in San Marco, 71F (tel: 26356), under the arcades of the piazza, open Monday to Saturday 9 a.m. to 12.30 p.m. and 3 to 7 p.m. There is an office also in the station (tel: 715016) open daily 8 a.m. to 7 p.m.

Almost every town in Italy has a **Touring Club Italiano** (TCI) office, which can provide free information about points of interest in the area. Telephone numbers are listed in the local phone book.

CREDITS

INDEX

N

O

Q - R

S

T